COLD PEACE
Russia's New Imperialism

JANUSZ BUGAJSKI

Published in cooperation with the
Center for Strategic and International Studies,
Washington, D.C.

PRAEGER

Westport, Connecticut
London

Library of Congress Cataloging-in-Publication Data

Bugajski, Janusz, 1954–
  Cold peace : Russia's new imperialism / Janusz Bugajski.
    p. cm.
  Includes bibliographical references and index.
  ISBN 0–275–98362–5 (alk. paper)
    1. Russia (Federation)—Foreign relations—1991– 2. Russia (Federation)—Politics and government—1991– I. Title.
  DK510.764.B84 2004
  327.47′009′051—dc22   2004011886

British Library Cataloguing in Publication Data is available.

Library of Congress Catalog Card Number: 2004011886
ISBN: 0–275–98362–5

First published in 2004

Praeger Publishers, 88 Post Road West, Westport, CT 06881
An imprint of Greenwood Publishing Group, Inc.
www.praeger.com

Printed in the United States of America

⊚™

The paper used in this book complies with the
Permanent Paper Standard issued by the National
Information Standards Organization (Z39.48–1984).

10 9 8 7 6 5 4 3 2 1

This book is dedicated to my parents, Jadwiga Bugajska and Piotr Bugajski, both of whom survived the Soviet Gulag and lived to see a free Poland. Their strength of character and directness of perception will always be an inspiration to me.

Contents

Acknowledgments

My utmost gratitude in completing this book is extended to all the assistants and interns at the Center for Strategic and International Studies (CSIS) who tirelessly conducted volumes of research, in both the written and the spoken word. I would especially like to thank Milena Staneva, Margaret Dobrydnio, Nathan Hulley, Irina Axene, Ivi Kolasi, Juliette Souchon, Plamen Ralchev, Elizabeth May, Marina Veljanovska, Natalie Zajicova, Eleonora Ibrani, Jonathan Nabavi, Marcin Bugajski, Iztok Bojović, Milena Rajović, and Lizabeta Paloka. Above all, I am grateful to my stalwart colleague and Fellow at CSIS, Ilona Teleki, who as usual made the entire endeavor possible. Thanks are also due to all my colleagues and interlocutors throughout Eastern Europe and Russia whose insights and information gave credence to my hypotheses.

1
Introduction:
Near or Temporary Abroad?

ORIGINAL SINS

Over a decade ago, Russia experienced the most profound economic, political, and military collapse by an empire not defeated in war. With the fall of Communist regimes and the withdrawal of Soviet military forces from Eastern Europe, Moscow surrendered its political and military domination.[1] But during the 1990s, the Kremlin sought to regain much of its influence and leverage and to limit Western penetration in the region. Above all, it endeavored to rebuild Russia as a great power on both the European and "Eurasian" stages.

An important measure of Russia's global role is the nature of its policies toward former East European vassals. Russian authorities are unwilling to acknowledge their subjugation of Eastern Europe under Tsarism and Communism. Material reparations were not forthcoming after the collapse of the Warsaw Pact and the Soviet Union, even though Russia inherited the Soviet administrative apparatus and most of its resources and assets. The Kremlin refused to recognize that Russian policies throughout the twentieth century stifled Eastern Europe's economic development, retarded its political evolution, and undermined the region's efforts to become part of an emerging European economic and security structure. Unlike Nazi Germany, Soviet Russia was not held accountable for its actions in the region and has not paid any restitution to the countless victims of Soviet Communism. This has contributed to breeding resentment and suspicion with regard to Russian motives and Western duplicity.

In the post–Cold War era, Russia has failed to take into account the national interests of its East European neighbors. Instead, it has constantly complained about its own endangered interests.[2] Moscow demands a higher degree of national security than any of its neighbors and this stance has been uncritically accepted in Western policy circles. In reality, the "interests" that have been most threatened since the demise of the USSR are Russia's renewed expansionism and regional domination. Enlargement of the North Atlantic Treaty Organization (NATO) was opposed because it could prevent future Russian enlargement by ensuring the permanent security of the East European members.

In Russia itself, there is little systematic analysis on the perspectives of East European states with regard to Moscow's policies. Policy statements and media coverage indicate that the public receives a distorted picture of East Europeans' views of their country.[3] Russian spokesmen claim that they cannot be held responsible for the actions of the Soviet Union (as Russia was allegedly the first victim of Communism), and complain that East Europeans are ungrateful for their "liberation" from the Third Reich and for reconstruction assistance. Paltry information about their Western neighbors fosters hostile stereotypes about the allegedly Russophobic East Europeans.

Russian–East European relations are imbued with negative perceptions among governments and publics and the Kremlin harbors deep suspicions over the ambitions of its former subordinates.[4] In the region, there is a prevailing sense that Russia has not atoned for its regressive policies. Indeed, there has been no Russian equivalent of the German apology uttered by Chancellor Helmut Kohl "on behalf of the German people."[5] In terms of Russian intentions, Moscow cannot be afforded the "benefit of the doubt" among former satellites as subterfuge and imperialistic ambitions have formed the core of Russian policy for generations. Observers concur that Great Russian chauvinism remains an active component of Moscow's foreign policy.[6] Most post-Communist states are strong proponents of Russia's containment and point to a history of dominance and interference.[7] They understand that Russia's economic weakness and internal turmoil limit any direct military threat, but they fear that latent imperial aspirations present a persistent challenge to their independence. In a thorough multinational analysis conducted at the end of the 1990s, it emerged that fears of Russia remain high in countries that experienced historical conflicts with Moscow[8]: "Throughout most of Central and Eastern Europe, fear of Russia and the memory of Russian domination first prompted the idea of joining NATO. . . . The 'East' is widely associated with backwardness, poverty, lack of freedom, and foreign domination. The 'West' or 'Europe' is associated with wealth, freedom, independence, and security."[9]

In their search for permanent security, most of the new democratic governments focused on institutional integration with the West. Such policies were reinforced after the failed coup attempt in Moscow in August 1991 and the collapse of the Soviet Union. Russia's neighbors began to clamor for entry into NATO as a guarantor of their independence and national security.[10] Even among states seeking opportunities for economic cooperation, reservations were voiced about Russia's reliability. Although the Kremlin claimed that it desired an equal partnership with all East European states, it was viewed as intent on regaining dominant political influence. In order to explore Russian state policy and its impact on neighbors, it is valuable to summarize the conceptual underpinnings of Muscovite policy: "Having been pushed back from a strategic border in mid-Germany to its 19th century frontiers, and facing a greater conventional superiority on NATO's part (before enlargement) than it itself enjoyed during the Cold War, it is in the West that Russia feels it has suffered the greatest relative loss of regional standing."[11]

After an initial period of policy confusion, Russian state nationalism has been on the rise since the unraveling of the USSR in 1991.[12] During the 1990s, nationalism and statism became important ideological and mobilizational devices for Russia's leaders. Only marginal extremist groups operated on the premise of exclusive ethnic nationalism. Instead, a pan-ethnic, Moscow-centered statism predominated, in which Russia was depicted as a significant power that needed to rebuild its zones of influence. The former Soviet bloc was viewed as one of the primary venues for Moscow's objectives. Although Russian politicians were divided on domestic issues, they proved united on the premise that international decline needed to be reversed and dominance rebuilt. After lying dormant in the early 1990s, "the greatness syndrome" resurfaced "with new intensity in the mid-1990s and once again began to play a major role in the country's foreign and domestic policies."[13]

Tsygankov offers a typology of five streams of Russian policy: pro-Western liberals, national democrats, statists, neo-Communists, and expansionists.[14] However, these positions are too rigid and fail to distinguish between strategies and tactics in differing international contexts. Even the "pro-Western liberals" adopted harsh rhetoric toward NATO or followed neoimperialist policies in the "near abroad" when it proved politically expedient. In the estimations of East European analysts, the "imperial temptation" resurfaced among the Russian elites soon after the loss of empire. It operates on the principles of "self-proclaimed spheres of influence abroad in more or less open disregard for the sovereignty of neighboring states."[15] Russia's "imperialist consciousness" has been reinflated, while the flexible and adaptable definition of what constitutes "Russian" contributes to making the state more expansive than if it was based on precise ethnic criteria: "The question of who belongs to the Russian nation and where 'the just' borders of the Russian nation-state is much less clear today in the case of Russia than in other European nations. . . . Russian state-building has stood in the way of Russian nation-building."[16]

Russia's masses also remain infused with an imperial mentality and a delusion of state grandeur. In detailed surveys conducted between 1993 and 2000, between 58 percent and 83 percent of respondents answered in the affirmative to the question "For the most part the national interests of Russia should extend beyond its current territory."[17] Over half of respondents agreed that Russia should send its army, if asked, "to aid countries of the former USSR." Even more telling, between 69 percent and 81 percent of those surveyed over a seven-year period asserted that "the defense of Russians abroad in the former republics of the USSR is a very important foreign policy goal." Russia's leadership in a pan-Slavic "third way" has deep roots in the country's political culture.[18] Although few individuals openly espouse the embodiment of any global mission, the definition of "Russian" includes coethnics, conationals, coreligionists, and colinguists, while Moscow also poses as the protector of smaller non-Russian nations. This is underpinned by an "expansionist siege mentality," in which the Russian state and its inhabitants need to be shielded against political, military, economic, and cultural encroachment from all sides.

With the loss of empire, Moscow's elites experienced a painful postimperial crisis, with intense debates over Russia's global role and continuing assertions about its superpower status.[19] Disputes have not revolved around dichotomies between pro- and anti-Westernism, despite the historical analogies of "Westernizers" against "Slavophiles." The debate is principally focused on the rationale, methods, and strategies for restoring Russia's global status.[20] The proponents of a "normal state," favoring noninvolvement in the former Soviet republics and a limited global role, have little political mileage because they are widely perceived as weak, cowering to the West, and in conflict with Russia's historical traditions. The question was how to revive Russia's strength and influence after an interlude of imperial collapse.

GORBACHEV'S SINATRA DOCTRINE: "I COULDN'T DO IT MY WAY"

Soviet rule crumbled in Eastern Europe in 1989–1990 because the binding principles of the international Communist system had expired. As the former Lithuanian president Vitautas Landsbergis once remarked, it was not so much that Moscow initiated a thaw in the region, but the fact that "the refrigerator finally broke down."[21] Claiming credit for reforming or dismantling a system that was coercively imposed on half of Europe for over forty-five years has not earned policymakers in Moscow any praise in states subjected to Soviet domination. Russian officials described the revolutions of 1989–1990 as an irreversible military withdrawal in a gesture of magnanimity. They refused to admit that Russia lost the Cold War and had little choice but to evacuate its military forces and enable satellite states to restore their independence. According to Soviet and Russian spokesmen, Secretary-General Mikhail Gorbachev "liberated" the region in order to encourage political cooperation with the West. However, such a policy was not implemented because of an overnight conversion to anti-imperialism or democratic rule but because of a sober calculation that the burdens of empire had become too onerous and Moscow was desperate for financial assistance from the West.

There were several causes for the sudden disintegration of the Soviet bloc. Soviet Communism, both as an ideology and a system of rule, was politically defunct and economically exhausted. Soviet "stagnation" did not begin under Gorbachev, but could be traced to the Brezhnev years from the 1970s onward. Moscow's global power was an illusion that could not be sustained without major economic growth that the system was incapable of generating. The Gorbachev leadership eventually grasped the necessity for radical reform to avert an economic meltdown and potential social revolution. However, the Soviet leader was convinced that he could salvage both the essence of the system and the USSR itself through economic restructuring:

> Gorbachev was a firm believer in the sovietization myth. The underlying assumption of *perestroika* itself was that a loyal Soviet people existed. Once freed from bureaucratic constraints by *glasnost* and *demokratizatsiya,* this Soviet people would use its newly found freedoms to pull the USSR from its stagnation, reinvigorate the Soviet economy, and accelerate the USSR's historical progress toward communism.[22]

Gorbachev seriously miscalculated as Communist rule evaporated, the satellites broke free, and the USSR fractured into its constituent republics. Cognizant of Russia's weakness and fearful of Russia's international isolation, Gorbachev disavowed the "Brezhnev Doctrine," which justified Soviet intervention in any satellite state where Communism was under threat.[23] The Kremlin altered its confrontational foreign policy and released the long-suppressed political aspirations of the East Europeans. In 1990–1991, the Warsaw Treaty Organization (Warsaw Pact) and the Council for Mutual Economic Assistance (CMEA or COMECON) were both dissolved. Gorbachev made it clear to East Europe's Communist leaders that military force would no longer be employed to preserve them in power. Moscow was unwilling to risk a military escapade that would bear high financial and political costs. Gorbachev's self-proclaimed "mutual security" concept was intended to foster collaboration with the West and nonthreatening relations with former satellites. However, the notion of "Russian interests" throughout Eastern

Europe was retained but without the military muscle and the dominant political controls.

In a rebuke to Western Russia-watchers who were looking for a
"Gorbachev Doctrine" toward Eastern Europe, Soviet leaders coined the glib
phrase the "Sinatra Doctrine" to signify that the satellites were freed from
Moscow's tutelage.[24] However, this did not mean that the region was at liberty to arrange its own security and foreign policies. It signaled that Russia
would no longer intervene militarily to subdue their independence and would
not maintain proxy Communist parties in power as the basis of its regional
control. The Red Army retreated from all satellites by the end of 1992 and
from the three Baltic states by 1994, but maintained a presence in Ukraine,
Belarus, and Moldova.[25] However, the former satellites were expected to
coordinate their foreign and security policies with Moscow and refrain from
entering any "hostile alliances." Ultimately, the "Sinatra Doctrine" proved
a failure either in preserving a reformed Soviet Union or in maintaining
dominance over the post-Communist states.

The Russia that emerged from the ruble of the Soviet Union was no
longer a superpower but a huge country possessing weak economic foundations and unrequited ambitions rooted in a long imperial history based
around an illusion of parity with the United States. Moscow sought to terminate its expensive economic and military commitments outside Russian
borders; but this often contradicted the deep-rooted desire to regain influence and control. Nationalists and Communists bemoaned the Soviet collapse
and the military retreat from Eastern Europe as capitulation to the West.
Meanwhile, liberals and reformers praised Moscow for "consenting" to the
reunification of Germany and the Red Army withdrawal. However, many
liberals and democrats sought to dismantle Communism and did not envisage that the Soviet state itself would collapse. According to official propaganda, Russia agreed to these steps without any pressure or coercion, thereby
displaying its cooperativeness.[26] As a result, Moscow expected various benefits from the West and became sorely disappointed. In reality:

> The Central-East European Countries (CEEC) achieved full (external) sover-
> eignty owing far more to Soviet weakness than to any fundamental change of
> attitudes in Soviet foreign policy toward the region. The internal weakness
> barred the Soviet Union from using (military) force in its relations with the
> CEEC, since political costs were considered far too high, and the ultimate
> success (given the massive resistance to Soviet rule in the CEEC) was highly
> doubtful.[27]

YELTSIN'S STRATEGIC INTOXICATION

Following the collapse of the Soviet bloc and after a brief period of tactical partnership between Yeltsin and the newly independent states, political,
security, economic, and cultural ties between Russia and the new East Europe

declined. Trade relations plummeted, sometimes with negative consequences for certain industrial branches, as the new democracies sought to reorient their trade westward and to limit their dependence on Moscow. They were also perturbed by unfulfilled supply obligations and Russia's failure to pay on time for deliveries. Tapping into Western markets was considered essential for bolstering national independence and promoting integration into the European Union (EU) and NATO. Moscow also curtailed its economic relations with Eastern Europe, as it was in competition for Western aid, trade, and investment.

Russia became the legal successor of the Soviet Union and inherited the USSR's permanent seat at the UN Security Council, the Soviet Union's nuclear and conventional military arsenal, a vast array of assets, and the bulk of territory that became the Russian Federation. This placed Moscow in a dominant position vis-à-vis the other former Union republics after Boris Yeltsin was elected president in June 1991. In the first few years of the Yeltsin administration, under the impact of the Gorbachev-Shevardnadze "new political thinking," Moscow was relatively accommodating toward its former satellites while pursuing a policy of "radical democratization" at home. The goals of securing Russian independence, undercutting pro-Soviet elements that challenged Yeltsin's legitimacy, and gaining Western economic assistance were considered more crucial than rapidly regaining influence in the collapsed empire. "Moscow's honeymoon with the West in 1991–1993 was motivated by shrewd calculation as well as wishful thinking. Russia's moderation was based on a sober appreciation of Russian weakness and recognition of Russia's need to get along with the West during a period of acute vulnerability."[28]

The Kremlin calculated that the United States would help rebuild Russia as a great power coresponsible for international security and incorporate it in the major international institutions. With such elevated and unrealistic expectations, Muscovite leaders subsequently felt profoundly disappointed if not humiliated. Between the middle of 1992 and early 1993, expansionist positions gained ground and Moscow's foreign policy became more confrontational.[29] The Kremlin adopted more assertive policies that were at odds with the West and used the pretext of unfulfilled promises of Western assistance to underscore its distinct "national interests." Even many former democrats shifted toward nationalist or "national patriotic" positions calling for a more combative Russian foreign policy. Officials failed to point out that Moscow's accommodation with the West did bring Russia significant financial benefits and political support and helped to avoid international isolation and internal fragmentation at a time of uncertainty and weakness.

The hardening of Russian policy was partly motivated by internal political considerations as the Yeltsin administration tried to outflank its nationalist and Communist challengers. It was also spurred by domestic accusations that Moscow had neglected the former Soviet republics and East European proxies and was ignoring the deteriorating fate of Russian ethnics in neighboring states. In return for their support in cracking down on a rebellious parliament in October 1993 and imposing presidential rule, Yeltsin promised military leaders that Russia would refocus its attention on its "vital interests" in the former Soviet zone and lessen its security cooperation with the West.[30] The objective was to "converge" extensive parts of the former USSR into a single political, military, and economic "space."

Harsher rhetoric was accompanied by more pressured policies in expanding Russian influences.[31] This approach became more coherent after 1993. Key policy documents adopted in the spring and fall of 1993, including the foreign policy concept and the new military doctrine, were characterized by marked suspicion of Western intentions, resentment against Russia's apparent subordination, complaints about painful economic reforms allegedly imposed by the West, and a resolve to restore the country's global position. The liberal reforms initiated by Prime Minister Igor Gaidar in 1992–1993 were viewed as destructive of Russian interests and pandering unnecessarily to American influences. Hard-liners, restorationists, Communists, and nationalists criticized the early Yeltsin years as a series of unilateral concessions to the West that had begun under Gorbachev. The military doctrine, signed by Yeltsin in November 1993, asserted a Russian sphere of influence that coincided with that of the USSR and its former satellites. The armed forces had several priority tasks, including establishing mobile forces to conduct operations in any threatened region, and providing security for other members of the Commonwealth of Independent States (CIS) by deploying Russian troops when necessary in neighboring countries. Moscow also repudiated the principle of "no first use" of nuclear weapons.

Even the "Westernizing" foreign minister Andrey Kozyrev adopted a more stridently imperialist posture, as Eastern Europe purportedly remained a "sphere of Russia's vitally important interests."[32] Kozyrev described the re-integration of the former Soviet republics as the chief objective of Russian foreign policy.[33] Meanwhile, the Russian population in other post-Soviet states was defined as an integral part of the Russian nation and its position became a central feature of a more assertive foreign policy.[34] Officials argued that Russians could not maintain their identity outside a Russian state; hence the re-creation of a larger unit to incorporate these territories was vital for the survival of the Russian people.[35]

Kozyrev alternatively adopted soft and hard positions depending on his audience and the intensity of domestic criticism from nationalists and Communists. His objective was to reassert Russian primacy in the former colonies despite the material weakness of the state. A more strident tone was adopted toward Eastern Europe as Moscow threateningly encroached on the region's independence especially when the new democracies canvassed for NATO membership and disregarded Russia's self-proclaimed "security interests." This new "Kozyrev Doctrine" did not explicitly prohibit the former satellites from entering NATO but was designed to obstruct and delay their integration. Any moves toward the West by neighboring capitals needed to be "coordinated" with Moscow, an approach that served to further alienate the region from Russia. In the fall of 1993, Kozyrev claimed that Russia possessed strategic interests in all former Soviet territories and warned that "power vacuums" open to "enemy forces" would not be tolerated.[36]

Despite his efforts at Russia's regional restoration and his more nationalistic foreign policy line, Kozyrev was distrusted by key sectors of the Russian establishment. He was criticized by nationalists, Communists, and the military for failing to perceive the danger that the West posed to Russia and for undermining the country's patriotic spirit and military morale. Hard-liners were not convinced by Kozyrev's tougher pronouncements. While a nationalist core sought to limit Western influence, Russia's leadership feared isolation and retardation in comparison to Western technological and economic advances. Nevertheless, many former liberals and pro-Westerners switched their positions and withdrew their support from Kozyrev when it became clear that Russian state nationalism was in the ascendancy.

The rise of "pragmatic nationalist" forces from the early to middle 1990s convinced Yeltsin to replace Kozyrev in January 1996 with Evgeniy Primakov, a strident champion of distinctively Russian interests.[37] A stricter policy line became evident under Primakov, especially in terms of opposition to NATO enlargement and the integration of the former Soviet republics.[38] Indeed, even before Primakov's appointment the anti-NATO card became a useful device to mobilize public opinion and underscore the government's patriotic credentials in response to political challenge from ultranationalists. In this context, the new Russian constitution in 1994 gave more powers to the president and strengthened his role in foreign policy.

Yeltsin's harder line was reinforced after the December 1993 Duma (parliamentary) elections, which boosted the influence of nationalist and Communist parties and steered the administration on a more aggressive course. Prominent Russian observers depicted the new parliament as split between an "anti-Western imperial majority" and a "Westernizing minority."[39] Voters had turned to the populist and nationalists largely because of economic dissatisfaction and poor living conditions blamed on Western-inspired reforms. Meanwhile, many liberals felt rejected by Western institutions, arguing that Russia was kept at arms length despite its early commitment to radical reforms.

Distrust of the Kremlin's pro-Western policies was especially evident in the Defense Ministry, in the security services, and in the Security Council. Each accused the government of lacking a comprehensive foreign policy concept. In their perceptions, Moscow's decreasing influence in Eastern Europe generated instability as it exposed the region to "internal contradictions" by removing the bipolar shield.[40] Moreover, the United States was evidently seeking to gain advantage from the "power vacuum" in order to project its hegemony further east.

> The Westernizers' liberal concept of foreign policy could not be anything but a passing phase in the genesis of a lasting Russian foreign policy. The liberal policy, a carryover from the foreign policy of the waning days of the Soviet Union, did not respond to the reality that emerged following the USSR's collapse, nor was it equipped to deal with an entirely new universe of issues that were bound to haunt post-Soviet Russia. The basic assumption that Russia could rapidly join the ranks of civilized nations, politically as well as economically, proved to be false.[41]

With Primakov's appointment as foreign minister, Russia took a more active role toward former satellites, although it avoided direct confrontation with Washington. According to Primakov, Russia and the West jointly won the Cold War.[42] Such arguments were designed to depict the Soviet Union and the West as equals, to minimize perceptions of any threat from Russia, and to present Moscow as a constructive international player without imperialist pretensions. Primakov's rise signaled a major shift from a Western orientation to a "great power" or "Eurasian" foreign policy as he was viewed as a "pragmatic anti-Westerner."[43] He sought to resurrect the Russian superpower while rejecting close affiliation with the West. The world was perceived as a struggle between the "Atlanticists," led by the United States, and the "Eurasianists," led by Russia.

Moscow's new policymakers criticized the lack of a coherent approach toward Eastern Europe after the dissolution of the Warsaw Pact. Under Primakov, clashes between the executive and the legislature became less frequent as the new foreign minister was widely respected as a "Russian patriot." Primakov's appointment signaled a more decisive break with the early Yeltsin years of integration with the West toward a policy of "multipolarity" designed to restore Russia's status and distinctiveness in the international arena.[44] Primakov emphasized the importance of Russia's relations with other "poles of power," some of which were hostile to the United States. The new foreign minister believed that too close a partnership with NATO would hinder Moscow's objective to develop into a distinct "center of power in a multipolar world." Primakov provided more consistency and steadiness in policy and insulated it from the turmoil in Russia's internal politics. His successor Igor Ivanov, under the Putin administration, upheld this "pragmatic" approach.

Commentators have noted a persistent lack of realism in Russia's assessments of its capabilities on the international arena given the economic and military weakness of the state.[45] Few if any political leaders resigned themselves to the permanent loss of the former Soviet republics, which were perceived as part of Russia's historical heritage. One overwhelming historical burden continued to cast a long shadow over the country—the fact that

Russia gained an empire before it became a state and a coherent nation. This helped to explain persistent Russian claims to the identity and territory of various neighbors and why the former Soviet republics were not considered fully sovereign entities but classified as the "near abroad." The borders of these new states were not perceived as international frontiers but as Russia's "outer border," which Moscow had a historical right to guard and guarantee.

The disintegration of the Soviet structure was viewed as a greater calamity than the collapse of the Communist system. The country's elites argued that Russia had to be the guarantor of political stability and military security throughout the former USSR and needed to ensure order within and among these states. They also viewed Russia as a protector of weaker neighbors against unwelcome Western and Islamic influences. Divisions materialized between ultranationalist restorationists, who favored forceful takeovers, and state leaders preferring a gradual process of domination through political, economic, and security levers. Nevertheless, the pursuit of great power status was supported by the military and security services. Russian commentators justified such expansionism on the grounds that Moscow was simply seeking "national security."[46]

FROM RUSSIA WITHOUT LOVE: PERSPECTIVES ON EASTERN EUROPE

Russian foreign policy analysts contend that Eastern Europe was neglected in the early years of the Yeltsin administration. Moscow was too preoccupied with establishing profitable relations with the West to pay much attention to former satellites. In addition, Russia inherited a system in which relations with other Communist states were not the responsibility of the Foreign Ministry but of a specialized Communist Party department. Relations with the Soviet republic were also handled within the Soviet Communist Party apparatus and there was confusion whether relations with the former republics constituted foreign or domestic policy. Russian leaders had to learn to deal with all the newly independent states as part of its foreign policy process.

Mixed messages emanating from Moscow perturbed the East Europeans and did not enhance confidence in Russian policy. Different politicians appeared hawkish or accommodating, and some leaders sent contradictory signals.[47] This often-confusing position gradually altered as the Kremlin realized that the region could drift irretrievably into the NATO security structure. During 1995, Russian Prime Minister Viktor Chernomyrdin made a tour of the region in order to halt its slide toward NATO membership and to offer each capital lucrative energy and economic deals.[48] However, Moscow failed to assuage fears about its ambitions and did not engage in meaningful dialogue on the region's security.

Despite its military withdrawal and the ouster of ruling proxy parties, Moscow asserted that it possessed "legitimate foreign and security interests" in the region. Suspicions intensified that the Kremlin was intent on regaining domination over each country's foreign and security policy and disabling NATO entry. The majority of capitals remained deeply skeptical of Moscow's aspirations and did not welcome inferior status. Vehement Kremlin opposition to NATO as the primary structure of European security was perceived as a threat by many East European governments because it was aimed at denying them the right to exercise their security options. In May 1992, General Igor Rodionov, chief of the General Staff Academy in Moscow, enumerated several Russian "vital interests":

> The neutrality of East European countries or their friendly relations with Russia; free Russian access to seaports in the Baltics; the exclusion of 'third country' military forces from the Baltics and non-membership of the Baltic states in military blocs directed at Russia' the prevention of the countries that constitute the CIS from becoming part of a buffer zone aimed at separating Russia from the West, South, or East; maintaining the CIS states under Russia's exclusive influence.[49]

To help justify their ambitions, officials warned that new West-East divisions were emerging within Europe. The United States was accused of undermining Russia as a competitor on the world market, especially in the arms trade and space technology.[50] The United States was described as a new hegemon that disguised its objectives with cooperative rhetoric. The Kremlin claimed that NATO enlargement was creating conflicts on the continent, but refused to acknowledge that persistent assertions about such divisions became a self-fulfilling prophecy. Moscow highlighted various divisions on the continent, including that between the "Orthodox East" and the "Catholic and Protestant West." Russian policy analysts claimed that NATO acquired a more pronounced anti-Russian position with the entry of Poland, Hungary, and the Czech Republic in 1999.[51] Moscow failed to point out that states opposing NATO accession, or which adopted a neutral position, were laggards in the reform process and controlled by special interest groups and populist or nationalist politicians.

Russian authorities depicted NATO as a "grand design" to "encircle" Russia, to achieve strategic superiority, to marginalize, isolate, and "de-Europeanize" the country, and to promote disintegration of the Russian Federation. Furthermore, NATO expansion would purportedly destabilize several neighboring countries and provoke civil wars that could eventually embroil Russia: "Russia's leadership uniformly views NATO as strictly an anti-Russian military alliance, ignores NATO's substantial demilitarization, sees European security in terms of rival blocs pursuing zero-sum and antagonistic goals, willfully distorts NATO's position on nuclear missiles, and greatly overrate Russia's power and position in Europe."[52]

By the end of 1993, Moscow understood that NATO enlargement would continue after the unification of Germany and that the Alliance would not be transformed into a harmless political institution. In official Russian calculations, NATO should either have been dissolved after the Warsaw Pact was terminated or transformed into a political association under overall control of the Organization for Security and Cooperation in Europe (OSCE). Envisaging an important role for Russia, Prime Minister Viktor Chernomyrdin openly called for a "collective security system" in Europe at the OSCE's Lisbon conference in December 1996.[53]

It is difficult to decide whether the "NATO threat" as trumpeted by Russian leaders was a genuinely perceived challenge or a "contrived threat evoked for political advantage."[54] Nevertheless, the threat was deliberately exaggerated in order to mobilize domestic public opinion, to elicit sympathy among Russophiles in Western capitals, and to gain leverage with the NATO states.[55] NATO, led by the United States, remained as the generic adversary and a focal point for Russian unity, even though cooperation with Washington in numerous arenas was deemed necessary. Even the avowed reformer, Deputy Prime Minister Anatoly Chubais, asserted to business and government leaders in Davos, Switzerland, in March 1997 that the admission of new NATO members would create a nationalist backlash and push Moscow into ending its cooperation with the International Monetary Fund (IMF) and the World Trade Organization (WTO).[56] In displays of political blackmail, the Kremlin periodically issued warnings that NATO enlargement would stimulate a nationalist response, strengthen the position of anti-Western hard-liners, and undermine cooperation on a range of issues, including arms control and weapons proliferation. Such threats carried some resonance in Western policy circles, but raised even greater fears in Eastern Europe that neoimperialism continued to be a central factor in Russian policy.

Moscow and its Western supporters claimed that Russia lacked the resources, capabilities, and intentions to dominate the Eurasian heartland and that it posed no threat to U.S. and European interests.[57] However, such contentions assumed that domination was necessarily military or that current capabilities necessarily matched ultimate objectives. The "front line" states of Eastern Europe were clearly not impressed by Russian arguments and pressed for NATO membership to guarantee their security regardless of leadership changes and tactical policy shifts. Kremlin opposition to NATO growth raised fears that Russia harbored hidden designs and accentuated East European aspirations for entry into the Alliance.

Russian policy analysts persistently warned about "isolating Russia" and creating an anti-Western reaction in the country. By "isolation" they understood ongoing NATO enlargement and the curtailment of any Russian role in the foreign and security policies of former Soviet satellites. According to this position, Russia had already offered the maximum "geopolitical concessions" to the West and remained a "regional superpower" that simply could not be ignored.[58] The Russian military doctrine, adopted in April 2000, described NATO expansion and cooperation with former Soviet republics as threats to Russian security. NATO's growth was assailed as an anti-Russian offensive that could eventually encompass all former Soviet republics and undermine their national interests.

Russia's military, for both institutional and political reasons, rang the alarm bells that NATO expansion constituted a major security threat to Moscow's traditional sphere of influence. Some commentators also accused the United States of encouraging conflicts within and between the CIS states or embroiling Russia's military in dispersed trouble spots in order to weaken its capabilities.[59] The military used the justification of a NATO threat to canvass for a larger defense budget. the Basic Principles of Military Doctrine of the Russian Federation, issued in 1993, defined as a military threat any "approach of military blocs and alliances toward Russia's borders."[60] The revised military doctrine, issued in April 2000, stated that a major security threat to Russia was the hegemonic policies of Washington and the potential "enlargement of military blocs and alliances" along Russia's borders.[61]

NATO actions were depicted as imperialistic U.S. attempts to dominate the European continent and eliminate Russia's influence. The United States was allegedly seeking to impose its political and economic dominance and a "cultural uniformity" throughout "Eurasia." NATO expansion and the process of globalization were highlighted as the Trojan horses for U.S. planetary control. The Washingtonian offensive was intended to prevent the "reintegration" of the post-Soviet countries and to create conflicts between these states and Moscow. NATO and the United States were purportedly intent on ousting Russia from "the regions of its traditional presence and influence."[62] Observers in Moscow claimed that NATO's Partnership for Peace, launched in 1993 to foster intermilitary cooperation, was a method for undermining the CIS and infringing on Russia's sphere of influence. In response to these "threats," anti-Western coalitions gained ground seeking a tighter integration of the CIS and adopting a more combative anti-NATO posture. Russia's political leaders only grudgingly accepted the NATO-Russia Founding Act in May 1997, which provided Moscow with a consultative voice in NATO debates.

Russia's leading politicians asserted that the country's international weakness was only temporary and that it would recover its global position once it underwent an internal "renewal." In the summer of 1998, Foreign Minister Primakov praised the early-eighteen-century achievements of Prince Aleksandr Gorchakov, who restored Russia's strength and geopolitical reach after the disastrous Crimean War.[63] Such statements highlighted how the elites found it difficult to adjust to a postcolonial status in which Russia had become a mid-level power with restricted international influence.

In order to revive Russia's status, it suited Moscow to periodically restoke the Cold War with NATO. Armed Forces Chief, General Anatoliy Kvashnin launched diatribes against Washington, claiming that NATO was a major security threat to Russia.[64] His arguments were reminiscent of the Soviet era. Russian officials periodically demonstrated how Russia remained surrounded by unfriendly powers or by regional trouble spots. For centuries, as the Muscovite empire expanded its borders largely through conquest, the perception of outside threat was manipulated to justify militarism, external hostility, and the imposition of an internal state of siege.

In February 1996, Colonel Valeriy Mironov, the principal military adviser to Russia's prime minister, stated that "the Cold War still goes on and only one definite period of it is over."[65] He indicated that Russia would adopt a more forthright position once the country's economy recovered and it could restore its military potential. In essence, despite its defeat in the Cold War, regardless of the collapse of the Communist bloc, and irrespective of the disintegration of the Soviet Union, political and military elites did not acknowledge their postimperial status. All former colonial powers, including Britain and France, have experienced psychological and political traumas in adjusting to their reduced role in world affairs. But in Russia, the deimperialization process has proved especially problematic because the imperial temptation served some vital political interests.

Russian officials, military commanders, and virtually the entire political establishment firmly believed that Russia remained a global power with crucial national security interests across Europe and Asia. In Kremlin estimations, without Russian supervision the entire area from the Baltic to the Pacific was threatened either by chaos or by NATO and U.S. domination. Officials exploited the NATO issue for two main purposes. First, by attacking the Alliance, they calculated that they would gain economic concessions from the West to help pacify their rhetoric. And second, Moscow consistently fed its populace with a diet of fear with regard to external dangers and foreign interference. Having lost its capacity to challenge NATO militarily, Moscow demonstrated to its own public that Russia was still capable of standing up to the United States in pursuing its own distinct agenda.

Irrespective of Moscow's perceptions, NATO's expansion is not a security threat to Russia, but a challenge to Russia's exertion of predominant influence in the post-Communist states. The notion of NATO as a pan-European security structure presented a problem for Moscow, which insisted that this would result in the recreation of two hostile camps. The majority of East European states viewed NATO as a security provider and not a regional destabilizer. They contended that their inclusion in the Alliance would actually lessen anti-Russian sentiments stemming from a historically grounded sense of threat. The prospect of incorporation also ensured that aspirant states implemented the required criteria for membership, including civil-military reform and the forging of interstate treaties. This process contributed significantly to stabilizing Russia's western borders. Rationally speaking, it would directly serve the interests of a democratic Russia to support NATO inclusion for all East European states as this would lessen security uncertainties and allow the Kremlin to focus on more pressing domestic and foreign security challenges. However, such an approach required a profound break with Russia's great power traditions.

Russia's expansive policies toward Eastern Europe have escalated because the region has become a major transit route for energy supplies to an expanding EU. In the framework of Moscow's revived assertiveness, energy dependency proved valuable in relations with former satellites. State-connected oil and gas companies assumed an important role in Moscow's foreign relations. Energy firms earned over half of the country's export revenues while their taxes constituted the largest part of Russia's federal budget. East Europeans remained highly suspicious of Russia's energy giants, especially as they were not managed in a transparent fashion and maintained close ties with the Kremlin. After it was privatized in 1993–1994, Gazprom became Russia's largest company, supplying about 20 percent of the world's gas production and owning about 40 percent of global gas reserves. It became an enormous business empire accounting for about 8 percent of Russia's gross domestic product (GDP) and the single largest source of hard currency for the state.[66] Government ownership in Gazprom by 2000 stood at 40 percent and state officials exerted an important influence in its operations. Viktor Chernomyrdin, who was instrumental in consolidating the company in the early 1990s, served as Yeltsin's prime minister in the late 1990s.

At critical times, companies such as Gazprom act as arms of government. They have on occasion cut off supplies to targeted countries and even diverted energy from lucrative western markets in order to gain political advantages for Moscow. In such instances, the expansion of political influence conflicts with the goal of profitability. Some analysts contend that rather than Russia's authorities simply manipulating the energy sector to achieve foreign policy goals, the energy sector also impacts on foreign policy. Loss of revenues through a supply boycott needs to be compensated, whether through financial benefits or personal favors. Energy is viewed as a key geostrategic tool and a crucial security question. Officials believe that Russia is being deliberately pushed out of the CIS countries, both politically and economically, in order for the United States to gain exclusive control over Caspian–Central Asian energy resources and Russia has to vigorously counter such pressures.[67]

The oligarchs who emerged from the Soviet system and were often privileged members of the Communist nomenklatura had an immense impact on economic development, political decisionmaking, and Russia's foreign policy. Under Yeltsin, a close symbiosis was forged between the oligarchs and the president, and their wealth was "grafted to his power."[68] Close connections were established between business monopolies and the Russian authorities. The new businessmen, many of whom operated as semilegal robber barons, created their own private fiefdoms and security units, and recruited senior officers from the former KGB.[69] They expanded their operations abroad through a massive outflow of Russian capital. Oligarchic groups intermeshed closely with officialdom, whether by gaining valuable contacts, contracts, assets, or loans through the state privatization process. They established business lobbies in the Duma and gained high-level supporters in the administration. The impact of the oligarchs under the Yeltsin administration was a form of "state capture" by narrow vested interests, including coalitions of businessmen, well-financed politicians, and well-connected factory directors.

The financial crisis in Russia in the summer of 1998 alerted policymakers to the destabilizing influence of oligarchs in pursuing personal interests sometimes at the expense of the Russian state. One of the objectives of the new Vladimir Putin presidency was to rein in independent businessmen and mobilize them in the service of the government. At the same time, Putin granted his predecessor and his business clan sweeping immunity from prosecution. Some of the oligarchs concluded by the late 1990s that it was in their interests to have a more effective state as all the major privatization deals were completed and they needed a strong but compliant government to safeguard their holdings.[70] They curried favor with the Putin presidency, based around the revitalized security network, which needed big business to assist in the reconstruction of Russia's domestic and international power.

INSPECTOR PUTIN TAKES CHARGE

Russia has traditionally been preoccupied with foreign policy often at the expense of domestic reforms, thus placing internal issues in the shadow of Moscow's ambition for international grandeur. Even though officials have acknowledged the limited resources available to pursue foreign policy goals, international objectives were a primary source of prestige and status. After Vladimir Putin captured the presidency in 2000, there was a renewed focus on consolidating a strong central government and pursuing a policy of *derzhavnost* and *gosudarstvennost,* or authoritarian statism that would restore Russia's great power status: "*Derzhavnost* can be interpreted as a call to create a strong, paternalist, and to some extent expansionist state. Rather than nationalism, this ideology is a return to a traditional Russian form of legitimacy characteristic of the tsarist and Soviet periods, in which the idea of a strong state replaces that of a nation and the state is situated above society."[71]

Putin's political philosophy emphasized that a strong state was the basis of solving Russia's accumulated problems. Such a policy would enable Russia to project its eroded international position, especially on the former Soviet territories, and was supported by a broad range of political forces—from liberal to nationalist. Putin sought to develop a stronger national identity as a strategic goal to fill the vacuum left by the eradication of Sovietism. He presented his mission as reviving the state, championing the Russian "national idea," combating separatism, and saving the country from disintegration.[72] Putin's "Russia First" policy was also a reaction to what was perceived as the failures of Westernization, the shortcomings of liberalism, and alleged U.S. aims to weaken Russia. Under Putin, statist nationalism was consolidated as the governing idea and modus operandi if not a fully formed ideology. It was backed by the political and intellectual elites, and following elections in March 2000, Russian foreign policy became more forceful, coherent, co-ordinated, and methodical in terms of goals and strategies.[73]

The military and security services gained ascendancy after 2000. Russia's democrats, moderates, and pro-Westerners were squeezed to the political margins. The second Chechen war mobilized the country's nationalist and imperialist forces, while Putin himself increasingly determined Moscow's strategies toward the West. Critics argued that under the Yeltsin adminis-tration, foreign policy had been too accommodating and failed to sufficiently project Russian "national interests."[74] The appointment of Foreign Minis-ter Igor Ivanov provided a degree of continuity with the hard-line Primakov but injected new vigor and assertiveness. While seeking cooperation and in-vestment from the West, the Kremlin played on nationalistic and patriotic themes and periodically employed anti-Western rhetoric domestically to maintain the support and motivation of the army and security services.

Russia's embryonic democratic institutions eroded as Putin's policies "di-minished the democratic legacy of the reform years."[75] The presidential ex-ecutive retained control over policy and succeeded in further undercutting parliamentary authority. Putin increased state supervision over all political parties and pressure groups. The president's retinue created a new "person-ality cult" in which Putin was depicted as a determined and virtually infal-lible leader who would save Russia from disintegration and restore its international glory.[76] Putin also promoted the image of a down-to-earth pragmatist and realist, especially when dealing with Western audiences, lead-ing some to believe that he was the first Russian leader "to move beyond Russia's traditional great power ambitions."[77] He was described as focused on economic modernization and Russia's integration into the global economy without any controversial long-term political ambitions.

Under Yeltsin, Russia did not develop a strong entrepreneurial middle class but a small group of powerful tycoons with inordinate political influence, who were less interested in the creation of effective legal institutions.[78] The new president used the economic groups to his political advantage in an ef-fort to weaken alternative sources of political and economic power that did not serve Kremlin interests and to harness business more closely to the state. These included many of the oligarchic groups, the independent media, and regional governors. "Private interests" barely existed in Russia at high levels as most organizations became interconnected with the state apparatus.[79]

Putin pledged a strong-arm government that would resolutely fight crime and corruption, eliminate terrorist and separatist groups, restore law and order, and shield the population from economic hardship. Such objectives seemed unlikely to be achieved by democratic means but through the imposition of quasi-authoritarianism. Putin sought to recentralize power and reign in Russia's regions and economic interest groups. This policy was styled as the "vertical line of power" in which the country was divided into seven federal super-regions that coincided with its military districts. Moscow appointed regional representatives answering directly to the Kremlin. Five of the seven initial appointees were former KGB or military officers whose role was to supervise local governors and report directly to the president's office. They also became members of the presidential Security Council.

In its self-proclaimed "managed democracy," the Kremlin was determined to wrest control over all crucial political, institutional, repressive, informational, financial, and economic instruments. The Duma became a more pliant and docile body than under Yeltsin. It was directed by the Kremlin in electing its leaders and voting on key legislation. Aside from the Communists, there was no significant political opposition and little sign of conflict with the executive. Putin also eliminated the political role of the Federal Council, or upper chamber of parliament. The existence of political parties was largely dependent on the will of the Kremlin and the newly created "party of power" (United Russia) became an additional instrument of political control.[80] Even though political freedoms were increasingly restricted, the majority of the population supported Putin's policies and favored his strong-arm approach. In the December 2003 parliamentary elections, United Russia captured a majority of seats together with two smaller ultranationalist parties favored by the Kremlin, as Putin intensified his authoritarian agenda Putin himself was re-elected president in a landslide victory in March 2004 in which his rivals were either politically discredited or ignored by the Russian media.

Despite the president's avowed backing for democracy, press censorship returned to Russia. Putin endorsed the Doctrine of Informational Security, which allowed the state to intervene in media policy and silence or change editorial teams, while critical journalists stood accused of sympathizing with terrorists and separatists.[81] Putin's election campaign chief proclaimed that the president held the right to control the media in order to achieve "national accord" and to "use all power at his disposal" to punish critics. The president also influenced public opinion through indirect controls over much of the mass media; companies such as Gazprom purchased media outlets with governmental approval.

Irrespective of repeated promises to fight corruption, Putin permitted violations of antimonopoly legislation by business owners closely connected to the Kremlin. He was more intent on combating businessmen who opposed his policies than in challenging the economic powers of loyal oligarchs who could serve his political ambitions. As with the state, the media, and civil society, Putin believed it necessary to concentrate power over big business and strengthen the role of the state in economic activities. He established close ties with many large entrepreneurs, calculating that they would be politically useful. During the summer and fall of 2003, police actions and criminal investigations were launched against business barons who planned to be involved in the December 2003 parliamentary elections and the March 2004 presidential ballot in opposition to Putin.[82] Fears heightened that the Kremlin was intent on nationalizing several large strategic companies.

Putin's commitment to a transparent and competitive market economy remains highly suspect despite a wide-ranging program of reforms announced during the summer of 2001.[83] The new presidency was determined to collect taxes for the state budget, regulate the economy, and fulfill Russia's external financial obligations in order to improve its global economic prospects. Putin was not averse to forging tactical alliances with Communists and nationalists where this could serve his goals. During his first term in office, he brokered a deal with the Communists on the nomination of the Duma speaker and on the division of parliamentary committees. The president expanded his political base beyond his close circle of security officials and military generals to include nationalists, Communists, and centrists.

Putin's system of government became a parody of democracy. Although he spoke often about the "rule of law," he also asserted his belief in a strong state as a "traditional Russian value" while rejecting the "Anglo-Saxon model of liberal governance" because it was "ill-suited for Russia." The independence of the judiciary was undermined and it became a punitive tool in the hands of the presidential administration.[84] The former KGB regained much of its power. Putin himself was a longtime KGB operative who served as an intelligence officer for fifteen years and was head of the Federal Security Service (Federalnaya Sluzhba Bezopasnosti [FSB]) in 1998–1999. The promotion of individuals with a security background to various state bodies concentrated power and threatened democratic development. The FSB pursued an integrated and centralized system of intelligence and counterintelligence, similar to the old KGB system, and Putin's former associate, Nikolai Patrushev, became its director. Putin actively promoted the Russian intelligence and security apparatus and their staffing and funding were no longer subject to budgetary scrutiny or parliamentary oversight. Many former high-ranking KGB officials were appointed to senior political and advisory positions in the administration. At least seventeen high-ranking former KGB officials were promoted to senior Kremlin posts within the first year of Putin's tenure. Many were responsible for political repression under the Soviet regime. By the end of his Putin's first year in office, the Duma included twenty-two generals either from the army or the former KGB.

Security agencies stepped up their harassment of human rights activists, Western nongovernmental organizations (NGOs), nonofficial religious groups, and Putin critics.[85] Domestic intelligence gathering was expanded; for example, through the creation of an eavesdropping network giving the security services the authority to monitor all Internet traffic. This contributed to instilling a pervasive sense of fear regarding arbitrary government measures. The intelligence services were also buttressed in their foreign operations given Russia's relative economic and military weakness and its greater reliance on information gathering and technological theft. Espionage activities were markedly beefed up in various regions, including Eastern Europe.

In January 2000, Acting President Putin approved a new National Security Concept and in April 2000 he signed a new military doctrine.[86] The National Security Concept focused on Russia's economic crisis as the main source of national insecurity.[87] While the political concept charged that Washington was intent on creating an international structure based on its own dominance, the military doctrine emphasized various possibilities to counteract NATO expansion and U.S. hegemony. The military budget was increased and the president sought to rally political and public support for Russia's defense and security agencies. Putin's attempts at military reform proved difficult, because of budgetary constraints and opposition from senior military figures against large-scale restructuring. In March 2001, Defense Minister Igor Sergeyev was replaced with Sergey Ivanov, Putin's close former KGB comrade. Nikolai Pankov, a career intelligence officer with close ties to both Putin and Ivanov, was appointed head of the Defense Ministry's chief personnel administration.

Officials from the intelligence agencies constituted around 13 percent of the federal government apparatus as Putin installed military and secret service personnel to all sectors of the state bureaucracy to consolidate his power. Prominent Russian analysts believed that Putin was laying the foundations for autocracy. In an interview for *Moskovskie Novosti* in July 2003, sociologist Olga Kryshtanovskaya claimed that "preparations for a transition to an authoritarian model have already been made. And at the first signal, the mechanism will go into motion."[88] Such a mechanism can work through the "vertical system of the federal districts." Security councils were created in each district and regional law enforcement officials were subordinated to district structures rather than to regional governors.

Putin appealed to the concept of Russia's greatness to create the image of a strong and successful leader.[89] In a speech to the federal assembly in July 2000, he promised to restore Russia to its former position as a great state.[90] Such an approach was necessary to rekindle faith in the presidency, to mobilize public opinion, and to unite Russia's disparate political forces. Although the Russian Federation inherited the foreign policy apparatus of the USSR, the absence of clear policy direction and regular policy shifts under Yeltsin complicated its operations. Putin injected a greater degree of coordination between state organs and business interests in pursuing a more united foreign policy. He increased the level of presidential involvement, established a clearer hierarchy of decisionmaking, introduced stricter discipline in the foreign policy machinery, allocated significant state resources, and insured greater secrecy in foreign policy operations.[91] Putin strengthened the role of the National Security Council in foreign policy, which he directed briefly in 1999 and where he helped to forge the new National Security Concept: "Security Council membership has again been expanded to include the armed forces chief of staff and the seven supraregional presidential representatives; the leaders of the two chambers of the parliament have also regained their seats. About 90% of the Council's 178 staff are reported to be former KGB personnel."[92]

The president appointed trusted comrades to key positions and closely consulted the security agencies, especially the Foreign Intelligence Service, on foreign policy issues. But he preferred to reach consensus in a smaller grouping than the Security Council. Putin's "power vertical" assumed the "unchallenged dominance of the Kremlin in managing domestic and foreign policy in Russia."[93] Analysts believed that in foreign policy Putin was attempting to balance various power interests, some of which were in conflict.[94] He pandered to anti-Western sentiments in the army and the security services while maintaining cordial relations with the United States.

Putin also drew the mammoth energy industries more closely into his foreign policy through personal connections, state ownership of energy shares, and government energy contracts. While Yeltsin used the oligarchs to guarantee his own power, Putin manipulates the oligarchs to maintain his preponderance and to expand Russian state interests. Businessmen became "one of the key domestic resources of the Kremlin in its foreign policy."[95] Gazprom is closely linked to the highest political levels and the government can apply irresistible leverage through the Ministry of Fuel and Energy and state-controlled pipelines in regulating amounts and schedules for export. Gazprom's chairman, Dmitry Medvedev, was also deputy chief of the presidential administration. While Russian businessmen view Putin's "pragmatism" as an opportunity to expand their contacts and profits in the West, for the Kremlin they provide a valuable resource for promoting Russia's international agendas and gaining economic benefits. The foreign policy concept issued in 2000, emphasized Russian "economic interests" as an important component of foreign policy.

Putin's Kremlin sets for itself several priority objectives in its foreign policy agenda. These include: restoring Russia's "global presence," promoting and projecting Russia's great power identity, undermining the United States as the sole superpower by inhibiting its range of maneuverability, creating alliances with countries that were wary of U.S. influence, exploiting conflicts between Washington and its European allies, and using strategic resources to gain economic and political influence in Russia's former empire. It also trumpets the notion in Western capitals that without the inclusion of Russia and consistent NATO-Russian cooperation, European security cannot be guaranteed. Key Russian analysts believe that with Putin's appointment the process of "consolidating Russia's geopolitical space" has accelerated.[96] Russia is now a much more active and influential international player and, unlike Yeltsin, Putin has not been viewed domestically as Washington's vassal.[97]

With the aim of centralizing foreign policy, Putin also sought to rein in the foreign relations of various regional and sectoral interests. This became a challenging task where twenty-seven of Russia's regions became international frontiers after the disintegration of the USSR. But it was deemed essential to prevent any moves toward separatism.[98] Seven super-regions were established and supervised by a new layer of presidential representatives and plans were drawn up to consolidate Russia's regions and autonomous territories. In January 2003, Putin urged the Foreign Ministry to help Russia's regions to coordinate their international ties in order to promote the country's objectives.[99]

In the initial phase of political consolidation, Putin sharpened Russia's relations with the West and depicted the United States as a strategic adversary. His priorities were to strengthen the central government, revive the economy, reinvigorate the armed forces, and reassert Russia's global power status. But even before 11 September 2001, Putin began to apply a more accommodating strategy toward Washington. The Kremlin devised a policy of cooperation and nonconfrontation that could bring Russia long-term economic and political dividends.[100] After 11 September, it avoided harsh attacks and even signaled that it would not oppose further NATO enlargement. Moscow was also prepared to share intelligence and make other contributions to America's struggle against international terrorism. Putin's willingness to collaborate with Washington brought him into friction with military leaders, but they are in a weak position to openly oppose his policies. Although the government adopted a pro-Western position, much of the leadership and bureaucracy remains resistant.[101] Few young people have entered the foreign and intelligence services and the bureaucracy only selects people holding similar precepts. This is particularly evident in the Defense Ministry, where young officers, similarly to the old generals, are distrustful of the West and view the world in Cold War terms.

Putin's foreign policy approach can be compared to that of the Tsarist foreign minister Aleksandr Gorchakov in the nineteenth century.[102] In aiming to alter the global distribution of power to Russia's advantage, the Putin presidency displays a nonaggressive foreign policy in which cooperation with the United States and integration into international economic institutions is pursued in order to generate resources and markets to help rebuild and modernize the Russian economy.[103] This lulls the West into a false sense of security and an illusion of permanent partnership while Moscow steadily seeks to rebuild the state as a global power. The strategy is designed to "lower the costs connected with an overturn of the existing order" in which the

United States is the dominant power.[104] Behind Russia's economic priorities lurks the specter of competitive politics aimed at the global redistribution of power to Moscow's advantage.

In sum, Putin's foreign policy, especially with respect to the United States, can be described as "strategic jiu jitsu" skillfully played by a seasoned judo master. In this strategy, the strengths and advantages of the adversary are exploited to benefit Russia without surrendering the ultimate objective of gaining parity with the United States and assuming predominance in regions adjacent to the Russian Federation. In this ploy, the economic, political, and military vulnerabilities of neighbors are methodically exploited to Moscow's advantage. The judo master is not necessarily a gentleman who respects weaker partners but a trained intelligence agent who perceives both strength and weakness as opportunity that is couched as pragmatism.

FROM CONFUSION TO CONCENTRATION: RUSSIAN DECISIONMAKING

It is valuable to assess Russia's decisionmaking process since the collapse of the USSR, as well as ties between government and business in the foreign policy arena. Observers of Kremlin politics believe that multiple actors with a great deal of latitude conducted Russian foreign policy especially in the early 1990s, including ministries, military lobbies, and commercial interests such as Gazprom and Lukoil.[105] Some analysts conclude that Russian decisionmaking for much of the 1990s was amorphous, unstructured, incoherent, inconsistent, and often ad hoc. Various state agencies pursued their own agendas regardless of state interests and compromises were difficult to reach.[106] Moreover, officials were often catering to two divergent audiences: domestic and international. This unpredictability was reinforced by the secretive nature of Russian decisionmaking, by the confusion that accompanied Soviet disintegration, and by "debilitating contradictions" in policymaking and implementation.[107] However, Lynch provides a more convincing interpretation; he asserts that Russian foreign policy since 1991 has proved relatively successful in upholding two central policy objectives that are sometimes conflictive: "Establishing Russian diplomatic and security hegemony throughout the territory of the former Soviet Union as well as Russia's 'great power' status in international councils while at the same time avoiding a rupture with the G-7 states, in the first place the United States, whose cooperation remains essential to Russia's internal as well as external prospects."[108]

The crumbling of the Soviet Communist Party disrupted and dispersed foreign policy among various decisionmakers, including the Foreign and Defense Ministries. Under Yeltsin, the presidential bureaucracy began to replicate the Communist apparatus at the apex of the policy process.[109] The presidential Security Council, formally a consultative body assembling key government officials, was propelled into a position of power, creating tensions in the foreign policy arena between the Security Council, the Foreign Ministry, and the parliamentary Committee on Foreign Affairs. Yeltsin established a superpresidential administration in which ministries and other state institutions were duplicated. It became almost impossible to remove the president from office and Yeltsin himself needed to approve any changes in the constitution. According to Article 86 of the 1993 Russian constitution, formal power over Russian foreign policy was vested in the president. The Foreign Ministry usually played a secondary role even though the appointment of Primakov injected greater prominence for the institution, which then played a more substantial coordinating role.

Although Yeltsin was often personally detached and uninterested in foreign policy, when it suited him he intervened in decisionmaking. Ministers responsible for security and foreign affairs reported directly to him rather than the prime minister. He balanced competing agencies and they were principally expected to implement foreign policy rather than to fashion it. However, without the Soviet Communist apparatus, the president did not have at his disposal a significant organization to coordinate policy. This exacerbated contradictions and confusion in decisionmaking.

In the absence of a firm center of coordination, various agencies pursued some elements of foreign policy by default. The military seemed to conduct its own policies in several conflict zones, such as Moldova and the Baltic states, in the early 1990s, where they supported separatist and autonomist movements among Russian speakers. By 1993, Yeltsin's administration regained the initiative and reigned in rogue actors as the new constitution gave the president appropriate powers. With greater assertiveness by the Kremlin, especially toward the CIS states, a compromise was reached between various interest groups and governmental departments:

> From 1993 onwards various arms of the government appeared to act in a much more vigorous, coordinated manner to assert Russian dominance, using military, political, and economic levers . . . and military basing rights for Russian troops were established in most states. This agreement among the executive agencies to harmonize their actions around a more assertive policy line was an essential prerequisite for the overall policy shift . . . in the direction of Pragmatic Nationalism. While military spokesmen still tended to take a more hawkish line than the Foreign Ministry and the President's office, this began to appear more often as evidence of a natural "division of labor" within a unified plan of action than of disunity over strategy.[110]

Struggles were visible within the decisionmaking structure over the definition of security threats and what these portended for the Russian military.[111] Threat definitions determine government doctrine, budgets, and policy. Throughout the 1990s, negative assessments of the NATO enlargement process favored the hard-line core of the military leadership and severely hampered cooperation with the North Atlantic Alliance. This position was fueled by NATO's New Strategic Concept, which broadened the mandate for Alliance security tasks, and by the war over Kosovo in the spring of 1999, which enabled military officials to argue that the threat to Russian security was escalating.[112] The NATO threat was exaggerated in policy circles in order to gain political mileage and more significant funding for the military and it generated fears among Russia's neighbors over the government's strategic ambitions. Moreover, the influence that the Russian General Staff exercised over the formulation of defense policy and in obstructing military reform was viewed as a primary source of threat in Eastern Europe.

Near the end of his tenure, Yeltsin on the advice of Primakov and several military and intelligence officials, handpicked Putin as his successor. Putin's administration accelerated the process of centralization and focused on controlling Russia's business interests. Under Yeltsin, powerful economic lobbies played a significant role in government decisions and often influenced parliamentary votes through financial or personal connections. The energy giants in particular were believed to exert an inordinate influence over Russian foreign policy as they sought to magnify their profits and supported policies that opened up markets for their supplies.

Connections between the presidential administration and the most significant energy companies were tightened during Putin's reign. The new president inserted a new team of executives into semiprivatized companies such as Gazprom, which became more dependent on his approval. Moreover, all crude oil pumped out of Russia still needed to pass through a central state-owned pipeline system and the government assigned oil companies quotas for access. This provided Moscow with ultimate control over the industry.[113] In January 2003, Prime Minister Mikhail Kasyanov reiterated that energy pipelines would remain under state control. He asserted that the government would not tolerate the construction of private pipelines in Russia.[114] All major oil pipelines are controlled by the state-run monopoly Transneft, while Gazprom runs all natural–gas pipelines. Kasyanov's statement put in doubt plans by Russian and foreign investors to build pipelines worth tens of billions of dollars.

There were congruencies between government and business where Moscow sensed advantages to secure favorable trade agreements and influence local interest groups in targeted states. Moreover, the Russian government held substantial shares in the energy companies and under Putin endeavored to exert more direct control over the most vital Russian industries. In the summer of 2003, Putin launched a crackdown on some of the obstreperous tycoons who refused to tow his political line. The Kremlin was concerned that some of the richest businessmen were planning to convert their wealth into political influence in the upcoming presidential and parliamentary elections. Putin also continued to place his former KGB colleagues in senior positions in the major energy companies.[115] Meanwhile, Gazprom remained the largest state-owned company that could provide resources for Putin's re-election bid.

Questions have arisen whether there are any significant internal conflicts over Russian policy toward Eastern Europe. At times the Ministry of Defense under Sergey Ivanov publicly declared a harder line than the Foreign Ministry or the presidency. However, some Russian analysts believe that most of these purported policy differences are willfully orchestrated in a "good cop–bad cop" routine.[116] Putin's election raised concerns among Russia's neighbors. The fortification and expansion of security, police, and intelligence forces were especially troubling for countries that had been prone to Russian pressure in the past.

The Putin government intended to rebuild a broad sphere of control in the former Soviet republics and to substantially increase its influence in parts of Central and South Eastern Europe. Numerous avenues were pursued to achieve such objectives, whether by forging alliances or by assisting authoritarian regimes or by supporting political groups and economic interests that were opposed to NATO membership and to growing U.S. influence. Despite the fact that Putin's Foreign Policy Concept no longer referred to the former satellites as lying within a "historical sphere of interest," East European governments were suspicious about the long-term objectives. Regardless of Moscow's episodic cooperation with the West, they believed that the Kremlin would endeavor to keep pro-U.S. governments off balance even if it could not dislodge them from power. This served Russia's "national security interests" because it maintained Moscow's involvement, created complications for the Alliance, stirred controversies between the United States and its European allies, thrust Moscow forward as a "mediator" or "partner" in resolving pressing security problems, and fortified Russia's ambition to become a significant "pole of power" vis-à-vis the United States.

2

Russia's Foreign Policy Arsenal

TARGETED ZONES AND GOALS

From Moscow's perspective, four major subzones can be distinguished in the eastern half of Europe: the European CIS, the Baltic region, Central Europe, and Southeast Europe. The European CIS (Belarus, Ukraine, Moldova) is as an important arena for regaining a broad sphere of Russian dominance and projecting Russia's rising international power toward Central and Western Europe. The reintegration of the "post-Soviet space" became a priority under Putin, as it would elevate Russia's contention that it was an important global player and a stabilizing factor in "Eurasia." Moscow opposes any significant foreign military presence in the region and seeks to dissuade its CIS neighbors from inviting U.S. forces or petitioning for NATO entry.

The Baltic states (Estonia, Latvia, Lithuania) are a vital buffer against Western encroachment on the former Soviet territories. The Kremlin has therefore sought to promote weak, isolated, and subservient Baltic neighbors, either devoid of close ties with Western security structures or maintained as small and irrelevant players by the Atlantic Allies and considered to be on NATO's periphery.

The Central Europeans (Poland, Hungary, Slovakia, Czech Republic) are viewed as a potentially negative source of influence over their CIS neighbors because of their progress toward Western integration. These countries are earmarked for neutralization or containment through targeted penetration. Central Europe also provides opportunities for Russian inroads toward the pan-European and transatlantic institutions. Moscow fears that the Central European and Baltic countries will inject Russophobic positions into the EU and it seeks ways of counteracting such trends through closer bilateral relations with West European states and the marginalization of East European newcomers in the EU's decisionmaking process.

The Southeast European or Balkan region (Slovenia, Croatia, Bosnia-Herzegovina, Serbia, Montenegro, Kosovo, Macedonia, Albania, Bulgaria, Romania) became a significant area of international competition for Moscow during the 1990s. Regional struggles with NATO and the United States were most pronounced during the armed conflicts in former Yugoslavia while the phase of postconflict reconstruction was also exploited by Russia despite its insignificant material contribution. The Kremlin has maneuvered to gain selected footholds in targeted countries, especially where political ties with Russia have been more pronounced in the past.

Within the four regions, Moscow has tried to influence each country's foreign and security policy, to benefit from local political, ethnic, subregional, religious, and social rivalries, to limit the progress of military integration with the United States, and to obstruct forms of regional cooperation that countered Russia's objectives to reestablish its zone of influence. The Kremlin's successes have varied. In some cases, it exerted critical leverage over a country's international priorities, in other instances its influences were limited or short-lived, and on occasion its policies have backfired as suspicions about Russia's motives contributed to propelling several capitals in a more determined westward direction. The Russian authorities realize that overt or direct control over Eastern Europe is impractical and expensive. Instead, they have determined several concrete and achievable policy targets. While some elements are attainable in a shorter time frame, other goals have a longer-term trajectory. Putin reinvigorated and clarified these objectives during his first term in office.

The first Kremlin goal is to achieve primary influence over the foreign orientations and security postures of nearby states. This is especially evident in the CIS area, where Moscow seeks exclusive control, but also applies to key countries in the other three subregions.[1] The Russian authorities have pursued influence over the smaller and weaker states in order to secure political allies on the international stage or to neutralize their potential opposition to Russian policy. Moscow wants to forestall rival alliances that could effectively block Russian goals. In the case of NATO and EU entrants, the Kremlin seeks to impact on Union policy by increasing its influence among the new East European members. Control over foreign and security policy was guaranteed within the Soviet bloc. Currently, the Kremlin needs to be more flexible and active in gaining influence over political actors in pluralistic political settings.

Second, Russia has endeavored to gain increasing economic benefits and monopolistic positions through targeted foreign investments and strategic infrastructural buyouts in Eastern Europe. This can supply Moscow with substantial influence over any country's economic, financial, trade, and investment policies. As Russian capital hemorrhaged from the country, government officials tried to direct this toward nearby regions where the state has long-term strategic interests. In specific economic sectors, such as energy supplies, Russia seeks to establish a monopolistic regional position. In addition, by reigning in some of the most influential oligarchs, the Putin administration has increased its influence over foreign investments, intensified its political leverage, and captured a greater share of revenues for the state.

Third, Moscow aims to convert East Europe's overwhelming dependence on Russian energy supplies and economic investments into long-term, constant, and predictable intergovernmental influence. Close connections between the Kremlin and the largest Russian companies, whether through executive appointments, through the promotion of overseas operations, or through financial, legal, and police instruments, demonstrate that foreign policy is closely coordinated. Russian enterprises have been encouraged to gain political influence through involvement with officials, parties, and media outlets in targeted East European states.

Fourth, Russia has attempted to limit the scope and pace of Western institutional enlargement and integration, especially in the security arena in the European CIS states. Moscow has obstructed the creation of alliances such as the GUUAM initiative (comprising Georgia, Ukraine, Uzbekistan, Azerbaijan, Moldova) that could block Russian inroads and deepen the region's ties with NATO. Officials have opposed the process of security integration with NATO in order to prevent these countries from participating in U.S.-led coalitions opposed by Moscow. They have simultaneously pursued closer military integration in Russian dominated "collective security" mechanisms. Putin understood that Russia was too weak to prevent NATO enlargement in three of the subzones and that any failed opposition would be domestically and internationally damaging. Instead, he tried to minimize the impact of NATO's growth by seeking a role in Alliance decisionmaking and weakening its effectiveness.

Fifth, Moscow is preparing to use the region, especially the European CIS, as a springboard for rebuilding a larger sphere of influence and global status and reversing Moscow's decline as a major international player. Strategists calculate that this can be accomplished with the help of Western resources and by establishing a regional "great power" status in Eastern Europe and Asia. Russia can then pose not as a junior partner of the United States but as a key player increasingly able to balance American influence throughout "Eurasia."

And sixth, by intensifying its involvement in the European arena, Moscow seeks to undercut or damage transatlantic relations or the Europe-America link. The objective is to strengthen the Europe-Russia or Eurasian strategic "pole" vis-à-vis the United States and to establish a Russia-EU system of international security for the old continent.

In order to achieve these six principal objectives, the Russian arsenal deployed toward Eastern Europe includes an assortment of weaponry. Some levers have proved more advantageous in certain countries, but often a combination of tools is employed to promote Russian interests and expand Moscow's influence. While several policies are intended to gain short-term benefits, others are designed to have a longer-term impact in targeted countries. In several cases, Moscow's pressures have proved to be unsuccessful or have actually had the reverse effect by stiffening rather than softening resistance to Russian demands. The following forms of pressure, suasion, incentive, and coercion have been employed by the Russian authorities and its assorted agencies in various parts of Eastern Europe.

DIPLOMATIC PRESSURES

An assortment of diplomatic devices are deployed to enhance Russian political influence among neighbors, minimize their independent foreign policy orientations, and curtail forms of regional cooperation that would exclude Russia. Moscow has historically benefited from disputes and divisions in the region and the divergent interests of the West European powers. The Kremlin has most visibly applied political pressures against states that emerged from the defunct Soviet Union in order to influence their security and foreign policy orientation. High-level and sometimes ostentatious visits by Russian dignitaries or the deliberate snubbing of certain governments serve as standard diplomatic devices to extract concessions and voice approval or disapproval for specific foreign policies. Diplomatic initiatives are undertaken to draw governments into a closer alliance with Russia, especially where Moscow provides support in an ongoing internal crisis.

Treaties and other interstate agreements are manipulated to exert pressure on specific governments. Even when bilateral treaties were signed with several neighbors, their ratification by parliament was delayed or indefinitely postponed without presidential opposition. The resistance displayed by the Russian legislature at vital times was a smokescreen for government noncompliance with an existing international agreement. This was reminiscent of the "good cop–bad cop" routine and was intended to extract maximum concessions from the targeted country by gaining greater advantage from reworking any interstate accord.

The Duma also influences the public mood and the political climate on various international issues. Frequent combative statements by deputies and party leaders in the Russian media have heated up the political environment and demonstrated to East Europeans that Moscow could adopt a harder approach against certain governments. Parliament has engaged in an indirect role in foreign policy by voicing controversial opinions that make the administration look moderate by comparison. It plays a useful role in putting forward more radical foreign policy proposals than the executive or issuing tough statements against Russia's neighbors. This often suits the government, which appears reasonable and accommodating. While under Yeltsin, the legislature was at times in considerable conflict with the presidency; under Putin it has consistently supported the president's foreign policy positions.

PROPAGANDA ATTACKS

Russian public opinion has been deliberately inflamed against certain East European governments in order to justify Kremlin pressures against recalcitrant neighbors. The capability to influence public opinion both at home and abroad is a key reasons why Putin tightened government controls over the broadcast media. Moscow's official or indirect control over numerous television outlets that broadcast programs to most former Soviet republics is a useful instrument for influencing public opinion and political elites in neighboring states. This has been plainly evident in Belarus, Ukraine, and Moldova, where a majority of citizens, and not only Russian ethnics, regularly watch the Moscow media.

An additional measure for influencing public and political opinion is the purchase of major media outlets in targeted states, especially television stations and popular newspapers with a wide audience. Russian businessmen with ties to the Moscow authorities have endeavored to acquire majority shares or outright ownership of media outlets in a number of countries. This provides a valuable means for airing opinions, commentaries, and discussions that enhance Moscow's foreign policy offensives. Moreover, the lack of professionalism and a penchant for sensationalism in much of the post-Communist media in Eastern Europe have assisted Moscow's objectives in planting damaging and misleading information for political ends.

DISINFORMATION CAMPAIGNS

Regular propaganda attacks by Russia's state media outlets are supplemented by more systematic disinformation campaigns in familiar KGB style operations. These have targeted particular governments, specific politicians, or pro-Western political parties in nearby states. These targets are depicted as dangerously "Russophobic" and thus their inclusion in NATO would allegedly poison the West's relations with Russia and introduce unstable states into the Alliance. The Russian press has frequently cited U.S. and European commentators who speak out against NATO enlargement on the grounds that it will undermine relations with Moscow by making the Alliance more anti-Russian.[2]

Russian officials have warned that including too many East European states would strengthen NATO's anti-Russian character and make the

Alliance more aggressive. Such assertions are intended to deter NATO leaders, as the acceptance of new members would allegedly engender conflicts with Russia. Moscow has regularly claimed that both NATO enlargement and its new missions in Kosovo and Bosnia-Herzegovina were unsuccessful and did not promote security on the European continent. Russian politicians and the media regularly claim that the NATO presence itself was responsible for ongoing instability in the Balkans rather than being a primary factor for disabling military hostilities, laying the groundwork for reconstrcution, and bringing war criminals to justice.

The Russian authorities have consistently used the traditional Soviet argument that any alleged threats to the country's security and attempts to "isolate" Russia would encourage extremist forces such as Communists and nationalists to challenge the moderate administration. A range of initiatives have been listed as constituting a threat to Russia, including NATO's absorption of Eastern Europe, new Alliance missions in Southeast Europe, the military modernization of the East European militaries, closer links between the United States and the CIS countries, and the building of U.S. bases in Eastern Europe.

MILITARY THREATS

Following the evacuation of the Red Army from Eastern Europe, the possibility of direct military intervention receded. Nevertheless, Russia's military and security apparatus inherited from the USSR has endeavored to maintain its influence and use its assets in much of the former Soviet Union, either through infiltration, covert intervention, or deliberate destabilization. Formally established in May 1992, the Russian military structure has tried to ensure itself a significant presence in virtually all former subject republics and has consistently lobbied the Kremlin for a tougher approach toward the "near abroad."[3] One key objective was to denuclearize the CIS and prevent the stationing of nuclear weapons in the former satellites. Russia sought to be the sole nuclear state in the region. According to the military doctrine issued in November 1993, Moscow extended the "nuclear umbrella" to all members of the CIS Collective Security Treaty, guaranteeing their territories against foreign invasion. Russia also sees both strategic and psychological value in maintaining forward military bases throughout the former USSR, as these are a source of visible power projection.

Military threats have been periodically issued in response to policies Moscow has opposed in Eastern Europe, such as NATO expansion, as this would purportedly provoke a renewed arms race. Russian policymakers claim that NATO aims to supplant its influences in all former Communist states. This provided justification for Russian military threats, seen as an essential defense of national interests. The threats themselves highlight East European contentions that Russia had not resigned itself to a loss of control in the region even though Moscow did not possess the capabilities to stage a massive re-armament against the "NATO threat."

Kremlin officials have regularly warned that Russia would suspend vari-ous nuclear and conventional arms control agreements, maintain tactical nuclear missiles in its western borderlands or even deploy additional war-heads, and form a strong military pact with CIS countries. Russia's military doctrine also provides for the first use of nuclear weapons under threaten-ing circumstances. All such statements and warnings are perceived by East European governments as direct threats to their security. Moscow also of-fered security guarantees to various states in order to woo them away from NATO and to discourage Alliance leaders from issuing invitations. These offers have been viewed in the Baltic capitals as attempts to entrap them in an unwelcome permanent alliance.

An additional reason for Moscow's opposition to NATO enlargement was fear that Russia's arms market could shrink as the East Europeans focused increasingly on Western suppliers for NATO-compatible equipment. Since Putin's appointment, Russia has redoubled its efforts to recapture the arms market among former satellites and establish more dependent military ties through economic instruments. Russia's military intelligence, much like its civilian counterpart, has also remained active in the former satellites.[4] According to General Valentin Korabelnikov, head of Russia's military-intelligence, the GRU, his agency continues to operate in even the most re-mote corners of the world. The GRU relies mostly on "special operations" to gain information and "active measures" to influence foreign agencies. In addition, Russian companies were eager to repair the military infrastructure of East European neighbors, thus giving them potential access to sensitive military information.

All CIS governments are systematically dissuaded by Moscow from join-ing alliances that are purportedly directed against Russia. The Federal Border Service (formerly the KGB Border Guard) also fulfills an important foreign policy role after assuming responsibility for guarding the outside borders of the entire CIS, which are viewed as vital to Russia's security. Internal bor-ders between the CIS states are still considered "transparent" and largely administrative.

Political and economic pressures are also applied to achieve the desired security results. After the appointment of Primakov as foreign minister in January 1996, Moscow redoubled its efforts at CIS military integration. The authorities issued warnings that the CIS treaty on collective security would be transformed into a more coherent military alliance in the event of NATO expansion to the old Soviet borders. This was a pointed threat aimed against Alliance aspirants in Central Europe. The threat failed to materialize after NATO enlargement. In some cases, military threats have been combined with enticements related to military contacts. In the case of allied governments in CIS countries, Russian officials promote closer military ties, whether for profitable arms trading or because it binds a nearby state closer to Russia.

In a disturbing development for Russia's neighbors, in October 2003 Defense Minister Sergey Ivanov outlined situations in which Moscow might carry out a preemptive military strike according to stipulations in a recently drafted military doctrine.[5] Russia reserved for itself the right to conduct such a strike if there was a distinct, clear, and inevitable military threat to the country, or if Moscow felt threatened by reduced access to regions where it possessed crucial economic or financial interests. Russia could also use its military might within the CIS if a "complex, unstable situation develops" or if there is a direct threat to Russian citizens or ethnic Russians. Such a flexible and wide-ranging doctrine will reinforce Russia's energy dominance, political influence, and economic penetration through a direct military threat.

PEACEKEEPING DEPLOYMENTS

During the 1990s, Moscow fomented, orchestrated, or capitalized on rebellions in neighboring CIS states and then pressed for the injection of Russian troops as long-term peacekeepers. Russia's 1993 military doctrine viewed the armed forces as an essential instrument of the country's foreign policy. This was clear in the nature of Moscow's peacekeeping missions, where Russian intervention under the guise of peacekeeping, "broke the cardinal rule of peacekeeping, which prohibits peacekeepers from siding with one of the combatants."[6] "Moscow often had a vested interest in the continuation of a 'controlled' level of violence: neither so great as to be seriously destabilizing, nor so minor as to obviate the need for a semi-permanent Russian force presence in the conflict zone."[7]

Russia established itself as the primary self-empowered peacekeeping force on the territory of the former Soviet Union. It has unilaterally decided which conflicts it should promote, at which juncture it should intercede as a mediator or crisis manager, and for how long its troops should remain on the disputed territory. Such a policy exerts enormous pressure on a targeted government, as its choices become limited between domestic war and territorial disintegration or foreign occupation disguised as peacekeeping. Russia's military doctrine posits various scenarios in which its peace-enforcement units can be deployed, including the possibility of unrest and secession in neighboring countries that necessitates a military mission to save the lives of Russian ethnics.

Russian units have been deployed in crisis points in several states, including Transnistria in Moldova. However, Russia is not a fully neutral party and has backed separatist movements in several newly independent states that enabled it to gain leverage over incumbent central governments. Russia has projected itself as "Eurasia's gendarme," whereby the entire space of the former USSR is proclaimed as a sphere of "vital interest" to Moscow. It has also sought UN recognition for the CIS as an "international organization" that would enable regional peacekeeping deployments decided by Moscow without prior UN Security Council approval.

ENERGY CONTROLS

Following Soviet disintegration, fossil fuels became Russia's key resource for rebuilding its economy, its military capabilities, and its foreign reach.[8] The Russian economy is reliant for about half of its foreign revenues on the export of crude and refined oil and natural gas. Other raw materials, such as metals, gold, and diamonds, are the next largest export items. The global rise in energy prices during the 1990s provided oil and gas companies and the Russian state with increasing revenues. Capital was used to acquire controlling shares in strategic industries in neighboring countries and to increase production to supply former satellites. The large energy companies were also intent on expanding and acquiring the major transportation infrastructures across the region to Western Europe.

Increasing energy sales provide a valuable lever for exerting foreign policy influence. As the dominant supplier of energy, Moscow has sought to prolong and deepen the dependence of all East European states. The promotion of economic vulnerability is a mechanism for both financial profit and political leverage. Energy and other strategic resources can be decreased or severed at important junctures to exert pressure on particular capitals to alter their policies. The threat of economic chaos resulting from energy sanctions has generated powerful pressures on governments to synchronize their policies with the Kremlin.

Putin has focused on energy as an important factor in foreign policy and the energy companies have become tools of the state leadership in which their mutual interests are closely intertwined.[9] Russia's pipeline network remains under state control through two state-owned companies: Transneft for oil and Gazprom for gas. The Kremlin calculates that it would be more profitable and politically advantageous not only to control energy supplies but also to refine and sell the final products. Russian company buyouts and ownership of key oil and gas infrastructure in Eastern Europe, such as pipelines, refineries, and storage sites, thereby enable Moscow to uphold additional leverage.[10] Control of energy transport systems has become one of the major elements in Russia's strategy toward former satellites. The energy industry became awash in cash during the last decade and could use these resources to purchase infrastructure and other assets.

The easiest targets for Russian investors are "debt-ridden, badly-run companies in poor, politically weak countries."[11] Once Russian energy giants gain a foothold in a country they endeavor to increase their share of ownership in local companies either directly or working through nominally independent subsidiaries. Most East Europeans remain weary of Russian investment and are only willing to allow entry when faced with no suitable alternatives. In addition to unwelcome political influences, Russian companies are riddled with criminality that threatens to corrupt local business practice.[12]

The energy giants have exerted influence over Russian politics through close connections between company directors and government officials. Moscow in turn uses energy diplomacy by exerting pressures and providing enticements to targeted neighbors. Putin has described Gazprom as "a powerful lever of political and economic influence in the world."[13] The government has been cautious in gas-sector reforms such as breaking-up Gazprom. Under a reform program drafted by the Economic Development and Trade Ministry, Gazprom was scheduled to lose control over its transport, storage, and distribution networks. Nonetheless, the Kremlin is seeking a balance between Gazprom's profitability and ultimate political direction over its operations. This will enable Moscow to transform its growing oil wealth into more expansive political power.

Moscow pursues geostrategic dominance in the energy sector by increasing the leverage of the main energy suppliers to consumer countries. Lukoil and Gazprom and their various subsidiaries have increased their share in energy markets and control a web of transit pipelines and energy outlets.[14] Both companies employ hundreds of former Soviet intelligence officers closely linked with the Putin administration. They utilize existing KGB networks throughout the region to advance the interests of the Russian state. Since 1992, Russian energy firms have created joint ventures with local private enterprises in many East European countries whose products were dependent on the import of Russian raw material. These industries invariably dominate gas and oil supplies. Such arrangements enable Russian energy conglomerates to create strong local consortiums fully dependent on Russian suppliers.

Some analysts posit that Russian investment in energy infrastructure abroad merely reflects the normal movement of capital into profitable ventures. Such explanations ignore the close ties between government and big business as well as the Kremlin's approval for a strategy that acquires strategic assets for state-connected Russian firms in countries where Moscow seeks to wield political clout. Moreover, the crackdown on big business in the fall of 2003 and greater state supervision of capital will intensify Moscow's direct economic influence in Eastern Europe. Government officials in the region contend that allowing Russian companies to purchase energy infrastructure compromises their national security, as the state will no longer have control over domestic production and distribution.

The Russian authorities and energy companies aim to balance political advantages with economic costs in applying their "fuel diplomacy" toward the various subzones of Eastern Europe.[15] Meanwhile, most countries in the region endeavor to diversify their energy sources in order to avoid dependence and potential political blackmail.[16] In some cases, dependence on Russia has been solidified in the absence of affordable alternatives. Moscow has also tried to lessen its vulnerability to East European blockages of energy supplies to the lucrative West European market. It purchases energy infrastructures in neighboring states, using a variety of transit outlets, and builds alternative routes to ensure transit diversity.

ECONOMIC LEVERAGE

In addition to energy supplies and infrastructure investments, Moscow holds trump cards vis-à-vis neighbors who remain dependent on Russia for credits, trade, and investment. In this "politicization of economics," Russia's objective is to enmesh states in a web of commercial and financial ties that buttress its political penetration. Foreign direct investment (FDI) outflow from Russia exceeded $3.2 billion in 2001 alone, and this figure covers only a small portion of total capital outflow abroad.[17] At least one third of Russian FDI has entered the former Soviet bloc. Conversely, through its high customs and tariff barriers, Moscow is very selective in the foreign business it allows to enter the country and favors companies tied with governments favorably disposed toward Russian policy.

In order to increase control over neighboring economies, Moscow focuses on acquiring strategic industries by business groups tied to the Russian state. This is not merely a question of seeking favorable conditions for Russian business, but of supporting companies that play a significant role in advancing Moscow's foreign policies. The official press has noted that business and government work in tandem to promote Russia's national interests. Firms with connections to state officials benefit from the privatization process in order to purchase key industries in accessible parts of the region. Russian companies often possess inbuilt advantages in competition with local enterprises, such as easier financing and cheaper raw materials. The main sectors targeted have included energy, banking, and telecommunications.

The Kremlin encourages state-connected companies or shell enterprises to acquire key sectors of the East European economies in order to gain political influence and favorable terms of trade. Gazprom has endeavored to obtain a share of lucrative telephone traffic between Russia and the rest of the continent via fiber-optic lines. Moscow also proposes building a wide-track railroad network through East Europe to enable it to transport its goods, a proposition that is widely opposed in the region. Vertically structured financial-industrial groups (FIGs) have acted as sectoral ministries and assisted in the process of supranational economic integration between Russia and its neighbors, especially following the privatization of strategic assets. Russia's multinational companies stand behind various economic takeovers in the region and some East European officials trace the directives for their operations back to the central government in Moscow. Clearly, the political risks associated with Russian investments are higher than that for other foreign powers economically active in the region.

Trade is also used as a weapon both as an enticement, through subsidies of various products and raw materials, and as a punishment, through partial or complete cutoffs in supply or the imposition of double tariffs on imports. In some instances, Moscow has reneged on fulfilling its trade agreements by refusing to pay for previous shipments on spurious financial grounds.[18] Large debts owed to Russia by CIS states such as Ukraine provide opportunities for Moscow's pressure, either by demands for prompt payment or debt forgiveness in exchange for Russian company ownership of strategic assets such as energy pipelines or military equipment.

EXPLOITING ETHNIC DIVISIONS

Over 25 million Russian ethnics or Russian-speakers are estimated to reside in the territories of nearby CIS states, of which the majority are permanent residents. Nearly half of this total resides in Ukraine, Belarus, and Moldova. The Russian diaspora does not everywhere consider itself to be interlinked, even though they were once part of the Soviet system. Nevertheless, the Russian authorities find it useful to consider all Russians residing abroad as an undifferentiated and uniform mass.[19] By seeking to preserve as many privileges for this population as possible, the Kremlin believes it is investing in a loyal social and political corpus that will be more amenable in backing Russian state policy. At the same time, it has discouraged immigration into Russia that could strain the country's social services and it contributes little material support for the diaspora.

Policymakers view the ethnic and Russian-speaking diaspora, irrespective of their citizenship, as a valuable form of regional influence. Moscow has applied intensive pressures on newly independent states to grant Russian-speakers an enhanced political status and through this channel it can increase its influence in each country. Kremlin officials and parliamentary deputies have pressed neighboring states to adopt dual-citizenship laws while offering all former Soviet citizens Russian citizenship The proindependence national leaders were labeled as nationalists while Russian-speaking or Sovietized minorities were depicted as progressive and internationalist forces. Moscow thrust itself forward as the arbiter in any resulting conflicts between nearby governments and the Russian diaspora.[20] Kremlin support for Russian minorities has radicalized their leadership and made the resolution of conflicts with incumbent governments more elusive. The diasporas have tended to vote for extremist Russian parties, including Communists and nationalists, who challenged the independence of newly formed states.[21]

The real or manufactured mistreatment of Russian minorities has "produced significant pressures in Moscow for interventionist policies."[22] Nationalist and Communist groups have lobbied the government to intervene on behalf of allegedly victimized Russians. Supportive or ambiguous signals from Moscow encourage local radicals to pursue their agendas in the belief that Russia will assist them. Through the threat of unrest and secession, officials in Moscow have pressured nearby countries to enhance the political representation of Russian minorities. This became a useful method for increasing influence and keeping a troublesome neighbor off balance. In some cases, Russia has pressed for territorial revisions by laying claims to areas considered traditionally Russian or whose transfer to a neighboring republic during Soviet times has been denounced as illegitimate.

The Russian authorities manipulate ethnic tensions among neighbors in order to benefit politically from the ensuing uncertainty. This was most obvious in the case of Latvia and Estonia containing the most substantial Russian-speaking minorities relative to the indigenous population. Persistent allegations of mistreatment enables Moscow to use the issue as a bargaining chip in dealing with questions such as military deployments, economic and trade relations, diplomatic recognition, and qualifications for membership of international organizations. Virtually all ethnic tensions involving Russian or Sovietized minorities are perceived in the former Soviet republics as Moscow's machinations. This makes national governments more intransigent, exacerbates ethnic relations, and increases Russian government involvement.

The Russian Orthodox Church is also vocal in defending the allegedly endangered Orthodox faithful especially in multidenominational neighboring states. It assists Moscow in intensifying political pressure on new governments. The Orthodox Church has a long tradition of serving as an instrument of Russian foreign policy before, during, and after the Communist interlude.[23] The Moscow patriarchate helps to maintain Russian influence within the former USSR among Orthodox believers and promotes anti-Western, anticapitalist, and antidemocratic values by stressing collectivism, antimaterialism, pan-Slavism, and Russian nationalism.

Additionally, numerous Russian media outlets zero in on indigenous ethnic frictions in several East European countries, especially with regard to the large Roma (Gypsy) population, as well as on manifestations of anti-Semitism, in order to depict some of the democratic governments as failing to meet "European standards" and thereby disqualifying them from NATO membership.

INFLAMING SOCIAL DISCONTENT

Russian propaganda and intelligence services exploit traditional social, regional, religious, and ethnic cleavages in Eastern Europe to sow mistrust, confusion, and conflict. Domestic tensions enable pressures to be exerted on governments disapproved by Moscow and to distance these countries from Euro-Atlantic institutions. Special agents are recruited within the targeted country or among neighbors to encourage social turmoil. Russia exploits the issue of declining living standards to promote social discontent in countries whose policies conflict with those of the Kremlin. Moscow also benefits from the inherent weakness of civil societies in nearby states and the immaturity of political elites in the CIS. It locates "soft spots" in the political systems to expand its influences, including parliamentary bodies and governmental ministries. Energy shortages caused by supply restrictions from Russia can also fuel social unrest and serve as a form of political pressure and blackmail.[24]

DISCREDITING GOVERNMENTS

Several avenues are pursued to undermine the credibility of pro-Western governments, parties, and politicians. The Kremlin has benefited from the political immaturity, inexperience, and weakness of many administrations in the region, especially in CIS countries. In the early days of post-Communist independence, government agencies in Moscow tried to exploit factional differences between the post-Soviet elites in order to gain policy advantage and place more trusted partners in neighboring governments.

In terms of NATO enlargement, Moscow seeks to undermine efforts by incumbent administrations to meet the criteria for Alliance membership. This has involved media campaigns and the promotion of alternative political parties that can expound policies closer to Russian goals. Press reports have listed reasons why the NATO contenders were allegedly ineligible for entry according to Alliance standards.[25] Russian companies in Eastern Europe have created their own political parties to influence policymaking or attack a government. Alternatively, some politicians have been bribed or blackmailed into promoting Moscow's regional agenda. The trustworthiness of East European officials is questioned by the Russian media or by planting disparaging information in the local media. Some have stood accused of corruption, dishonesty, susceptibility to blackmail, or maintaining contacts with foreign intelligence services. This is particularly troubling to NATO leaders where local officials are expected to deal with sensitive Alliance information. Disinformation campaigns are also conducted against opposition leaders and political formations whose policies run counter to Russian interests in an effort to prevent their accession to government.

Russian intelligence services and media outlets exacerbate domestic political conflicts and focus on discrediting politicians opposing Moscow's interests or favoring NATO membership and close ties with the United States. Kremlin agencies possess volumes of personal information acquired during the Soviet era, which they can publicize and manipulate against uncooperative politicians. Where Moscow cannot obtain significant political influence, it acts as a spoiler by promoting corruption among targeted officials and by fostering confusion and conflict among nonallies.

A useful development for Moscow has been the emergence of several weak states in the region. Countries such as Ukraine or Moldova have been institutionally brittle, politically unstable, and economically vulnerable. This has enabled greater Russian penetration, whether through political, intelligence, security, economic, or criminal channels. In such conditions, Moscow is able to foster divisions and conflicts between various political groups over appropriate security and foreign policies. It is clearly in Moscow's interest to keep targeted states weak and dependent.

POLITICAL INFLUENCES

The Kremlin benefits from its Soviet-era political connections with an assortment of politicians, academics, journalists, economic managers, and regional leaders. It methodically tries to entwine each targeted country in a web of institutional linkages and personal connections to register political impact. Former Communist contacts remain useful in reviving old alliances regardless of current ideological colorations. In nearby CIS states, the Kremlin exercises increasing control over the police, security, military, and intelligence organizations, and in some cases applies direct pressure, as in Belarus, Ukraine, and Moldova, to implant pro-Russian sympathizers in key official positions.

Moscow has developed strong local economic interests and funded parties, media outlets, or other organizations that can promote its goals. Russian capital sponsors political and public relations campaigns to influence or replace uncooperative governments. Political competition and fund raising for political parties remains in an embryonic state in much of the region. Hence, the Kremlin exploits cash-starved politicians and parties to fund suitable individuals and organizations. It also uses such influence to block efforts at energy diversity and closer security arrangements with Western powers. Russian companies tied to mother organizations in Russia have developed political lobbies in some countries. Lukoil established dummy companies that offered campaign contributions to pro-Russian political parties in Ukraine and the Baltic states. The appointment of high-ranking or well-connected Russian politicians as ambassadors to neighboring states also engenders a more intensive involvement in domestic politics and resembles a quasi-colonial or protectorate relationship.

Orthodox churches in Eastern Europe are also valuable in assisting Russian state policy. Moscow steers the Russian patriarchate to exert its influence in states such as Ukraine, Belarus, and Moldova and to use the issue of an international religious community to maintain pro-Russian sentiments and undermine the position of autocephalous Orthodox churches that support disassociation from Russia. The Russian patriarchate seeks an "Orthodox commonwealth" to span the Russian Federation, the two neighboring Slavic states, and nearby countries with sizable Russian-speaking minorities.[26]

Russian Orthodox patriarch Aleksey II is a strong supporter of CIS integration and a "Eurasian union" and established an Inter-Religious Council to expand church activities throughout the CIS. Aleksey views the church as an advocate of ethnic Russians outside the motherland and an important force for Eastern Slavic integration. Secular leaders also raise the notion of a new global moral mission for Russia in which Orthodoxy is a core element.[27]

SUPPORTING ISOLATIONISM

Moscow established close ties with political leaders and parties who were criticized or ostracized by the West for their democratic shortcomings. Russia prefers to deal with authoritarian figures who can thwart differing political opinions on the question of relations with Moscow and the West. Russia has supported undemocratic, nationalist, or populist regimes in Serbia, Slovakia, and Belarus that allied themselves with the Kremlin's foreign and security policies. Moscow does not distinguish between diverse ideological interests and deliberately cultivates ties with the extreme left, the radical right, the populist "center," and anarchist militants if it serves its agenda. Estrangement or self-isolation from the West by particular regimes assists the Kremlin in carving out valuable spheres of influence. Antireformist administrations in Eastern Europe can also discourage those Western business investments which are viewed by Moscow as exerting unwanted influence over the targeted country's political system and security posture. Western businesses are also competitors for Russian companies seeking to purchase strategic industries and they encourage greater legality and transparency in business practice that is detrimental to the operations of some Russian firms.

MANIPULATING CRIMINAL NETWORKS

East European governments remain deeply concerned over the activities of Russian criminal networks both as a destabilizing socioeconomic element and as a tool of Moscow's political and economic interests. Unfortunately, Western law enforcement agencies have conducted limited analysis of the origins and operations of criminal groups tied to Russian intelligence agencies. Criminal enterprises are not a new phenomenon in Russia. They existed under Communism, where the black market was an instrument of privilege for party officials. Close linkages are maintained between former Communist leaders, intelligence services, and criminal networks across the region, which officials in Moscow can exploit to their advantage. The Russian diaspora also provides a source of criminals familiar with local conditions. Many of those involved in money laundering and smuggling are former KGB personnel who moved funds abroad during the last gasp of the Soviet system.[28] Communist Party and KGB officials clandestinely transferred massive quantities of diamonds and $4 billion in gold and other precious minerals to secret accounts in the West.[29]

The post-KGB maintains close links with several internationally organized criminal syndicates and both networks benefit substantially from the relationship.[30] While the criminals obtain a high level of protection and clandestine state sponsorship, the post-KGB gains additional funds and access to valuable economic and political connections through the mafia. According to Czech analysts:

> Seemingly incapable, for historical and other reasons, of creating genuine democracy in Russia, the current Russian strategy appears to be to sow discord, distrust, and criminal activity wherever they can, in a perverse effort to prevent others from achieving democratic pluralism and a better life. To achieve these objectives, they may use substantial financial resources to infiltrate both public and private institutions around the world. This aspect of Russian foreign policy will probably not change despite the hopes entertained by politicians like Tony Blair; indeed, given President Putin's KGB background, it will likely grow.[31]

The Kremlin uses organized crime as leverage to benefit Russian state interests, whether by creating networks of piratelike penetration into neighboring economies or by corrupting, blackmailing, and intimidating specific government officials. Criminal organizations provide a shadow intelligence agency for the Kremlin. During the collapse of the Soviet Union, the KGB laundered money and established dummy companies to protect the financial assets of the former Communist nomenklatura. Because the KGB did not possess sufficient resources for a vast and sustained operation, it went into business with the mafia, which substantially expanded its operations under KGB protection. The KGB provided the criminal networks with sophisticated communications and modern technology and in effect: "An unholy troika gradually coalesced: the *mafia,* the *nomenklatura,* and current and former members of the government, military, and security services. They came into their own after the collapse of communism."[32]

Post-Soviet criminal networks operate across the former USSR and its satellites and possess important transit links into Western Europe. Former and current members of the Soviet and post-Soviet security services play important roles in organized crime inside Russia and among its neighbors. They uphold extensive international ties, have vast knowledge of business and finance, are involved in various commercial and financial ventures, and "almost every one of the organized criminal groups has its own high-ranking official who provides protection and support."[33] Intelligence officers have been encouraged to work abroad as businessmen and to engage in economic espionage and money raising for Russia's security services.

The Russian mafia greatly expanded its activities during the 1990s and penetrated or established a number of regional networks in such illicit endeavors as migrant smuggling, drug trafficking, arms smuggling, money laundering, human trafficking, international prostitution, auto theft, embezzlement of state property, corruption, extortion, racketeering, assassinations, counterfeiting currency and documentation, art theft, illegal gambling, contract killing, infiltration of legitimate businesses, creating false companies, engaging in financial "pyramid" schemes, and smuggling radioactive materials. Russian syndicates have either been in competition with local gangs or collaborated and complemented each other. Collaboration allows Russian groups to expand their penetration of East European economies and to invest in purchasing real estate and local companies.

Criminal organizations enable Russian security services to attain a wider reach in targeted countries. Analysts in the region contend that Russian intelligence services coordinate several criminal groups and direct a proportion of their resources to exert economic and political influence throughout Eastern Europe. Some criminal networks assist in the economic and political infiltration of targeted countries and ultimately serve both Russian business interests and the Kremlin's political ambitions.

PENETRATING INTELLIGENCE SERVICES

During Communist times, the security services, intelligence branches, and government structures of all Warsaw Pact states were saturated with KGB officers who ensured that their policies conformed to Moscow's objectives. After the collapse of the USSR, the state security apparatus was appropriated by Russia. Key Russian intelligence agencies include: the Foreign Intelligence Service (Sluzba Vneshnei Razvedki [SVR]), the Main Intelligence Directorate of the Military General Staff (GRU), the Federal Security Service (Federalnaya Sluzba Bezopastnosti [FSB]), the Federal Agency of Governmental Communications and Information (FAPSI), the Federal Protection Service (FSO), and the Main Directorate of Special Programs of the Russian President. Although Moscow concluded agreements on the "mutual nonperformance of intelligence operations" with all CIS countries, in practice this made Russian espionage activities either more direct or elusive.

In the process of centralization, in March 2003 Putin abolished FAPSI and the Federal Border Guard Service, subordinating their functions to the FSB. Under a decree issued in August 2003, the new FSB consisted of the departments of Counterintelligence, Protection of the Constitutional Order, Analysis and Strategic Planning, Military Counterintelligence, and the Border Guard Service. The agency also formed a nineteen-member collegium as its top administrative body.[34] All of these organizations, except the GRU, were formerly elements of the KGB. The SVR was previously the chief directorate of the KGB and its first head was Evgeniy Primakov, one of Yeltsin's foreign ministers. The vast intelligence network assumed an important role in Russian foreign policy and according to the Law on Foreign Intelligence, passed in August 1992, the SVR reported directly to the president with little parliamentary oversight. "Together with the military, the intelligence service was another 'power-wielding' institutional actor that regularly found a place at the table when foreign policy decisions were made in the Soviet Union. It continues to do so, without having undergone significant reform, in democratizing Russia."[35]

After the dismantling of the Warsaw Pact, Russia's revamped intelligence agencies became more active throughout Eastern Europe. Indeed, Russian espionage intensified when the process of NATO enlargement accelerated. The equipment, facilities, and personnel of the KGB security apparatus were largely left intact:

> This vast apparatus, numbering hundreds of thousands of employees in total, is only partly accountable to elected authorities. Most observers inside and outside Russia agree that democratic control of the intelligence/security complex is tenuous at best and, in some cases, nonexistent. Russia's intelligence and security forces enjoy extraordinary powers—both formal and informal—to act on their own.[36]

Unlike in Communist times, almost the entire East European region is now viewed as a potentially hostile international environment. Moscow no longer controls a guaranteed conduit of information and decisionmaking through the subordinate governing Communist Parties and other institutions. KGB defector Oleg Gordievsky, the UK's highest-ranking Cold War agent, confirmed that paradoxically the KGB's successor organs are more active in Eastern Europe than they were before the unraveling of the Soviet bloc.[37] Moscow views the new NATO members and aspirants as its principal enemies and uses active measures to weaken their standing internationally while surreptitiously penetrating their economies.

Foreign intelligence activities were substantially reinforced under Putin and questions arose as to Moscow's ability to influence leading politicians in the region because of its possession of secret files from the Communist era:

> Under Vladimir Putin—himself a former senior-ranking KGB officer—Soviet-era intelligence networks have been reactivated in an effort to rebuild Moscow's influence throughout Central and Eastern Europe. While some agents work willingly with Russia's intelligence agencies, those who are more reluctant can often be persuaded through the use of *Kompromat*—damaging material contained in the many individual personnel files held in Moscow.[38]

Former intelligence and counterintelligence contacts are utilized, especially as many East European governments have a limited new pool of agents and continue to employ experienced professionals with former KGB connections. Western intelligence services remain concerned about Communist-era links between some new NATO members and Russia and have demanded extensive reform including the protection of intelligence sources and a thorough screening of operatives.[39] Following NATO enlargement in Central Europe, Russian espionage services benefited from still existing network to penetrate Alliance secrets. Political and intelligence penetration among new members facilitates the infiltration of various security bodies within the Alliance. Among NATO newcomers, many thousands of military personnel and bureaucrats have been denied access to classified papers because of refusal to comply with strict vetting procedures. A substantial number of intelligence officers previously worked for Communist spy agencies and their presence poses a security headache for the Alliance as it can be exploited by Moscow.

Muscovite intelligence officers do not merely seek information, but conduct campaigns of active influence in targeted countries. Russian services seek to penetrate the secret and regular police of all neighboring states. Wherever possible, Putin has encouraged FSB influence or control over the police, security, and intelligence institutions of CIS states and seeks to replace their leaders with persons more loyal to Moscow.[40] Russian foreign services recruit new agents among local government employees, academics, journalists, and parliamentarians. The East European media, which have access to much more detailed information than during Communist times, are one of the major targets for Russian espionage.[41] Russian spokesmen indicate that NATO enlargement could lead to instability in Eastern Europe and threaten to use their intelligence assets to foment conflicts to their advantage in the region. Russian intelligence services are instrumental in undermining trust between member and candidate countries and are mobilized to counter Western attempts to absorb the CIS countries:

> Contrary to public perceptions, the confrontation between intelligence services since the Cold War had actually intensified. NATO enlargement and the desire of other countries to join increase the need to be active in those states. . . . Millions of Russians now live outside the country and this provides fertile ground for recruitment. Rich Russians are of special interest especially if they are businessmen. A trade-off can be arranged for services rendered.[42]

A substantial increase in Russian embassy staff was also recorded in every East European capital during the 1990s, indicating that espionage activities greatly had expanded. Media publicity and periodic revelations about the extent of Russian espionage also serve Moscow's objectives by discrediting the competence of government agencies in states aspiring to NATO membership and seeking closer ties with Western services. It is also not inconceivable that Russian services could engage in assassination and sabotage if those were to be considered expedient by the Kremlin.[43]

3

Retaining a Union:
Belarus and Kaliningrad

GREAT POWER SYNDROMES

The Commonwealth of Independent States is a centerpiece through which Moscow has re-created its sphere of influence and dominance on the territories of the former Soviet Union.[1] The CIS was established in December 1991 following the annulment of the Union Treaty of 1922, which had created the USSR. The CIS was conceived as a mechanism to bind smaller and weaker neighbors closer to Russia and prevent their drifting permanently away from Moscow's orbit. Russia depicts itself as the stable central pillar for a new multinational structure that would prevent the country's marginalization. Politicians also assert that the CIS would salvage the national identities of newly independent states in danger of being swallowed by the West. Moscow's acceptance of the independence of the new states therefore remains conditional and restricted.

> The CIS is an instrument of Russian foreign policy in two ways. It serves as a means of coordination of policies among its members. It is also a mechanism for asserting Russian hegemony over the other eleven states. Both goals have been pursued simultaneously. Initially prominence was given to the former, but with the passage of time the latter has become an important feature of Russian policy.[2]

Russia's objective is the creation of a political superstructure under its supervision that would coordinate foreign and security policy. Within the

CIS, Russia operates according to a modified "Brezhnev Doctrine" of "limited sovereignty."[3] Yeltsin evidently took the decision to form the CIS in order to "reassure the Soviet military that a new security structure would be created to replace the USSR."[4] Despite attempts to retain a unified armed force, all CIS states insisted on creating their own national militaries. Consequently, Moscow focused on establishing a joint overall command primarily responsible for the control of strategic nuclear weapons. Under intensive pressure from Moscow and Washington, Ukraine, Belarus, and Kazakhstan surrendered their nuclear weapons ensuring that Russia remained the sole post-Soviet nuclear power.

Russia's relationship with the CIS is akin to its previous connections with the former East European satellites—independent in form but subordinate in content. The speed and depth of CIS integration depends on economic, political, and security conditions. In the early 1990s, Russia was too preoccupied with domestic issues and improving its relations with the West to pay intensive attention to the Soviet successor states. The CIS focus became more pronounced after 1992 when the Commonwealth was defined as a zone of Russia's "primary interests" or "historic territory." Yeltsin became committed to "defending" the outer borders of the CIS states. Meanwhile, the term "near abroad" began to dominate official views of Russia's neighborhood, signifying the necessity of a "special relationship" with Moscow for all former republics regardless of their internal developments.[5]

Russian minorities in CIS states were officially elevated by Moscow as an "integral part of the Russian nation"—a maneuver designed to justify close state interference on the pretext of defending minority interests. Russians in these countries became known as the *rossiyskaya* diaspora, for whom the federation was the homeland, or *rodina,* even though only a small proportion were actually Russian citizens. Moscow considers it a duty to "defend" these populations against the policies of independent governments, even though they constituted a diverse and dispersed group. It pressures neighboring capitals to permit dual citizenship for Russian speakers. Most states refuse to agree to these demands and the citizenship question is a form of political pressure. The Kremlin uses all available means to foster CIS integration and tries to manufacture a shared Commonwealth identity through common citizenship.

The CIS did not become a cohesive entity and failed to gain international recognition as a viable regional organization. Russian efforts to construct a fully integrated post-Soviet space as a countervailing alliance to NATO fell short of expectations.[6] Because of political resistance and insufficient resources, the CIS did not evolve a military union or an economic association. Moscow did not invest sufficient resources into reintegration because market-oriented forces prevailed and were unwilling to subsidize Russia's weaker neighbors.[7] Economic reformers are weary of rapid integration lest this destabilize the Russian economy through onerous debts sustaining obsolete government-controlled industries in nearby republics.

There is resentment at Moscow's attempted dominance and some governments endeavor to diversify their trade, investment, and foreign and security policies.[8] Several states resisted the creation of an integrated military with a CIS Joint Command subordinate to the Russian High Command. Instead of exclusively promoting CIS integration, which was a long-term prospect, and to avoid burdensome economic obligations, Moscow focused on developing tighter subregional ties and bilateral relations with the most strategically important republics, particularly its two Slavic neighbors. In December 1991, the association between Russia, Belarus, and Ukraine was initially named the Commonwealth of Slavic States (CSS). This was expanded to include all the non-Slavic republics and renamed as the CIS that same month. This "near abroad" (*blizhnee zarubezhe*) was depicted as a priority area and Moscow required predominant influence over these states, underpinned by a common Russian sentiment:

> So far there is one part of the Russian imperial legacy where very little rethinking and change of attitude has taken place. This concerns Russia's relations with the two other east Slavic states—Ukraine and Belorussia. Most Russians continue to regard the citizens of these states as, in effect, belonging, together with the Russians, to one pan-Russian nation.[9]

Russians have internalized the state-sponsored position that the three East Slavic nations are essentially of "one blood" (*edinokrovnye*) and that Ukraine and Belarus formed parts of "Mother Russia." During the 1940s and 1950s, Soviet policy codified the East Slavs as historically belonging to one Russian people (*Ruskiy narod*). Belarusians and Ukrainians were no longer classified as distinct nations but as regional Russians.[10] The notion of *sblizhenie* (drawing together) of the three Slavic peoples was the cornerstone of Soviet nationality policy during the final years of the USSR. Such sentiments were also displayed in Russia's 2000 National Concept, which declared that the spiritual regeneration of society was impossible without preserving the role of the Russian language as a means of "intergovernmental communication of the peoples of the states constituting the CIS."[11] Divisions surfaced between hard-liners and pragmatists on the speed of integration between former Soviet republics. While conservatives favor rapid incorporation in a centralized CIS, pragmatists back incremental control over the most important institutions, including the military and security services: "Russia's political elites, divided on domestic programmatic grounds, are nevertheless united on a core pragmatic nationalist consensus that Russia is in a rapid decline that must be reversed, that primary foreign policy focus must be in the CIS region and that Russia's nuclear superpower status must be maintained."[12]

Although the term "near abroad" largely fell into disuse by the late 1990s, state objectives toward immediate neighbors did not fundamentally alter. The entire CIS region is seen as vital because of its alleged historical, ethnic, cultural, linguistic, and political interconnectedness. Russian leaders consider the CIS as a natural sphere for their political, economic, and security interests while outside influences were deemed to be a threat to achieving these goals.[13] There was also an important economic calculation, as Moscow wanted to ensure control over the major transportation routes and energy pipelines that crosscut the region.

Yeltsin needed the CIS to prove to the public and to elites that although the Soviet Union was dissolved, a Greater Russian sphere of interest continued to exist. Russia's liberals also supported the CIS concept, viewing it as an important step toward genuine confederation along democratic lines. Russia was not intent on full incorporation because this was viewed as an economically expensive proposition. Instead, it focused on selective domination in key spheres such as energy, business, and military. Through such channels it could strongly influence a country's foreign and security policies. While Russian nationalists and Communists, in a more strident neoimperialist approach, insisted on rapid absorption of the "near abroad," the Kremlin views CIS integration as a long-term process with no set timetables. Its pace and depth remain contingent upon economic costs and benefits. Security interests also need to be balanced with budgetary requirements, as Moscow does not envisage assuming major new burdens beyond essential military expenditures. The more realistic policy voices understand the gap between ambitions and capabilities and plan to ensure economic viability in a longer-term pursuit of integrationist goals.

The CIS and other instruments enable Moscow to apply a "Eurasian" version of the U.S. "Monroe Doctrine" in its former dominions. The doctrine was first expounded publicly in 1992 by Evgeniy Ambartsumov, chairman of the Duma's Foreign Affairs Committee.[14] The objective is to reintegrate the former Soviet territories around the Russian core primarily through economic instruments. Russia's Foreign Intelligence Service (SVR) also issued a report in 1994 stating that Russia must play a dominant role in the territory of the former Soviet Union.[15] The policy was elaborated in May 1996 by the Council on Defense and Foreign Policy, an institution closely linked to the government. It underscored that Moscow needed to exert leadership and expand economic domination rather than seeking outright political control.[16] Even if the CIS structure was not fully integrated, it provided a vehicle for political dominance through various organisms and gave Russia a sense of continuity as a global power. It also helped to counter attempts by Western governments to integrate these states. Some officials also argued that with American encouragement several CIS neighbors would make territorial claims on Russia; hence their Western links needed to be curtailed.[17]

Moscow was unable to establish an integrated Commonwealth military. Instead, it concentrated on pursuing closer links with the Russian military as the core.[18] Under the CIS umbrella, Russia gained access to the military facilities of former dominions, controlled their air defenses, and used the outer CIS border as its military frontier. Russian leaders view themselves as the leaders of security on the entire territory of the former USSR. They underpin their policies with a "civilizing" mission of bringing democracy and prosperity to the Soviet successor states.[19] Although it depicts the CIS as a voluntary association, the Kremlin affirms that its support for other CIS governments remains conditional on their acceptance of the Russian model of integration. Moscow reserves for itself all key positions in the CIS structure that ensure dominance over its most important institutions. Additionally, Moscow has not formalized its Soviet-era frontiers with CIS states, agreeing only to delimit them on maps but not to demarcate them on the ground. It also campaigns to have Russia declared an official working language in the CIS.

Moscow's long-term objective for the CIS is to establish a tighter federation highly dependent on the Russian center but without necessarily expanding Russian territory.[20] This entails the development of supranational organs in the political, economic, and military domains. The goals include an economic union patterned on the EU and styled as the Eurasian Economic Community (EEC). Economic integration has proved uneven as the majority of states are protectionist in their orientation and the EEC has not developed into an integrated structure.[21] Of the hundreds of documents drafted by the CIS by 1998 only 130 were signed by all member states.[22] In addition, Russia and its neighbors continue to impose tariffs on imports in order to protect their domestic producers and to raise revenues. There is also stiff resistance to draining the Russian budget to subsidize ailing or mismanaged economies. Some analysts calculate that the turnover of goods among CIS countries actually declined during the 1990s given the dissolution of the Soviet internal market, economic depression, severe financial constraints, and trade diversification among member states.

Political cooperation proved weak under Yeltsin and the CIS was not transformed into a single state entity. Unlike with EU integration, the CIS process is not viewed as a "pooling of sovereignty" in which Russia would surrender some of its powers to supranational institutions. Moscow presses for "asymmetrical sovereignty" in which CIS neighbors surrender elements of their independence to the Kremlin, which assumes the decisive voice in Commonwealth affairs. The majority of CIS members have defended their sovereignty against Moscow's encroachment and there is little sense of common identity or joint citizenship. This is compounded by the organization's bureaucratism and lack of meaningful resources from each member state.

The model of reintegration adopted by the Kremlin is not the restoration of a centralized post-Soviet state or the re-creation of a broader Russian empire in which CIS countries became administrative units. Moscow maintains the formal independence of its neighbors while pursuing economic and military integration and gaining influence over foreign policy. These objectives were concretized in two official documents: the Basic Concept of the Foreign Policy of the Russian Federation, issued in January 1993, and the Basic Military Doctrine of the Russian Federation, released in November 1993. Various pretexts are employed to justify Russian domination over the CIS. Among the most frequent is defense against a radical Islamic threat from the Caucasus and Central Asia that could spill onto Russian territory and precipitate Western intervention.

Putin has sought to reinvigorate the CIS as a viable economic union and the CIS free trade zone was due to become operational by 2004. The Kremlin seeks two main goals in creating a CIS free trade zone: to subordinate the foreign and trade policies of Commonwealth states so that Russia can speak on behalf of the entire CIS and to represent the CIS in relations with the World Trade Organization.[23] The new CIS economic structure would thereby coordinate its relations with the EU, the WTO, and the UN. Russian leaders calculate that their claims to great power status will only be taken seriously if the CIS acts as one coordinated body, much like the defunct USSR.

Russian officials have depicted NATO as a hostile alliance and a dangerous competitor in the former Soviet region, seeking to lure the CIS states westward and to isolate Russia from Europe. Any weakening of integrative processes within the CIS is portrayed as a direct security threat to Russia itself. Conversely, the West is allegedly fearful that an effective CIS would revive competition with NATO.[24] A Russian-led Commonwealth is presented as a potential equal pillar with NATO in ensuring "Eurasian" security: "Russia's neuralgic sensitivity to CIS military cooperation with NATO comes from a perception that the West, particularly the U.S. and Turkey, seeks to push Russia out of the region and confine Moscow's influence to within Russia's borders."[25]

Officials in Moscow stress that attempts to interfere with the integrative processes in any former Soviet republic would be viewed as unfriendly acts.[26] CIS integration is also allegedly threatened by efforts of Western powers and transnational corporations to establish control over key industries, communications, transportation, and natural resources. In justifying CIS integration around a Moscow center, NATO's Partnership for Peace (PfP) program has been attacked as a mechanism to bind the CIS militaries with their NATO counterparts. Bilateral military cooperation and NATO training programs for CIS officers supposedly hamper the progress of CIS integration. The assimilation of any former Soviet republic into the Western sphere has been condemned as a means for building a cordon sanitaire around Russia and permanently replacing its presence in the CIS. Moves to draw Ukraine, Belarus, or Moldova into the Visegrad initiative in Central Europe or more intensive cooperation between Polish and Ukrainian militaries are perceived as part of a Western strategy of subterfuge. There is pronounced fear that CIS states could act outside of Russia's ambit amid criticisms of the feeble nature of Commonwealth security structures.[27]

A persistent theme of Kremlin policy has been its purported concern for Russian minorities in neighboring states, especially in countries that opposed Russia's integrative efforts or were determined to join NATO. Defense of Russian coethnics has been a component of all major foreign policy documents and military doctrines. Deployment of the Russian military in CIS states is described as a form of protection for Russian minorities. Moscow also attempts to pursue a common foreign policy among CIS members by seeking joint position, but such efforts proved difficult because of the diversity of priorities among CIS governments.[28]

Moscow has promoted various security initiatives within the CIS framework, including military accords such as the Tashkent Treaty on Collective Security.[29] In March 1996, a Joint Chiefs of Staff of the CIS was established under the chairmanship of Russia's general staff and an "Integration Agreement" was signed in Moscow the same month. The Kremlin pursues the notion of a broad CIS defense alliance under overall Russian command in which there would be a common patrolling of external CIS borders and the construction of Russian military bases in all CIS states. Moscow claims that the creation of a unified armed force would ease the burden of maintaining several small armies. The common defense of the "outer borders" is evidently in the interest of all states especially as their "internal borders" are extremely porous. In October 2000, the presidents of Russia, Belarus, Kazakhstan, Kyrgyzstan, and Tajikistan (RBKKT) upgraded their 1992 Collective Security Treaty and gave Russia a dominant military position. Officials claimed that they were defending the country's security interests against outside threats and alternative alliances.

Despite these efforts, Russia failed to establish an effective CIS military alliance that could counteract an enlarged NATO.[30] Moscow's anti-NATO position contributed to distancing some states from the process of CIS military integration for fear of alienating NATO and isolating themselves from the West. Most CIS states do not recognize the Commonwealth as an authoritative organ deciding on the deployment of combat and peacekeeping forces. This resistance led to the creation of the GUUAM initiative in November 1997. Moscow is staunchly opposed to any subregional grouping that excludes Russia: "any closed military-political alliances whatsoever by the former Union republics, either with one another or with third countries that have an anti-Russian orientation" constituted a potential security threat.[31] The GUUAM states (Georgia, Ukraine, Uzbekistan, Azerbaijan, Moldova) oppose any onerous security agreements with Russia and seek closer ties with NATO.[32] They are suspicious of Russia's motives and view the CIS as an impediment to their freedom of maneuver. For GUUAM, integration into "transatlantic and European structures" has been viewed as the only solution to combating threats to their sovereignty.

The GUUAM initiative was also undertaken to prevent the use of energy supplies as a form of blackmail by Moscow. A primary economic motive was to ensure the supply of Azeri oil by pipeline through Georgia and then by tanker across the Black Sea to Ukraine and Moldova, thereby bypassing Russia.[33] This has been called the "New Silk Road" or the "Eurasian Corridor." In addition, GUUAM aspired to closer economic ties with Western countries, a genuine free trade area to counter Russian protectionism, and visa free travel between member states. GUUAM enabled these states to better coordinate their response to various pressures, such as Moscow's attempts to revise the Conventional Forces in Europe (CFE) treaty in order to permit the concentration of a higher number of Russian forces near GUUAM countries. In the security arena, several GUUAM capitals aim to exclude Russia and include the United States in future regional arrangements. Moscow condemned the GUAAM initiative as a policy coordinated by Washington to destroy the CIS from within. U.S. support for GUUAM allegedly obstructed Moscow's efforts to establish a CIS collective security system and was the spearhead for creating an "anti-Russian military bloc." Russian officials considered Ukraine as the driving force of this "anti-Russian axis" aimed at the "destruction of Russian statehood."[34]

The Kremlin became increasingly concerned about the involvement of CIS states in NATO's PfP program. Anxieties were also voiced over proposals to include non-CIS states such as Romania in GUUAM. Such moves were viewed as a direct challenge to Russian interests in the former Soviet territories because they encouraged the expansion of hostile alliances.[35] NATO intervention in the Balkans was depicted as a trial run for future missions in the southern CIS under the pretext of supporting human rights while cutting Russia out of the developing Caspian-Europe transport corridor.[36] In September 2003, Deputy Foreign Minister Vyacheslav Trubnikov, a former director of Russia's Foreign Intelligence Service, claimed that Russia was playing a decisive role in combating organized crime and terrorism and expressed skepticism about a U.S. initiative for a regional antiterrorism center inside GUUAM.[37]

SOBER CALCULATIONS: PUTIN AND THE CIS

Under Putin, pressures increased to forge a more effective CIS and project an invigorated Russia as a distinct pole of global influence. The principle of "integration at different speeds" was applied, with a greater focus on differentiated bilateral and sub-CIS relations. Russia's new Foreign Policy Concept asserted that the CIS states must be subordinated to Moscow's interests in questions of security, in coordinating the use of natural resources, and in the rights of Russian speakers. Early in 2000, the president created the CIS

Counter-Terrorism Center and a CIS Rapid Reaction Force allowing Russian security forces to intervene in all CIS countries.[38] Most CIS members view such initiatives as a covert threat to their national independence.

The new Kremlin leadership also declared during 2000 the existence of a "red line" against NATO inclusion of the Baltic states. It issued warnings that crossing this line by encompassing any former Soviet republics would provoke confrontation with Russia. The transformation of the CIS into an integrated security organism was depicted as a defensive move against further NATO encroachment. Russia regards itself as the primary defender of post-Soviet borders and declares its right to preserve military bases and border guard troops in all CIS countries and to maintain mutual air defense agreements. Officials and security experts favor the reintegration of much of the former USSR through Russia's economic dominance.[39] Such a strategy also entails limitations on other external powers. In criticizing Western meddling in the CIS, Moscow has positioned itself as the economic, political, and cultural "center of gravity" in "Eurasia."[40]

In the first two years of his administration, Putin took several steps toward consolidating a Russian-led bloc in "Eurasia."[41] He was intent on reestablishing economic interdependence among Russia, Ukraine, Moldova, Armenia, and Belarus. A vital objective is to gain control of the strategic energy sectors. In the case of heavily dependent CIS states, Russian gas and oil enterprises created joint ventures with local private energy-related firms or with industries dependent on raw materials imported from Russia. These concerns dominate the energy sector and become financially powerful while remaining fully dependent on Russian "mother" companies. Local enterprises developed into strong domestic interest groups lobbying on behalf of Russian "partners" for favorable trade deals and investment opportunities while supporting Moscow's foreign policy goals. The most vulnerable states are ones holding burdensome debts to Russia or remaining fully dependent on Russian energy and raw materials. Moscow has been eager to exchange debts for a share in the ownership of strategically important industries. However, some Russian commentators voice concern that CIS countries will become economic liabilities for Moscow rather than political assets, the recipients of substantial Russian aid rather than productive partners.[42]

In a further attempt at economic integration, in July 2001, the International Exchange Association of CIS member countries and the Moscow Interbank Currency Exchange signed an agreement calling for the creation of "a single financial space." The agreement established rules for clearing mechanisms within the CIS and for common legal arrangements on currency matters. In April 2003, Putin claimed progress on a draft agreement to create a "unified economic zone" encompassing Ukraine, Kazakhstan, Belarus, and Russia.[43] During a meeting with Deputy Prime Minister Viktor Khristenko, who headed the working group on the unification of trade and tariff legislation, Putin stated that the four countries should be able to enter the WTO as "a single economic space." According to the draft agreement, economic activity would be based on the free movement of goods, services, capital, and labor, while a single policy on foreign trade, tax, monetary, credit, currency, and finance would be pursued.

Putin's economic approach toward neighbors is dictated by a desire to control the oil and gas export infrastructure, especially as countries such as Belarus and Ukraine are primarily energy transit corridors.[44] In October 2003, he asserted that Russia would not relinquish control over the pipeline infrastructure on CIS territory as the system was built by the Soviet Union and only Russia was in a position to keep it in working order.[45] To elicit EU support for Russian energy control, Putin claimed that it would only be possible to provide cheap Russian energy to the EU if Moscow keeps the pipeline system functioning under its supervision. He added that Russia would maintain state control over the pipeline network and over Gazprom.

Moscow may harbor a more ambitious long-term objectives in attaching portions of neighboring territories to a "Greater Russia" or incorporating the entire state within an expanding Russian Federation. Putin has called for a "Russian revival" that questions the permanence of several post-Soviet frontiers. At the end of 2001, the Duma passed a new law that officially codified procedures for expanding Russia's borders.[46] According to an article in Moscow's *Nezavisimaya Gazeta* on 5 July 2001, the provisions of the law allowing Russia to incorporate either all or part of other countries acutely disturbed several CIS capitals. Some governments view such legislation as a form of pressure to follow Moscow's lead or face disintegration. In this context, they grew alarmed by Moscow's plans to promote Russian language use among their citizens; this was perceived as an ominous step toward future territorial claims.

In the wake of 11 September 2001 and the U.S. antiterrorism campaign in Central Asia, Moscow pushed for closer CIS military integration.[47] At the CIS summit in Moldova in October 2002, the presidents of Russia, Belarus, Armenia, Kazakhstan, Kyrgyzstan, and Tajikistan launched the founding documents of a Collective Security Organization (CSO), the renamed Collective Security Treaty (CST).[48] The treaty was signed in Dushanbe, Tajikistan, in April 2003.[49] The CSO was designed to operationalize the 1992 CST by turning it into a concrete military structure. The provisions of the CSO founding document strengthened Moscow's role in the security of neighboring states. It included a status-of-forces agreement that legitimized the entry, transit, and operations of Russian troops and multilateral frameworks for joint military exercises.

CSO signatories agreed to establish a rapid reaction force to combat terrorism, drug trafficking, and threats to the security of member states. The new military structure was to have a joint general staff headed by a Russian, Nikolai Bordyuzha, a former secretary of the Russian Security Council.[50] The CSO military doctrine is modeled on that of the Warsaw Pact, with Belarusian president Alyaksandr Lukashenka claiming that the organization was established in direct response to U.S. military intervention in Iraq without UN Security Council authorization. The CSO ensured that doctrine, planning, procurement, and training would be controlled from Moscow and that Russian officers would dominate the collective staffs and joint forces. This would provide international legitimacy to any Russian military operations. Three "regional groups of forces" were to be established, including a Western group consisting of Russia and Belarus. In case of any security emergency they would act under a "joint command" led by Russian generals.

An additional mechanism for reintegration is military service. Russia's Defense Minister Ivanov proposed that citizens of CIS member states be allowed to serve in Russia's armed forces.[51] Legislation to this effect was submitted to the Duma. As the Russian military is to be transformed into a partly professional and contract force, Moscow will seek to attract young people from neighboring countries. They will be offered Russian citizenship in return for three years of military service. This can further weaken and deplete the armed forces of CIS states while buttressing Moscow's dominance in military affairs.

In strengthening the CIS, Putin also sought to eliminate the GUUAM initiative.[52] GUUAM's importance began to decline after 2000 when Ukraine, its largest member, reoriented its foreign policy toward Moscow as President Kuchma became isolated internationally. The election of Communists in Moldova also undermined the pro-NATO initiative. Of the five original GUUAM members only Uzbekistan and Azerbaijan continued to espouse pro-U.S. policies and opposed Russian initiatives to bolster Kremlin influence.

In addition to CIS integration, Russia's relations with Belarus, Ukraine, and Moldova are considered to be of the highest priority and a vital foreign policy interest.[53] All three states are defined as "strategic partners" and bilateral relations take precedence over broader multilateral groupings. Russia's guiding objective is to integrate the zone economically and militarily and to exclude unwelcome foreign influences. Policymakers view Ukraine, Belarus, and Moldova as artificial creations that would sooner or later merge into a wider political structure. They use various historical and strategic arguments to justify their policies toward Belarus and Ukraine. A common Slavic and Orthodox heritage is frequently invoked, as the three nations are purportedly components of one ethnos needing to remain in a single political and security structure. In June 2000, Duma chairman Genadiy Seleznyov participated in the First Congress of Russian, Belarusian, and Ukrainian Nations and described the event as a platform for national unification. Russia's Orthodox Church claims that the three peoples cannot live apart as they converted to Christianity at the same time and share a common history.

Moscow exploits economic difficulties and political turmoil among its CIS neighbors. This has proved easier in Belarus, a country characterized by a

weak sense of national identity and whose president maintains a tight dicta-
torship and harbors ambitions to become a pan-Slavic leader. In Ukraine,
Moscow's exertions proved more difficult because of the pro-Western orientation of a sector of the Ukrainian political elite. In Moldova, peacekeeping (*mirotvorchestvo*) is a useful tool to exert influence over a recalcitrant and
unstable state and to maintain Moscow's strategic position.[54] Unlike the UN,
Russia has not been constrained in its peacekeeping operations in the "near
abroad" in terms of legitimacy, rules of engagement, collateral damage, or
public scrutiny. In several unstable CIS states, Moscow combines peacekeeping with counterinsurgency, or has defended one side in the conflicts, such
as the Transnistrian separatists in Moldova. The conflict itself became a means
for exercising influence over political developments in Russia's favor.

Moscow has taken upon itself the role of "Eurasian peacekeeper," even
without a formal UN mandate and despite its complaints that NATO was
acting unilaterally in Southeast Europe. The Kremlin presents its peacekeeping missions as CIS operations even though it has not received such a
mandate from other states and most remained hesitant in participating in
Russian-led missions. Moscow has not permitted either the UN or the OSCE
to assume peacekeeping operations in former Soviet territories, despite the
fact that it demanded such missions in the Balkans while pushing for NATO's
exclusion. In its peacekeeping interventions, Moscow has frozen armed confrontation to "establish Russia as indispensable to any solution of that conflict."[55] It thereby developed strong leverage over incumbent governments
and its troops were transformed into a quasi-permanent occupation force.
Russia condemns any challenge to its dominance in the CIS as a threat to
its security. In this context, Moscow has been anxious that the U.S.-led campaign against international terrorists and "rogue states" would increasingly
embroil the CIS and challenge Russia's preeminent influence. Although
Moscow is too weak to prevent American military deployments in Central
Asia and the Caucasus, it is determined to restrict growing U.S. influence.

BELARUS

For the Russian authorities, a close relationship with Belarus is deemed a
strategic imperative, as the country now borders three NATO members and
facilitates mainland links with Russia's Kaliningrad oblast. An integrated
Belarus eliminates the prospect of a Baltic–Black Sea "belt" around Russia
and enables Moscow to project a semblance of great power status. Despite
its statehood, Belarus remains highly dependent, politically, economically, and
militarily, on Russia and only reluctantly opted for independence once it was
clear that the USSR was defunct.

The first Belarusian president, Stanislau Shushkevich, attempted to steer
a neutral course for Minsk even after establishing the CIS with the Russian
and Ukrainian presidents. He wanted to subordinate former Soviet troops

to Belarusian control and desisted from signing the CIS Collective Security Treaty. But his moves proved unpopular with parliament and the general population, over 80 percent of whom had voted in favor of preserving the Soviet Union in March 1991. In June 1994, Shushkevich relented and signed the CIS Treaty, which expressly forbade the country from entering into alliances with nonmember states. Subsequently, Belarusian foreign and security policy remained focused on a close relationship with Russia.[56]

With the assumption of power by Lukashenka in July 1994, the pro-Russian orientation became more forthright.[57] Lukashenka moved to undercut the country's independence and pursued a close union with Russia. He preferred a strong bilateral relationship with Russia or a mini-USSR with Kazakhstan and Ukraine rather than supporting Moscow's attempts to establish a disparate CIS. Lukashenka's approach involved a mix of pan-Slavic solidarity and nostalgic Sovietism that appealed to wide sectors of Belarusian society. He envisioned Belarus as the vanguard of an emerging Slavic union that would save Russia from an aggressive Western offensive. Lukashenka was backed by senior figures among the Russian elite, including Prime Minister Viktor Chernomyrdin and Foreign Minister Evgeniy Primakov, who sought to restore a unified state out of the former Soviet republics.[58] However, some of Russia's prominent economic reformers placed brakes on unification, fearing that Belarus would become a major burden on the Russian economy.

In February 1995, Moscow and Minsk concluded a treaty of "friendship and cooperation." Between 1995 and 1997, they signed agreements abolishing border controls and creating a monetary union. In April 1996, a treaty was initialed establishing the Community of Sovereign States. In April 1997, Yeltsin and Lukashenka called for a union between the two countries and in May 1997 they formally signed a union charter. Lukashenka was convinced to sign the treaty on terms favorable to Moscow in exchange for a $1 billion energy debt relief to Minsk. Lukashenka's objective was to obtain a senior position in the interstate structure and to assure his regime of long-term economic support, including the management of its energy debt and beneficial trading agreements. In December 1998, an additional series of documents were signed furthering the integration process.[59] President Yeltsin needed the Belarusian connection to uphold some measure of public support for his "Greater Russian" foreign policy and to remove the issue as a rallying point among nationalists and Communists.

Although Moscow desired close political supervision and military dominance, it steered clear of substantial economic commitments and remained concerned that Belarus could become an enormous drain on Russia's budget. The December 1998 agreement declared the unification of the two states and in December 1999, the two Presidents signed a treaty committing Russia and Belarus to a confederal state. Lukashenka's move was overwhelmingly popular in Belarus where almost 90 percent of the population supported integration with Russia. Belarus proved to be Russia's staunchest foreign policy supporter and was the only country consistently mentioned as the highest priority in Moscow's international relations.[60] Russia's neighbors fear that Belarusian-Russian integration could serve as a precedent for other former Soviet republics.

Early on in his presidency, Putin stated that he took the integration issue seriously and would avoid symbolic and declaratory politics about "Slavic brotherhood" characteristic of the Yeltsin era. The Kremlin sought to out-flank Lukashenka by proposing in August 2002 the creation of a unified fed-eral state over an eighteen-month period; this would include referenda on the Union in both countries by May 2004.[61] Following the plebiscites, both countries could elect a joint parliament, introduce the Russian ruble as the union's single currency, and elect a supreme president of the new state. Putin also stressed that the institutions of the joint state should function in accor-dance with the Russian and not the Belarusian constitution.

Such moves threatened to marginalize Lukashenka as real power in a unified structure would revert to Moscow. Instead of a union of two equal states with the same voting rights, Putin's plan called for swallowing Belarus as the ninetieth unit of the Russian Federation. Such a full-scale union with Russia would mean the termination of the Belarusian state and the end of Lukashenka's presidency. Demands by Minsk for a state of two symmetrical and equal units was unacceptable to Moscow, especially as it could encour-age Russia's diverse federal units to demand a similar status.[62] Andrey Ryabov, an analyst with the Carnegie Moscow Center, told *Izvestiya* on 14 August 2002 that Putin was exploiting Belarus's international isolation to force Lukashenka to agree to a rigid unification model on Russia's terms. Putin transformed himself into the driving force of integration and cast Lukashenka as a potentially obstructive nationalist. Such an image was likely to further boost Putin's popularity during the 2004 Russian presidential campaign by portraying him as a "gatherer of the Slavic lands."

In March 2003, an intergovernmental commission agreed on the basic provisions of a Constitutional Act of the Belarus-Russia Union. The act con-firmed that Belarus and Russia would retain their sovereignty in the Union state, which would have its own legislature and government that would in-teract with two national administrations.[63] The Supreme State Council was to be the Union's supreme governing body. Other executive bodies included a bicameral parliament, the Council of Ministers, and the Union court. Belarusian and Russian leaders would rotate the chairmanship of the Supreme State Council. The Belarusian-Russian state would have a flag, an emblem, and other attributes of statehood. The Union would possess a single cur-rency, a common market, a common transport and energy system, and syn-chronized trade, customs, tariff, monetary, tax, and pricing policies. The two capitals also committed themselves to unifying foreign investment and other laws. Observers envisage the steady transfer of decisionmaking powers from Minsk to Moscow as a more integrated and centralized joint state emerges.[64]

Russia's propaganda ploys vis-à-vis Belarus have rarely attacked the incumbent government but focused on alleged attempts by the West to destabilize the country and pull it away from Moscow. Claims were made that Belarus was isolated by the West as a form of punishment for seeking unification with Russia. Moscow positions itself as the sole defender of Belarusia's "normalization" on the international arena, even while it tolerates the authoritarian and ostracized Lukashenka regime. Lukashenka presented the planned union with Russia as an important counterweight to the "unipolar" world and to "American hegemony." This was intended to raise the prestige of a pauperized country on the edge of Europe dominated by an obsolete dictator.[65] Russian spokesmen also periodically use arguments about a growing "Slavic union" to demonstrate that NATO expansion is not unopposed and that Moscow is taking practical measures to expand its area of influence.

For Yeltsin, a close relationship with Belarus was useful to demonstrate his patriotic "Greater Russian" credentials to his political opponents. He could pose as the creator of a new large Slavic space that would re-create much of the Soviet Union and also helped buttress Lukashenka's image as the "incorporator of the Slavic peoples." Lukashenka enlisted the support of Russian parliamentarians and the Orthodox patriarch Aleksey II to reinforce his calls for union. Putin subsequently sought to deprive the Belarusian President of this image by proposing a full union with Russia that Lukashenka opposed because it threatened his own position.

The Russian authorities exert substantial influence on Belarusian politics not only through their support for Lukashenka but also by exploiting state television, which is widely viewed in Belarus. During the summer of 2001, a number of critical programs were aired on pro-Kremlin Russian television channels pressuring Minsk to make compromises with Moscow on various economic deals. Observers believed it highly unlikely that Lukashenka would have won the September 2001 presidential elections if the Russian media had campaigned to discredit him and presented the programs of opposition candidates.[66]

The role of the Russian media gained more attention after the public dispute between Putin and Lukashenka over the Kremlin's proposal to turn Belarus into a Russian federal unit.[67] In a sign of resentment at Moscow's pressure, seven regional transmitters airing Russia's RTR Television were scheduled to be taken over by Belarusian regional television channels. Belarus's State Broadcasting Company chairman Yahor Rybakou claimed that the move was prompted by the need to develop regional television because "Belarusian viewers are always confused by the existence of the three imperial channels (Russia's RTR, ORT, and NTV) here. We are a sovereign state and we will be developing our own television." In January 2003, Belarus stopped retransmitting programs from Russia's Mayak, Golos Rossii, and Yunost radio stations.

A key component of the Russia-Belarus Union is in the military arena. Belarusia's military has a preponderance of Russian officers and 40,000 Russian troops remained in the country after independence. The military contained pro-Belarusian and pro-Russian organizations.[68] The Russian dominated Union of Officers of Belarus opposed the proindependence groupings and assailed the concept of neutrality as a method for tearing Belarus away from Russia and creating a Baltic–to–Black Sea *cordon sanitaire*. Moscow has pursued close military integration and control over the country's borders and air space as Belarus forms the most direct link for Russia to Central Europe. Moscow planned to unify defense systems and military structures as Belarus reintegrated its air defense, intelligence networks, and arms production with Russia and began to merge its ground forces.

A plan was devised in Moscow to create three coalition military units within the CIS Collective Security Treaty: in Central Asia, Caucasus, and Belarus, with a joint headquarters in Moscow. The objective was to develop a common strategy and special military structures focused on peacekeeping missions conducted by and within CIS countries. The Kremlin also proposed the creation of a 300,000-strong military corps combining Russian and Belarusian forces that would be deployed along the borders of the Baltic states if they gained NATO membership. A proposal to permanently station some 25,000 Russian soldiers in Belarus was also agreed with Minsk.

To guarantee Belarusian compliance with Russia's security objectives, Moscow exerts influence in determining personnel policy in the Ministry of Defense, including the identity of the minister. Such moves were assisted by the fact that Belarus had undergone minimal reform of the state apparatus, the military, and internal security networks, while Russian aid guaranteed the maintenance of a sizable Belarusian military structure. Moscow and Minsk made plans for a joint military doctrine, a common command structure, legislative integration, a joint defense industry, and the common use of military infrastructure and bases. A number of joint military exercises have been conducted and the forces of both countries were so closely intertwined that reunification seemed only a matter of time.[69]

Moscow views Belarus as a forward base against NATO's eastward expansion. Hence it needs to guarantee the permanent presence of Russian forces and complete command over Belarusian airspace. Moscow believes that a significant military presence in Belarus and in Kaliningrad would discourage further NATO growth or deter any stationing of NATO troops on the territories of new members such as Poland. Moscow and Minsk also proposed the creation of an "East European" regional force to purportedly counter terrorism and contribute to the emerging "Eurasian security architecture." The suggested name presupposes a regionwide scope regardless of the views of most East European states. Moscow wanted to establish a buffer zone as protection against further Alliance penetration. Once Putin understood that he could not block or bluff NATO enlargement eastward, the idea of a

"300,000-strong joint Belarusian-Russian military group" fell by the way-side especially as the "strategic partnership" with Ukraine became more important for Moscow than the union with Belarus.

Similarly to most former Soviet republics, Belarus is almost totally dependent on Russian energy supplies. The country receives highly subsidized energy, for about half the price Russia charges Ukraine and a third of what Russian energy companies receive in the West. Moscow has remained one of Minsk's major trading partners, accounting for roughly 80 percent of its imports and 90 percent of its exports, and its economic interest groups maintain close connections. Most of Russia's regions also pursue direct trade links with Belarus. Moreover, nearly 70 percent of Russia's exports to Europe pass through Belarus, one of the major transit countries in the region. Hence Moscow itself is highly dependent on Minsk's cooperativeness and compliance.

Under Putin, the pace of controlling Belarus's energy infrastructure accelerated and economic pressures have been applied to gain Minsk's agreement. In November 2002, Gazprom warned that it might halt gas supplies if Minsk did not accept a higher price for consumption beyond the amount contracted for 2002.[70] According to Gazprom, the company had almost reached its subsidized gas-export target to Belarus at the price of $24 per 1,000 cubic meters. It wanted Minsk to pay $36 per 1,000 cubic meters for any additional supplies. Gazprom subsequently reduced its gas supplies by half, prompting Belarusia's Foreign Ministry to condemn this tactic as a "deliberate action to exert economic pressure on Belarus."

Lukashenka asserted that the Kremlin was resorting to unprecedented political pressure to force through the sale of the Beltranshaz gas transportation and storage company to Gazprom. According to him, the cut in energy supplies was a political decision by the Kremlin, because Gazprom wanted shares in Beltranshaz as repayment for the Belarus gas debt. Lukashenka also ordered the government to look for ways of supplying Belarus with alternative energy resources because "we cannot suffer such dependence on and humiliation at the hands of a single state."[71] Despite Lukashenka's verbal bravado, in April 2002 Minsk succumbed to pressure and signed an intergovernmental agreement to expand cooperation in the gas sector. It also pushed through various legal amendments that allowed for transforming Beltranshaz into a joint Russian-Belarusian enterprise.[72] Gazprom was due to receive 25 percent to 30 percent of Beltranshaz shares in return for writing off $80 million in government arrears. The Kremlin authorized Gazprom to make this arrangement just before winter when the leverage of suppliers was strongest. A further $280 million of unpaid debt will enable Gazprom to obtain additional Belarusian assets as payment. Lukashenka also failed to convince Putin that Gazprom should continue to supply gas at heavily subsidized prices beyond the 10 billion cubic meters set by an intergovernmental agreement.

The Beltranshaz deal was put on hold in June 2003 as the issue of price and controlling influence came to the fore. The two companies had agreed on the timetable for creating a joint venture but not on the purchase price. Lukashenka vowed that he would not sell Beltranshaz to Gazprom "for nothing" and backed away from Minsk's previous pledge to form a joint-stock company with Gazprom to run Beltranshaz.[73] Gazprom insisted on acquiring more than 50 percent of the shares on the assumption that the price of Beltranshaz was no more than $1 billion. Belarus demanded between $2.5 and $4 billion and was unwilling to give Gazprom a majority stake in the company. In the course of negotiations, Belarusian representatives experienced intense pressure and their intransigence resulted in the imposition of Russian sanctions.[74] Gazprom threatened to triple its price and in response Minsk was expected to raise duties on the transit of Russian gas across Belarus. In January 2004, Gazprom cut its supplies after repeated failures to reach agreement over Beltranshaz.

Russia's periodic pressures and strong-arm tactics have led to complaints by Minsk. Lukashenka was outraged when plans emerged in October 2002 that a Russian-Ukrainian consortium intended to build new gas pipelines that would bypass Belarus and thus adversely affect the country's revenues. Russian companies also looked poised to purchase the Belarusian petrochemical industry consisting of the Naftan and Polimir state enterprises. In February 2003, Minsk announced that arrangements had been made to sell the sector's leading companies, including the Polimir conglomerate in Navapolatsk and the Azot and Khimvalakno chemical plants in Hrodna.[75] Several Russian companies expressed interest in these enterprises, including oil giants Surgutneftegaz, Sidanko, Sibneft, and Lukoil. However, the privatization offer would only allow investors to gain full control if they fulfilled several investment obligations. This arrangement was vehemently opposed by Russian companies who viewed it as a means for Lukashenka to assure himself of their economic and political support for his reelection bid.

Throughout the Soviet era, the Belarusian economy was one of the most tightly integrated in the all-Union system.[76] During the early independence period, Minsk was unable to gain access to foreign markets and Russia remained the country's main trading partner and the chief supplier of raw materials. Russian economic support contributed to salvaging the Lukashenka regime, especially through cheap energy supplies, currency-supported credits, and a customs union that favored Minsk. A major reason why Lukashenka favored a close link with Moscow was to secure dependable access to Russian raw materials for low prices as this would help postpone the implementation of market reforms that could dislodge him from power.[77]

Moscow has been reluctant to shoulder the economic costs associated with rapid and full integration. On the eve of the signing of the Russian-Belarusian Charter in May 1997, Moscow pressured Minsk to substantially slim down the original draft document by deleting clauses committing Russia to costly subsidization. Instead, the agreement focused on coordinating security policy and joint border patrols. Skeptics believe that full details of the charter were not made public and a separate secret document was prepared to accompany the formal charter.[78] The Kremlin was not prepared to bail out the faltering Belarusian economy by allowing Minsk's central bank to print rubles following a currency merger. Instead, economic assistance has been conditional in order to gain direct control over Belarusia's economy. In December 2002, Russia pledged to make available a $40 million loan to Belarus if the government met a number of requirements.[79] These included unification of export and import tariffs and agreement on procedures for collecting export duties on petroleum products.

Although Lukashenka spoke out against selling Belarusian enterprises to Russian oligarchs, an increasing number of enterprises have become dependent on Russian capital. Russian companies are seeking primary access in any eventual privatization of key sectors of Belarusian industry and have supported a Russia-Belarus monetary union. Lukashenka has uneasily viewed the activities of Russian companies, not because they may enhance the country's dependence on Russia but because they may precipitate pressures for genuine economic reform and encourage Belarusia's anti-Lukashenka opposition.[80]

Lukashenka and Putin participated in a meeting of the Russia-Belarus Union Supreme Council in Minsk in January 2003. They stressed their commitment to introduce the Russian ruble as the legal tender as of 1 January 2005 and the adoption of a common currency on 1 January 2008. The two countries faced disagreements over currency and monetary controls, which Russia wanted to orchestrate from Moscow, while Belarus sought to create a joint central bank.[81] In June 2003, Minsk agreed in principle that Moscow would control its crediting and monetary policy and the right to issue rubles would be reserved by the Central Bank in Moscow.[82] The currency union would give Russia a major lever in influencing economic and foreign policy decisions.[83] However, only a few days after agreeing to Moscow's terms, Lukashenka unexpectedly asserted that Belarus would agree to adopt the ruble only if this contributed to raising living standards and did not damage the country's economic security.[84] He warned against subordination to Russia. Minsk would henceforth commit itself to a monetary union only after all other bilateral agreements regarding the Union were implemented. Belarus also expected Moscow to pay Minsk over $4 billion before the currency merger could take effect.

In January 2003 in Moscow, the Parliamentary Assembly of the Russia-Belarus Union approved a Union budget. The two countries earmarked funds for thirty-six Union programs, including reinforcement of the Union's external border, protection of common information resources, training of Belarusian servicemen at Russian military schools, and the development of railways.[85] Russia also wants Belarus to privatize its largest industries, as this will give opportunities for buyouts. In order to survive in power, Lukashenka may need to acquiesce to Russian economic demands, even though in the long-term losing his grip over the Belarusian economy could also precipitate his political suicide.[86] Above all, Moscow wants to secure full control over economic decisionmaking and monetary policy in the Union state.

Putin calculated that the strategic and symbolic position of Belarus outweighed the economic costs of full-scale integration. However, he is still reluctant to pump resources into Minsk that would prop up the unreformed economic structure. Moscow feared that further degeneration of the Belarusian economy could result in immense economic costs for Russia. Officials pushed for the "harmonization" of economic policy; this would undermine the system of rigid central planning and allow Russia to gain control over the most profitable industrial sectors.[87] Full-scale economic integration will thereby give Moscow more substantive and predictable political control over the country.

Moscow has had little need to play the ethnic card against Belarus as the Lukashenka government promoted the notion that Belarusians and Russians constituted two components of the same ethnolinguistic group. Russian officials have applauded Minsk on its stance and in the 1995 referendum, 83 percent of citizens voted for Russian as the country's second official language. Lukashenka made little effort to cultivate a distinct Belarusian identity and largely removed the Belarusian language and the country's history from school curricula. Minsk also reverted to the Soviet era Belarusian republic flag and adopted a variant of the Soviet Belarusian anthem. There has been no reported discrimination against Russian ethnics, who constitute approximately 13 percent of the population, and no conflictive interethnic incidents. Nonetheless, in the wake of Putin's offensive to trump Lukashenka's ambitions for a Union, Belarusia's President pledged to defend the country's independence.[88] He claimed to have at his disposal "various methods, including extraordinary measures." He stressed that Belarus can enter a currency union only if the country's sovereignty is preserved and "financial guarantees" are offered by the Russian side. He appeared to be reaching for the nationalist card in his dispute with Moscow.

Russian authorities have benefited from international criticism and ostracism of some allied governments as this drew such states closer to Moscow. Opposition activists contend that since the mid-1990s Belarus has played an important role in the global market for conventional weapons and has become one of the top ten exporters even though it remains an insignificant producer of arms. Minsk is an intermediary in selling Russian-produced arms. Russian companies channel weapons through Belarus for sale to sanctioned regimes, especially specialized military use equipment.[89] This provided a useful cover for Moscow, which coordinated its exports with Minsk on global arms markets. Such arrangements ensured that any disclosures about clandestine deals would reverberate negatively on Belarus while leaving Russia largely unscathed.

Under Soviet rule, Moscow's control over Belarus was all-pervasive and Russians occupied most republican leadership positions. Following Belarus's independence, Moscow had little reason to interfere constantly with Minsk as Lukashenka's foreign policies were either in tune with Russian interests or displayed Moscow in a relatively moderate light. Belarus supported all of Russia's foreign policy positions, such as opposition to NATO enlargement and support for Milošević's Yugoslavia. The Yeltsin government was displeased with Lukashenka's courting of the Communist and nationalist opposition in Russia and his steps to establish closer economic links with neighboring Russian regions. However, this did not precipitate a break with Minsk or spark pressures to replace the Belarusian president.

Despite calls by Western powers for Russia to take a more active pro-democracy role, the Kremlin was little concerned with democratization, human rights, or the rule of law in Belarus. It was content to let Lukashenka determine the outcome of the September 2001 presidential elections through the regime's tight media controls and harassment of the opposition. Russian officials declared the elections free and fair contrary to the findings of international organizations. The post-Soviet elite in Belarus views Russia as the ultimate guarantor of their authoritarian regime. Meanwhile, the nationalist and democratic opposition grew increasingly anti-Russian as a result of Lukashenka's links with Moscow. This also served Lukashenka's interests as the Kremlin viewed him as the only dependable pro-Russian partner in the country. Attempts by the opposition to gain Russian support were largely ignored. Moscow did not relish the prospect of an independence-minded government reversing Russia's strategic gains and seeking to move Belarus into Western institutions. The pro-Western movement remained relatively weak and isolated and of limited threat to Russian interests. Minsk's anti-NATO rhetoric suited Moscow even when Lukashenka's eccentric behavior appeared embarrassing. His survival in power assured Moscow of a compliant junior partner who could deliver on Russia's demands.

At some point, Lukashenka will either have served his purpose in bringing the two states closer together or he may be considered a hindrance to further integration. In such a scenario, the Kremlin possesses the tools to find a suitable pro-Moscow replacement. During 2003, Moscow was sounding out members of the opposition who would be willing to maintain the country's loyalty toward Russia. Valyantsin Holubeu, a member of the opposition Belarusian Popular Front (BNF), stated in August 2003 that the stance of Russia's political elite could be changing following a roundtable in Moscow, which brought together Russian political scientists and lawmakers as well as representatives of the BNF and another Belarusian opposition organization, the United Civic Party. [90]

Belarusian political commentator Valery Karbalevich believed that the Kremlin was establishing contacts with alternative forces as a form of pressure on Lukashenka with a view toward gaining concessions from him on privatization. In a move designed to silence opposition voices and their Russian supporters, Minsk closed the offices of Russia's television company NTV in July 2003. Most Russian parties criticized the Belarusian assault. Deputy Duma speaker Irina Khakamada described this decision as an indication of Belarus's unwillingness to build a single state with Russia. Russia's small democratic parties, including Yabloko, claimed that the Belarusian authorities were deliberately trying to sour relations with Moscow and called on the Kremlin to apply tough economic and political measures.[91] They also demanded that Russia make it clear that it was strongly opposed to Lukashenka's reelection to a third presidential term. The Kremlin gave little indication that it had decided on such a step. Union with Russia and a change of government in Minsk did not guarantee an improvement in the country's human rights record or the development of pluralism and civil society, as these were of lesser concern to Moscow.

The Kremlin's direct political influence has been evident in the selection and monitoring of key officials responsible for implementing foreign policy. Mikhail Khvastou, the new Belarus ambassador to the United States, met with Russian deputy foreign minister Georgiy Mamedov in Moscow in March 2003. According to a Belarusian Foreign Ministry spokesman, Khvastou went to Moscow to prepare for his future mission in Washington.[92] Additionally, Russian officials hold several top posts in Lukashenka's presidential administration, government, and security services.[93] Moscow relished the spectacle of Lukashenka's increasing dependence at a time when he was ostracized internationally. Lukashenka's unusual docility during his meeting with Putin in Moscow in November 2002 indicated that he was seeking Kremlin approval for a referendum in support of constitutional amendments allowing him to run for a third term in 2006.[94]

As in all CIS states, powerful Russian criminal cartels penetrate Belarus and cooperate closely with local criminal organizations. According to opposition sources, mutually beneficial ties exist between criminal enterprises, Russian security services, and Belarusian officials. Even official sources admit that mafia clans are capable of financing parliamentary elections and emplacing their own candidates.[95] Mafia leaders have also expanded their penetration into the legal economy. Some groups are based around sports clubs and have infiltrated the political system by fielding election candidates.[96]

Similarly to the military and security structures, the intelligence services of Belarus and Russia have remained closely interwoven. This enables Moscow to maintain an additional lever of monitoring, influence, and control over Belarusian politics. Lukashenka has promoted Russian former KGB operatives to high positions in the security apparatus, while his internal security force, estimated at some 120,000 personnel, was larger and better equipped than the regular army.[97] Reports also appeared that Putin's administration included senior analysts and former employees of the Belarusian KGB.

KALININGRAD

Russia's Kaliningrad exclave bordering Poland and Lithuania constitutes Moscow's remaining outpost on the Baltic Sea and is viewed as a significant security asset containing a major military base. It is also one of the poorest and most neglected corners of Europe and a major source and transit point for organized crime. Both Warsaw and Vilnius endeavored to establish cooperative relations with the Kaliningrad authorities and to integrate the territory into emerging regional structures. This raised consternation in Moscow that Poland and Lithuania were seeking to gain control over the region in order to sever it from Russia.[98] Debates have raged in Kaliningrad and Moscow on the extent of the oblast's autonomy and whether it was advisable to establish close relations with neighboring states and EU countries. Some policymakers favored turning the area into a free economic zone in order to attract foreign investment. But this would necessitate major economic reforms and political decentralization that could undermine Kaliningrad's ties with Moscow.

The Kremlin proved unwilling to give Kaliningrad a special status, fearful of creating a precedent for other Russian regions that may seek greater autonomy. Central European policy analysts argue that the status of Kaliningrad with regard to EU visa requirements should be based on the principles of parity. In other words, Russia's demands for special treatment should correspond to "parallel expectations from Brussels concerning special treatment of the oblast by Moscow."[99] In return for "nonstandard" visa solutions for Kaliningrad residents, Moscow should commit itself to allowing maximum opportunities of travel between the oblast and EU member states and the development of consular and border crossing facilities.

But instead of decentralization that would allow Kaliningrad to integrate into the Baltic Euro–region, Putin tightened controls over the local governor especially in the latter's foreign contacts. This included the blocking of several projects between Kaliningrad and neighboring states. The speaker of the Kaliningrad Duma, Valeriy Ustyugov, warned of the economic isolation of his territory from European-Baltic energy and transport projects.[100] The authorities in Kaliningrad needed to clear all their political, security, and economic initiatives with Moscow, such as the construction of a highway linking the capital with the northern Polish city of Elblag. The Kremlin's intention was to control the exclave more effectively and determine its level of crossborder interaction, out of fear that the oblast could evolve toward autonomy and independence.

In July 2003, the Kaliningrad administration rejected a proposal by Dmitriy Rogozin, the presidential envoy on Kaliningrad issues and Duma

Foreign Affairs Committee chairman, to transform the oblast into a separate federal district. Kaliningrad leaders believed that such a change would create confusion between competing authorities that would be impossible to administer. Other suggestions to turn the oblast into an offshore zone were also rejected as it could lead to a massive inflow of quasi-criminal enterprises from Russia's shadow economy. Oblast leaders wanted to improve existing tax and customs regimes, to bring accounting procedures into line with global standards, and to liberalize banking regulations.[101]

Most of Russia's propaganda attacks have been aimed at neighboring states for allegedly harboring aspirations toward Kaliningrad. Kremlin fears of secession and annexation in the early 1990s were compounded by statements from some politicians in Vilnius and Warsaw over the legality of Muscovite control over the region.[102] Officials in Moscow also purposely tied the danger of Kaliningrad's annexation by Poland and Lithuania to NATO enlargement. They cautioned Western powers not to attempt any revision of international agreements on Kaliningrad's status. Rumors were spread that Warsaw and Vilnius had doubled their military personnel in the border regions in preparation for a potential invasion with Alliance backing. Such propaganda ploys served to reassert Moscow's control over Kaliningrad, discouraged other regions from aspiring to genuine autonomy or independence, and depicted NATO expansion as destabilizing for the region.

The loss of the Baltic states and NATO's inclusion of Poland raised the strategic importance of Kaliningrad in the traditional mind-set of the Russian military. Commanders claimed that a defenseless Kaliningrad would gravely undermine Moscow's maritime interests in the Baltic Sea and render the country vulnerable to future blockades. NATO enlargement allegedly threatened the survival of Kaliningrad and its close link with Russia, as the exclave would be surrounded by NATO countries.[103] Kaliningrad has been visualized as the front-line against NATO and a potential source of military pressure against neighboring countries. In early 2001, in order to deter Lithuanian and Latvian entry into NATO, reports appeared that Moscow was storing tactical battlefield nuclear weapons in the exclave and threatening NATO aspirants.[104] Poland and the three Baltic countries viewed such measures as a challenge to their security, especially as Moscow had previously threatened to forward deploy short-range nuclear weapons in response to NATO enlargement. Although no tangible proof emerged to confirm the charges, the incident served to sour relations between Moscow and Vilnius. Both the Polish and Lithuanian Defense Ministries complained that the accumulation of military arms in Kaliningrad is "disproportionate to the defensive needs of the region."[105]

Kaliningrad remains completely dependent on energy supplies from Russia and has little opportunity, motivation, or prospect to diversify its sources. This has suited Moscow by keeping the region's leaders from contemplating autonomy. However, in terms of economic and social assistance, infrastructural modernization, and business investment Moscow has contributed little to Kaliningrad's development. The exclave concentrates on finished products for the Russian economy and has attracted little Western investment. Only a handful of foreign companies established businesses in the region and Kaliningrad's goods invariably fail to meet EU quality standards. As Poland and Lithuania move into the Union, Kaliningrad is likely to fall further behind in its development. Poverty is widespread, as Moscow has failed to provide basic social services and public health.

In September 1991, the Kremlin granted the oblast the status of a free economic zone (FEZ) in order to attract foreign investment at a time when Moscow was cutting its subsidies. But the FEZ was terminated in 1995 and replaced with a less beneficial special economic zone (SEZ). Russian companies complained of unfair competition in the FEZ because enterprises in Kaliningrad were exempt from customs duties, while some politicians feared that economic success in the exclave and openness to nearby markets would stimulate separatism. The SEZ had little success because of confused decisionmaking between center and periphery and the failure to reform local economic institutions. According to the deputy presidential envoy for Kaliningrad, Andrey Stepanov, a major objective was the transfer of control over the SEZ from the oblast to the presidential administration.[106]

The region lacks the functional autonomy to pursue policies essential for attracting substantial foreign investment, and the blame for its stagnation lies primarily in Moscow. Some of Russia's economic moves have proved counterproductive politically. In early 2001, Russian custom services removed some of the region's tax privileges and deepened Kaliningrad's economic crisis. While seeking to increase state revenues, such a policy actually increased autonomist sentiments.[107] The Kremlin attempts to control the exclave's economic valve with its two Westernizing neighbors. Efforts by Warsaw and Vilnius to modernize Kaliningrad through crossborder trade and investments are constrained by Moscow, which views such efforts as separatism. Only a few Polish and Lithuanian businesses established themselves in the territory because of Moscow's bureaucratic interference and rampant official corruption. Putin and his staff remain displeased with the extensive cooperation that Kaliningrad Governor Yegorin developed with Lithuania, Poland, and the Nordic states.[108]

The Kaliningrad exclave has a predominantly Slavic or Sovietized population with small Lithuanian, Polish, and other minorities. The ethnic question has therefore not figured in Moscow's equation to sow division and conflict in the exclave from which the Center could reap benefits. Ethnicity has not been a source of dispute with either Lithuania or Poland and seems unlikely to become a source of friction in the future. The question of regional identity and relations with Moscow is of graver long-term concern for the Kremlin.

Moscow has desisted from discrediting the regional administration in Kaliningrad, although it has occasionally voiced displeasure when it acted without central authorization in its relations with Poland and Lithuania. Only the government in Moscow was empowered to conduct foreign relations, which were often broadly defined to include economic contacts and invariably led to conflicts between federal and regional administrations.

Moscow has blocked decentralizing trends in Kaliningrad in case the leadership moved closer to Poland and Lithuania. Political leaders in the exclave have been less concerned about Baltic and Central European accession to NATO than their Moscow counterparts and favor closer ties with both Warsaw and Vilnius.[109] Yuriy Matochkin, the first governor of Kaliningrad after the collapse of the USSR, proposed in 1993 a regional referendum to transform the oblast into a republic within the Russian Federation. The proposal was abandoned when Yeltsin tightened federal controls over all the regions at the end of 1995. Moscow continues to give mixed signals about Kaliningrad's economic development. Intensive ties with neighboring Poland and Lithuania could pull the region away from Russia, while neglect and deterioration could also spur separatist feelings. In an effort to more effectively control the region, Putin favored a constitutional amendment that would make the Kaliningrad governor an appointee of the Kremlin rather than a democratically elected local leader.

In an example of its destructive policies, Moscow has opposed the establishment of modern border crossings between Kaliningrad and Poland and Lithuania. The center also decides on such issues as passports for local residents, the extension of sea and air connections, and the access of foreign citizens to the enclave. The process of obtaining a Russian visa to visit Kaliningrad can be prolonged and costly and has to be approved by the Ministry of Foreign Affairs in Moscow. In sum, Kaliningrad has been far more isolated by Moscow's policies than by its oblast government or by its immediate neighbors.[110]

Poland and Lithuania were adamantly opposed to the Russian idea of a special transit corridor to Kaliningrad from Russia proper. As both states moved closer toward EU accession they needed to adopt the Schengen criteria, according to which the EU drops internal border controls but adopts a strict visa regime for countries outside the Union, including Russia. This could exacerbate social and economic disparities between Kaliningrad and its neighbors and generate instability in the isolated territory. Meanwhile, EU officials were concerned that Kaliningrad's well-established networks of organized crime could compound existing problems if border security failed to be strictly enforced.

Through its obstruction of Kaliningrad's relations with neighboring democracies, Moscow has supported the more isolationist currents in the region, which invariably maintain close ties with criminal interests. In November 2000, Admiral Vladimir Yegorov, Commander of the Baltic Sea Fleet, won the gubernatorial elections in Kaliningrad over the incumbent governor Leonid Gorbenko. Yegorov benefited from Putin's confidence and was considered a more loyal and reliable leader. The Kremlin has opposed a NATO role in converting Kaliningrad's military industry, disposing of its chemical weapons stocks, and developing a civil emergency response plan. While Kaliningrad could become an opportunity for Russia to develop productive and practical relations with its neighbors, if the political, social, and economic situation continues to deteriorate, "the area may become a 'black hole' and a source of instability for the entire Baltic Sea region."[111]

In Kaliningrad, Russia's criminal networks operate on their home turf and have ample opportunity to expand their activities through a lucrative illicit trade in weapons, narcotics, contraband goods, and human cargo. The Russian mafia exercises a high level of influence on the territory and officialdom is thoroughly corrupt from the regional government down to local police officers.[112] Under governor Gorbenko, several criminal leaders also made their way into Kaliningrad's official structures to head district administrations.[113] Moreover, Kaliningrad's intelligence and security services are fully integrated with the wider Russian system so there has been no necessity for hostile penetration and manipulation. Nonetheless, Russian services are constantly vigilant to monitor any developing ties between Kaliningrad and foreign businesses and agencies. As a result, espionage activities are widespread and pervasive in the exclave.

4

Regaining a Commonwealth: Ukraine and Moldova

UKRAINE

Ukraine, by its size, location, and population, formed the most strategically important country (other than Russia) that emerged from the Soviet Union. Few Russian politicians have been willing to accept the permanent independence of Ukraine, a country that is viewed as the historical origin of Russian statehood and the westernmost province of "Mother Russia." Russian elites hold a patronizing if not disdainful attitude toward Ukrainians, denying them not only a separate history and unique culture but also questioning their distinct national identity.[1] Ukraine's statehood is viewed as a temporary aberration, although the Kremlin did not plan for a military invasion or a wholesale takeover. Its ideal scenario is Ukraine's "Belarusification," by softening or disregarding interstate borders and creating a close political and military alliance directed from Moscow.[2] The internal characteristics of the Ukrainian regime and the political and economic systems were of lesser interest to Moscow as long as Kyiv followed Russia's foreign and security policies and did not succeed in gaining NATO or EU membership.

Under both the Leonid Kravchuk and the first Leonid Kuchma presidencies during the 1990s, Kyiv resisted pressures for close integration with either the CIS or with Russia.[3] It insisted on only participating in bilateral and CIS projects that directly benefited Ukrainian interests. It opposed the establishment of CIS coordinating structures and supranational bodies and avoided integration in the political and military spheres by refusing to sign the collective security treaty in Tashkent in May 1992. Although some analysts argued that Moscow's policy toward Ukraine was incoherent under Yeltsin, this may have been a consequence of the Kremlin's limited efforts. Russian officials believed that Ukrainian independence was temporary and there was little need to develop a long-range interstate policy.[4] During the late 1990s, Ukraine became more vulnerable to Russian pressures as the Kremlin exploited the political turmoil and Kuchma's ostracism in the West by posing as a more reliable ally. Power struggles among political interests, industrial lobbies, and state structures continued to swirl around the country and provided opportunities to pull Ukraine into a tighter Russian orbit.

The Central Europeans were especially concerned over Ukraine's stability and strategic orientation because a weak or Russian-dominated Ukraine could become a source of regional insecurity while encouraging Moscow's ambitions. By contrast, a secure, independent, and democratic Ukraine would present a more effective barrier against instability and Russian expansionism.[5] The Kremlin viewed Ukraine as the major tug-of-war between West and East, although most Western states were unwilling to damage relations with Moscow by pressing for Ukraine's membership in NATO and the EU.

To a greater extent than with other post-Soviet countries, Russian policy toward Ukraine was centralized and controlled by the president and his close advisers. Yeltsin defined Russia's relationship with Ukraine as the "priority of priorities."[6] The president paid one of his first foreign visits to Kyiv in November 1990 and signed an interrepublican agreement, which stipulated that Russia and Ukraine recognized each other's sovereignty and the inviolability of borders. However, Yeltsin's attitude changed after Ukraine declared its independence in August 1991 and Russia's political elites expressed outrage. Independence was confirmed in a public referendum in December 1991 supported by over 90 percent of voters. Soviet President Gorbachev warned that Russia would lay claims to the Crimean peninsula and other Russian-populated regions. Yeltsin's office stated that Russia reserved the right to raise border questions with any former Soviet republic.[7] Moscow drew back from the provisions of the November 1990 agreement as officials threatened that Ukrainian statehood would have dire consequences. In response, Kyiv boycotted all meetings at which Gorbachev sought to forge a new Union treaty and Kravchuk asserted that Ukraine was not interested in new treaties. When Moscow realized that its efforts were futile, it dropped the idea of a new Union, pushed for the dissolution of the USSR, and declared the creation of a looser CIS.

Although Ukraine was one of the founding members of the CIS and ratified its initial statutes, it raised reservations on issues such as a single currency, military affairs, and foreign policy in order to prevent the new structure from becoming a Soviet replica. Kyiv proved successful in thwarting Kremlin designs to construct a unified economic and security policy. The

Kravchuk leadership calculated that Russia remained the gravest threat to Ukraine's existence and that sooner or later Muscovite imperialism would resurface to threaten the country's independence: "Within the CIS, Ukraine should steadfastly block any efforts by Russia to turn the organization into a supranational, neo-imperialist Russian puppet, but instead support other independent-minded CIS states to resist potential Russian aggression."[8]

In order to return Kyiv more firmly under its control, Moscow engaged in various forms of subterfuge and subversion. The diverse methods included energy blackmail, economic buyouts, media propaganda, discrediting pro-independence politicians, attempts at diplomatic isolation, manipulation of ethnic and regional issues, threats of direct military intervention to protect Russian ethnics, lingering territorial claims, and challenges over the ownership of the Sevastopol naval base in Crimea. Pro-Moscow positions by political elites in neighboring Belarus and Moldova also squeezed Ukraine into the position of an outpost of "Westernism." The only political formations in Ukraine that supported a union with Russia and Belarus were extreme leftists, such as the Communists, Progressive Socialists, and Slavic Unity.[9]

Various diplomatic channels were employed by Moscow to solidify bilateral relations, especially after the election of Kuchma in June 1994. In March 1996, an Intergovernmental commission was created between the two prime ministers. In September 1997, a Russian-Ukrainian Consultative Council was established to meet annually and make recommendations for resolving bilateral disputes. Kuchma's premise was that repairing relations with Moscow would lessen Russian opposition to Ukrainian independence. In May 1997, to help avert Ukraine from revising its security neutrality, Moscow finally signed the Russian-Ukrainian Treaty of Friendship, Cooperation, and Partnership, which recognized the irreversibility of the disintegration of the USSR. The Duma ratified the treaty in December 1998 and the upper chamber of the Russian parliament ratified it in February 1999. Both houses had persistently raised objections and thereby maintained pressure on Ukraine. An agreement over the naval port of Sevastopol, which authorized the basing of the Russian Black Sea fleet on Ukrainian territory, also helped to ease tensions and created a foundation for more constructive relations between Russian and Ukrainian militaries.[10] Throughout most of the 1990s, the Russian legislature claimed that Sevastopol was a Russian city and part of the Russian Federation.

The importance of Ukraine to the Kremlin was underscored with the appointment of former Prime Minister Viktor Chernomyrdin as Russia's new ambassador to Kyiv in May 2001. Chernomyrdin was also declared Putin's economic and trade envoy with a mission to strengthen economic ties between the two countries. The new ambassador promptly criticized Kyiv's policy of neutrality and intimated that such a stance could undermine Ukraine's "strategic interests."[11] He openly interfered in Ukraine's parliamentary elections in March 2002 by publicly supporting the pro-presidential parties. The Russian embassy in Kyiv became more assertive in expressing its "concerns" over the rights of Russian ethnics and speakers.

As Russian influences increased, Kyiv largely accepted Moscow's demands that Ukraine put aside its pursuit of physical border demarcations. After years of prevarication by Moscow, Kuchma and Putin finally signed a treaty in Kyiv in January 2003 defining the land border. The two states still needed to sign a separate accord on the division of the Azov Sea as Moscow wanted to treat the sea as the internal waters of both countries. One important calculation for the Kremlin was that a full treaty with Russia could help dissuade Kyiv from moving closer to NATO and the United States as a potential protector against Russian demands. Moscow and Kyiv also signed nine agreements relating to cooperation in such fields as education and culture. In January 2001, Foreign Minister Anatoliy Zlenko claimed that the relationship with Russia was an "inseparable part" of Kyiv's "Europe-oriented policy."[12] Ukraine's future membership in the EU and NATO were "substantially dependent upon good relations with neighbors, particularly with Russia." Ukraine would evidently coordinate its westward integration with Moscow and not adopt any positions that were at odds with the Kremlin.

Under Putin, foreign policy toward Kyiv was energized in terms of objectives, enticements, and pressures. The Kremlin became more assertive with an extensive and expansive blueprint for dominating the country. This was evident in Russia's new military doctrine that gave Moscow the right to intervene in neighboring states containing large Russian populations. Ukraine's attempts to avoid integration in the CIS military and political structures vexed Russian leaders who viewed Ukraine as the strategic centerpiece of Moscow's European projection. In order to entice Ukraine into closer CIS assimilation, Kuchma was elected to chair the Council of CIS Heads of State at the group's summit in January 2003. Ukraine's status within the CIS remained in dispute, since Ukrainian officials claimed that the country was only an "associate member" because parliament never ratified the 1994 CIS Charter. However, in December 2002, Kuchma claimed that the Charter made no mention of "associate member" status, while Putin confirmed that Kuchma was elected on his initiative.

Some Ukrainian officials and opposition politicians remained anxious that Moscow could employ blackmail and intimidation to ensure Kyiv's compliance with its strategic goals. Such machinations could contribute to splitting society between a pro-Western and independence minded western Ukraine and a pro-Russian and anti-NATO eastern Ukraine. In a worst-case scenario, Russian pressure, coupled with economic hardship and political unrest, could precipitate a territorial breakdown. An increasingly polarized society could become ripe for political manipulation by ultranationalists and Greater Russian chauvinists. Internal divisions could paralyze the central government and give Russian agencies an opportunity to disqualify Ukraine from closer association with the West. Ukraine's neighbors, especially Poland, have pursued a policy of Ukraine's Europeanization, seeking to draw Kyiv into the Western orbit.[13] They argued that Moscow's reintegration of a large state such as Ukraine could serve as a negative example to other republics susceptible to Russian pressures.

The authorities in Kyiv tried to counterbalance Moscow by establishing closer relations within GUUAM, a grouping formed in 1997 and consisting initially of four states that feared Russian domination: Georgia, Ukraine, Azerbaijan, and Moldova. They were later joined by Uzbekistan. GUUAM rejected Russian pressures to join a CIS collective security agreement. Kyiv was fearful of exposure to Russian overtures after NATO's expansion into Central Europe. It grew concerned that such enlargement would assign Ukraine to a Russian sphere of influence and divide up the continent into two competing blocs. The political crisis in the fall of 2000, following the assassination of the investigative journalist Georgiy Gongadze, provided an opportunity for the Kremlin to move closer to Kyiv by offering support to a politically besieged president. As a result, Ukraine increasingly coordinated its foreign policy with Russia as evident in the slogan "Ukraine goes to Europe with Russia."

Russia's growing assertiveness was on display in October 2003 when workers constructed a causeway across the Kerch Strait that links the Black and Azov seas between Russia's Taman Peninsula and Ukraine's Tuzla islet.[14] Ukraine's Foreign Ministry warned Moscow that the construction of the dam violated Ukraine's territorial integrity. Moscow sought to influence ongoing talks over maritime border delineations, as it wanted to share sovereignty through the Kerch Strait that lay within Ukrainian territory.[15] In a victory for Moscow, in December 2003 Putin and Kuchma signed an agreement defining the Azov Sea as the internal waters of both states and provided for free navigation by Ukrainian and Russian vessels.

The Kerch incident demonstrated how Moscow unilaterally assumed the role of a guarantor or violator of Ukraine's territorial integrity. Its actions were carefully monitored by other countries that did not possess ratified border agreements with Russia. The Kremlin staged the provocation to gain territorial concessions from Kyiv and to test the international response to Ukraine's difficult predicament. Russian officials thereby publicly challenged the legitimacy of an existing CIS border, setting a dangerous new precedent, while the muted Western response could encourage bolder moves in the future.[16]

A major target of Russian propaganda attacks was the concept of "geopolitical pluralism," advocated initially by former U.S. national security adviser Zbigniew Brzezinski. This was described in Moscow as part of a sustained U.S. policy to steer all the CIS states away from Russia. "Certain forces" in Washington were evidently intent on "ousting Russia from the so-called post-Soviet space and to declare certain regions of the CIS as an

'American zone of special interest.'"[17] The Ukrainian authorities through-out most of the 1990s were criticized for resisting the reintegration of the "post-Soviet space" and obstructing Russian overtures for a closer union. A list of such damaging initiatives by Kyiv was posted in the Russian press, including attempts to create a Transcaucasian oil transport corridor bypass-ing Russia, the GUUAM initiative, efforts to construct a Black Sea–Baltic Sea union, Kyiv's support for NATO expansion, and Ukrainian aspirations to join the Alliance.[18]

In 2001, Kuchma stood accused by his opponents of cracking down on media freedoms and of playing a role in the disappearance and murder of investigative journalist Gongadze. Russian services were suspected of play-ing a role in his abduction. Although the President survived the ensuing storm, the Ukrainian parliament, dominated by a coalition of Communists, Socialists, Russophiles, and regional oligarchs, turned its fire on Prime Min-ister Viktor Yushchenko. The Ukrainian legislature passed a vote of no con-fidence in the reformist and pro-Western Yushchenko government, which promptly resigned while Kuchma survived. The Russian media broadcast-ing to Ukraine contributed to Yushchenko's downfall by branding him an "ultra-nationalist in hock to foreigners."[19] Moscow was especially angered by Yushchenko's determination to prevent Russian corporate takeovers. His replacement, Anatoly Kinakh, proved a more dependable pro-Moscow fig-ure tied to Russian business interests.[20]

The Ukrainian state remains precariously balanced between West and East. Moscow was perturbed that the "younger brother" had moved closer to NATO through various initiatives such as the Partnership for Peace program and the Gore-Kuchma Commission. Kravchuk also floated the idea of a Baltic–Black Sea axis to limit Russian influence, although Kuchma subse-quently discarded the initiative. Hard-liners in Moscow described Kravchuk's posture in the military arena as decidedly anti-Russian. As evidence, they cited a series of joint exercises by Ukraine's armed forces and NATO armies, the reorientation of Ukraine's space programs toward America, and pressures purportedly exerted against Russia's Black Sea fleet.

Although Ukraine opposed an outright CIS military alliance, it agreed to participate in a CIS joint air defense system and launched a program of joint officer training. In July 2003, Ukrainian premier Viktor Yanukovych and his Russian counterpart Mikhail Kasyanov signed an agreement on cooperation in military exports to third countries.[21] In January 2001, Moscow and Kyiv concluded a cooperation treaty that undermined any future Ukrainian par-ticipation in NATO's partnership programs. According to the fifty-two-point military cooperation agreement, Russia would participate in planning all multinational military exercises on Ukrainian territory, form common naval units, and jointly produce armaments.[22] Although Kyiv opposed the creation of any new military blocs on the territory of the former USSR, this position weakened as Russian influence expanded. When Kyiv declared in May 2002 that Ukraine had the ambition of eventually joining NATO, the Russian reaction was surprisingly muted.[23] Putin understood the obstacles Ukraine faced in entering the Alliance and dismissed such aspirations as unrealistic.

In an indication of the symbolic importance of Russia's military presence in Ukraine, Defense Minister Sergey Ivanov asserted in July 2003 that Russia was speeding up the pace of construction of a new naval base at Novorossiysk for some elements of the Black Sea Fleet, but parts of the fleet would remain in Sevastopol.[24] Ivanov noted that it was preferable to possess several bases and emphasized that Russia would not be leaving Sevastopol even after the Novorossiysk base was completed. In return for Russian support for Kuchma, Moscow was also aiming to extend the twenty-year lease of the Sevastopol naval base to ninety-nine years.

Energy supply, price, and credit have been manipulated as major economic tools of Russian policy. Ukraine remains dependent for more than 70 percent of its oil and gas needs on Russia and heavily indebted to Russia's energy monopolies.[25] Moscow's ability to injure Ukraine's economy through energy blackmail, raising prices, or by calling in debts challenged the country's social and political stability.[26] Moreover, pressures to integrate into the CIS reduce Ukraine's sovereignty while bilateral arrangements between Moscow and Kyiv undermine Ukraine's ability to administer its own economy.

Russia engaged in an "energy war" with Ukraine between 1992 and 1994, during which cuts in energy deliveries were politically motivated and crippled sizable parts of the economy. In 1992, Moscow cut by half the amount of oil it had guaranteed to Kyiv. The Ukrainian authorities were convinced that economic pressures were being applied to punish them for their rejection of various CIS agreements. By contrast, politically compliant Belarus was charged only half the price that Ukraine was required to pay for energy deliveries.[27] The Kremlin sought specific Ukrainian concessions to guarantee increased energy supplies, including full Russian control over the Black Sea Fleet and the surrender of Ukraine's nuclear warheads.

Moscow desisted from imposing a complete energy embargo partly because of the negative impact on its own energy revenues and because it wanted to hold this weapon in reserve. However, Moscow faced a dilemma as the closure of Ukrainian industries through energy shortages could harm Russian enterprises. With Ukraine also heavily dependent on Russian markets for its industry, the Kremlin possessed a powerful trade weapon at its disposal that led to a major energy crunch in Ukraine during the winter of 1993–1994. To ensure that Kyiv's attempts at energy diversity would have limited scope, Moscow stalled the demarcation of its borders with Ukraine. This delayed the exploration of new oil and gas fields in the Black Sea shelf, as state ownership could not be legalized until the border issue was resolved.

Another attempted energy weapon was the imposition in 1995 of excise duties on Ukraine's oil and gas imports so that Kyiv had to pay above-market prices. Moscow asserted that the duties would remain until Ukraine agreed to enter the Russia-Belarus-Kazakhstan customs union.[28] In a switch of strategy, from 1994 onward Moscow desisted from energy blackmail and sought instead to gain outright ownership of Ukraine's energy facilities. The Kremlin calculated that too much energy pressure could rebound negatively on Russia's ability to transport natural gas to Western Europe and thus affect its hard currency revenues. Nevertheless, between December 1999 and February 2000, Russia again engaged in an oil blockade against Kyiv. Although the issue of debt arrears was stated as the cause of the embargo, political considerations played a major role, especially in maneuvering Russian energy companies into a stronger position within the Ukrainian economy.

The purchase of energy-related industries and infrastructure has "revitalized the interlocking relationship between the Russian and Ukrainian elites."[29] Gazprom sought a majority stake in the pipelines crossing Ukraine. Its schemes were initially blocked as the Ukrainian parliament had prohibited the privatization of the oil and gas industries. Moscow's 1999–2000 blockade on shipments was intended to improve the position of Russian companies in the imminent privatization of Ukraine's pipeline system. In an effort to weaken Ukraine's bargaining position, during the mid-1990s Moscow also floated a plan to build new oil and gas pipelines through Belarus to Central Europe that would bypass Ukraine. Such a scheme would have severely damaged the Ukrainian economy because of losses from shrinking energy transits. The idea was shelved when the Kuchma administration became more accommodating to Moscow.

Concerted attempts to dominate Ukraine's energy sector continued under Putin. Lukoil purchased the Odessa oil refinery in May 2000 and Tyumen Oil acquired 67 percent of the Lisichansk refinery in July 2000. Moscow pressured Kyiv to use the Odessa-Brody pipeline to pump Russian oil to the Black Sea rather than Central Asian oil to Central Europe. In August 2001, Prime Minister Kasyanov and his Ukrainian counterpart Kinakh agreed to establish an "energy union." In October 2002, the two presidents signed an accord to form an interstate gas consortium to include Ukrainian pipelines and storage sites. Gazprom sought a 51 percent share in Ukrainian gas lines and other major assets, such as aviation industries, as payment for Kyiv's energy debts.[30] In December 2002, additional agreements were signed with Gazprom that increased the company's control over Ukraine's gas monopoly NAK Naftogaz. The Gazprom intermediary was Eural TransGas, a newly registered company linked with crime figure Semyon Mogilevich, who had been indicted in the United States.[31] Additionally, while Kyiv endeavored to increase its gas purchases from Turkmenistan, Gazprom maneuvered to purchase Turkmenistan's gas production capacity, beginning in 2007. This would make Ukraine fully dependent on the Russian monopolist for its gas imports.

In return for Moscow's support for Kuchma, the energy system was to be placed under Gazprom's control.[32] The agreement became valid for thirty years plus a five-year automatic extension. The Russian gas company thereby maneuvered itself into a position to directly influence Kyiv's energy policy including its deals with other countries. In addition, if Russia develops new energy pipelines through Belarus to Central Europe, Ukraine's leverage over Moscow will further decrease and Russia's dominance will solidify.[33] Nevertheless, the decision to create a Russian-Ukrainian gas consortium temporarily buried the idea of building a pipeline through Belarus and reflected Moscow's renewed confidence in Ukraine as a strategic asset.[34] The secret deal with Gazprom led to protests from the Ukrainian opposition, claiming that the agreement violated Ukrainian legislation, because the country's pipelines were not subject to privatization. Kuchma insisted that such an agreement did not require parliamentary approval and in June 2002 he signed an accord with Putin and German chancellor Gerhard Schroeder to establish an international consortium to use Ukraine's transit gas pipelines and ensure the uninterrupted transit of Russian gas to Europe.[35]

In October 2002, deals were signed between Gazprom and Ukraine's Naftogaz on gas transit, but the texts of the agreements were not publicized. Analysts speculated that Ukrainian ownership in the network was to be reduced to about 30 percent. When Prime Minister Kinakh voiced objections to the terms of the new gas consortium, claiming it contravened Ukraine's national interests, he was dismissed from office in November 2002. Kinakh's replacement was a pro-Russian politician from the Donbas region, Viktor Yanukovych, a strong supporter of the gas consortium. Ukraine would lose an estimated $1 billion in transit fees annually as a result of the gas deal that primarily benefited Russia. The agreement would also increase Moscow's leverage over consumers throughout Europe, in its control of both gas supply and transit, and prevent Western purchases of significant shares in Ukraine's transit system.

Russia's Unified Energy Systems (EES) planned to buy stakes in ten regional Ukrainian electricity distributors. The two governments also declared that they would initiate the parallel operation of their electrical grids. Such synchronization of power systems will allow Russia to export electricity to the West. Putin issued a statement claiming that this accord would "significantly strengthen" the position of the two countries on the international energy market.

Moscow has also pursued the transfer of ownership and operating rights to Russian companies as a form of debt collection. Premier Kasyanov noted that Moscow and Kyiv were finalizing an agreement on Ukrainian debts for Russian gas. Kyiv agreed to offer its national oil and gas company to Russia as a deposit for its future payments for Russian gas supplies.[36] Kyiv also moved nearer to joining the Eurasian Economic Community (EEC), a group comprising Russia, Belarus, Tajikistan, Kazakhstan, and Kyrgyzstan, amid reports that Ukraine was promised cheaper energy if it agreed to join the Russia-Belarus Union.[37] In July 2003, the Ukrainian government approved a draft fifteen-year agreement with Russia on the transit of oil through Ukraine, applying to all Ukrainian pipelines except the Odessa-Brody project. In sum, Russia's energy policy toward Ukraine has assured Moscow of greater control over the country's energy policy and a veto over Kyiv's energy deals with other states.[38]

Kyiv is dependent on Russia in three major economic dimensions: energy supplies, credits, and trade.[39] In addition, Russian capital investment has accelerated as the country's political uncertainty discouraged potential Western investors from participating in the privatization process. Russian enterprises acquired oil refineries, banks, aluminum plants, and parts of the broadcast media. These sizable Russian buyouts could jeopardize Ukraine's sovereignty especially as Putin seemed intent on making Russian business serve state policy. Close ties exist between Russian and Ukrainian business elites in several sectors, including energy and metallurgy. Most of these were based on prior Soviet-era political connections, enabling Russian businesses to cheaply acquire Ukrainian industries and to exert influence on Ukrainian politics.

Russian economic interests expanded under Putin and several companies invested heavily in strategic industries. In 2000 alone over $200 million was spent in buying up important Ukrainian assets, including oil companies, refineries, banks, metallurgical complexes, and chemical factories. According to Sergey Markov, the director of the Institute of Political Research, with close ties to the Kremlin, improving relations between Russia and Ukraine was the result of a calculated policy.[40] It was intended to engender a closed economic alliance or an "East European common market," to include countries that were "unwanted by Europe."

The level of Russian-Ukrainian trade by the late 1990s exceeded that of Soviet times. Russia accounted for approximately 45 percent of Ukraine's trade while Russia became the primary destination of Ukraine's emigrant labor. Putin asserted that trade in energy, defense, and technology would be stepped up so that Moscow and Kyiv could "influence the development of Europe's economy" and ensure that both states were "taken more seriously and our own economies will be more stable." Kuchma claimed that Ukraine would become a focus for gas and oil provisions to Europe from Russia and the Caspian region.[41]

Ukrainian parties alerted the public to the perils of Russian economic dominance. In February 2003, the Socialist Party's Valentyna Semenyuk, chairwoman of the parliamentary Monitoring Commission for Privatization, informed the legislature that Russian businesses jeopardized Ukraine's national security by acquiring "oil refineries, raw-aluminum production, communications, and many other strategic enterprises" during the privatization process.[42] Under Russian ownership, the economic effectiveness of these privatized companies declined, while investments in their modernization remained low.

Kuchma has increasingly allowed Russian capital to participate in Ukrainian privatization. By 2005, 70 percent of commodities made in Ukraine will be produced with the participation of Russian capital. Russian industries acquired control over aluminum production, including the Zaporizhia aluminum smelter (the largest chemical factory) bought by Russian car maker Avtovaz, two of the four most important oil refineries, and several banks, television outlets, and radio stations. The progress of Poland and other Central European states toward EU membership has also reinforced the dependence of Belarus, Ukraine, and Moldova on the Russian market.

CIS presidents signed an agreement to create a CIS free trade zone in April 1994, but this was not systematically implemented under Yeltsin. Putin encouraged Ukraine to join the Eurasian Economic Community (EEC) as this would enable Moscow and Kyiv to more effectively settle problems connected with the creation of a free trade zone and bilateral tax, tariff, and customs policies.[43] The EEC comprised Russia, Belarus, Kazakhstan, Kyrgyzstan, and Tajikistan. In December 2002, Ukrainian prime minister Viktor Yanukovych and Russia's premier, Kasyanov, announced the imminent creation of a free trade zone that would "open a new stage in the development of trade relations within the CIS."[44] In May 2003, Putin met Kuchma in the Crimea for a five-day summit without advisers—their nineteenth summit in two years. Putin was seeking closer ties in the security and energy sectors and focused on the creation of a CIS free trade zone, an international gas transportation consortium, and cooperation between Russian and Ukrainian military-industrial complexes. He also wanted to ensure that all CIS states coordinated their arms export policies.

A draft accord for the creation of a Single Economic Space (SES), comprising Russia, Ukraine, Belarus, and Kazakhstan, was approved in August 2003. Ukrainian lawmakers protested that it contravened the constitution and undercut the country's sovereignty as Russia was seeking to expand economic instruments into political controls.[45] The treaty envisages a free trade area, a joint economic policy, a customs union, coordinated accession to the WTO, and a central commission that could impose decisions on member states. In return, Kyiv will obtain cheaper energy and more equitable access to the Russian market. However, the SES would also entail the monopolization of Russian capital in the entire zone.

Ukraine has pursued an accommodating interethnic policy and there have been no reports of official anti-Russian actions. President Kuchma introduced a series of measures to strengthen ethnic coexistence by decentralizing language policy and rebuilding economic relations with Russia, especially in the military-industrial sector. He needed to maintain some equilibrium in his ties with Moscow in order not to alienate the large Russian-speaking population or the still powerful former *nomenklatura* that maintained its traditional political links. Yeltsin did not directly raise territorial or minority questions, although Russian parliamentarians periodically threatened Kyiv by staking claims to

Sevastopol and Crimea. In July 1993, the Duma declared Sevastopol a Russian city and encouraged separatism among Crimea's Russian majority. Yeltsin
officially distanced himself from such initiatives but did not completely subdue them as he calculated that they helped to exert pressures on Kyiv.

At the core of the Russian ethnic problem has been the question of identity.[46] Many Russians resident in the newly independent states continue to
identify themselves as citizens of the Soviet Union or whatever multinational
entity replaced this structure. They perceived new state borders as artificial
and after the collapse of Communism this population became susceptible to
populist and nationalist propaganda. Their "Russianness" was often magnified when the government adopted an anti-Moscow position, which was
interpreted as anti-Russian. Periodic opinion polls, posing the question
whether Ukraine should "reunite with Russia," were based on the premise
that Ukrainian independence was provisional and conditional.

The Russian minority has been exploited by Moscow to apply political
pressures on Kyiv. Russian officials demanded dual citizenship for coethnics
in Ukraine and used this as a pretext to delay signing a bilateral treaty. Kyiv
rejected such proposals, as they would allow Moscow to claim some jurisdiction over regions where Russian-speakers predominated. Moscow also
raised the specter of creeping "Ukrainization" directed against Russian
ethnics. To inject more venom into such attacks, this policy was described
as "Galicianization." This implied an attempt by West Ukrainian nationalists to oust the Russian language from all official communications, to thwart
Russian cultural influences, to limit the Russian Orthodox Church, and to
consolidate a "Ukrainian political nation," which remains an anathema to
Russia's political elite.

Kyiv remains concerned about possible Kremlin support for separatism in
Crimea and eastern areas of the country, especially as the permanence of
Ukraine's borders is questioned by Russian politicians. Nonetheless, it did
not serve Russia's interests to provoke a full-scale separatist conflict in eastern or southern Ukraine, as this would have a negative impact along Russia's
borders. Moreover, support for Russophone secessionism in eastern Ukraine
would be tantamount to recognizing the permanent separation of western
Ukraine. However, the Crimean issue has been manipulated by Russian
nationalists to prevent the Ukrainian government from fully consolidating
the country's independence and territorial integrity and moving in a pro-
Western direction. Officials repeatedly referred to Crimea as "ancient Russian land." In May 1992, Russia's parliament declared the illegality of
Crimea's transfer from Russian to Ukrainian jurisdiction in 1954.[47] It claimed
that the status of the territory should be determined through negotiations
with the participation of Crimean political representatives.

Although neither Yeltsin nor Putin openly questioned the status of Crimea
or any other part of Ukraine, they evidently approved of such debates as a

means of influencing Ukrainian policy. Russia gained the right to deploy troops in Crimea until 2017, primarily based in Sevastopol. This had a strong influence over local politics and emboldened leaders of the Russian majority on the peninsula. A local Crimean secessionist movement, led by the Republican Movement for Crimea, and was supported by the Duma and a number of senior political figures, including Vice President Aleksandr Rutskoi, declared that Crimea should belong to Russia and demanded a referendum on the peninsula for rejoining Russia.[48]

Duma deputies raised the Crimean issue to demonstrate their patriotism and to interfere directly in Ukraine's internal politics. In March 1995, the chairman of the Committee on CIS Affairs claimed that parliament succeeded in reuniting the splintered Russian separatist bloc, Rossiya, in Crimea.[49] Crimean controversies were also linked with festering disputes over the final territorial status of Sevastopol and the division and basing of the post-Soviet Black Sea Fleet. Formal agreements were reached on the latter question in May 1997 while postponing the resolution of the most contentious elements. Kyiv was confronted with an ultimatum from Moscow: either to make concessions on the Black Sea Fleet or face more intensive pressures over its control over the Crimean peninsula. Despite Moscow's subsequent calming of the dispute, none of the legislation passed by Russia's parliament, staking claim to Crimea, has been repealed.

One significant tool for Moscow in its "divide and rule" strategy has been the Russian Orthodox Church, which has stoked social tensions in Ukraine. The Moscow patriarchate was permitted to launch a major media crusade against the acceptance of an autocephalous Ukrainian Orthodox Church.[50] This campaign found a receptive audience among some former Communist *apparatchiks,* members of parliament and the administration, and among the large Russian minority. It also stirred communal frictions between adherents of the two Churches. In April 1999, violent scuffles took place in the city of Mariupol between supporters of the Moscow and Kyiv Patriarchates after Ukrainian Patriarch Filaret arrived to consecrate a cross, erected on the future site of a Kyiv Patriarchate Church. Filaret accused the regional authorities in Donetsk of complicity in provoking the incident and of actively supporting the Moscow Patriarchate.[51]

In the March 2002 parliamentary elections, priests of various Orthodox communities were accused of endorsing particular political parties or candidates in their sermons. This too had a negative impact on already tense inter-Orthodox relations.[52] Many prominent Ukrainians remained convinced that only through the creation of a fully legitimate and separate Orthodox Church administration in Ukraine could Moscow's influence in the country be curtailed. Hence, the Russian patriarchate, through the support it receives in the Kremlin, remains a major obstacle to consolidating Ukrainian independence.

Special interest groups in Ukraine linked with Moscow were determined to derail the Yushchenko reform program in the late 1990s, which threatened their semilegal or corrupt business enterprises. The relative success of Yushchenko's administration in stabilizing the economy and pursuing structural reform was undermined by oligarchic groups fearful of legalism and Western business competition. Meanwhile, Kuchma was willing to sacrifice Yushchenko in order to remain as head of state, deflect attention from his political problems, strike a deal with the oligarchs, and move closer to Moscow. Kuchma's domestic travails reinforced Ukraine's "tilt to the East" while discouraging Western governments and businessmen from dealing with a repressive and corrupt government.[53] The Kremlin exploited opportunities presented by Ukraine's political unrest in 2000 and backed the boosting of presidential powers at the expense of parliament. The presidential administration and the Council for National Security and Defense concentrated authority in their hands. This led to political protests and international criticism, but Kuchma retained support among Ukrainian businessmen linked with Russia.

Putin visited Kyiv in the midst of political turmoil in a display of support for Kuchma just as criticisms increased in the West against the president's tolerance of human rights abuses and his crackdown on independent journalists. At the Putin-Kuchma summit in Dnipropetrovsk in February 2001, the two leaders agreed to deepen economic and technological cooperation. Kuchma became increasingly dependent on Russian oligarchs and Putin's personal support for his political survival. Moscow calculated that unlike in the Baltic region, the West would be less resistant to a gradual reabsorption of Ukraine by Russia, especially if it encouraged greater predictability in the country's domestic and foreign policies.

Under Yeltsin, direct political backing was given to elect Kuchma in competition with the more independence-minded Kravchuk. In the June–July 1994 presidential elections, the Russian authorities gave financial support for Kuchma's campaign. Yeltsin appeared on Ukrainian television and appealed to citizens to vote for Kuchma.[54] Putin also played an influential role in the composition of the Ukrainian government from which individuals with close ties to the West were excluded. After a visit to Ukraine in October 2000, Putin pressured Kyiv to dismiss the pro-Western foreign minister Boris Tarasyuk and replace him with the more pliant Anatoliy Zlenko.[55] Tarasyuk was a thorn in Russia's paw as he favored a close security relationship with NATO. Also replaced at that time was Mykola Zhulinsky, deputy prime minister for cultural affairs. The government, in close consultation with Moscow, also launched judicial proceedings against Deputy Prime Minister Yuliya Tymoshenko, who sought to reform the energy sector and eliminate corruption.[56]

Moscow contributed to influencing the outcome of Ukraine's parliamentary elections in March 2002 through its media and financial support. The

Kremlin was keen to capitalize upon its growing success in reorienting Ukraine's foreign policy eastward. The main threat to Kremlin policy and Russia's increasing influence was former premier Yushchenko and his Our Ukraine bloc.[57] In order to promote Russian state interests, a Russian Bloc political movement was formed in July 2001 with the explicit goal of uniting all "Russian people" in one state. It organized demonstrations in dozens of Ukrainian towns to support this cause.

Russophile oligarchic clans and their media outlets in Ukraine manufactured a "Brzezinski plan," a conspiracy supposedly concocted by a group of U.S. policymakers and advisers to overthrow Kuchma and replace him with Yushchenko. The scheme was allegedly modeled on the ouster of Yugoslav president Slobodan Milošević. Yushchenko's purported allies in this plot were two wings of the anti-Kuchma opposition, Yuliya Tymoshenko, his former deputy prime minister, and Socialist leader Oleksandr Moroz. According to Russian sources, the "Brzezinski plan" was behind the "Kuchmagate" scandal that erupted in November 2000, when incriminating tapes made in Kuchma's office were released, leading to Ukraine's largest opposition demonstrations. The trumpeting of a "Brzezinski plan" is a classic example of disinformation that deflects attention from probable Russian involvement in the "Kuchmagate" scandal. Controversial Kremlin strategists and Putin image-makers Gleb Pavlovskii and Merat Gelman, joint owners of the Fund for Effective Politics (FEP), provided maximum publicity for the "Brzezinski plan." The FEP engaged in various disinformation activities during the Ukrainian elections together with the pro-Moscow Social Democratic Party (United) (SDPU-O), whose main target was Yushchenko. The SDPU-O, together with the Communist Party, supported Ukraine's membership of the Russia-Belarus Union. SDPU-O leaders also raised the question of changing the 1989 language law by adding Russian as a second "official language."

The SDPU-O was the main backer of the extreme nationalist and anti-Western Rukh for Unity (NRU-ye) splinter group, created only three days before the "Kuchmagate" scandal began. The NRU-ye and the Progressive Socialists played the role of "radical opposition" parties on the right and left of the political spectrum respectively, but closely controlled or influenced by the executive. This was similar to the position occupied by Vladimir Zhirinovsky's Liberal Democratic Party in Russia. The NRU-ye controlled the Ternopil-based Tryzub paramilitaries, led by Colonel Yevhen Fil, who orchestrated violence at demonstrations in order to discredit the anti-Kuchma opposition. The SDPU-O also attempted to blacken former premier Yushchenko's character. It forged an agreement with the FEP to provide "campaign advice" and created a fake Yushchenko Web site. FEP and its SDPU-O allies were also behind Ukraine's second taping scandal, that of Yushchenko and Kyiv Mayor Oleksandr Omelchenko in January 2002. The tape was released by the civic group For Trustworthiness in Politics, which was closely linked to the SDPU-O and the NRU-ye and which aimed to discredit Yushchenko.

Moscow consistently attempted to gain influence over Ukrainian politics and parliamentary elections became the scene of fierce competition over the country's future direction. While the pro-Russian parties and most of the large economic interest groups prefer to see Ukraine "rejoin Europe together with Russia," the pro-Western organizations seek rapid integration regardless of Russia. The latter option is promoted by Yushchenko and his allies; the former alternative by Russian officials and their Ukrainian partners.

On the eve of Ukraine's March 2002 parliamentary elections, Yushchenko claimed that statements issued by Russian officials constituted "direct interference in Ukraine's internal affairs and its electoral process."[58] He was referring to a pronouncement by Russian presidential administration chief Aleksandr Voloshin singling out specific parties for praise in strengthening Russian-Ukrainian relations while condemning others for their allegedly "anti-Russian positions." Our Ukraine also accused Russian politicians of provoking anti-Western sentiments and blocking Ukraine's access to Euro-Atlantic structures by artificially fanning anti-Western hysteria. All major political candidates in the March 2002 elections made pilgrimages to Moscow to display their pro-Russian credentials, fearing that their absence would rebound negatively on their chances during the election.

Russian state-controlled television stations, widely viewed in Ukraine, were mobilized to launch attacks on political parties that were not favored by the Kremlin. Following the elections, Moscow encouraged Kuchma to exclude reformist and pro-Western parties from gaining positions in the new government, while supporting the inclusion of representatives of oligarchic factions linked to Russian business. Russian Ambassador Chernomyrdin advised Ukrainian deputies to approve Kuchma's choice of Anatoliy Kinakh as the new prime minister because he was amenable to Russian influences. The Putin regime made preparations for the post-Kuchma era by cultivating candidates for the October 2004 Ukrainian presidential elections and discrediting pro-Western politicians such as Yushchenko.[59] The Kremlin supports East Ukrainian business interests with close ties to Russia and fears that a Yushchenko victory would jeopardize its influence and reverse Kyiv's course toward Russia. Putin sought to ensure that a loyal successor to Kuchma would guarantee strong support for Moscow's policies.[60] Prime Minister Viktor Yanukevych was a leading candidate for the position as he could undercut the anti-Kuchma Socialist vote in eastern Ukraine.

Moscow played on both the fears and realities of Ukraine's limited economic and political reforms. Russian political, security, and business interests sought to benefit from Kyiv's exclusion from NATO and EU enlargement. Ukraine's political elites were instead offered closer links with Russia. Despite Moscow's strategy, Ukraine's younger generation is less nostalgic about the Soviet past and has fewer bonds with Russia. Sociological surveys con-

ducted between 1999 and 2002 show that young people are less isolationist or Russo-focused and more pro-Western than elders. Young people generally support Ukraine's membership in NATO and the EU and are critical
of the serious obstacles to democratic development.[61] Nonetheless, pro-
Russian forces encouraged attacks on pro-Western groups, including incidents such as in Donetsk in October 2003, when the congress of the Our
Ukraine movement was officially canceled. Statements by Western diplomats
that such actions would disqualify Ukraine as a democratic state and a serious
contender for NATO accession were not criticized by Moscow.

The criminal-political nexus is strongest in Ukraine's banking sector. With
Russian banking interests dominant throughout the region, corruption and
criminality in Russia cannot be isolated from Ukraine.[62] Criminal bosses
operate freely between the two states and are able to bribe and corrupt
officialdom or operate with the knowledge of intelligence and security services. The latter employ criminals to engage in espionage, sabotage, harassment, abductions, and assassinations that benefit the Russian authorities.
High-level intelligence and security contacts from the Soviet period have been
maintained between Kyiv and Moscow.[63] Russian secret services help their
Ukrainian counterparts to investigate, harass, and arrest selected members
of the political opposition. The latter included the former energy minister
Yuliya Timoshenko, who voiced concern about Russia's energy policy toward
Ukraine. Under Putin, Russian and Ukrainian agencies have become even
more interdependent and fully engaged to undercut any political opposition
to closer ties between Moscow and Kyiv.

MOLDOVA

During the last months of the Soviet Union, the Yeltsin government supported the independence movement in Moldova and other republics as useful
levers against Gorbachev and the Soviet regime. Paradoxically, during this
period the Moldovan administration, led by the Moldovan Popular Front
(MPF), backed unification with Romania and engaged in some discriminatory measures against the Russian minority in the Transnistria region. Meanwhile, leaders of the Transnistrian separatists supported the August 1991
hard-line coup against Gorbachev and did not support Yeltsin's objective to
terminate the USSR and declare Russia's independence. Yeltsin supported
the Moldovan authorities and at one point labeled Transnistrian separatism
as a "threatening precedent." Moscow was also concerned that it not lose
Western support through any kind of crackdown against Chisinau.

Russia's policy toward Moldova changed during 1992 as Yeltsin adopted
a more assertive nationalist position cognizant of criticism from the military
and security apparatus.[64] Moscow took aboard the issue of "protecting" the
large Russian population stranded in the newly independent states and the supposed legitimacy of Transnistrian demands. Even though the pro-Romanian

faction lost most of the key leadership positions in Chisinau, Russian authorities condemned the Moldovan government for its "Romanianism" and its purported attempts to subdue the Slavic populations along the Dnistr River. The Transnistrian standoff was depicted as defense of the rights of Russians in the "near abroad," even though Russian ethnics accounted for only 25 percent of the population in the enclave.[65] Under Foreign Minister Primakov, Moscow lobbied for the creation of a federal "common state" of Moldova-Transnistria.

In the early years of independence, Moldova was hesitant about CIS integration, even though it was an original signatory to the organization's founding documents in December 1991. Its position at that time was similar to Ukraine's. Chisinau was suspicious of Russian proposals to create any supranational security, political, or economic structures.[66] The government resisted ratifying the CIS Charter in January 1993 and did not participate in the Tashkent Collective Security Agreement. Moldova's parliament declined to ratify CIS membership in August 1993. Moscow then applied economic pressures, including the imposition of punitive agricultural tariffs, pricing Moldovan goods out of the Russian market. The country's ability to purchase raw materials and fuel from Russia was seriously jeopardized and Moldova's energy debt greatly increased. Under intensive pressure from Moscow, parliament relented and voted to join the CIS in April 1994. However, Chisinau stipulated that it would not participate in any military pacts or in the ruble zone and demanded the withdrawal of Russia's Fourteenth Army from Transnistria.

Russian legislators in 1999 had refused to ratify a Russian-Moldovan treaty, initially signed in 1990, because of the document's failure to reflect Transnistria's secession. Yeltsin withdrew the document from the state Duma and initiated negotiations on a new bilateral treaty. The completion of a treaty was stepped up after the Communist victory in Moldova in both parliamentary and presidential elections. Upon his election in April 2001, President Vladimir Voronin, a Russian by nationality, asserted that improving ties with Russia was a top priority.[67] The two foreign ministers, Igor Ivanov and Nicolae Dudau, initialed the bilateral friendship and cooperation treaty in November 2001.[68] Voronin and Putin signed the accord during the Moldovan leader's visit to Moscow that same month. Both legislatures ratified the document by an overwhelming majority.

The treaty was a disappointment to Transnistria's pro-Russian leaders, who wanted the document to mention the existence of a "common state," composed of Moldova and Transnistria. Russia recognized Moldova's independence and territorial integrity and pledged to work toward a political settlement of the Transnistria dispute. Ivanov also asserted that Russia would observe a 2002 deadline for completing the withdrawal of troops and weapons from Transnistria and believed the agreement would inaugurate a "strategic partnership" between the two countries. The treaty was also declared to be a first step in Moldova's progress toward the Russia-Belarus Union. In August 2001, a new political movement was created in Moldova that strongly supported unification with Russia, Belarus, and Ukraine. The movement's leader, Valery Klimenko, asserted that a referendum would be held on joining the Russia-Belarus Union.[69] However, shortly after assuming office Voronin stepped back from a Union with Russia, partly due to fears of provoking domestic opposition.

Transnistrian leaders wanted the treaty to declare their right to establish separate economic, cultural, and social ties with Russia and to provide for a Russian consulate in Transnistria. But Moscow refused to include any of these provisions in the treaty without Moldovan consent. Moldova agreed to various compromises in the document. In order to gain official recognition of its independence and territorial integrity, Chisinau complied with Moscow's insistence that Russia was the main arbiter and guarantor in the Transnistrian dispute. Moscow exercised political and economic pressures on the Transnistrian leadership to abide with the Kremlin's more accommodating stance toward Chisinau. In February 2002, Gazprom cut gas supplies to a major Transnistrian steel enterprise because it had not paid for its deliveries. The separatist foreign minister Valeriy Litskay accused Russia of trying to impose economic pressure on the self-proclaimed republic. He stated that the decision to cut supplies coincided with the visit of Russian first deputy foreign minister Vyacheslav Trubnikov.

The Transnistrian issue plagued relations between Chisinau and Moscow despite the cordial relations between the Communist government and the Putin regime. Even Voronin appealed to Moscow to remove its troops and weaponry from the territory and to "recall his subordinates" from Transnistria to allow for the holding of free elections.[70] On the other hand, Moscow views Transnistria as a guarantee that Moldova will follow an Eastern orientation, especially if its leaders join the central government in the power-sharing proposal envisaged in the various federalization plans.[71]

Propaganda attacks were conducted by Moscow, initially against Moldovan statehood and then in opposition to Chisinau's closer links with Romania and the West. The Transnistrian rebellion was portrayed by Russian hard-liners and military leaders as a base from which the reconstruction of the Soviet Union would begin.[72] The rebels were presented as patriots and genuine internationalists against a radical nationalist Moldovan administration. Even Russian democrats and moderates reinforced this propaganda barrage.[73] Russian media and intelligence units of the Odessa Military Command engaged in a massive pro-Transnistrian and anti-Moldovan media campaign, which further emboldened the secessionists. They were assisted by the fact that Russian television channels are widely watched throughout Moldova, even among Moldovan speakers. With a Communist government in place in Chisinau in the late 1990s, Russian authorities turned their attention to the opposition Christian Democratic Popular Party, which they accused of being aggressive nationalists and instigating a "xenophobic public mood and inter-ethnic strife."[74]

During the Soviet period, the state propagated the image of Romania as a negative and primitive influence alien to Moldovan identity. The USSR and later Russia were depicted as the chief protector of Moldovan statehood and national identity against "Romanian assimilationism." But Moscow's claims that the Transnistrian revolt was sparked by Moldovan moves to unify with Romania had little substance. Indeed, the separation of this enclave with a large non-Moldovan population could actually encourage the remainder of Moldova to seek a merger with Bucharest.[75] Contrary to Moscow's assertions, Transnistrian separatism did not prevent Romanian-Moldovan unification and was not a "strategic response" to such an initiative. The Transnistrian issue was deliberately heated up by Moscow after Chisinau had already declared that unification with Romania was not feasible because the majority of the population rejected it. Moscow's support for Transnistria accelerated at a time when Chisinau was making significant concessions to the separatists and was willing to grant the region special status and its leaders positions in a coalition government. Pressures on Moldova continued even though Chisinau backed Yeltsin during Moscow's parliamentary revolt in October 1993, while the Transnistrian leadership actively fought on the side of the president's opponents. Continuing Russian threats and pressures actually energized sectors of the Moldovan elite and society that desired closer ties with Bucharest.

In effect, the Russian authorities helped to create a second Kaliningrad in the Transnistrian region. The area became a heavily militarized exclave strategically located between Ukraine and the Balkans that received much of the weaponry and ammunition relocated from Central Europe by the Red Army. The commander of Russia's Fourteenth Army, stationed in the Transnistrian capital of Tiraspol, General Aleksander Lebed, declared that Transnistria was part of Russia, the "key to the Balkans" and a "strategic crossroad" between Ukraine, Romania, and the Black Sea: according to him, "if Russia lost this area, it will lose influence in the entire region." Moscow also insisted that any action in the Danube Basin and the Black Sea required its prior agreement, because these were areas of "traditional Russian interest."[76]

Russian proposals for closer military ties were rejected by the Moldovan authorities. Although Moscow and Chisinau signed an interstate treaty in 1990, Russia's parliament failed to ratify it as the Kremlin expected Moldova to include protocols enhancing Russian influence over Moldovan security and foreign policy. The Moldovan case demonstrated how the Duma was employed to delay the implementation of bilateral treaties and apply pressure on the "near abroad." Moscow persisted in drawing Moldova into a tight military pact. Pressures were exerted to form a joint council on regional security issues in which Moldova would need to consult with Russia before it adopted any policy initiatives. General Anatoly Kvashnin, chief of the General Staff of Russia's armed forces, even proposed that Chisinau legalize Russia's military presence and confer basing rights for Russian troops.[77] Moldovan officials responded that the constitution prohibited the stationing of foreign troops on its territory. The Transnistrian war and subsequent peacekeeping duties provided a valuable opportunity for Russia to maintain a troop presence, even though foreign forces on any part of Moldova's territory violated the constitution, which declared the country's neutrality after the demise of the USSR.

Peacekeeping was employed as a weapon to intensify Moscow's political influence. Russia's Fourteenth Army assisted the Transnistrian separatists through supplies of weapons, resources, and training.[78] By early 1992, Russian troops began to take a more direct role in the fighting on the side of the secessionists. There were long-standing ties between the Russian military and Transnistria's post-Soviet leadership. Because some officials in Moscow feared that the Fourteenth Army could become an independent political actor, the local commander was replaced by General Lebed, a Yeltsin supporter with broad backing in Russia. Lebed was successful in disarming wayward paramilitary and Cossack units and bringing the military under stricter central control. Under Lebed's command and with the authorization of the Ministry of Defense, the Fourteenth Army adopted an openly pro-Transnistrian position and claimed it would back the secessionists with force if necessary. Yeltsin did not interfere with military decisions and implicitly supported the rebellion. The defense establishment set the pattern for Russian foreign policy in subsequent peacekeeping deployments in CIS countries even though the Kremlin had no CIS mandate for such missions. Despite denials and smokescreens from Moscow:

> Presidential advisor Sergey Stankevich and others have echoed the belief that the Russian government supported the Fourteenth Army's involvement. Several Western analysts have cited the fact that the intervention by Russia is one facet of the pattern of Russian involvement in the domestic affairs of the other former Soviet states and therefore not an anomalous act. Two years after the incident, the Russian paper, *Rossiyskie Vesti,* concluded: "Only now, summing up all the facts, we have come to understand: every step of (Lebed in Moldova) was authorized by the hierarchy of Russia's Ministry of Defense."[79]

The Moldovan case helped Moscow to reestablish its dominant position in the former Soviet Union with the "tacit acquiescence of the Western powers, including the United States."[80] The failure of Western capitals to challenge Russian intervention in Moldova in 1992 convinced Muscovite leaders that they could act assertively in the "post-Soviet space" without negative repercussions from the West. Washington feared that any sanctions against the Yeltsin administration would benefit revisionist and nationalist forces in

Moscow. This enabled Yeltsin to pursue a more aggressive policy without fear of opprobrium. Western inaction also convinced the Moldovan leadership that they would not receive political support and encouraged them to join the CIS largely on Moscow's terms.

In October 2002, Russian Duma speaker Genadiy Seleznev declared in Chisinau that Russia had directly supported the Transnistria separatists in the early 1990s when Russia supposedly feared that Moldova was on the verge of merging with Romania.[81] Moldovan Popular Party Christian Democratic (PPCD) chairman Iurie Rosca asserted that Seleznev disclosed the duplicity of Russian diplomacy, which had insisted that it had no influence on the Tiraspol regime. Seleznev also claimed that Moldova's aspirations to merge with Romania had weakened and that Moscow had urged the Transnistrian leader Igor Smirnov to help Moldovan president Voronin win the parliamentary elections.

Moscow's policies reinforced the pro-Russian separatist regime in Transnistria, which was used as a political counterweight to the Moldovan government. In the light of potential Romanian membership in NATO, Russia's military deployment in Moldova was also depicted as an understandable "countermeasure."[82] Moreover, Russia proved reluctant to accept the authority of the UN in its peacekeeping missions in areas viewed as part of Moscow's "vital strategic interests." Chisinau complained in vain that Russian forces were not neutral in the conflict and were not suitable peacekeepers because they openly supported the Transnistrians. Moscow persistently delayed implementing agreements on evacuating its troops from Transnistria.[83] It wanted an open-ended deployment and Moldovan compliance. Russian forces, numbering approximately 2,500 troops by early 2003, remained in Transnistria despite an agreement on troop withdrawal arranged in 1994 that all forces and equipment would be evacuated by the close of 2001. Under a 1999 OSCE agreement signed in Istanbul, Moscow pledged to liquidate its heavy weaponry by December 2001 and to withdraw its troops by December 2002.

Putin backtracked on Yeltsin's pledge and was willing to use his veto power in the OSCE to prevent any reaction to the violation of the Istanbul accord. An OSCE document signed in December 2002 merely acknowledged a Russian "intention" to withdraw its forces from Moldova within a year, "provided the necessary conditions are in place," thus leaving substantial room for interpretation.[84] The Kremlin connected the issue of troop withdrawal with the final status of Transnistria in which Moldova would be turned into a loose federation under Russian tutelage. The OSCE's December summit in Portugal set 31 December 2003 as the new deadline for removing Russian troops and armaments from Transnistria.[85] Moscow claimed in the summer of 2003 that the Transnistrian authorities were blocking the troop evacuation and that the December 2003 deadline was endangered. The notion that Russian forces were held hostage by Tiraspol seemed hardly credible; placing blame on the separatists clearly suited the Russian authorities.

According to a Defense Ministry statement in January 2003, Russia intended to keep its military contingent in Moldova even after the full evacuation of its arsenal. While Russian troops would no longer be needed to guard the evacuated munitions depots, they would "perform new tasks and functions" in the region, especially "the safeguarding of peace and stability." General Valeriy Yevnevich, head of the Russian operations group in Transnistria and deputy commander in chief of Russia's ground forces, confirmed that Russia did not intend to withdraw its troops from the separatist region by the end of 2003.[86] In January 2003, General Anatoliy Kvashnin, chief of Russia's General Staff, suspended his previous order to disband the Operative Group of Russian Forces in Moldova.

Russia promoted the "pentagonal" format (Russian, Ukraine, OSCE, Moldova, and Transnistria) to keep Western powers at a distance in any decisions on Transnistria's political future and the role of foreign peacekeepers. Putin's plenipotentiary representative for negotiations on Moldova, Vyacheslav Trubnikov, a career FSB general and first deputy foreign affairs minister, was adamant that any final settlement must include agreement by the Transnistrian administration. This provides a camouflage for obstruction and delay as officials in Tiraspol seek a Russian military presence to help perpetuate their quasi-criminal enterprises.

Russian generals have urged the Kremlin to repudiate the OSCE agreement and maintain a permanent military base in Moldova as a staging point for Russia's military projection toward the Balkans.[87] Moscow also asked Chisinau to join the CIS treaty on the "joint protection of external borders." This would involve the deployment of additional Russian troops and their basing in western Moldova, outside the Transnistria region. Russian military commanders have a geostrategic objective in "keeping Moldova within Russia's sphere of influence as a strategic crossroads between the Black Sea and the Balkans."[88] Additionally, Transnistrian separatism allows the military to maintain a substantial infrastructure of military bases, arms and ammunitions stores, and communications facilities near the outer borders of the CIS.

Moldova is a landlocked country with no indigenous fossil fuels. It imports all of its oil and gas from Russia via pipelines that run through Transnistria. Moldova is almost completely dependent on Russian energy and other raw materials, and its foreign trade is geared toward Russia. During the 1990s, Gazprom gained control over Moldova's gas pipelines while some of Chisinau's gas debts were transformed into Russian assets. Russian firms have garnered much of Moldova's energy infrastructure, including the hydroelectric power plant in Dubăsari, which supplies the bulk of Moldova's electricity output. In March 2003, Gazprom announced it was prepared to reduce the price of gas to Moldova in return for allowing Russian business to buy up assets. Moldova's debt for gas deliveries until July 2003 stood at

$121.1 million and Gazprom wanted to swap the debt for ownership of several Moldovan companies, including electricity distributors, wine and brandy producers, cigarette and glass factories, and former components of the Soviet military-industrial complex.[89] Alternatively, Gazprom was willing to accept an additional 35 percent stake in Moldovagaz in exchange for writing off the debt.

The Transnistrian region is also fully dependent on Russian energy supplies and is indebted to Russian gas and oil companies to the tune of $483.7 million. In effect, Russian subsidies keep the separatist region solvent. Moscow views Moldova as one of the major transit countries for energy exports to the Balkans. Russian energy is either resold as a source of income or used to maintain the region's large military-industrial complex. Among the pretexts issued by Moscow for not abiding by its international agreements to withdraw troops from the enclave was that during 2003 Tiraspol blocked the departure of trains loaded with Russian weaponry and ammunition because it had not obtained a write-off from Moscow for Transnistria's gas debt.

Following the election victory of the Communist Party in 2001, Moscow made plans for further inroads into the Moldovan economy and a dominant position in its mass media. During Prime Minister Mikhail Kasyanov's visit to Chisinau in October 2001 he was given a list of sixty Moldovan enterprises that were slated for sale and seeking Russian investments. Moldova was the number one destination per capita for Russian direct investment, followed by Belarus and Ukraine. Russian companies with close ties to the Kremlin have bought up Moldovan industries on favorable terms or acquired properties to offset Chisinau's unpaid debts.

Moldovan opposition leaders charged that Moscow was pursuing expansionist policies by taking over some of the most profitable businesses while investing little in the local economy. The acquisition of a controlling stake by Gazprom in Moldova's gas supply company Moldovgaz, in payment for Chisinau's gas debt was cited as the most glaring example.[90] Gazprom did not invest in the development of the gas supply network but simply pocketed the earnings. By 2002, Russian companies invested little more than $10 million in the Moldovan economy although they were buying up the most lucrative strategic industries. The Russian company MGTS was the only bidder in the privatization of Moldova's fixed-line telephone monopoly Moldtelecom, leading to complaints that Russia aimed to control the country's telecommunication system.

In Transnistria, many of the largest businesses have majority Russian ownership. Russia's Itera gas company has major shares in the Rybnitsa steelworks, which generates about two thirds of Transnistria's tax revenues. The enclave also produces arms and ammunition for Russian companies and many Transnistrian officials and businessmen carry Russian passports.

Moscow exploited the fact that much of the Transnistrian population possessed a distinct regional if not a single ethnic identity that had been promoted by Moscow throughout the twentieth century. The Russian authorities, similarly to their Soviet predecessors, endeavored to exploit the "dual identity of the titular group (Moldovan versus Romanian) to foster tension and confrontation" with Romania and to prevent Chisinau from forging closer political and security ties with Bucharest.[91] The independent Moldovan authorities were initially labeled "adventurist" pro-Romanians by Russian spokesmen for seeking the termination of the Transnistria republic. Although the Transnistrian population was predominantly Moldovan, the overwhelming majority of the leadership were Russian or citizens of Russia who held positions in Moscow's military and intelligence services. Various Russian political groups, officials, and parliamentarians gave financial and political backing to the rebels against Moldovan independence. Pro-Soviet Transnistria, led by the pro-Soviet Union of Workers' Collectives (Obedinennyi Sovet Trudovykh Kollektivov), broke away from Moldova in 1990 over alleged fears that Moldova would seek reunification with Romania.[92] A quasi-independent state was established styled as the Transnistrian Moldovan Republic (Pridniestrovskaya Moldovskaya Respublika [PMR]). In September 1990, troops from the Soviet Interior Ministry protected the congress in Transnistria that declared the region's independence.

The separatists formed well-equipped paramilitary units and were supported by Russian military commanders. Volunteer units, including Cossack bands, were also recruited in Russia and Russia's Fourteenth Army supplied the local militia with weapons. This force, styled as the republican guard, eventually reached 12,000 fighters and took control over the region's infrastructure, administration, security forces, and economic enterprises. The Yeltsin government provided economic support to the Transnistrian leadership through a major credit of 1 billion rubles in 1992.[93] Armed conflicts followed and approximately six hundred people died in seven months of fighting between separatists and Moldovan security forces. Fighting subsided in July 1992 with a Moscow-mediated settlement enforced by Russian troops already stationed in the region.

Hard-line politicians in Russia exploited other ethnic tensions in Moldova in order to unsettle the government. Activists among the Gagauz (Christian Turkic) minority in southern Moldova also began to agitate for autonomy and special status. Many Gagauz leaders were members of the Communist Party hierarchy and supported the continuation of a Moscow-centered system. The majority of Gagauz voted to stay in the USSR in the March 1991 referendum on the future of the Union and their leaders supported the hardline coup attempt in August 1991. Chisinau accused them of separatism backed by Transnistria and Moscow and lay siege to Gagauz territory. Tensions were defused in 1993 when the new government in Chisinau sought accommodation by granting the Gagauz region a "special status" through political, cultural, and linguistic autonomy. It recognized a national Gagauz territory with its own legislative and executive organs and the Gagauz abandoned claims for separate statehood.

Numerous moves have been made to enhance Russian influences in Moldova. The 2001 treaty gave the Russian language a prominent status in a country where some 65 percent of the population of 4.4 million spoke Moldovan, a language virtually identical to Romanian. Moldova pledged in the treaty to provide "necessary conditions in accordance with Moldovan law" for those who want to study in Russian. In February 2003, Voronin asserted that the Russian language would be granted official status by the end of the year. Opposition leaders claimed that any attempt to provide such status would be provocative and generate political destabilization.[94] Moscow also supported Moldova's return to Soviet-era education policies when the Russian language was again made compulsory in Moldovan schools.[95] In reaction, pro-Romanian activists formed a Committee for the De-Russification of Moldovan Education and collected a petition with 100,000 signatures against compulsory Russian language classes.

Pro-Romanian and independence activists grew especially anxious over creeping Russification in Moldova after the 2001 elections. Protests were staged in the capital between January and April 2002 against what was viewed as the elimination of Romanian national identity. Demonstrators objected to the introduction of compulsory Russian language classes and the inauguration of new history textbooks that questioned Moldova's Romanian heritage. In February 2002, with public protests escalating, the government declared a moratorium on the decision to replace the teaching of the "History of Romanians" with the "History of Moldovans." The crisis threatened to challenge the legitimacy of the government and soured relations between Russia and Romania, who mutually accused each other of interference in Moldova's internal affairs.

The federalization proposal for Moldova backed by the OSCE and the Western countries was supported by Russia, as it would provide Moscow with additional political leverage vis-à-vis Chisinau.[96] Moldovan opposition activists and independent analysts believed that the proposal was designed to push the country firmly into the Russian orbit and was implicitly condoned by Washington.[97] It would serve to legalize the regime in Tiraspol by providing it with an important voice in the central government while making Moscow a guarantor of the arrangement, thus ensuring that Moldova becomes a Russian protectorate.

The main source of instability in Moldova was the Transnistrian issue and to a lesser extent the Gagauz Turkish minority in southern Moldova. Moscow contributed to inflaming social discontent in the early 1990s by manipulating ethnic issues through the mass media and by encouraging local calls for autonomy if not outright territorial secession. The Kremlin held these cards in reserve as it enticed and cajoled Chisinau into a closer political relationship. Russia's support for the Transnistria rebellion promoted populism and isolationism in the enclave. Russian political parties backing unification with Russia surfaced in Transnistria, including the Unity party, which was financed and equipped by the parent movement in Moscow. Unity encouraged local residents to apply for Russian citizenship and sought to undermine the Smirnov leadership, which was considered unreliable and self-serving. While Transnistria is in effect self-isolated from Europe, it forms an important hub for Russian security forces, intelligence networks, and criminal organizations.

In the early 1990s, the Russian authorities used propaganda techniques, disinformation campaigns, and active support for the rebellion in Moldova to discredit the Chisinau government. The campaign subsided as Moldova linked itself more closely with the CIS. During Voronin's tenure, Russian authorities have been less critical of Chisinau as the government became more compliant and accommodating to Russian interests. After the Communist victory in the February 2001 parliamentary elections, Moscow concluded that Moldova would veer more closely toward it. The Party of Moldovan Communists (PCM) won two-thirds of the 101 parliamentary seats and set a new course for the country's foreign policy. All talk of the country uniting with Romania or cooperating with Bucharest under the slogan "One Nation, Two Countries" was dropped. The victors declared that Russia was Moldova's "strategic partner" despite its formal neutrality. The Communist triumph was a public protest against rising poverty and the widespread belief that a closer link with Russia would halt the sharp decline in living standards. Soviet-era nostalgia for a predictable economic life played an important role among the Moldovan electorate.[98]

The election results cooled relations between Moscow and Transnistria as the Kremlin calculated that Moldova as a whole would move closer to Russia. Nevertheless, the separatist card was not totally discarded, as it could prove useful in future confrontations with Chisinau. In October 2002, Moscow began diplomatic procedures for opening a consulate in Transnistria. Russian ambassador to Chisinau Pavel Petrovskiy negotiated with Voronin after the Duma adopted a decision about the consulate.[99] Before the Communist victory, the Moldovan authorities and the opposition parties alike objected to foreign consulates in Tiraspol, as this would signify official recognition of the breakaway region.

Communist electoral pledges included closer integration with the CIS and the restoration of economic ties with Russia, which provided a mirage of prosperity. Officials claimed that a majority of Moldovans wanted to speak Russian and join the Russia-Belarus Union. Shortly after the February 2001 elections, Voronin claimed that there was no hurry to enter the Union and that a referendum might be called on the issue. In early 2003, the Moldovan authorities stated that they had not abandoned this goal.[100] According to parliamentary leaders, as soon as the Russia-Belarus Union Parliamentary Assembly agreed on a constitution for the Union, Moldova would begin "to take steps in this direction." In the meantime, Transnistrian officials made a failed attempt to appoint an ambassador to the Russia-Belarus Union. The move was disapproved by Moscow because it would alienate the Moldovan authorities at a time when the Kremlin was bringing the country under its wing.

In December 2002, a plan for Moldova's federalization under the "Kiev Document" was drafted by Moscow and accepted by international players. The state would have two loosely tied federal units, thus legitimizing the Transnistrian administration. Moreover, Tiraspol would have the right to veto the Moldovan government's foreign and security policies, thus giving Moscow indirect control over decisionmaking in Chisinau. The country's constitutional arrangements and institutions would be supervised by Russia, Ukraine, and the OSCE. In effect, Moldova would move closer to the status of a Russian satellite.[101] The Voronin government partially accepted the federalization proposal, but also reached out to Western governments for greater involvement in defending Moldovan interests. The opposition Christian Democrats claimed that Voronin's proposal to develop a new constitution in cooperation with the Tiraspol authorities was a dangerous step toward confederation and a Russian protectorate because it would grant Russian troops a permanent status on Moldovan territory.[102]

Moldova's opposition staunchly opposed federalization and claimed that this would terminate the country's neutrality as Russia would maintain its military presence. The separatist region would enjoy large-scale economic autonomy and make only symbolic contributions to the federal budget. In a two-entity federation, Tiraspol would gain half the seats in the upper chamber of the legislature and opportunities to block Moldovan legislation when it suited Moscow. Military and security structures would be unified, but Tiraspol would maintain a separate militia. Moreover, Tiraspol would have the right of veto over federal legislation. Such an arrangement would give Moscow a permanent lever of influence over Moldova as the plan would be guaranteed by Russia, Ukraine, and the OSCE. In November 2003, a new variant of federalization was drafted at Putin's insistence by Dmitriy Kozak, deputy head of the presidential administration.[103] The plan was supported by Transnistrian leaders with the intent of turning Moldova into a demilitarized confederation in which Russia could intervene in the event of new conflicts.

Defense Minister Ivanov declared that Russian troops would remain in Moldova as guarantors of any federal arrangement for a "transitional period" of up to twenty years. Protests in Moldova escalated and the opposition established a broad Committee to Defend Moldova's Independence and Constitution. Voronin rejected the Kozak plan and negotiations over federalism were restarted with the United States supporting a multinational peacekeeping force to replace the Russian contingent in Transnistria, a proposal that the Kremlin opposed.[104] The Moldovan government expected that such a force could function under an OSCE mandate and meet the standards of UN peacekeeping forces. Meanwhile, Moscow planned for its peacekeepers to be transformed into a more permanent forward military base that could operate throughout Moldova. In June 2003, Russia's Trubnikov asserted that Russia intended to "play the dominant role in the operation of military guarantees in Transdniester."[105]

Criminal networks in Transnistria have become notorious throughout the region and they negatively affect Moldova's chances for EU integration. Leaders in Tiraspol gain massive profits from contraband and other forms of illegal trafficking. Organized crime generates an income of some $3 to $4 billion annually. Many of the criminal organizations are closely tied to Russian intelligence services and Russian mafia groups who use Transnistria as a transit point for regional enterprises in human trafficking, arms smuggling, and other illicit activities. Transnistria is widely known as a "black hole" on Europe's doorstep, and both the EU and the United States have imposed travel bans on Transnistrian officials.

The son of the Transnistrian leader, Vladimir Smirnov, runs the Sheriff company, which controls virtually the entire economy in the statelet and is closely linked with the Russian and Ukrainian mafias.[106] The only genuine industry in Transnistria consists of arms factories that manufacture components for small arms and electronics systems assembled in Russia and Ukraine. In recent years, Transnistria has developed closed production cycles for small arms and mortar and missile launchers.[107] One of the major money earners in both Moldova and Transnistria is the smuggling of tobacco, alcohol, and oil from Russia, with official complicity. Transnistria also houses the Klobasna ammunition depot for the former Soviet Fourteenth Army. Despite the destruction of tons of ammunition due to international prodding, the Russian army profits from the stores by clandestinely selling arms to several "rogue states" and members of Russian and Ukrainian organized crime groups. The Russian authorities, whether by design or default, have played a key role in the survival of Transnistria as a smugglers' paradise.[108] Illicitly exported weapons have reportedly become the mainstays of the Transnistrian economy.[109]

Tiraspol has also become a shelter for some notorious figures implicated in violence and civilian murders on the eve of the Soviet Union's meltdown. Vadim Antyufeyev and other former officers of the Soviet special police force OMON (Otryad Militsii Osobogo Naznacheniya) assumed high positions in the Transnistrian security forces. Antyufeyev and his comrades were sought by Interpol for crimes committed in Riga, Latvia, in 1990–1991 where they attempted to thwart the movement for independence.[110] Such characters certainly do not welcome any final settlement of the dispute with Chisinau as this could lead to their arrest, extradition, trial, and imprisonment.

Moldova's and Transnistria's intelligence services are comprehensively penetrated by Russian operatives and informers. To further develop their interconnectedness, in June 2003 a prolonged incognito visit was paid to

Moldova by Sergey Lebedev, director of Russia's Foreign Intelligence Service.[111] The official purpose of the visit was to discuss security issues with Moldovan officials, including President Voronin, the interior minister, and the director of the country's Security and Intelligence Service. Russia has established a major espionage and logistic base in Moldova that includes a telephone-bugging center called FAPSI on the grounds of the Russian embassy. Moldovan ministries and commercial structures are penetrated by Russian spies and Moldova's secret services dispatch their agents to Russia for training.[112] Opposition leaders also charge that Moldova's SIS has been instructed by the FSB to reopen a department to combat pro-Romanian activities in the country.[113]

5

Blocking Western Encroachment: The Baltic States

SMALL IS NOT BEAUTIFUL: RUSSIA'S BALTIC CONUNDRUM

Russia's leaders did not believe that they could realistically integrate the three Baltic countries into the CIS or any other superstate structure. Instead, they sought to place Estonia, Latvia, and Lithuania in an undefined "neutral zone" between NATO and the CIS and between Central Europe and Russia. In this way, Western influences would be minimized and Russian security and national interests safeguarded. Russian officials warned throughout the 1990s that NATO admission for the Baltics would terminate Moscow's relations with the North Atlantic Alliance and usher in a new era of conflict. The future of the Baltic states was symbolically important for Russia, as it could be emblematic for the future of all former Soviet republics.

In the Kremlin's view, former Soviet borders, including the outside borders of the Baltic republics, retain a measure of validity as the major parameters of exclusively Russian influence and a barrier against Western penetration. Russian officials persistently claim that the Baltic states entered the USSR voluntarily and legally at the close of World War II and failed to acknowledge that Estonia, Latvia, and Lithuania were under Soviet occupation for fifty years. This position outraged the Baltic governments and reinforced their assertions that Moscow possessed a grand design to reabsorb their territories, especially as officials periodically claimed that Baltic borders were adjustable.

Soon after regaining independence, the Baltic republics dismissed any prospect of joining the CIS because membership was seen as incompatible with NATO and EU integration. The Commonwealth was viewed as another attempt to promote centralized Muscovite control over neighboring states. After an initial period of cordiality with the Russian government during the Soviet demise, the Kremlin position hardened. The Soviet and later Russian troop withdrawal was made an issue in bilateral negotiations. The Kremlin expected additional conditions to be fulfilled by the Baltic side, especially in the area of minority rights, to allow for a phased evacuation of approximately 130,000 troops. Soviet forces on these territories were under the command of the North West Group, whose objective was to defend the USSR from an alleged NATO threat while ensuring the loyalty of the three Baltic states.

Due largely to Western pressures and incentives, the Russian troop withdrawal was completed by 1994 despite Moscow's persistent charges about Baltic mistreatment of the Russian minorities.[1] On several occasions, Russia declared that the troop evacuation would be delayed or suspended on the pretext that Baltic minority policies were failing to meet international standard. It also claimed that the troop evacuation caused major logistical challenges. In reality, Moscow sought to benefit from its pressure politics by gaining financial and other benefits from the West.[2] The Baltic governments appealed to the UN General Assembly to help persuade Russia to fully remove its troops from their territories.[3]

Moscow broadened the category of the Russian minority by including Russian-speakers (*russkoyazychnye*) of different Slavic ethnicities in order to raise the number of alleged victims of Baltic discrimination. Including non-Russian populations among the victims of mistreatment made the issue more universal, less ethnic-based, and potentially more damaging to the Baltic governments who were depicted as rabid nationalists and xenophobes.[4] The Russian-dominated "Inter" groupings in all three Baltic states were presented by Russian officials as multiethnic and international to distinguish them from the alleged ethnonationalists within movements demanding independence from Moscow. Russian post–World War II migrants were locally perceived as "imperial colonizers" and tools of Moscow intent on eradicating indigenous cultures. This was reinforced by the fact that most Russians displayed little inclination to assimilate or learn local languages but expected the Balts to become Russified Soviets. The new governments made a distinction between economic migrants, who settled in the three countries in order to improve their material conditions, and "occupiers" or "colonials," consisting of military and police personnel and party functionaries whose aim was to eliminate the independence of the Baltic republics.

Claims by officials that the Baltic governments actively discriminated against Russians, despite the conclusions of international human rights organizations, contributed to heightening international tensions. Moreover,

Russia's long, drawn out process of signing and ratifying border treaties contributed to maintaining the sense of threat. The purpose was to disqualify these countries from NATO and EU membership because they had outstanding disputes with Moscow. In reality, Baltic Russians benefit from higher living standards and better conditions than their brethren in Russia and many who left after the Soviet collapse sought to return to the Baltic region. The number of stateless Russians steadily declined during the 1990s, either as a result of emigration or citizenship: the figure dipped to under half a million by early 2003, from a total Russian ethnic or Russian-speaking population of some 1.5 million.

Moscow vehemently opposed the entry of the Baltic states into NATO and warned that such a move would bring hard-liners to power in Russia who would precipitate a conflict with the Alliance.[5] The Kremlin charged that Baltic admission would create a serious barrier with Russia and demanded a decisive voice in the security policies of the Baltic republics. Russian authorities wanted the demilitarization of the Baltic littoral and offered unilateral guarantees for Baltic security that were promptly rejected as unrealistic by all three governments. Prime Minister Evgeniy Primakov and other officials warned about a "red line" between NATO and any former Soviet republic that Russia would not allow the Alliance to cross.

Unable to influence internal political developments, the Kremlin instead sought to isolate the three states internationally. It promoted tensions with and within the three Baltic countries to block their NATO accession, especially as good relations with neighbors was an important prerequisite for Alliance membership. It manipulated the minority question in order to depict the three governments as failing to meet European standards for minority protection and human rights.[6] The Kremlin claimed the right to represent and defend the interests of "Russian-speakers," whose primary language was the result of decades of Russification. Foreign Minister Kozyrev asserted that the position of minorities was a vital strategic issue for Russian diplomacy.[7] Statements were issued about a massive exodus of Russians provoked by discrimination and a policy of apartheid. The minority issue became less acute in the latter part of the 1990s, as all three Baltic governments adopted policies of greater inclusion and met Western standards. But Moscow continued to manipulate the ethnic issue at convenient venues, including UN Human Rights Commission sessions. This heightened concerns that a future nationalist regime could employ military means to support secessionist movements and establish new Russian enclaves in the pursuit of a Greater Russia.

During the first two years of Putin's tenure, stress was placed on preventing NATO entry for the Baltic countries. Their inclusion was condemned as an attempt to isolate Russia from Europe through the construction of a cordon sanitaire. Officials asserted that membership for any Baltic country would permanently sour relations with Moscow and provoke countermeasures. It would change the "balance of forces" in the region and derail relations between Russia and NATO. Putin intensified ethnic tensions in 2001.[8] He urged Russian-speakers in all three countries to demand the status of a second official language and for numerical quotas in government bodies according to Russian proportions of the population. He cited the Macedonian peace agreement of August 2001 in claiming that Russians should gain the same status in Estonia, Latvia, and Lithuania as the Albanian community in Macedonia. Delegates at a "Russian compatriots" congress in Moscow in October 2001 also supported the idea proposed by the Russian government to establish a permanent organization of Russians residing abroad, including those in the Baltic republics. In raising the minority issue, Putin may have been motivated by the fact that the OSCE was closing its monitoring missions in Estonia and Latvia, on the grounds that human and minority rights were sufficiently respected. The Kremlin was acutely concerned about Russian assimilation into Baltic societies and improvements in their conditions as this could remove a potentially useful element for political exploitation.

Moscow also raised territorial issues with Estonia and Latvia to maintain pressure on their governments. Final frontier delineations remained unratified in a shrewd calculation that unsettled borders would make a country ineligible for NATO. About $50 million was spent in the late 1990s by the Russian authorities in anti-NATO disinformation campaigns, mostly directed against the Baltic states. However, Russian state propaganda proved counterproductive as it stirred animosity against Moscow and stiffened Baltic determination to enter NATO. All three countries remained anxious about Russia's long-term intentions and petitioned for full membership in all major Western institutions.[9]

Russia's authorities threatened the Baltic countries, advocated economic warfare, and claimed that the Baltics were positioning themselves as a launching pad for NATO aggression against Russia.[10] Some politicians called for military measures to coerce the three republics into submission, while Foreign Minister Primakov demanded a revision of certain post-Soviet borders. When outright threat did not have the desired effect, the Kremlin resorted to offering enticements. At the Vilnius summit for East European leaders in September 1997, Prime Minister Chernomyrdin proposed various confidence-building measures styled as the "Baltic Initiative." This included proposals for unilateral Russian security guarantees if Estonia, Latvia, and Lithuania remained outside NATO and bilateral guarantees from Russia and NATO. Moscow also proposed the demilitarization of Kaliningrad to assuage Baltic fears of a military threat and offered joint control of Baltic airspace and joint military exercises. The Baltic governments dismissed these proposals as tactical maneuvers to regain a Russian sphere of influence through "protectorate arrangements" designed to limit Baltic sovereignty.[11]

By the end of 2001, the Kremlin calculated that open opposition to NATO enlargement would be ineffective and damaging to Russia's prestige.

Alliance consensus on a second wave of expansion would once again demonstrate Russia's waning regional and global influence. Unable to dissuade NATO leaders from crossing the "red line," Moscow continued to disqualify the Baltic states as worthy Alliance contenders. It manufactured domestic and external problems so that NATO leaders would consider Baltic accession as too risky because it would import fresh problems into the organization. In this strategy of foreign policy blackmail, Moscow could derail relations with any country and then claim a deterioration in bilateral relations.

Although the Kremlin accepted the inevitability of Baltic NATO membership by the time of the Prague summit in November 2002, it continued to threaten unspecified actions if Russian interests were violated. In December 2002, presidential aide Sergey Yastrzhembskiy asserted that once Latvia, Lithuania, and Estonia join NATO, their attitude toward their Russian-speaking populations would deteriorate. He warned that Moscow will "keep an eye" on developments because "the Russian public is very sensitive to the policies pursued regarding our compatriots in the Baltic states."[12] In the propaganda arena, Moscow sought to depict the Baltic governments as fascistic and xenophobic, whose leaders were either tied to former Nazi collaborators or provided them with protection.

Russian authorities were also outraged by demands for compensation payments to the victims of Stalinist occupation and mass deportation from the Baltic states. The Lithuanian parliament adopted a law on compensation for material damages sustained by the country as a result of Soviet annexation. The Estonian and Latvian governments expressed political support for the Lithuanian initiative. Such moves provoked Moscow to claim that Baltic incorporation into the USSR was a voluntary act. Officials even asserted that Vilnius, Tallinn, and Riga should be grateful for the Soviet contribution to their economic development and the Duma approved a resolution in December 2002 claiming that the Baltic states owed Russia billions of dollars for the military installations left behind by the retreating Red Army.

Moscow disrupted the Baltic economies in order to gain political advantages. Each government tried to steer the economy westward and to limit their dependence on Russia and their susceptibility to blackmail. In particular, Moscow endeavored to control energy transit routes, as this was both financially and politically profitable. Oil supplies were used as leverage to purchase shares in local refining and transportation systems. Periodic threats to reduce or halt supplies were a means of extracting concessions to allow for Russian buyouts. Some Russian business interests were opposed to economic warfare, arguing that this could rebound negatively on Russian exports. Attempts have also been engineered to discredit the Baltic intelligence and security services, whether to increase interstate animosities or to disqualify them from NATO.

Moscow also tried to foster divisions between Baltic leaders claiming that Estonian and Latvian businessmen were skeptical about NATO accession and would prefer to expand trade and political ties with Russia. Nonetheless, Russian trade with the Baltics has not grown significantly, although the ice-free Baltic ports served as major transit points for Russian exports. A policy of deliberate differentiation was practiced by Moscow.[13] While Lithuania appeared to be favored in the late 1990s, Latvia was depicted as a major anti-Russian offender and intensive pressures were applied. Primakov introduced these wedge tactics to disrupt Balkan solidarity. The pressure on Estonia was more consistent and predictable, while it has intensified on different occasions toward Latvia. The undermining of inter-Baltic cooperation was designed to disrupt a united foreign policy and weaken arguments that the Balts generated regional stability.

Moscow falsely believed that it had to be rewarded for its support of the post–11 September 2001 antiterrorist coalition through a halt in further NATO expansion. When Putin realized that NATO's growth would continue, he calculated that acquiescence on Baltic membership, coupled with a more pronounced voice for Moscow in NATO's deliberations, would weaken the Alliance and undercut the relevance of enlargement. Baltic officials argued that it was important to include all three countries in NATO simultaneously. This would prevent future conflicts with Moscow over subsequent membership, lessen the opportunities for stoking rivalries, and provide a secure framework for economic development. Delays in Baltic accession would enable Russia to increase its international leverage by gaining firmer control over strategic sectors of the local economies.

Russia experienced several disappointments in its Baltic policy. It failed to draw the three independent states into a Russian security orbit and it proved unable to prevent them moving westward politically and establishing close relations with the United States. Moscow was left with a policy of limiting the Baltic states from exerting a magnetic influence on Russia's neighboring regions, especially the exclave of Kaliningrad. It feared that close cross-border relations could weaken Russian control and alienate the oblast economically and politically from the center: "The Russian leadership was more interested in maintaining or expanding its diluted influence in the Baltic states than in participating in regional cooperation."[14] The Russian authorities and interlinked business interests were also seeking to benefit economically from investment opportunities and to exert political influence through major economic levers, especially in control over strategic infrastructure. Such inroads and influences could also benefit the Kremlin as the three Baltic countries entered the European Union.

ESTONIA

Yeltsin initially encouraged the independence of all three Baltic states as a useful weapon against the Soviet authorities. After Russia proclaimed its sovereignty in June 1990, Yeltsin advocated Estonian independence and maintained cordial relations with the proindependence movement. He also opposed the bloody actions of Soviet Ministry of Interior troops (OMON) in Latvia and Lithuania and traveled to Tallinn in early 1991 to back the embattled Baltic leaders. At that time, he also opposed separatist moves among Russian radicals in Estonia who claimed the Narva region in the northeast of the country as part of Russia.

Neither the outgoing Soviet government nor the incoming Russian administration accepted responsibility for the forcible annexation of Estonia in 1940. This generated resentment and suspicion in Tallinn that Russia's imperialist policies had not been fully discarded. In August 1991, Russia recognized Estonian independence shortly after it was declared. But the honeymoon was short-lived, as Yeltsin increasingly turned to nationalist themes in order to rebuild Russian influence. One of the most readily available mechanisms was to manipulate the status of the large Russian-speaking minority. In its efforts to depict Estonia as a repressive state vis-à-vis its minorities, Moscow delayed signing a treaty and a border agreement. Estonian and Latvian insistence that the 1920 Treaties of Tartu and Riga be recognized led to charges that both countries harbored claims to Russian territory. In reality, Tallinn and Riga accepted as unchangeable the forcible Russian annexation of several thousand square kilometers of land in eastern Estonia and eastern Latvia at the close of World War II.

Alleged territorial aspirations by the Baltic governments were presented as evidence that Estonia and Latvia had failed to meet the criteria for NATO and EU accession. Even though both countries acceded to Russia's demands over frontier demarcations, Moscow still refused to formalize a border agreement. Tallinn dropped language referring to the 1920 Tartu Treaty, which marked the first Russian recognition of Estonian independence, but to no avail. Russia's parliament, with the tacit approval of the Kremlin, continued to delay the ratification of a border accord. The Kremlin even put forward demands that a bilateral commission be established allowing Moscow to monitor interethnic relations in Estonia. This proposition was rejected by Tallinn, which viewed it as a mechanism for interfering in its internal politics. Continuing Russian pressures and the unilateral demarcation of the common border in 1994 by Russian troops was received in Estonia as evidence of neoimperialism.

Even with Estonia's imminent entry into NATO and the EU, Moscow continued to exert pressure on Tallinn to meet its demands. In November 2002, Russian deputy prime minister Valentina Matvienko said her country expected EU support in pressuring Estonia to address seven points connected with minorities, languages, and Communist-era crimes.[15] Matvienko reiterated these demands in meetings with Prime Minister Siim Kallas and President Arnold Rüütel. They included granting citizenship to more ethnic Russians, improving the position of the Russian language, ending the prosecution of former KGB agents and officers accused of crimes against the Estonian people, abolishing restrictions enacted by the Estonian parliament in ratifying the convention on the protection of minorities, granting residence and work permits to former KGB officials, and allowing the Russian embassy to expand its staff.

In February 2002, Estonia's Foreign Ministry decided not to respond to seven demands submitted by Russian deputy foreign minister Evgeniy Gusarov as preconditions for improving bilateral relations.[16] The demands included accelerating the tempo of the naturalization process, so that 15,000 to 20,000 Russians would be granted Estonian citizenship each year; registering the Estonian Orthodox Church subject to the Moscow Patriarchate; creating favorable conditions for the Russian language in regions where a majority was Russian-speaking; allocating more funds for Russian-language higher education; providing social guarantees to former KGB officers and their families by changing the relevant provisions in Estonia's law on aliens; and halting any investigation into crimes against humanity committed by former Soviet army veterans. Such demands contributed to worsening relations between Moscow and Tallinn.

Russian state propaganda depicted the Estonians as racist and anti-Russian and routinely exploited ethnic incidents to denounce Estonia as a fascist state.[17] Following an incident in the former Soviet naval base of Paldiski in August 2001, in which young Estonian peacekeeping recruits assaulted several local Russians, the Foreign Ministry issued a strongly worded statement claiming that the episode was fanned by Tallinn's official policy toward its nonnative population. This media barrage had a significant impact on Russian public opinion and was designed to exert psychological pressure on Tallinn. In an opinion poll conducted by the Russian Center for Study of Public Opinion in May 2001, Estonia was viewed as the "biggest threat to Russia," even scoring ahead of the United States.[18]

In order to gain domestic support and international sympathy, Moscow accused Tallinn of practicing genocide against its Russian and Sovietized population. Yeltsin condemned Tallinn for engaging in "apartheid" and warned that the Russian minority had a right to self-defense and protection from Russia.[19] The Russian ambassador to the UN, Yuliy Vorontsov, charged in December 1993 that Estonia and Latvia were applying a policy of "velvet-gloved ethnic cleansing."[20] In the security arena, Tallinn has been accused of undermining Russian security by cutting off the country from the Baltic Sea, establishing an anti-Russian structure in Northern Europe, and acting as a Trojan Horse for American influences. The signing of the U.S.-Baltic Partnership Charter in January 1998 by all three Baltic capitals was stridently denounced in Moscow as a step toward NATO entry and as a method for isolating Russia.

In the first few years after the restoration of Estonian independence, the question of Russia's troop presence was of prime importance for Tallinn.

Although only a few thousand soldiers remained in Estonia by 1993, they contributed to maintaining tensions between the two states especially as Moscow was reluctant to formalize an agreement on their withdrawal. The Russian government and parliament sought to postpone the evacuation, often linking the troop issue with the treatment of the Russian minority.[21] An accord between Yeltsin and President Lennart Meri was finally concluded in July 1994 when Moscow agreed to remove its forces while Tallinn accepted the principle of "social guarantees" for thousands of retired Soviet military officers living in Estonia. Foreign Minister Kozyrev claimed that Russian troops should remain in the former republics to protect Russian coethnics and avoid a "security vacuum" that could be filled by "unfriendly forces."[22]

It was "convenient for the Kremlin every now and then to have the military frighten Riga and Tallinn."[23] In June 1992, Russian and Estonian soldiers exchanged shots when Estonian troops attempted to take control of a Russian naval building in Tallinn and Russian soldiers occasionally staged incidents on the borders to heighten Estonia's sense of insecurity. In the fall of 1998, Russian troops stationed close to the Estonian border undertook a war game in which they conquered a small country.[24] The exercise, codenamed "Operation Return," was viewed as a major provocation by Tallinn. The reported deployment in January 2001 of tactical nuclear missiles in Kaliningrad also alarmed the Baltic capitals. Despite these incidents and threats, Moscow was careful not to escalate tensions into a full-scale conflict as it could face political and economic reprisals from the West.

Tallinn was strongly opposed to Russian attempts to gain an international peacekeeping mandate throughout the former Soviet Union. Estonia's Foreign Minister Trivimi Velliste pointed out that the enhanced role sought by Moscow "departed from the general principles of peacekeeping."[25] Estonian military specialists also warned that a more expansionist regime in Moscow might be tempted to support secessionist Russian radicals in Estonia in order to inject Russian peacekeeping forces into the country.[26] Despite Russia's grudging acquiescence to the inclusion of the three Baltic states in NATO, the Foreign Ministry claimed that Russia continued to be concerned over the military consequences of eastward expansion.[27] At the NATO-Russia Council meeting in Madrid in June 2003, Russian spokesmen insisted on "clear and unambiguous guarantees that armed forces of other countries will not be deployed on the territory of the Baltic states." They did not rule out the possibility of Moscow taking appropriate military steps in response.

Russia exerted direct pressure on the Estonian government by initiating an energy squeeze between 1992 and 1994, including cutoffs in gas supplies, on the pretext of protesting against violations of minority rights. While Moscow attempted to alter Talinn's policies and to obtain favorable trade and investment concessions, Estonia endeavored to reduce its dependence on Russian energy by diversifying its sources. In order to discourage further Russian pressures, Tallinn allowed Gazprom to invest in its national gas company while selling an equal share to Germany's Ruhrgas.[28] The Estonian authorities argued that such a balancing act would give Russia a stake in the country's prosperity without creating a monopoly. By 2001, the biggest Russian investor in Estonia was Gazprom, which held one third of the stake in Estonia's gas company Eesti Gaas while the second Russian gas giant Itera acquired almost 10 percent.

Of all three Baltic countries, Estonia proved most successful in preventing Russian businesses from gaining control over strategic domestic industries. Estonia's high economic growth rate and its turn to Western markets also enabled Tallinn to resist Moscow's economic influences. At different times, Moscow threatened and imposed economic sanctions and blockades in protest against the treatment of the Russian minority, Tallinn's insistence on the withdrawal of all Russian troops, and its ambition to join NATO. This included periodic bans on food imports and the imposition of double customs duties on Estonian products. The effect of such economic pressures was to convince the Baltic governments that they needed to speed up their integration into Western economic structures and to limit their dependence on Russia. Estonia embarked on a process of economic diversification and closer contacts with the Western economies. By the late 1990s, the EU had become Estonia's major trading partner and this process would intensify with impending EU membership. This could further estrange Tallinn from Moscow, as Estonia will be required to introduce Union standards, thus limiting Russian labor migration and the import of inferior Russian products. Russian businessmen were also likely to see some shrinkage of their access to the Estonian market.

The Russian or Sovietized population in Estonia, numbering about 30 percent of a total of some 1.6 million in the early 1990s, became a major bone of contention between Tallinn and Moscow. The Estonian parliament reimposed the 1938 citizenship law, whereby all post-1940 settlers and their descendants were required to submit to a naturalization procedure mandating a two-year residency, basic proficiency in the Estonian language, and proof of a permanent source of income. This and several other laws geared toward the re-Estonianization of the country's institutions provoked outrage in Moscow, even though the human rights of all citizens were respected. Moscow's preoccupation with the minority issue generated suspicion that the Kremlin was engaging in cynical manipulation to destabilize the independent state.[29] As a result, Russian minorities in Estonia and Latvia came to be widely distrusted as potential fifth columns representing Moscow's imperial designs. Threats from the Kremlin and the Duma against Estonian sovereignty reinforced these suspicions.[30] The pro-Soviet Interfront movement and the Russian minority United Council of Labor Collectives were widely viewed as Moscow's proxies especially after Russian demonstrators attempted to storm the Estonian parliament in May 1990 and minority representatives openly opposed Estonian independence.[31] In fact, both minority movements were supported by conservative Communists in Moscow rather than by the emerging Russian government.

Russian minority organizations tended to employ antinationalist or internationalist slogans and Socialist phraseology that outraged the Estonian majority. It proved difficult to distinguish between pro-Soviet elements and the anti-Soviet Russian authorities in terms of the support offered to minority activists. When the USSR disintegrated, the Russian movements found themselves temporarily without a dependable sponsor in Moscow until Yeltsin understood the political value of exploiting the ethnic question. The Russian authorities also exaggerated the number of Russian ethnics in Estonia and Latvia to accentuate the extent of alleged official discrimination.[32]

In fomenting ethnic tensions, in June 1993 Russians in the city of Narva publicly protested against Estonian legislation on citizenship. In July 1993, Narva's city council held a referendum on autonomy, a move that was supported by 97 percent of the city's residents even though it was declared illegal by Tallinn. Attempts at autonomy were unsuccessful as much of the rural population around Narva was Estonian and the minority leadership did not possess a coherent organization or program. Estonian leaders argued that minority representatives were not so much fearful of human rights violations, but of losing the privileged positions they held under the previous system. Moscow's use of the minority issue as an instrument of pressure was weakened by three factors: the international response to Estonia's independence, the decline of the ethnic Russian population, and the proindependence or neutral stance of a substantial part of the Russian minority. The OSCE and the Council of Europe found no pattern of officially sponsored discrimination, thus Estonia's and Latvia's citizenship laws were declared consistent with European standards, to the chagrin of Russian officials. In December 2001, the OSCE missions in the two Baltic states were closed down despite Moscow's objections.[33]

With regard to Russian demographics, from a total of some 474,800 people in Estonia in 1989, the numbers declined to about 353,000 a decade later.[34] This was reflective of a more general Russian demographic collapse as well as the assimilation and out-migration from the former Soviet republics. Statistics also demonstrated that Russians were not evacuating the "oppressive" Baltic states any faster than they were the "fraternal" countries of Belarus or Armenia. Indeed, more Russians were likely to stay in Estonia because of greater economic opportunities and higher living standards than in Russia itself.

Members of the Russian minority have on occasion heated up social discontent. Political leaders and parliamentarians in Moscow maintain close connections with former comrades in Estonia and have supported protest actions to discredit the incumbent government. Demonstrations have been staged on various pretexts against Tallinn's policies, such as the trials of KGB veterans who participated in massacres and deportations of Estonian resistance fighters after World War II. Russian ultranationalist parties, such as National Unity, have also been active in Estonia seeking to provoke interethnic conflicts.[35] Estonia has produced no significant extremist groups that would be amenable to Russian state intrigues. Populists and isolationists, which could damage relations with Western powers and institutions, have been absent, while ultranationalist elements have been marginalized.

Moscow has also depicted Tallinn in a negative light by claiming that it still harbors territorial pretensions to former Estonian lands in the Narva and Petseri regions that were annexed by the Russian Federation after World War II. Although the issue was dropped soon after Estonia's independence, except among radical nationalists, it suited the Kremlin to claim outstanding border disputes as a means of disqualifying Estonia from international organizations. Russia's 1993 military doctrine even mentioned the possibility of territorial disputes and Russian minority attempts to secede from Estonia as creating a pretext for military intervention.

As in the other Baltic states, Moscow had little direct political influence over the Estonian governments, which sought to distance themselves from Moscow's tutelage. In March 1999, claims were made by Duma deputy Yuriy Kuznetsov that Russian companies helped finance the campaign of several ethnic Estonian parties in order to gain a foothold for lobbying.[36] All the accused parties categorically denied the allegations. Reform Party secretary-general Heiki Kranich charged that the allegations looked like a provocation to foster political conflicts in Estonia, especially as Kuznetsov was a member of Zhirinovsky's ultranationalist Liberal Democratic Party in Russia.

During the disintegration of the USSR, Estonian and other Baltic leaders stated that the Russian military was forging links with the mafia-controlled shadow economy. This was especially worrying as Tallinn exercised little control over the former Soviet military areas while the remaining troops felt demoralized, betrayed, and abandoned by Moscow.[37] The criminal gangs crosscutting the region also stoked fears that Moscow could exploit them to its economic and political advantage. Russian criminal groups have fomented ethnic tensions inside Estonia and Latvia and the Baltic governments believe that Moscow encourages or directs such operations by channeling funds and operatives into the mafia network.[38]

Russian criminal activities became more sophisticated and less violent after Estonia enacted more effective legislation and law enforcement in the mid-1990s. Organized crime was less able to penetrate the upper echelons of power as Estonia introduced stringent criteria for citizenship and Estonian nationals dominated top positions in government and the security services.[39] Estonian authorities are also concerned with the smuggling of illegal immigrants to Western Europe through Estonia.[40] Much of the business is run from Moscow and involves smuggling people to the EU as tourists. Estonia's border guard has warned that this business is expanding.

Lacking any direct political controls and fearing closer ties between Estonia and Western institutions, Russian intelligence services magnified their espionage operations in the country. The size of Russia's diplomatic corps in Estonia has grown significantly and includes officials working in the embassy in Tallinn and consular offices in Narva and Tartu, with special service agents disguised as diplomats. In August 2000, Estonia ordered two Russian diplomats accused of spying to vacate the country.[41] Russian missions are likely to expand in the light of Estonia's accession to NATO and the military intelligence that will thereby be acquired. Russian authorities also endeavored to discredit the Estonian intelligence services. In February 2000, Prime Minister Mart Laar blamed Moscow for organizing scandals around Estonia's security organizations, which he called a "permanent process."[42] The campaign included reports in the Russian media that a powerful intelligence center was operating in Estonia for NATO interests and that the United States had established a center to train personnel for conducting subversive acts and gathering intelligence In the fall of 2003, Estonian authorities reported that Russian intelligence services were increasing pressure on their diplomats to divulge classified information on NATO and the EU.[43] Head of the Estonian intelligence service, Tarmo Turkson, asserted that attempts to recruit Estonian diplomats are made in Russia and in the West. Russian intelligence views the Baltic states as easier targets for obtaining information than their EU counterparts.

LATVIA

Latvia became a prime object of Russian diplomatic pressures soon after gaining independence. The border treaty between the two countries remained unratified by the Russian parliament and Latvian officials believed ratification would be postponed until after the December 2003 Duma elections. Russian parliamentarians routinely justified the delay by accusing Riga of human rights violations against the Russian minority and calculated that nonratification would delay Latvia's NATO entry.[44] Moscow officials brought the issue to the UN in order to stimulate international criticism of Riga's minority policies. It applauded the UN Committee on the Elimination of Racial Discrimination, which expressed concerns over the status of non-citizens in Latvia.[45] Latvian president Vaira Vike-Freiberga pointed out in May 2000 that Russia was eager to split the unity of the three Baltic states as this would enable Moscow to restore its influence in the region.[46] She also suggested that Russia had drafted a special program to exert diplomatic pressure on the Baltic nations. Even after Latvia's invitation to NATO, the Duma continued to issue resolutions condemning alleged human rights violations by Riga.

Russia's executive and parliament have systematically portrayed Latvia in a negative light through the mass media. Moscow exploited the presence of

small numbers of Latvian Waffen Schutzstaffel (SS) veterans to claim that
the country was veering toward fascism and threatening its Russian minority with genocide. In 1998, the televised participation of the commander in
chief of the Latvian armed forces in a march of SS veterans in Riga provoked
a tough Russian response. A similar outcry was generated when a Russian
World War II "antifascist partisan" was convicted on charges of war crimes
for murdering Latvian anti-Communists. The Latvian authorities condemned
Moscow's frequent criticisms of legitimate war crimes trials.[47] A major Russian media assault was conducted in March 1998 when Latvian police dispersed an unauthorized march by Russian pensioners. Moscow accused Riga
of massive human rights violations. Small explosive devices were also discovered near the Russian embassy and close to a synagogue. Latvia was branded
in the Russian press as pro-Nazi, anti-Russian, and anti-Semitic. Russia restricted its imports from Latvia and stopped transborder bank transfers. Some
Russian politicians also demanded a cutoff in energy supplies.

In March 2000, Latvian secretary of state Maris Riekstins accused Moscow of waging a propaganda campaign against his country. He claimed that
almost every day Russia's Foreign Ministry would issue statements about the
revival of fascism and human rights violations.[48] In June 2003, the Latvian
media reported that the country's Russian-language newspapers were assisting politicians in Moscow to besmirch Riga.[49] Many of the interviews with
selected Russian parliamentarians involved routine attacks on the Latvian
government. The two most quoted anti-Latvian voices in Moscow were
Dmitriy Rogozin, chairman of the Duma's International Affairs Committee,
and Andrey Kokoshin, chairman of the Duma's CIS Commission.

The line between propaganda and outright disinformation has often been
crossed by Moscow. The mayor of Moscow, Yuriy Luzhkov, accused the
Latvian authorities of genocide and ethnic cleansing in order to raise tensions between the two states and terminate the hesitant policy of rapprochement. A number of Russian leaders called for greater protection by the state
of its diaspora, implying more direct interference in neighboring states.[50] In
an imaginative twist, one Russian security expert charged that Latvia and
Estonia were deliberately conducting "soft ethnic cleansing" campaigns
against the Russian population in order to elicit a harsh nationalist response
from Moscow that could then be presented as a Russian threat in order to
gain Western sympathy.[51] Russia's representative on the Council of Europe
distributed a document in March 2002, claiming that Latvia resembled
Macedonia in its policies toward national minorities. He implied that a bi-
national accord needed to be forged between Latvians and Russians similar
to the Ohrid agreement in Macedonia.[52]

Russian special forces and military units attempted to stage a bloody
provocation in Riga in January 1991 in order to thwart the drive toward
independence. A handful of Latvians died in the clashes but the episode was

short-lived.[53] As in Estonia during much of the 1990s, the Russian army after its withdrawal rehearsed various invasion and occupation scenarios. It vastly exaggerated the threats posed by this small state to Russian security. Some officials even threatened to attack the Baltic countries with conventional or nuclear weapons if their cooperation with NATO intensified.[54] Latvian officials publicly accused the Russian government of planning to invade the country. Latvia's invitation to join NATO in November 2002 was criticized in Moscow for fostering disunity, mistrust, and destabilization, but no threatening countermeasures were envisaged. However, Russian officials demanded NATO guarantees that Alliance troops and weapons would not be deployed in any Baltic republic.

Following a period of energy blackmail, through the withholding of oil and gas supplies in the early 1990s, Russia adopted an alternative approach in seeking to capture control over energy markets and infrastructure. Russian corporations invested over $130 million in Latvia; the biggest investments included Lastrostrans (Russia's Transneftprodukt, specializing in oil transit products), Latvijas Gaze (Gazprom), and Lukoil Baltija (Lukoil). Russia also announced plans to build pipelines that would bypass Latvia in case of "political complications" between the two countries. During 2002–2003, Russian companies exerted economic pressures on Latvia by severely cutting back oil supplies to the Ventspils terminal, the largest oil port in the Baltic region, and threatening it with bankruptcy.[55] The objective was to persuade Riga to sell its shares in the terminal to Russia's state oil-pipeline operator Transneft, which would obtain a controlling stake in the facilities. Prime Minister Kasyanov opposed the resumption of supplies by Lukoil and Yukos in order to push through the Transneft deal. As in other countries, Russian enterprises in coordination with state officials were intent on taking on the multiple monopoly functions of energy supplier, distributor, and owner of generating plants and transport systems. This would provide substantial economic and political leverage over a targeted government.

In January 2003, Latvia lodged a complaint with the WTO over a decision by Russia's state-owned oil exporter Transneft not to ship oil to Ventspils in the first quarter of 2003.[56] Foreign Minister Sandra Kalniete dispatched a letter to the EU commissioner for external relations, Chris Patten, expressing concern that Russia could wield undue political influence through its decisions on the transit of oil through Latvia's ports. In February 2003, Russia officially halted the shipment of oil for two months. The objective was to lower the value of the oil-terminal operator Ventspils Nafta as Transneft aimed to acquire a stake in the company. Transneft vice president Sergey Grigoriev confirmed his company's interest in Ventspils Nafta and asserted that the moratorium on oil shipments would be lifted if management of the terminal were handed over to Russia in exchange for $143 million offered by a group of Russian oil majors. Representatives of the Latvian side insisted on payment of at least $200 million.

In February 2003, the Latvian Foreign Ministry protested that Moscow that was not fulfilling the Latvian-Russian government agreement of June 1993 on joint utilization and operation of oil pipelines in Latvia. Riga complained that while it had invested significant funds in modernizing the pipeline, which was owned by the joint enterprise LatRosTrans, Transneft decided unilaterally to halt oil shipments to Ventspils. Employees of LatRosTrans signed a letter to Putin asking the government to resume oil supplies. Ninety-five percent of the company's employees were Russian-speaking residents of Latvia. Moscow responded that accusations that it was not fulfilling its obligations were groundless. It argued that that the contentious Latvian-Russian agreement only provided for setting up a joint venture but did not regulate practical operations.

The Latvian energy crisis was part of a broader effort by Moscow to assert control over energy routes in the region while lessening Russia's dependence on transit lines running through particular states. Russian companies have been systematically purchasing refineries, pipelines, and terminals to reintegrate their former Soviet supply chains.[57] Because Riga resisted such pressures, oil supplies were terminated. Some Russian companies linked to the state were willing to incur financial losses in order to assert their dominance. Others protested to the Russian premier that they were losing revenues because of the blockade. Moscow's reaction was mute, indicating approval for Transneft's pressures. In the gas arena, Gazprom and its allied company Itera acquired a major stake in Latvia's gas utility while increasing the price of gas supplies to Latvia by some 20 percent in 2002. As a result of such policies, Latvian officials claim that Moscow is seeking "energy-based economic control" over the country.

The Russian authorities crafted a long-term strategy for dominating the Latvian economy. According to parliament's Foreign Affairs Committee, these plans included the control of the rail system, gas and oil pipeline links to the Baltic coast, the shipping service, and the ports of Riga, Ventspils, and Liepaja. Russian business heavily penetrated Latvian farming and the food-processing industry. Government and business interests also seek to funnel money through Latvia's banking system and Riga has become one of the biggest offshore financial centers for Russian businessmen seeking a safe home for their money.[58] Russian-linked banks in Latvia also exert political influence and Riga voices anxiety over their long-term impact on Latvian politics.

Moscow has blocked Latvian exports and imports in order to inflict pain on the economy and to display its dissatisfaction with Riga's policies toward the Russian minority. In April 1998, the mayor of Moscow and leaders of several other cities called for a boycott of Latvian goods and the termination of cooperation with Latvian companies. An embargo imposed in July 1998 effected Latvia's fishing industry, which lost some half a million dollars that year, as well as milk processing and dairy products, whose export to Russia was dramatically cut. Also affected were the pharmaceutical and machine-building sectors. There was a danger that Latvia stood to lose its most favored trading status with Russia. Opinion polls in Russia demonstrated that a majority of citizens approved of sanctions against Riga.

Officials also obstructed the development of crossborder regional projects with Latvia and Estonia, this despite the willingness of local authorities in Russia's regions to work more closely with their western neighbors. Moscow informed local governments that crossborder cooperation, especially through private initiatives, was not in Russia's national interest. The governor of Pskov oblast pulled back from several joint projects so as not to contradict Kremlin policy.[59] Moscow feared centrifugal tendencies in the Pskov region encouraged by its Baltic neighbors and was opposed to devolving power to the oblasts. Paradoxically, greater interregional openness could favor the position of Russian and other Slavic minorities in the Baltic republics by increasing their cooperation with coethnics in Russia. The Kremlin perceives this as a threat to territorial integrity despite the aspirations of Russians on both sides of the border.

In a striking example of economic pressure, in December 2002 the Latvian Border Guard Service declared a state of emergency at the Terehova border checkpoint because of actions by Russian customs officials who refused to admit Russian passenger cars with transit numbers unless drivers paid a tax and convoying charges.[60] The move resulted in a massive queue of hundreds of trucks and passenger cars at the checkpoint. Latvian officials concluded that only full integration into the EU would enable the country to resist pressures by Russian business, criminal networks, and intelligence services.

The Kremlin has exploited internal political and ethnic tensions in Latvia to its advantage. Of the three Baltic republics, Latvia has received the most intensive attention over its treatment of the minorities. Both government and Duma have exacerbated conflicts over Latvia's language and citizenship laws in order to present the large Russian minority, forming some 30 percent of the population, as a victim of discriminatory policies.[61] The local Russian leadership also contributed to stoking tensions in consultation with officials in Moscow.

As the Latvian share of the population has risen during the past decade, Moscow accused Riga of persecuting minorities. It insisted that before ratifying a border agreement, Latvia had to abide by Kremlin demands on the position of the Russian minority. Russian ethnics decreased in Latvia from approximately 905,500 in 1989 to around 710,000 by the late 1990s. Moscow feared that its leverage would decline alongside the demographic contraction and that Russian ethnics would play a shrinking role in Latvia's political and economic life and prove unable to advance Moscow's interests. Cognizant of its potentially declining influence, the Kremlin persistently attacked Riga for thwarting the naturalization of ethnic Russians, even though countries such as Germany imposed tougher restrictions on citizenship. Moscow's pressure was useful for minority leaders as it enabled them to secure additional economic and social benefits.

Writing in *Nezavisimaya Gazeta* on 13 January 2001, Igor Igoshin, a Russian foreign policy analyst, urged Moscow to use its nationality policy to promote its foreign policy goals.[62] The ethnic question was identified as a core issue in which the Russian government could promote its agenda by intensively supporting the Russophone population in all former Soviet republics. The diasporas were capable of becoming a serious internal political factor, which would have a "positive influence" by lobbying on behalf of Russian state interests. Russia's economic presence, its ability to direct the flow of goods, and its propaganda campaigns gave Moscow the means to have an impact on diaspora communities and through them on the indigenous governments. Each year, new issues provoked verbal barrages by Russian officials and parliamentarians and by minority leaders in Latvia. In the summer of 2003, Riga announced that from September 2004, all Latvian high schools had to teach 60 percent of classes in Latvian, even though most schools already followed this stipulation.[63] This led to renewed protests by Russian officials.

Russian authorities have used the minority issue to warn of social unrest and chaos in Latvia. In July 2003, Latvia's Foreign Ministry protested against a Russian representative's claims at a meeting of the Council of Europe that tensions over educational reform could lead to civil unrest and conflict.[64] Riga accused Russian officials of unilaterally claiming to speak on behalf of Latvia's minorities and deliberately stirring social tensions in the country. The government called upon Moscow to provide any information they had regarding the possibility of civil unrest or to retract the statement. Although the scenario painted by Russian representatives was dismissed as a fabrication, it stirred tensions and encouraged militants among the minority.

In May 2003, the Latvian authorities declared Duma deputy Iosef Kobzon *persona non grata,* because he posed a "threat to Latvia's national security."[65] The ban prompted Russia's Foreign Ministry to demand an explanation, while Riga asked Moscow to "avoid an unnecessary provocation of controversial situations." Kobzon asserted that the ban humiliated "all of Russia and all Russian compatriots in Latvia" and would negatively affect Russian-Latvian relations. The ban came in response to his participation in a 9 May Victory Day performance organized by the Russian embassy and his criticism of Latvia's treatment of Russian veterans. Moscow was also culpable in the activities of the extremist National Bolshevik Party (NBP). In October 2003, Russia's Office of the Prosecutor-General refused to extradite Vladimir Linderman, the NBP's deputy chairman, to

Latvia to face charges of illegal possession of explosives and preparing to overthrow the Latvian authorities.

Russian officials claimed that Linderman was being persecuted in Latvia for his political activities and convictions.[66] No significant non-Russian extremist groups have surfaced in Latvia that would enable Moscow's special services to discredit the country in Western eyes. Populists and isolationists who could damage relations with Western powers are marginal phenomena in the country.

Each Latvian government since independence has been portrayed in Moscow as racist and xenophobic and as having fascistic tendencies. In addition to propaganda and disinformation campaigns, open rifts with Riga were intended to persuade Western institutions that Latvia was an unsuitable candidate for membership. Various events in Latvia were blown out of proportion and exploited by the Russian media as governmental plots. This included the vandalizing in March 1998 of a Russian war memorial in Liepaja and the march of veterans of Latvia's voluntary SS Legion that same month. Such incidents were denounced as an official conspiracy to force ethnic Russians to emigrate from Latvia and as indicating that the country was an extremist anomaly in Europe.[67]

Energy and economic pressures on Latvia are intended not only to influence Riga's policies but also to destabilize governments viewed as particularly anti-Russian.[68] Cuts in trade, energy squeezes, and resulting budgetary pressures have had a sobering effect on the Latvian authorities. Russian energy revenues are also channeled into funding political parties that are favorably disposed toward Moscow's interests. Local politicians complain that Russian capital is corrupting the political process and leading to intensive lobbying activities by interest groups in Moscow. In November 2001, Latvia's Bureau to Protect the Constitution investigated the supposed collaboration of Latvia's Socialist Party with the radical Russian Union of Communist Parties (UCP).[69] The UCP promotes the re-creation of the USSR, which contravenes the Latvian constitution. The presence of Russian energy companies and other businesses is treated with enormous suspicion in the Baltic states even where their major interest may be profit over politics. This mistrust has grown under Putin's tenure as the energy companies have been brought under closer Kremlin supervision.

Russian organized crime exerts a bigger influence in Latvia than the other two Baltic republics. One explanation for this is the number of ethnic Russians in Latvian institutions, including in the security agencies. They changed their names after independence but maintained links with Moscow and were prone to corrupt practices and criminal connections. Latvian banks became susceptible to money laundering operations and for channeling cash from Russia to political parties, media outlets, and other pro-Moscow interest groups throughout the Baltic region. Russian criminals confessed to fomenting ethnic conflicts in Latvia and Estonia and that Moscow directed such operations.[70] The Russian authorities viewed Latvia as the "weakest link" in the Baltic chain and the laggard candidate for both NATO and EU accession. Sanctions periodically imposed by Moscow against Riga also contributed to criminalizing economic activities.[71]

LITHUANIA

Moscow delayed ratifying a border treaty with Vilnius for several years. An agreement was finally signed in October 1997 but was opposed by a range of political forces who believed Moscow was unnecessarily surrendering an important policy lever. Territorial pressures continued with a Duma resolution in 1998, claiming that the Klaipeda area along the Baltic coast was Russian soil. Although this did not represent the official government position, it nevertheless increased bilateral tensions. In the military arena, Moscow wanted a free hand in transiting its military across Lithuania to its outpost in Kaliningrad, but Vilnius successfully arranged a transit regime that required prior notification and no stopovers for rail and road traffic.

The Kremlin fomented disputes between the three Baltic states to weaken prospects for crossborder cooperation. Under both Yeltsin and Putin, the authorities verbally reassured their neighbors that Russia's national interests were nonimperial and indistinguishable from those of other democratic global powers.[72] Baltic leaders were not convinced by such pronouncements and the drive for a NATO umbrella continued unabated. Vilnius and other capitals believed that postponing the accession of the Baltic republics would simply encourage Russia to be more assertive, thus worsening relations with Moscow at a time when the West was seeking to expand Europe's sphere of security. While NATO's ambiguity invariably stimulated Russian adventurism, clear policy decisions dispelled confusion and undercut opposition.

In May 2003, the Duma finally ratified several treaties with Lithuania on the delineation of borders, including the division of the Baltic Sea shelf.[73] The treaties formed part of the agreement reached in November 2002 by Russia, Lithuania, and the EU on transit between the Kaliningrad exclave and the rest of Russia in the run-up to Lithuania's entry into the EU. The treaties formally bestow the status of an international frontier on the administrative border that separated the Russian and Lithuanian Soviet republics. Opposition politicians urged Putin to block ratification, as this would purportedly obstruct Lithuania's entry into NATO because the Alliance only accepted countries that have no disputed international borders.

Both the Russian government and parliament have orchestrated verbal assaults on Vilnius. When the Lithuanian legislature voted in 2000 to demand compensation from Moscow for losses that the country sustained during half a century of Soviet occupation, senior Russian political figures suggested that Vilnius return the territories that it had acquired under Moscow's rule. They were referring in particular to the capital Vilnius (in prewar Poland) and the main port of Klaipeda (in prewar Germany).[74]

Military threat became a reality when the country asserted its independence from the Soviet Union. In January 1991, Soviet troops stormed and captured the television tower in Vilnius in an attempt to reverse the tide of independence. During the ensuing protests, fifteen unarmed civilians were murdered by Red Army soldiers and dozens were injured. Tensions eased with the withdrawal of Soviet troops, but Moscow failed to honor Lithuanian request for the extradition of Soviet paramilitary and military figures responsible for the killings.

The question of Russian military transit to Kaliningrad through Lithuanian territory has been a source of conflict and it provided an opportunity for the Kremlin to exert pressure.[75] If Vilnius acceded to Kremlin demands for unchecked transit this would have legitimized Russia's military presence. With an invitation to join NATO in November 2002, Lithuania felt more secure in resisting such pressures and reducing the political significance of the military transit question. In August 2002, Putin's special envoy for Kaliningrad, Dmitriy Rogozin, reported after talks with Lithuanian prime minister Algirdas Brazauskas that Russia may attempt to block Lithuania's entry into the EU by not ratifying a bilateral accord on border delineation. Such a measure would make it impossible for Vilnius to comply with an EU requirement that members have no outstanding border disputes. Rogozin believed that Lithuania would agree to a compromise allowing Russians free access to Kaliningrad.

In January 2003, the Kaliningrad legislature passed a nonbinding resolution asking the Duma to postpone consideration of the border treaty between Russia and Lithuania.[76] Deputies argued that the treaty did not take into account the needs of Kaliningrad oblast residents following Lithuania's EU accession The resolution stated that the oblast legislature would submit its recommended modifications to the Duma. Muscovite officials complained that visa stipulations infringed on the rights of Russians to move freely "within their own country" and therefore posed an assault on Russian sovereignty. The Kaliningrad transit issue seemed settled in early 2003 after Lithuania agreed to certain concessions.[77] The new rules, to be incorporated into the Schengen agreement governing border crossings, called for simplified transit documents for Russians for three year terms. The procedure, which went into effect in July 2003, allows Russians a twenty-four-hour period in which to pass through Lithuania. Foreign Minister Antanas Valionis asserted that Vilnius made several concessions by dropping its refusal to have consular workers handle transit procedures aboard trains and shortening the time needed for issuing transit documents.

On several occasions, Russia used energy as a weapon of sanctions, either by withholding scheduled deliveries or imposing higher prices. When Lithuania pushed for independence in 1990, Moscow closed the oil pipeline to the Mazeikiai refinery and created major shortages in the country.

This was intended to pressurize the authorities by raising the prospect of social unrest through a painful energy squeeze. Russia was determined to penetrate the energy chain through control over production, processing, transit, distribution, and associated services. Moscow has also tried to incorporate Lithuania into its electricity grid that spans much of the Baltic region. As an indication of Lithuania's concerns over growing Russian influence, in 1999 the government sold a large stake in the Mazeikiai oil refinery to a U.S. company, Williams International, rather than to Russia's Lukoil. Mazeikiai generated about 10 percent of Lithuania's gross national product (GNP). This decision was based primarily on political calculations rather than purely economic criteria as Vilnius wanted to avoid more intensive dependence on Russia.

Lithuania was given several ultimatums that Lukoil would cut off its supplies unless the company was allowed to acquire majority shares in the pipeline from Belarus to the Baltic Sea and in the Mazeikiai refinery. After Vilnius disregarded Russian threats, Lukoil shut off crude supplies to the country nine times for brief periods between 1999 and 2001. In 2002, Lukoil, through Euro Oil Invest, made a concerted effort to take over Mazeikiai, including a large refinery, the Butinge maritime terminal.[78] This enterprise constituted Lithuania's largest economic entity and the major refinery in the Baltic region. Lukoil indicated that it would restore supplies if Lithuania and Williams ceded a large equity portion and full operating rights. The cutoffs forced Mazeikiai into heavy debts and deprived Lithuania of crucial tax revenue. In August 2002, Russia's second-largest oil producer, Yukos, offered a new deal to Mazeikiai, promising adequate supplies while buying out Williams.[79] It acquired a 54 percent stake in the refinery along with operational control over the entire complex, following a government decision not to buy a 27 percent stake. Lithuanian politicians voiced concern over the implications of the takeover by a substantial Russian company in the absence of a Western partner.[80]

In September 2001, Russian premier Kasyanov proposed to his Lithuanian counterpart Algirdas Brazauskas the purchase of substantial shares of the Lithuanian gas company Lietuvos Dujos by Gazprom and its Lithuanian affiliates. Vilnius proved extremely reluctant to agree to this target of Russian investment and in November 2002 postponed the wider liberalization of the gas distribution sector. However, in September 2003 Vilnius finally approved the sale of a 34 percent stake in Lietuvos Dujos at a price offered by Gazprom.[81] The German companies Ruhrgas and EON Energie also bought a 34 percent stake in the company. The deal with Gazprom involved guarantees for the long-term supply of Russian gas at stable prices. Several leading politicians were anxious about the deal, arguing that it would make Lithuania even more vulnerable to economic pressure. However, Vilnius had little alternative, as it cannot afford to buy large quantities of gas from western suppliers.

A consortium comprising Gazprom, the U.S.-based Clement Power Venture, and the local company Dujotekana (controlled by Gazprom) signed an agreement in March 2003 to purchase the Kaunas thermal-power plant (Lithuania's largest) from the utility Kauno Energija (Kaunas Energy).[82] Gazprom purchased 99 percent of the plant's shares and the other two partners 0.5 percent each. However, by December 2003 the shares were to be redistributed so that Gazprom would own 51 percent; Clement Power Venture, 25 percent; and Dujotekana, 24 percent. Gazprom will be responsible for supplying natural gas to the plant, Clement Power Venture will deal with the plant's expansion and upgrading, and Dujotekana (Lithuania's largest natural gas importer) will oversee operations.

During 1999, Lithuania refused to sign a deal with Russia, Belarus, and the other two Baltic states for the integration of their energy systems. Such an arrangement would increase Russia's control over each country and deter European investors from the energy sector. Russia's state electricity company, Unified Energy System, was poised to purchase Lithuanian power plants and electricity distribution grids. Vilnius may also need Russian cooperation in storing the nuclear waste from the Soviet-built Ignalina nuclear power plant whose reactors are of similar design to that of Chernobyl. Lithuania is due to close two of the reactors as a condition for entering the EU. The planned decommissioning of the Ignalina facility will make Lithuania more dependent on Russia.[83] Almost 76 percent of Lithuania's domestic energy needs would be generated at thermal electric power stations, which import heavy fuel oil from Russia.

Premier Kasyanov promoted the extension of a transit corridor from Kaliningrad to the Lithuanian border at Klaipeda, which Russian companies were pursuing. Russia's moves were accompanied by a media campaign aimed at discrediting Western capital in the Baltic states. In popular perceptions in Lithuania, Russia already controls the country's energy system, which in turn generates distrust in the government's handling of foreign and economic policies.[84] Plans by Lukoil to extract oil from the Baltic Sea near the Lithuanian coast also became a highly charged political issue.

Russian-speaking groups engaged in business relations with Russia gained some political influence. In 1998, the Association of Russian Businessmen "Compatriots" was founded, comprising twenty-four Lithuanian enterprises employing mostly Russian ethnics. The Compatriots belonged to the International Union of Public Associations' Rusj Jedinaja, established in September 2000 with the objective of creating independent Russian economic, educational, and cultural structures in the "near abroad." However, Russian-speaking inhabitants did not pose any significant threat to Lithuania's national interests.

Companies from the Russian Federation were interested in purchasing major transportation companies that Lithuania was in the process of privatizing. Several intermediary companies, such as Stella Vitae and Itera Lietuva, were purchased by a combination of Lithuanian private investors and Gazprom. Although Lithuania had less Russian investment than either Latvia or Estonia, Russian companies sought to acquire several important industries. In 2002, they purchased one third of the shares in the fertilizer plant at Lifosa, the Lithuanian phosphate company. Lukoil gained petrol distribution rights in Lithuania but remained in competition with other companies.

In October 2003, Russia's Konversbank and its subsidiary, Incorion Investment Holding Company, increased its ownership stake in Lithuania's commercial bank Snoras to 57.6 percent and assumed management control of the company.[85] A number of Russian firms and their subsidiaries were seeking a larger stake in the Baltic economies especially as the prospect of EU membership loomed closer and could prove beneficial to their business interests. To protect itself against unwelcome economic penetration, Vilnius introduced laws to prevent an investor from a foreign state to dominate strategically important economic sectors. The government also focused on investigating "capital of unclear origin" to prevent it from gaining a foothold in the economy.

The Russian minority in Lithuania is small in comparison to Estonia and Latvia. Moscow has been less successful in sponsoring ethnic conflicts in the country as the Russian share of the population at the time of independence in 1991 stood at only 8 percent. This figure since declined from 344,500 in 1989 to about 280,000 in 1999. Moreover, Vilnius granted citizenship to all ethnic Russians resident in the country soon after gaining independence. Although few official complaints were lodged by Moscow, minority issues have been raised on occasion to depict Lithuania in a poor light when it suited the Kremlin's foreign policy goals. Reports on anti-Jewish and anti-Russian incidents have featured in the Russian media to damage Vilnius in Western eyes during the country's candidacy for NATO.

Moscow has endeavored to discredit Lithuania's intelligence and security services in order to disqualify the country from NATO entry. In June 2000, Russia's Federal Security Service (FSB) announced that it had uncovered a Lithuanian agent in the double employ of Lithuania's State Security Department and the U.S. Central Intelligence Agency (CIA) who was tasked with collecting information about FSB operations and sabotaging its counterintelligence activities. The political objective of the Lithuanian authorities, according to the FSB, was to discredit Russia in the eyes of Washington. This supposedly demonstrated Vilnius's unreliability as a partner and an ally even as the country was becoming a credible contender for the Alliance.

Russian authorities pursued their agenda in Lithuania by either working through minority organizations or establishing their own small but well-endowed political parties. Gazprom and Lukoil created such organizations and financed election campaigns. A company named Vaizga, whose main shareholder was the wife of the president of Lukoil-Baltija, contributed generously to the Social Democratic coalition (the Lithuanian Democratic Labor

Party and the Social Democratic Party), headed by former president Algirdas Brazauskas, during the October 2000 parliamentary elections.[86] Vaizga was the second largest financial contributor in the elections. Lukoil-Baltija is a subsidiary of Russia's Lukoil, which was engaged in arranging the acquisition of Mazeikiai.

In January 2003, opposition leaders claimed that Russia was spending large sums to gain influence over Lithuania's political life.[87] Moscow invested up to $2.8 million on the presidential election campaign and bought access to the Lithuanian media. Politicians complained that political party funding was undeveloped in Lithuania, thus leaving the space open to foreign influences. In November 2003, the prosecutor-general's office launched a criminal investigation into allegations that Yuriy Borisov, the owner of the helicopter firm Aviabaltika, who contributed $400,000 to Rolandas Paksas's successful presidential campaign, made threats against the president. Borisov allegedly complained that Paksas had refused to abide by an agreement to make him a presidential adviser. Vilnius imposed a ban on Borisov leaving the country and confiscated his Russian and Lithuanian passports.[88] Allegations were also made that the president's closest aides were tied to the Russian underworld and a parliamentary commission investigated the potential threat to national security. It concluded that Russian public relations firm Almax, with suspected links to Russia's secret services, was "seeking to influence and control political processes in Lithuania" through the president's office.

Russian diplomats have attempted to bribe parliamentarians into opposing NATO accession. Russian media moguls purchased several local media outlets enabling Russian commentators to interject in the domestic debate on NATO enlargement. They raised doubts about the advisability of Alliance accession by arguing that new NATO members were performing poorly economically. To undercut the drive for NATO, Russian propaganda also focused on the EU as a much more prescient priority and raised the prospect of a European security structure outside of NATO as a preferable solution for Lithuania's security.

The proximity of Kaliningrad helps account for the high percentage of Lithuanian-based criminal networks involved in illegal weapons sales.[89] Other contraband products have also traversed Lithuania between the Belarus border and the port of Klaipeda. In 1993, a popular investigative journalist, Vitautas Lingys, was murdered in Vilnius by members of a Russian criminal gang. This led to a major trial and conviction of four criminal bosses, one of whom, Boris Dekanidze (a Georgian Russian), was executed in 1995. In October 2003, Mecys Laurinkus, the outgoing head of Lithuania's State Security Department, warned about a number of organized criminal groups that had penetrated Lithuania. They included the Moscow-based Luzniki group and the 21st Century Company, whose chief, Anzori Aksentev, maintained contacts with leaders of Lithuania's criminal groups.[90]

In November 2003, premier Brazauskas asserted that officials named in a classified State Security Department document who maintained ties with crime boss Aksentev should resign.[91] The officials included the Lithuanian president's National Security Adviser and the head of the State Border Guard Service. A parliamentary commission investigated possible threats to national security and concluded in December 2003 that the president was vulnerable to Russian pressure and blackmail. Paksas faced impeachment proceedings for violating the constitution through his links to the Russian mafia and secret services.[92] An intelligence report claimed that Paksas's main financial backer, Yuriy Borisov, was involved in illegal arms deals and some presidential aides had links with crime rings, while Lithuania served as a base for financing international terrorists.

According to Lithuania's State Security Department, Russia's Foreign Intelligence Service, the Federal Security Service, and military intelligence have stepped up their operations in the Baltic states.[93] All three agencies have revived Soviet-era contacts and actively recruited new informants especially in the civil service, the Defense Ministry, and the security services. At a meeting of Baltic security chiefs in August 1998, discussions focused on improving the exchange of information on Russian espionage networks and on recruiting people with no prior links to the KGB or the GRU. In December 1999, the media reported on a successful operation by Lithuanian counterintelligence when the aide of Russia's defense attaché attempted to recruit an officer in Lithuania's Defense Ministry.[94] He was asked to supply information on arms purchases, relations with NATO, military plans, foreign instructors, and military installations. Disclosures about the arrest of alleged Lithuanian spies were issued by Moscow to discredit Vilnius. In July 2000, the head of Lithuania's State Security Department, Mecys Laurinkus, ridiculed a Russian report about the arrest of a Lithuanian spy recruited by the CIA to hack into FSB computers.[95] Lithuanian officials, including Alvydas Sadeckas, head of parliament's defense and security committee, also noted a surge of interest in their diplomats by Russian intelligence agencies.[96]

6

Neutralizing the Core: Central Europe

A BRIDGE TOO FAR: CENTRAL EUROPE ON RUSSIA'S MAP

The Central European region that was once part of the Soviet bloc has been categorized in Moscow as either the "far abroad" or the "middle abroad," thus giving the area a special status for Russian penetration. The region is then further subdivided into the Central European and Balkan zones, with a distinctive role assigned for each.[1] In the Central European states of Poland, Hungary, the Czech Republic, and Slovakia, Russian policy has been de-militarized and de-ideologized.[2] However, the region's importance has re-mained twofold: as a bridge to the wealthy EU and as a buffer against Western penetration of the CIS. Economic ties, especially in the energy and financial sectors, and enhanced Russian intelligence operations serve as the primary mechanisms for regaining influence in these new democracies.

Soon after the Central European states regained their independence in 1989–1990, the Russian government attempted to place limitations on their foreign policy decisions particularly in the security arena. The objective was to guarantee their neutrality and nonalignment with NATO. Moscow was assisted by Western powers, which urged a cautious approach to severing Soviet domination for fear of upsetting the Kremlin. NATO leaders envis-aged the Central Europeans as a belt of neutral states modeled on the Finnish example. Pressures were exerted to sign bilateral agreements with Moscow that contained security clauses restricting any feasible alternatives. In 1990–

1991 the "Kvitsinsky-Falin Doctrine" aimed to convince the Central Euro-peans to agree to a permanent "nonbloc" status in treaties they concluded with the USSR.[3] Such attempts were rejected by Warsaw, Budapest, and Prague, which viewed their independence as a result of Moscow's weakness rather than any fundamental change in Russian foreign policy.

Governments in the region feared that Russia could in the future revert to a more aggressive posture. A potentially narrow window of opportunity had opened to catapult the newly liberated states into the Western security structures as a guarantee against future Kremlin ambitions. Until the time Poland, Hungary, and the Czech Republic were admitted into NATO, Russian officials believed that their pro-Western orientations were reversible. Central European governments concluded that Russian policymakers refused to accept them as equal players but as pawns in a broader struggle for domi-nance on the European continent.

The first few years of the 1990s were marked by some confusion in Krem-lin policy. A "Kozyrev Doctrine" emerged in 1992, named after Russia's foreign minister, stating that Moscow's "strategic task" was to prevent the Central Europeans from forming a buffer that would isolate Russia from the West. It was equally important for Moscow to prevent the West from push-ing Russia out of the region.[4] Russia's 1992 Foreign Policy Concept under-scored these objectives, while Moscow expected significant Western economic assistance for its domestic reform program and as a reward for its withdrawal from Central Europe. When the Western response was viewed as disappoint-ing, Russian policy toward its former satellites was heavily criticized by the foreign policy elite.[5] A tougher policy line emerged during 1993–1994, when it became apparent that three former Warsaw Pact states were pushing stri-dently for NATO membership.[6] The leaders of all major Russian parties opposed Central European inclusion in the Alliance, considering this a di-rect challenge to Russia's security interests. In deflecting such an outcome, Moscow consistently tried to deal with NATO over the heads of the Cen-tral Europeans and to broker a deal regardless of their aspirations.

According to foreign policy expert Aleksander Dubin, Moscow needed to promote "neutrality" in Central Europe, with a maximum degree of do-mestic freedoms but ultimately dependent on Russia for its security. This was a post-Soviet version of "Finlandization."[7] At no point did the Kremlin de-clare that with the dissolution of the Warsaw Pact the Central Europeans were outside of any distinct sphere of Russian geopolitical interest.[8] Moscow en-visaged a zone of nonaligned and weak states. This would serve two strate-gic purposes: to promote a conduit for Russian ties to the EU and to forestall "negative influences" from Central Europe toward CIS neighbors that would draw them away from Russia. The Central Europeans were unwilling to act as bridge-builders for Russia and expressed their weariness about Moscow's long-term intentions. A primary Kremlin objective was to prevent these coun-tries from moving into NATO and from diminishing Russia's strategic maneuverability. Moscow sought the region's demilitarization and neutral-ization so that it would constitute a security buffer between NATO and the CIS: "A majority of Russian policy makers still refuse to accept the CEEC as players endowed with equal rights on the international stage. They still maintain the traditional perception of the people and the countries in the Central and Eastern European regions as pawns in a broader struggle for dominance and hegemony by the great powers of Europe."[9]

Foreign Minister Primakov proposed that Russia and NATO jointly issue security guarantees for the four Visegrad states as an alternative to NATO entry. Such an indeterminate "gray zone" in Central Europe would have given Moscow more options in reestablishing its predominance. The former satellites would have become bargaining chips with the West rather than independent international players. The Central Europeans were determined to avoid the status of a buffer and pressed to become interlocked with NATO and to expand the "sphere of security" eastward. In November 1993, a new Russian military doctrine was issued that underscored the need to maintain the "friendly neutrality" of the Central European countries. Membership of any of these states in the Atlantic Alliance was described as a direct threat to Russian security. As an alternative to NATO, Moscow proposed the trans-formation of the OSCE into a security mechanism to which NATO, the West European Union, and the Council of Europe would be subordinate, thus effectively providing the Kremlin with veto powers over NATO policies.

When it became evident that NATO would expand into Central Europe regardless of Russia's objections, with Poland, Hungary, and the Czech Republic invited to join in July 1997, the Kremlin downplayed the signifi-cance of NATO enlargement. It did not want to jeopardize inflows of West-ern investment or face isolation while appearing weak and ineffectual. Moscow endeavored to water down the implications of NATO growth by limiting the role of new members.[10] Enlargement was to be denuded of any military significance while Russia was to play a more prominent security role through the NATO-Russia Council. Moscow also demanded assurances that NATO's military infrastructure, including airfields and headquarters, would not be extended to new members, that the incoming states would be nuclear-free, and that they would not host any integrated NATO military units.

Despite Moscow's misleading suppositions, NATO was not planning ei-ther to position nuclear weapons or combined Allied forces on the territory of new members. However, the Alliance was not prepared to lower the ceil-ings set by the Conventional Forces in Europe (CFE) Treaty on military equipment held by new members. Moreover, NATO's pledge not to deploy any sizable military forces or weapons systems was a political declaration and not a legally binding accord. The Kremlin complained that the moderniza-tion of the Central European military and infrastructure, including airfields, bases, ports, and communications lines, would in itself undermine Russian security by making these countries into effective bridgeheads for any future

NATO assault. For the Central Europeans, the question of NATO entry was not negotiable and neither was the Kremlin notion of "partial membership." Russian proposals and demands were dismissed as displays of arrogant imperialism. In the words of one Russian commentator:

> How is it that Kremlin officials failed to realize that, in and of itself, the very method chosen to block our neighbors' admission into NATO is a convincing argument in favor of their prompt entry? How is it that they failed to anticipate the passions with which the entire "near abroad," from big to small, from the Baltics to Kyrgyzstan, watched to see how the dispute would end, holding its breath and praying to God that Clinton would stand firm and that Havel would succeed? Some expressed this openly, while others, more circumspect, whispered it in the corridors. But the driving force for all was the same—fear.[11]

Russia's adamant opposition to NATO expansion had the reverse effect. It convinced these countries to strengthen their Western integration and avoid exposure to Kremlin pressures. Government officials argued that NATO accession would enhance their self-confidence and improve their future relations with Moscow by placing them on a more equitable footing without fear of domination. Russia also expressed concern about the Visegrad Group initiative as a pro-Western and anti-Russian bloc. The initiative was launched by Warsaw, Budapest, Prague, and Bratislava in the early 1990s to help coordinate their foreign and security policies.[12] The signing of the NATO-Russia Founding Act in May 1997 and Moscow's search for a special role in relations with the Alliance, created consternations in Central European capitals that Russia was diluting their security. This perception was buttressed under Putin when Moscow offered far-reaching cooperation with the West in combating international terrorism and a new NATO-Russia Council was established.

Moscow employed an assortment of economic instruments to gain political influence over its former satellites. This policy was formulated by Prime Minister Chernomyrdin and Minister of Foreign Economic Relations Oleg Davydov and supplemented by Primakov when he became foreign minister in 1995.[13] The central objective was to build "bridgeheads" for Russian state and private capital in the region, to gain control or influence over strategic sectors of the Central European economies, and to use the region as a springboard for economic expansion westward. Four main areas were earmarked for penetration: energy, armaments, banking, and trade. It was difficult to estimate the precise level of Russian investment, especially as much of this reached the region as non-Russian capital through third countries as well as semilegal businesses and illegal money-laundering activities. Russian authorities also tried to create debt relationships with the Central Europeans especially through energy dependence and negative trade balances that could promote their political goals.

After the breakup of the COMECON economic bloc, commercial ties between Russia and its neighbors broke down as both sides turned their attention toward Western markets and investments. The East Europeans and Russians had little to offer each other by way of trade, investment, capital, and technology. To try and regain its Central European market, Moscow proposed the creation of a "COMECON II" as an integrated economic alliance and a counterpart to the EU. Such vaporous proposals without any economic substance were dismissed as nonstarters throughout the region. A new economic union would have had little practical value because of the poor economic condition of each state, the legal chaos and criminalization of the Russian economy, and the persistent fears of Russian economic domination. Furthermore, Russia still held debts with all the Central European states from the "COMECON I" era. Although Russian authorities were not opposed to Central European accession to the EU, they expressed reservations about the negative impact on Russia.[14] They were fearful of economic discrimination through more stringent border controls and visa regimes that could further estrange the former satellites and isolate Russia from the European mainstream.

Russian analysts criticize the alleged anti-Russian postures of the Central European states. Officials claim that these governments attempt to counteract the integration processes within the CIS and act as negative influences within Russia's "near abroad" by encouraging pro-U.S. political forces. Contacts between Central European and CIS militaries, parliamentary bodies, media outlets, and business concerns have been condemned. Moscow also periodically plays the pan-Slavic card, not based on notions of political unification but on anxieties about Germanization, globalization, and the elimination of distinct Slavic cultures.[15] According to Russian policymakers, only the influence of Russia can prevent foreign domination, while a balanced Russian-German alliance would ensure security, identity, and development in the region.

Moscow calculates that after an initial spell of separation, each Central European state will turn toward its eastern neighbor because of the importance of energy supplies, raw materials, and markets. It hopes to use economic levers to foster political collaboration. In reality, political, economic, and cultural ties between the Central European states and Russia have greatly diminished. This was especially the case in the early 1990s as each state with the exception of Slovakia endeavored to nullify its post-Soviet dependence. The various bilateral friendship societies and exchange programs were also terminated and educational and scholarly contacts were curtailed. Nonetheless, ongoing dependence on Russian energy and the sale of sectors of the domestic energy industry to Russian companies maintains vulnerability to Muscovite pressures.[16]

With Putin's election, Moscow injected more methodical pragmatism into its relations with the four Visegrad states. During 2000–2001, political relations with Russia were enhanced as demonstrated by the mutual visits of foreign ministers. Putin's Kremlin realizes that it needs to adapt to an enlarging EU and to harness its potential. At the same time, Moscow remains concerned that the Central Europeans can serve as attractive models for neighboring CIS states and undermine their growing dependence on Russia. Hence the twin objectives of political containment and security neutralization have been upheld.

POLAND

Although the Russian authorities resigned themselves to the loss of Poland as a satellite, they perceived the country's integration into NATO as an obstacle to their influence in the region. All Polish governments, whatever their political pedigree, were treated with suspicion and mistrust. Warsaw in turn remained skeptical over Russian motives and policies. In an interview in 1993, Foreign Minister Kozyrev included Poland and its neighbors as part of Russia's "near abroad."[17] Kozyrev warned Warsaw that joining NATO would strengthen reactionary forces in Russia and transform the region into a "buffer zone that could be crushed in any situation." In this context, Russia's moves toward union with Belarus were perceived in Warsaw as expansionist maneuvers that exacerbated tensions along Poland's eastern border. Efforts at neutralizing Polish regional influences are deemed essential by the Russian authorities. Moscow is suspicious of close cooperation between Warsaw and its CIS neighbors and fearful of Western influences that could permanently tear Ukraine and Belarus away. Thus Muscovite spokesmen stridently attack Polish political, cultural, and economic influences.

Successive Polish governments pursued the normalization of relations with Moscow and did not adopt any overtly hostile positions. Warsaw dropped all financial claims resulting from the environmental damage caused by Soviet troops stationed on Polish territory. In October 1990, Poland established relations with the Russian Federation and soon after signed a Declaration on Friendship and Good Neighborliness. Although contacts between Moscow and Warsaw were initially cordial, a number of problems arose as a consequence of Russian attempts to restrict Poland's security and foreign policy options. The Kremlin was perturbed that Warsaw was intent on pursuing close ties with Kyiv and depicted Poland as an aspiring regional power seeking to replace Russia. Warsaw was allegedly pursuing the formation of a belt of states between the Baltic and Black Seas and constructing a cordon sanitaire around Russia.

Even before the collapse of the Soviet Union, the Polish government appropriated to itself the role of Europeanizing these emerging countries and bringing them into the West, seeing it as an opportunity to bolster Poland's international role. This belief was reinforced by the nearly universal assumption that Ukraine, unlike Russia, would make the transformation to democracy and a market economy relatively quickly and painlessly and that without Ukraine, Russia would cease to be a superpower.[18]

Yeltsin's confrontation with the Russian parliament in August 1991 and his use of the army against recalcitrant deputies convinced Warsaw that Moscow was set on a more assertive course. Kozyrev exemplified the Russian position during a visit to Warsaw in February 1994 when he claimed that Poland's NATO entry would undermine its relations with Moscow.[19] Each Polish government underscored that it was intent on NATO admission regardless of Russian objections. They also insisted that Warsaw preferred to have good relations with Moscow in order to help bring the country westward. Such an approach was treated with suspicion and cynicism in Russia.

Under Putin, a new dose of "pragmatism" was injected by the Kremlin in order to elicit benefits for Moscow. The left-of-center Polish government, formed in October 2001, attempted to give a new impetus to Polish-Russian relations. Prime Minister Leszek Miller visited Russia in December 2001 and signed a declaration on economic, trade, financial, and scientific cooperation. In January 2002, Putin became the first Russian leader to visit Warsaw since 1993. Moscow primarily sought improved economic relations and repayments of Poland's sizable energy debt to Russia. Polish businesses also began to view Russia as a promising market while Moscow negotiated the building of a new gas pipeline through Poland to western Europe.

The chief purpose of accusing Poland and its neighbors of alleged Russophobic tendencies was to disqualify them as NATO candidates. Their poor relations with Russia would purportedly have a negative impact on Alliance-Russian relations. An additional goal was to create doubts and rifts between Polish politicians over the country's security and foreign policies, which it was claimed were antagonizing a powerful neighbor. An example of Moscow's tactics was an incident in October 1994 at a Warsaw railway station when Russian travelers were allegedly roughly treated by Polish police. This event was exploited by the Foreign Ministry as evidence of rising anti-Russian sentiments. A similar reaction was recorded in February 2000 after a group of Polish demonstrators protesting the war in Chechnya broke into the Russian consulate in Poznań and tore up the Russian flag. An official apology from Warsaw was ignored, while anti-Polish demonstrations, in which Polish flags were ceremoniously burned, were staged with official approval outside Polish diplomatic missions in Russia. Both the Russian Foreign Ministry and the parliament appeared to be competing with each other to condemn the "bandit" attacks against Russia.[20] On several occasions, the state-directed Russian media fanned the image of growing Polish-Russian tensions, especially after Warsaw petitioned for NATO inclusion.

Russian propaganda strenuously attacked Poland's efforts to establish regional groupings with its post-Soviet and Central European neighbors. Moscow was perturbed that structures such as the Visegrad Group would exclude Russia and draw the CIS states into the Western orbit. The most virulent attacks were reserved for Polish-Ukrainian rapprochement. Ukrainian President Kravchuk's proposal for a Baltic–to–Black Sea security zone, issued in February 1993, was denounced as a dangerous ploy to permanently undercut Russian interests throughout Eastern Europe. Seeing itself as a regional superpower, Moscow does not countenance any rivals such as Poland for this position.[21] Indeed, it seeks to lock the country into the role of a minor player in an enlarging Europe. Russian officials openly oppose close security ties between Warsaw and Kyiv, while Poland remains fearful that Ukraine could become a weak buffer between Russia and Central Europe facilitating renewed Russian pressures throughout the region. Warsaw therefore supports the development of closer links between Ukraine and NATO.[22] Ukrainian military participation in peacekeeping exercises in Poland and the creation of a Polish-Ukrainian peacekeeping battalion in 1995 were derided in the Russian press as evidence of Warsaw's anti-Russian ambitions that would pull Ukraine into NATO.

As Poland was determined to expand its relations with Ukraine, Lithuania, and other post-Soviet republics, Warsaw was accused of ambitions to become a "quasi-imperial regional power" intent on damaging its relations with Moscow. Polish influences in neighboring Kaliningrad are also viewed as potentially threatening to Russia's territorial integrity.[23] Moscow perceived Poland as its main regional competitor in exerting influence over the CIS states. The Vilnius initiative, launched by Poland and Lithuania in the fall of 1997, was condemned as an attempt to isolate Russia from Europe by building a "geopolitical cordon" across the region. Both Moscow and Minsk regularly berate the Polish authorities for allowing the Belarusian opposition to establish a base in Poland. As Warsaw moves into the EU, it will canvass for a more active Eastern Dimension in Union policy, focusing on Ukraine, Belarus, and Moldova.[24] This will rekindle frictions over regional influence with Moscow, as Poland stands accused of "antagonizing Russian efforts for reintegration with Ukraine and Belarus."[25]

Russia's Orthodox Church has been instrumental in attacking Poland for its alleged attempts to missionize and Catholicize Russia through the actions of the Polish Pope. The Vatican's decision in early 2002 to reorganize its structure inside Russia into full diocese stirred outrage in the Orthodox hierarchy and led to expulsions and entry bars for several Polish Catholic priests, including Bishop Jerzy Mazur of Irkutsk in April 2002. This led to protests by Warsaw and the Vatican but the Kremlin remained silent and Warsaw endeavored not to escalate the incidents.[26] Russia's Orthodox Church has leaned heavily on the government to make the work of non-Orthodox denominations difficult in Russia through legal, administrative, and financial harassment. The Kremlin has also included "cultural-religious expansionism" by other states onto Russian territory as a national security threat.[27]

The Polish authorities are criticized by Moscow for providing assistance to human rights activists in Belarus and Ukraine. This is depicted as an attempt to influence internal politics and pull these countries into the NATO orbit. The activities of various Polish NGOs, foundations, and media outlets are denounced as the work of the Warsaw authorities rather than as private initiatives. Russia's disinformation campaign is underscored by a basic conflict of interest as Warsaw seeks to intensify contacts with the CIS states, while Moscow aims to restore its predominant influence in the same countries.[28] A classic example of Russia's public disinformation campaign, intent on achieving specific political objectives, was the Yeltsin declaration in August 1993 that Moscow would no longer oppose Poland's NATO membership. The aim was to limit Poland's contacts with Ukraine as it evidently obtained a free hand to move westward. Yeltsin's statement was subsequently retracted but not before it had damaged Warsaw's relations with Kyiv. There is also evidence that in exchange for Russia's decision to build a natural gas pipeline across Poland, Warsaw agreed to lessen its support for both Ukraine and Belarus in international fora.

Russia's defense doctrine, issued in 1993, classified Poland as a potential threat to its security and placed the country firmly within Russia's sphere of interest. Relations with Russia were further strained after Poland's accession to NATO in 1999. The Kremlin endeavored to demonstrate that new NATO members would have an adversarial relationship with Russia. Officials complained about increasing NATO activity close to the country's borders, including military overflights of Kaliningrad oblast. On this pretext, Russian commanders revised their plans for combat readiness in the region and the Belarusian authorities issued several threatening statements in support of a Russian military presence along the Polish border and the repositioning of nuclear weapons in Belarus. At the beginning of 2001, U.S. intelligence reports indicated that Moscow had moved short-range nuclear weapons to Kaliningrad.[29] Rumors also surfaced that Russia could deploy tactical nuclear missiles on ships in the Black Sea fleet if NATO deployed nuclear weapons in Poland.[30]

Various Russian proposals were viewed as provocative security threats by Warsaw. In the mid-1990s, a plan to build and control a rail and road corridor from Belarus to Kaliningrad through Poland (the so-called Suwałki corridor) sparked outrage in Warsaw.[31] Moscow was seen as acting unilaterally and disregarding the security interests and territorial sovereignty of the Polish state. Warsaw retooled its military arsenal largely with purchases from the West, in an effort to become technically compatible with NATO. This had an impact on the traditional arms trade with Russia. Military agreements with Moscow principally covered the servicing and repair of military equipment sold by Russia to Poland during the Soviet era, including a fleet of MiG-29 fighter jets. Russian officials also complained about Polish participation in NATO-led peacekeeping missions in Bosnia-Herzegovina and Kosovo and Warsaw's support for military actions against Iraq, which they described as serving U.S. hegemonic interests.[32]

Reports during 2003 that the United States planned to move some of its military bases and personnel from Germany to Poland caused consternation in Russia and Belarus.[33] In June 2003, Belarusian president Alyaksandr Lukashenka, who was believed to vent Russia's harsher rhetoric, asserted that the potential redeployment of U.S. troops would be an "unwise" move and that Belarus would take "adequate measures." Russia itself is strongly opposed to the stationing of U.S. troops on Polish soil as this purportedly breaks the pledges given to Moscow when Poland and its neighbors joined NATO.[34] Russian analysts claim that such a move will ruin both relations between the United States and Russia, and between Central Europe and Moscow, especially if the Baltic states are involved.[35] According to commentaries calling for more assertive action:

> Russia does not have a policy of strategic interests. Russia was in the same situation under Gorbachev. He could demand that NATO stop its expansion eastward, and the West would have had to obey. Gorbachev preferred to keep silence and withdraw Russian troops from Europe. The consequences are evident: the USSR fell apart, and military airdromes and military settlements were seized by "implacable friends." The US has decided to move its troops from Germany to Poland, Romania and Bulgaria, closer to Russia. . . . U.S. aircraft and ground units will be stationed in Poland, Romania and Bulgaria near the border of the zone of Moscow's strategic influence. In addition, NATO is cherishing plans to create military bases in Azerbaijan, Georgia and the Baltic States.[36]

Although Warsaw reoriented much of its foreign trade westward, it remained highly dependent on Russia for energy supplies. Approximately 90 percent of Russian exports to Poland consist of natural resources (oil, gas, petrochemicals, and metals) and the bulk of Russian investment in the country revolves around Gazprom. Among the oil giants, Yukos established a firmer foothold than Lukoil in Poland and gained a six-year contract in December 2002 that would enable the company to capture about 7 percent of the Polish market by 2009.

Moscow uses its "energy diplomacy" to score political points. During 1993, Warsaw was informed that secure gas supplies would be contingent on the joint construction of a second Yamal pipeline through Poland to Western Europe that would bypass both Ukraine and Lithuania.[37] Such plans were designed to negatively affect Poland's relations with both states and enhance regional wedges that would benefit Russia. Warsaw and Kyiv suddenly found themselves in potential competition for gas transit revenues.[38]

The proposal also served to undermine relations between Poland and Brussels, as there was an impression in Warsaw that the EU was negotiating with Moscow about future gas supplies without considering the interests of the transit states in Central Europe. In this fashion, energy was manipulated by Moscow to promote its foreign and security policies.

Russia's energy giants have purchased large shares in local energy enterprises and sought to control Polish pipelines and refineries in what officials in Warsaw describe as "nontransparent tactics." Moreover, representatives of several Russian companies and financial institutions engage in economic espionage and other covert operations under the camouflage of legitimate business activities. Polish sources regularly complain that Russian energy companies have nontransparent management procedures and some of their activities are suspect. Their attempts at penetration and control could make the Central European economies more vulnerable to sabotage and criminality. Polish officials have also expressed worries about shadowy Polish intermediaries backed by Russia who have gained prominent roles in the country's oil business: "The Polish energy market is murky, full of unclear deals and suspicions of links between business and politics. *Lukoil* knows very well how to exploit this, because the Russian market is even more opaque. . . . By letting in the Russians we will ultimately lose any chance to regulate and make the Polish energy sector more civilized."[39]

In a move to ensure energy diversity and lessen dependence on Russia, in September 2001 Poland signed an agreement with Norway even though Norwegian gas supplies were some 30 percent more expensive than Russian.[40] Moscow tried to counter this energy diversification: Gazprom and its Polish subsidiary Bartimpeks lobbied hard to discourage Poland from building new pipelines that would transmit gas from Norway. Gazprom also refused for several years to renegotiate the 1996 gas supply contract that was disadvantageous for Poland unless Warsaw renounced the Polish-Norwegian agreement.[41] The agreement was finally settled in March 2003, in which the volume of Russian gas imports was reduced but the supply period was increased by two years through 2020. The deal led to furious protests by Polish opposition parties, accusing the government of turning the country into a Russian vassal and placing it under a "strategic threat" from Moscow.[42]

Warsaw resisted the sale of Rafineria Gdańska, the country's second largest oil refinery, to Russian bidders. Instead, it searched for sound domestic alternatives in order to keep the refinery in Polish hands. Russian companies have faced substantial opposition, as local firms want the government to restructure the entire Polish oil sector while politicians remain suspicious of Moscow's political intentions.[43] Several other proposals to lessen energy dependence include building a natural gas terminal in Swinoujscie on the Baltic coast that could import gas by ships from Algeria, Nigeria, or Libya, and importing oil from Azerbaijan through alternative oil pipelines that bypass Russia.

Both energy blackmail and inducements are core elements of Russian diplomacy. Moscow's decision in June 2003 not to route increased energy supplies through Poland was linked by the Putin administration with the "hard line" taken by Warsaw and the EU against visa free travel between Russia and Kaliningrad.[44] Warsaw stood to lose a lucrative pipeline and several billion dollars worth of related development projects. Moscow signaled that it considered Ukraine a more reliable partner while Gazprom calculated that modernizing and maintaining the existing route through Ukraine, which carried 90 percent of Russia's gas exports to Europe, was cheaper than building a new pipeline through Poland.

According to Polish statistics, about $1.3 billion of Russian capital entered the country by 2001, making Russia the tenth largest investor. Gazprom is recorded as the fifth largest foreign company in Poland, with most of its holdings in Europol Gaz. In the financial sphere, Russian capital has tried to secure a foothold in Polish banking and to establish branches of Russian banks and other financial agencies. Several financial structures were created with funds transferred by the FSB, Komsomol, and privatized state enterprises:

> The shadowy connections between the business and financial sectors on the one hand and the world of politics, the secret services, and the *mafia* on the other, have been made still more complicated by the establishment of the so-called Financial-Industrial Groups (FIGs). FIGs complicate the situation because they bring under one roof industrial and financial concerns, so making them an even more formidable lobbying force.[45]

In 2002, Gazprom suffered a setback when one of its illicit schemes was exposed and terminated by Warsaw. The company had built a new pipeline across the country, which began to pump gas in September 2000. However, three months later it transpired that Gazprom was also using the route for a high-capacity fiber-optic cable and failed to inform or pay Poland for the contract.[46] Officials accused Gazprom of trying to deny them profits from the cable's lucrative telephone traffic. This incident greatly raised suspicions over Russian tactics and intentions and delayed negotiations over the planned gas pipeline from the Belarusian border to Slovakia.[47] Opinion polls indicated that the majority of citizens viewed investments by large Russian companies as contrary to Poland's national interests. Gazprom also came under suspicion for its close connections with a Polish partner Bartimpeks, which gained a franchise for the country's gas imports. Bartimpeks claimed seventeen former ministers and senior officials on its payroll and its owner, Aleksander Gudzowaty, maintained close ties with several Russian oligarchs. His political influence both in Poland and in Russia remains a subject of police investigation.

Moscow has made it difficult for Polish investors in Russia evidently fearing the growth of Polish and pro-Western influences in the country. For years, the Russian parliament refused to ratify an agreement with Warsaw on the protection of foreign investment although most other states had already implemented such accords with Poland. Polish exports have also been limited as the Russian side often makes imports contingent on Warsaw's purchase of additional raw materials and energy.[48] This has negatively affected Poland's trade balance with Russia.

Due to Poland's ethnic homogeneity and the absence of any sizable autonomist movements involving Russian-speaking populations, there has been little opportunity for Moscow to exploit ethnicity to its advantage. Nonetheless, on certain occasions, officials in Moscow and the Russian media presented Russian visitors, traders, and workers in Poland as being subject to abuse. In November 1994, a planned visit to Warsaw by Viktor Chernomyrdin was postponed to protest the alleged mistreatment by the Polish police of Russian passengers on a long distance train bound for Moscow.

Russian services have had little opportunity to provoke ethnic, social, religious, or regional unrest in Poland or to inflame antigovernmental sentiments. As one of the most homogeneous states in Eastern Europe, with a reasonable record on minority rights and a tiny Russian ethnic population, Warsaw escaped some of the charges leveled against its Baltic neighbors. The only points of attack have consisted of media reports alleging the mistreatment of Russian, Ukrainian, and Belarusian workers and visitors by Polish police. Populism and international isolationism has a limited following in Poland as the overwhelming majority of the population expressed a strong desire to join both NATO and the EU. As a result, there has been little opportunity for Russian manipulation of these issues. National extremists are also commonly anti-Russian and rarely amenable to political exploitation by Moscow. However, suspicions have been aired that Russian money was channeled to radical populist groupings such as the Farmers' Defense organization, which staged numerous anti-European protests and vehemently attacked government ministers.

Moscow persistently tried to discredit the Polish authorities in order to disqualify the country from NATO entry. It exploited policy divisions within the Polish leadership with regard to Warsaw's "eastern policy." Fissures occasionally appeared regarding Warsaw's policy toward Ukraine and Belarus, with some politicians arguing that too much preoccupation with the East could distance Poland from the West as Brussels was concerned that Warsaw was deliberately provoking Moscow. Russian officials also tried to prove that Poland was an unreliable partner for Western institutions by reporting that Polish and other Central European secret services continued to spy on the Alliance.[49]

As in other former satellites, Russian authorities benefited from contacts with former Communist functionaries. The short-lived government of Waldemar Pawlak installed in October 1993 provided such an opportunity. Pawlak sought to establish barter trade in energy and agricultural goods with Russia and seemed more willing to make political concessions to Moscow. Russian officials attempted to play on divisions within the Polish leadership and favored a prime minister who was less enthusiastic about NATO integration than his colleagues. Pawlak also seemed well disposed to Moscow's proposal for a permanent Berlin-Warsaw-Moscow consultative group that would have given Russia influence over the unfolding Polish-German relationship. Such notions were opposed by most Polish officials and discarded when the Pawlak government was replaced in March 1995. The election of President Aleksander Kwaśniewski in November 1995 also raised hopes that the new leader would be more accommodating toward Russia. Moscow's ambassador mentioned at a press interview that Kwaśniewski's intelligence and professionalism were superior to that of outgoing President Lech Wałęsa, because apparently "he knows us and will refrain from stirring up historical matters that are irritants in Polish-Russian relations."[50] Russian praise failed to deter the president from pursuing NATO membership much like his predecessor.

As elsewhere in the region, Russian mafia networks have been active in Poland. Officials have stated that some senior representatives of Russian organized crime have traveled to Poland on diplomatic passports.[51] Additionally, suspicions have been raised that energy companies such as Gazprom conducted their financial transactions through shadowy firms registered in various tax havens. There is a prevalent supposition that their funding is connected with money laundering from illegal energy exports at the expense of the budgets of transit countries in Central Europe.

Moscow employed various tools to thwart or complicate Poland's NATO entry. Russian intelligence services were reportedly involved in discrediting Prime Minister Józef Oleksy. Oleksy resigned in January 1996 following allegations by Poland's Interior Minister that he spied for Moscow when he was a military intelligence agent under the former Communist regime. The leaked details emerged from the files of the former Communist secret police. Russian services had an interest in fabricating or exaggerating the disclosures to heighten suspicions in the West about Poland's reliability as a NATO partner and the trustworthiness of its top politicians.[52] The allegations were dismissed after a prosecutor found there was insufficient evidence to pursue the case.

In July 1999, Polish counterintelligence agents arrested three Polish army officers on charges of spying for Russia since the early 1990s.[53] All three were colonels in military counterintelligence, the nerve center of Poland's armed forces, and were unmasked by a double agent. In a previous incident in 1993, Polish agents caught Major Marek Zieleński, a secret policeman, as he handed papers to a Russian military attaché. The military officers worked for the Soviet Union until its collapse and then for Russia. Russian intelligence retained high-quality espionage networks and kept a vast store of intelligence material gathered during the Communist period. This top-secret archive is known as the "Blackmailer's Treasurehouse" and contains details on the private lives of tens of thousands of citizens in Central Europe.

A major public feud erupted between Warsaw and Moscow in January 2000 as disclosures were made over extensive Russian espionage activities. Nine Russian diplomats were declared *personae non grata* and expelled from the country, many of them caught on videotape picking up or leaving material at hidden drops. They had penetrated sectors of the Polish government and used "aggressive operational resources" to gather classified information illegally.[54] Moscow responded by declaring the move an "anti-Russian provocation" and expelling nine Polish diplomats from Moscow. The authorities capitalized on the expulsions to heat up tensions with Warsaw and to support demonstrations outside the Polish embassy in Moscow. The conflict led Foreign Minister Ivanov to cancel a visit to Warsaw in February 2000. In addition, Gazprom's clandestine high-capacity fiber-optic cable was viewed as a means of providing a permanent intelligence carrier across Poland.

Poland's former defense minister Jan Parys confirmed in April 2001 that Russia's intelligence services have agents ensconced within the Polish banking sector, the government, and even Poland's security services and parliamentary parties, especially inside the post-Communist Party of the Democratic Left (PDL).[55] In March 1999, Poland expelled fifteen Russian businessmen on the grounds of a threat to national security and other spy-business networks are believed to be operational.[56] Warsaw attempted to uncover sleepers and active agents during its domestic political lustration campaign, but thousands of pages of relevant documentation disappeared before a proper investigation could be undertaken. Polish analysts also reported that Gazprom's activities in Central Europe included intelligence gathering. Former Polish premier Jan Olszewski believes that dozens of government officials who regulated the gas and oil sector are now working for the Gazprom joint venture in Poland.

HUNGARY

Hungary and Russia signed a treaty of friendship and cooperation in December 1991, although ratification was delayed by the Duma. In November 1992, Yeltsin visited Budapest and the two sides signed seven agreements, including financial settlements related to the Red Army withdrawal and the repayment of Russia's debt. Yeltsin also condemned the 1956 Soviet invasion and crushing of the Hungarian revolution, but soured this with a reference to Hungary's supposed "liberation" by the Red Army in 1945. Moscow's position hardened after Hungary petitioned for NATO membership. In a speech delivered in Budapest in November 1994, Yeltsin lambasted NATO and the new aspirant states for seeking to enlarge the Alliance. He warned about the dawn of a "cold peace" between Russia and NATO and threatened the Central European democracies for their desire to join the Alliance. Although relations between Budapest and Moscow subsequently stabilized, a strong element of mistrust remained on the Hungarian side. In Hungary's National Security Strategy issued in May 2002, Russia was qualified as a country with "a significant impact on the security of Hungary. . . though the threats connected to domestic instability have decreased, they have not been ruled out completely."[57]

Russia's propaganda attacks on Hungary have been more muted than against Poland, especially as the country does not occupy such a strategically sensitive position next to the CIS region. Moreover, Budapest's ambitions to join NATO were less strident than in the case of Warsaw, while Hungary seemed less concerned with the CIS than with northern and southern neighbors containing sizable Magyar populations. Nonetheless, Budapest's NATO decision was described as erroneous by Russian officials.

During the withdrawal of the Red Army, threats were issued by General Burlakov, the commander of Soviet troops, who asserted that he would slow down or halt the evacuation if Moscow's financial demands from Budapest were not realized.[58] Burlakov's comments led to high-level government protests and the military threat did not materialize. However, they aptly illustrated the impunity and arrogance of Russian military commanders and the disdain in which they held their East European former satellites. Moscow did not issue any specific threats against Hungary, but the criticisms it lodged against Poland as that country prepared for NATO membership applied to other Central European states. Prime Minister Viktor Orbán's comment in October 1999 that his government would consider allowing the United States to deploy nuclear weapons in Hungary "during a crisis" outraged Russian officials and led to the postponement of premier Kasyanov's visit to Budapest.[59]

Since Putin's appointment, Moscow has endeavored to boost its arms sales to former Warsaw Pact states and recapture some of this market from the West. In 2001, Russia's MiG company signed an agreement with Budapest guaranteeing operations of its MiG-29 planes until the end of 2005.[60] Similar contracts were initialed with Poland, Slovakia, and Bulgaria. However, Budapest remained wary of Russian military dependence and in September 2001 opted to lease fourteen Swedish-British Gripen JAS-39 fighter jets instead of rebuilding its MiG 29-s.[61]

In terms of Russia's "energy diplomacy," in 2000 the petrochemical firm Sibur, a Gazprom subsidiary, purchased substantial shares in Hungary's two largest chemical enterprises, BorsodChem and Tiszai Vegyi Művek (TVK). Several foreign companies, including Millford Holdings, a nominally Irish firm that tried to purchase BorsodChem, were fronts for Gazprom. These efforts provoked consternation in government circles and created a panic on the Hungarian stock exchange as officials and investors feared that Gazprom could capture control over a lucrative sector of Hungarian industry. Hungary's National Financial Supervisory Agency also began investigations of money-laundering allegations. Despite the protests, Gazprom obtained majority control over BorsodChem through Sibur and installed its representatives on the Hungarian company's board.

Gazprom's takeover precipitated an official investigation on suspicion that it had violated several Hungarian laws. Balázs Horváth, the former head of Hungary's security service, called the takeover "an extremely serious national security risk."[62] Government spokesmen claimed that "dirty money laundering operations" were behind the BorsodChem affair as greater volumes of money flowed through the accounts of companies involved than their disposable capital would warrant. A member of the parliament's Committee for National Security, in referring to secret service analyses, asserted that the entry of Gazprom and its subsidiaries into the Hungarian chemical company represented a danger to national security.[63] The deal also prompted MOL, Hungary's leading oil and gas company, and Polish oil giant PKN Orlen to pledge to join forces to prevent future takeovers by Russian companies.

Russian business is seeking to become more integrated into Hungary's energy sector through privatization. In the early 1990s, they were hampered by state regulation and the strong position of national companies. In the mid-1990s, five Hungarian gas companies were privatized while Gazprom was banned from participating in the tenders. This changed after 1998 when oil prices increased and Russian companies possessed extensive resources to purchase shares abroad. Russian firms sought to acquire control over Hungarian energy distribution companies. In early 2002, Yukos reached an agreement with MOL to become partners in pumping oil from one of the Siberian oilfields. This could significantly enhance Yukos expansion throughout Central Europe. A substantial percentage of MOL itself is controlled by Russian economic interests.

Russian capital has increased its role in Hungary over the past decade. Hungarian authorities have viewed this trend with some trepidation and imposed restrictions. According to official records, around $51 million of CIS capital has been invested in Hungarian privatization, but the actual amount is estimated to be in excess of $200 million.[64] In September 2003, Moscow and Budapest signed an agreement on cooperation in the sphere of information technology.[65] This would include intergovernmental collaboration in the development of telecommunication services, especially satellite communications and digital TV broadcasting, and a Russian-Hungarian task force for information technologies would be formed. Russian companies were also hoping to win a tender for the privatization of the Dunaferr steel mill.

In January 2003, Moscow and Budapest initialed an agreement settling Russia's debt, worth $467 million plus interest. Much of this sum was scheduled to be repaid through the supply of Russian goods.[66] Russian companies have also moved into Hungary's banking sector.[67] In June 1996, Gazprom purchased the Általános Értékforgalmi Bank (AEB), enabling it to better handle its transactions with Hungarian gas importers. Russia is also interested in investing in Hungary's steel industry and building the new metro extension in Budapest. While the Socialist administration seemed more amenable to Russian investment, the previous center-right government was extremely suspicious. In an address delivered in February 2002, Prime Minister Viktor Orbán alluded to Russian economic penetration by pointing out that for the first time in history Russian capital was flowing into Central Europe rather than Central European capital flowing out to Russia. However, according to the premier, the question remained whether this "can be considered foreign trade or foreign policy."[68]

Russia has tried to find common ground with its former satellites as an enticement for establishing a new alliance. One of the ploys adopted by Moscow vis-à-vis Budapest was to try and link the Russian and Hungarian minority issues as a basis for interstate cooperation.[69] A declaration of cooperation in "Assuring the Rights of National, Ethnic, Religious, and Linguistic Minorities" was signed in November 1992. However, it remained a paper accord only as Hungary avoided becoming associated with Russia's more aggressive policy toward its neighbors in defense of its large diaspora.

Russia made attempts to discredit the pro-Western and pro-NATO Hungarian government by playing on the Roma question, which it calculated was sensitive in Western capitals. In early 2001, a small group of Roma left Hungary to apply for political asylum in Strasbourg and alleged massive discrimination in Hungary. The incident led to suspicions of involvement by Russian intelligence services and Budapest did not deny the allegations. Members of the Roma community of Zámoly were encouraged by Russian operatives to plead persecution and violation of human rights before EU bodies and to request political asylum in order to damage Hungary's reputation.[70] The Roma question was precisely the issue over which the EU had persistently criticized Budapest. This method of active disinformation by manipulating innocent third parties was reportedly first attempted by Russian secret services in the Czech Republic before being transplanted to Hungary.

Some center-right politicians suspect that the Socialist Party, similarly to other post-Communist formations, has long-standing personal connections with Moscow and is more likely to enable Russian companies to enter the country. Former senior officials in Budapest also claim that Russian agents have penetrated Hungarian intelligence and security services primarily to gain information on the country's integration westward.

Dozens of Russian criminal groups operate in Hungary and have been responsible for a series of violent incidents.[71] As a result of their activities, the U.S. Federal Bureau of Investigation (FBI) opened an office in the Hungarian capital in March 2000 and works closely with local law enforcement personnel.[72] Budapest requested help from Washington in both breaking up Russian gangs and sharing criminal intelligence. One target of the authorities was Semyon Mogilevich, a Russian operating out of Budapest who trafficked drugs, refugees, and weapons. Another major Russian crime group, the Solntsevskaya organization, also stepped up its operations out of Budapest. An FBI report issued in 1995 described Solntsevskaya as the most powerful "Eurasian" crime organization in terms of wealth, influence, and financial control.

CZECH REPUBLIC

In April 1992, Presidents Václav Havel and Boris Yeltsin initialed a treaty of friendship and cooperation between Czechoslovakia and Russia. The text referred to the 1968 Soviet-led invasion of Czechoslovakia as an unjustified use of force and the two sides agreed on financial issues pertaining to the withdrawal of Red Army forces. However, the subsequent treaty in August 1993 between the Czech Republic and Russia (following Czech independence), as well as the one signed with Slovakia, lacked any apology for the 1968 intervention.[73] This was a consequence of the hardening of Russian foreign policy after 1992. Relations between Russia and the Czech Republic were devoid of major controversies but they also fell short of cordiality and partnership. Havel himself is unpopular in Moscow as a major symbol of anti-Communism and anti-Sovietism. On the other hand, concern about Russia is not as pronounced in the Czech Republic as in Poland, Hungary, or the Baltic states. Reportedly, only 3 percent of the population express fear of Russia in public opinion polls and geographical distance plays an important role. Apprehensions about Russian policies and intentions surface when there are international crises, such as over Iraq, Kosovo, or Bosnia.

Prague adopted a pragmatic position vis-à-vis Moscow as it was primarily interested in developing productive economic ties while lessening its dependence on Russian energy and recovering the bulk of Russia's debt. In February 2001, Czech and Russian foreign ministers agreed on the need to establish a regular dialogue.[74] Igor Ivanov was the first Russian foreign minister to visit the Czech Republic after 1994. Czech foreign minister Jan Kavan admitted that a "certain slowing down" and cooling of mutual relations had taken place in previous years. Ivanov also met with Havel and there was agreement that Czech membership in NATO was not an obstacle to relations with Russia. Under President Václav Klaus relations with Russia continued to improve and Moscow welcomed a Czech head of state who was less critical or suspicious of Russian policy than his predecessor.[75]

The Russian authorities have periodically voiced opposition to Prague's security and foreign policies, especially with regard to NATO enlargement. However, public campaigns have never been as vociferous as in the case of Poland. Russian capital has also attempted to gain control of some parts of the Czech media. Following a major financial scandal, it was widely suspected that the private TV Nova was purchased by Russian business.[76] TV Nova was the most influential television station in the Czech Republic and one of four national stations. In March 2000, the director of TV Duha, Karel Soukup, revealed that he was offered ten million crowns by Russian businessmen for a stake in the regional television station: "they promised that they would provide enough millions to equip the studio on condition that the broadcast will continue under their guidelines."[77] The offer was rejected, as the businessmen demanded a deciding stake in the station, which is watched by owners of cable televisions and satellite dishes.

A major theme of Russian state propaganda in opposition to NATO enlargement was that the economies and living standards of the new members would deteriorate. Moscow claimed that the cost of NATO entry would be astronomical and that the Western powers were unwilling to pay for the new burdens. The Russian press actively campaigned vis-à-vis the Czech Republic, where public support for NATO absorption was lackluster, to present the image of a pauperized country needing to upgrade its military spending in order to meet stringent Alliance requirements.[78]

In January 1990, Prague announced that the Treaty on the Temporary Stationing of Soviet Troops on Czechoslovak Territory was invalid and insisted on the withdrawal of all Red Army troops. During Havel's visit to Moscow in February 1990, an agreement was signed on the evacuation of over 73,000 Soviet soldiers, with a deadline set for June 1991. Prague also urged the dissolution of the Warsaw Treaty Organization, which finally occurred in July 1991. Since that time there has been no significant security link between Prague and Moscow other than some law enforcement cooperation in combating organized crime.

Moscow has not issued any specific threats against the Czech Republic, although it strongly criticized Prague's preparations for NATO entry. Russian authorities were angered by Havel's comments prior to the first round of NATO enlargement that he could not imagine Russia as a member as it was too big to absorb and had not fully discarded its imperial impulses. Havel also urged cooperation between the Alliance and the Russian Federation. In a visit to Prague in March 2001, Yegor Stroyev, the chairman of the Russian Federation Council (upper house of parliament), expressed fears about the alleged "militarization of Europe" in connection with NATO enlargement to include countries of the former Soviet bloc.[79] The chairman of the Czech Senate, Petr Pithart, told journalists after the meeting: "We tried to explain to him that our entry to NATO does not mean the militarization of Europe and we have proved this with figures." Evidently, the Russian official was not persuaded.

Havel strongly supported further rounds of NATO expansion to include the Baltic states. Shortly after Putin's appointment in January 2000, Havel asserted that Russia had "no right to oppose NATO enlargement" and comments by Putin that NATO expansion eastward was "unacceptable" and harkened back to the Cold War.[80] According to Havel, Moscow apparently still believed that "the principal mission of NATO is to confront Russia, for whom the enlargement of the Alliance constitutes a threat." He restated his position during the visit to Prague of Russia's Foreign Minister Ivanov that same month. In a major speech in Bratislava in May 2001, Havel vigorously supported swift NATO expansion into the Baltic states and reprimanded Moscow for its "absurd" opposition to enlargement.[81]

Revelations surfaced at the Czech Defense Ministry indicating penetration by Russian intelligence. In March 2003, the minister of defense, Jaroslav Tvrdík, announced that he had ordered purges of the Czech army's Military Intelligence Service (Vojenská Zpravodajská Služba, VZS).[82] About 100 officers with ties to the former Communist regime were to be sacked in the wake of a scandal involving a former VZ intelligence agent facing criminal charges. VZ ranks included Soviet-era intelligence officers who maintained their positions despite the democratic changes. Some of these individuals were suspected of maintaining links with their counterparts in Moscow. It was discovered that several officers had been duplicating secret documents and storing copies in their office safes. This incident raised suspicions that classified information related to NATO may have been supplied to third parties. Several VZS officers obtained their intelligence training in the former USSR at academies operated by either Soviet military intelligence (GRU) or the KGB. Even if they were not suspected of illegal activities, they were viewed as security risks owing to the Russian practice of maintaining personnel files containing compromising material for purposes of blackmail. Tvrdík asserted that the VZS would have to be completely reorganized as a result of the scandals.

Political turmoil and unpredictability in Russia for much of the 1990s was viewed as a serious economic and security risk by Prague.[83] One Czech priority was to build a technical infrastructure enabling it to import gas and oil from alternative sources. This included supplies of gas from deposits in the North Sea to gradually reduce dependence on Russia. However, by 2001 Russian gas and oil still accounted for 74 percent and 68 percent of total imports, respectively. Energy supplies were used as a lever by Moscow as the momentum for the Czech Republic's NATO accession accelerated. Prior to the July 1997 NATO summit in Madrid, the Russian ambassador indicated that Czech entry into the Alliance could have negative consequences for deliveries of gas supplies. Although the Foreign Ministry reassured the Czechs that the threat was unwarranted, Prague endeavored to lessen its dependence by signing a deal with Norway on supplies of natural gas despite the higher price. Some Czech energy companies, including the Moravian Oil Mines, were also believed to be penetrated by Russian crime syndicates.[84]

Soon after restoring its independence, Prague pushed to reorient its economy and markets westward and to attain EU membership. It also wanted to regain Russia's debts and ensure the steady supply of energy resources. By 2002, about 80 percent of Russian exports to the Czech Republic consisted of fuel and raw materials. Moscow's debt to the Czechs by the late 1990s amounted to around $3.7 billion and was the largest foreign debt owed to Prague. It proved a serious obstacle to economic relations, as the debtor nation was unable or unwilling to pay. Moscow repeatedly broke repayment schedules and obstructed effective debt restructuring. Trade and investment have also been restricted because Czech businesses have feared the risks involved in dealing with Russia.

According to Czech reports, Russian capital is flowing into the country at an "alarming rate." These deals have ranged from property buyouts to investments in strategic industries.[85] Prior to retiring from office in June 2002, former Czech Social Democratic prime minister Miloš Zeman inaugurated the costly D-47 highway project that will link the economically depressed region of Northern Moravia with the rest of the country. No public tender was issued, while ostensibly the construction company selected by the government to build the highway was Israeli. However, the company's management consisted of Russian émigrés with strong links to the Kremlin, while Russian mafia ties were also suspected.

A further illustration of corrupting Russian influences was the deal brokered in October 2001 to settle the $3.7 billion debt. The Social Democratic government selected Falcon Capital to resolve the debt issue. This was a financial group with close relations to Russian officials and with criminal connections. By 2003, only one third of the Russian debt was recovered by the Czechs through Falcon amid suspicions of corruption and bribery.[86] This highly secretive deal involved the sale of $2.5 billion of the debt to Falcon in exchange for an upfront payment of $547 million. A further 46 percent of the total sum owed by Moscow was written off. As part of the agreement, Prague accepted Russian arms supplies and a fleet of civilian transport ships. Moscow also tried to coax the Czechs into accepting military hardware, including MiG-29 fighters, as a means of settling its debt. Their offers were rejected on the grounds that the Czech Republic intended to join NATO and preferred to procure Western weapons systems compatible with its new allies. Prague would have to upgrade the MiGs to NATO standards, which is an extremely costly proposition.

Moscow has largely desisted from exploiting ethnic issues in the Czech Republic. However, the position of the Roma minority has sometimes been highlighted by Russian officials and media to paint the Czech Republic as a flawed democracy. Moscow has also voiced concern about the alleged mistreatment of Russian nationals by the Czech authorities after a new law on foreigners came into effect in January 2000.[87] Russia also expressed regret at Prague's introduction of visa regulations for Russian citizens.

It is unclear whether all scandals involving government officials are simply linked with corruption or if they are politically motivated. In July 2002, a major scandal in Prague involved a senior Czech foreign ministry official who paid for the assassination of award-winning investigative journalist Sabina Slonková from the Mladá Fronta Dnes newspaper. Slonková was investigating former Foreign Ministry Secretary-General Karel Srba's involvement in a corruption scandal related to Czech government-owned property in Moscow.[88] The accusations centered on the leasing of the Český Dům (Czech House) in Moscow to a Russian hotel group linked to the Putin government for a rate much lower than the property's actual market value. This deal resulted in a $3.3 million loss to the Czech state. Srba, a key aide to former Foreign Minister Kavan, resigned in March 2001 but denied any criminal activity. He was subsequently arrested in connection with the Slonková assassination plot. He had served as a Czech army intelligence agent since the 1980s with close ties to Russia. As a result of this scandal, Czech Minister of Defense Jaroslav Tvrdík dismissed the head of Czech army intelligence Andor Sandor. The incident tarnished the reputation of Czech intelligence services in the eyes of other NATO members.

As in other East European states, contacts between members of former Communist parties have been maintained. However, the Czech case is unique in the region, as the Communist Party of Bohemia and Moravia has upheld political continuity, a substantial support base, and a respectable parliamentary presence. It maintains ties with the Russian Communist Party, as they are the two largest Communist parties in the post-Soviet era. Although these ties are not seen as a threat to the democratic system, they nevertheless indicate a continuing Russian influence in Czech politics and the ongoing manipulation of social discontent with economic conditions that remain harsh among some sectors of society.

According to Slovak government reports, Russian intelligence agencies subcontracted Slovak secret policemen to sabotage NATO expansion by discrediting the country's pro-Western neighbors.[89] The report accused members of the SIS, the Slovak intelligence agency under the Mečiar regime, of subcontracting itself to Moscow for various plots in the Czech Republic and Hungary. These aimed to exploit traditional rivalries and inflame doubts about suitability for NATO membership. Some schemes employed members of organized criminal gangs. Among the campaigns was one designed to aid the Czech skinhead movement. According to the report: "As part of *Operation Dezo,* active measures were to be implemented to provoke among ordinary Czechs neo-fascist campaigns and racist moods and to sour the Romany issue to prevent the Czech Republic from being admitted to Euro-Atlantic structures. The goal of *Operation Neutron* was to provoke discussion among the Czech public on the country's entry to NATO." The plans were concocted by Ivan Lexa, a former SIS head, and Vladimír Mečiar, confidant. In return, Moscow helped to train SIS agents in 1996 and 1997.

The close ties that developed between the Mečiar regime in Slovakia and Moscow during the 1990s, while not threatening to Prague, were considered to be regionally destabilizing. Bratislava was feared to be a "playground" for Moscow. Also troubling have been alleged ties between Czech radical leftist groups and Russian government bodies.[90] According to a report on the state of extremism in the Czech Republic drafted in 1999 by the Interior and Justice Ministries, Czech neo-Bolsheviks maintain contacts in former Soviet republics, "including ties with official state structures." Anarchists, the Party of Czechoslovak Communists (KSČ), led by the pre-1989 Communist functionary Miroslav Štěpán, and supporters of the idea of "Slavic brotherhood" are also listed in the report. According to Czech intelligence, Russian agents operating on Czech territory maintain clandestine contacts with members of extremist groups. The purpose is to reinforce negative dispositions toward NATO and the United States. The number of leftist extremists exceeds that of rightist radicals; they possess higher social credit, are more tightly linked to civic society, and have better opportunities to reach the public. However, Czech involvement in NATO is also opposed by rightist extremists and in this respect they cooperate with leftist agitators.

According to Czech counterintelligence, international organized crime in the country was most often linked to Russian-speakers.[91] During the 1990s, the Czech lands became a central location for Russian criminal organizations in the region. They engaged in financial fraud and the infiltration of business and governmental structures. Some maintained close contacts with Czech businesses and banks or established trading companies that focused on the purchase of real estate, particularly luxury buildings. Moreover, illicit organizations were switching from criminal activities to legal business using fraudulently gained capital. Russian criminals seek influence in strategic branches of the economy, corrupt the state administration, and impact on its decisionmaking. They also endeavored to penetrate the major political parties and local administrations. The Russian mafia primarily operates in the hotel and restaurant businesses, drug trafficking, and prostitution. The Czech police have not been effective in combating these mobsters, leading to speculation of corruption and criminal payoffs. According to National Drug Squad director Jiří Komorous, drug gangs from the former Soviet Union appeared on the Czech drug scene in 1999. During that year, customs officials seized a large number of illegally exported weapons destined for the Russian drug mafia, which trades in various kinds of narcotics, including highly concentrated heroin.

Thousands of Russian businessmen, both legitimate and illicit, operate in the Czech Republic. Russian intelligence services primarily target such individuals to gain information on Czech economic and political life.[92] The Bohemian city of Karlovy Vary has become a notorious center of Russian immigration and criminality. Prague's intelligence service report that the KGB successors have gained a foothold in western Bohemia and have bought up property worth $30 million. Karlovy Vary has become a western bastion for Russian money launderers, illegal immigrants, and intelligence agents.[93] Real estate and land have also been purchased by the Russian embassy, while organized immigration has become a lucrative illicit venture.[94] Migrant smuggling is a major problem in the Czech Republic as the country is an important transit route to Western Europe and smugglers often dump migrants in Czech cities.

Czech intelligence and security officials have expressed grave concern that the country continues to be drawn closer into the Russian camp. Security Information Service (Bezpečnostní Informační Služba, BIS) officers have regularly submitted security reports to the government regarding the high level of Russian intelligence and organized criminal activity in the country, and the attempted penetration of Czech politics at the national, regional, and municipal levels. However, no significant action was taken to combat the threat.[95] Although the Czech police have found it difficult to effectively combat the mafia because of poor cooperation with Russian police, they have occasionally registered success. In December 2000, police in Prague and Brno arrested seven high-ranking members of the "Luhansk brigade," one of the strongest Russian-speaking criminal organizations operating in the country.[96] The Luhansk brigade is responsible for blackmailing businessmen, arms trafficking, money forging, and violent crimes. Besides the Czech Republic, the gang's terrain included Slovakia and Hungary.

In unveiling banking scandals in the Czech Republic, especially in the largest privatized Czech bank, Komerční Banka (KB), investigators discovered a labyrinth of unsavory connections. These included money laundering from the post-Soviet territories and links with Russian grain exporters, a known cover for the activities of the notorious Russian criminal, Semjon Mogilevic. He is suspected of having organized in the Czech Republic and elsewhere in Central Europe a major tax fraud in the import of heating oil and diesel fuel from Russia. Some Czech officials and "privatization speculators" evidently benefited from the deals. Mogilevic was also reported to be the mastermind behind the transfers of billions of dollars from Russia to the Bank of New York, embezzled from the IMF's disbursements to Russia. "Disturbing patterns of possible networking between some Czech government officials, political parties, state-owned companies, and Russian organized crime seem to appear in the picture, with potentially far-reaching consequences."[97]

A sizable illicit trade involving criminal and official Russian connections has been linked to arms sales on Czech territory. Russian banks were behind the Czech company Agroplast, based in Liberec, north Bohemia, on which the United States imposed sanctions on suspicion of mediating the sale of forty MiG-21 fighter planes to North Korea.[98] Agroplast was described as one of the largest international arms smuggling groups, trading in weapons manufactured in Russia and other CIS states. In 1999, Agroplast managers were also suspected of signing contracts for supplies of engines for MiG-29 fighter jets to Iran. Russian banks were behind the Kazakh firm Metallist, also involved in the deal. The participation of Russian banks may have been connected with an intervention by Moscow Mayor Yuriy Luzhkov, after which two Agroplast managers were released following their detention earlier in the year. The Czech police accused the two entrepreneurs of unauthorized trade in weapons and prosecuted them as fugitives.

Czech agencies report a significant increase in espionage and special influence activities by Russia's intelligence services during the 1990s.[99] Russian agents maintain contacts with extremist groupings, police, military personnel, and local government officials. In addition, Russian military intelligence has endeavored to penetrate several Czech ministries, including Transport and Defense, in order to obtain classified information and strategic technologies. The purchase of media outlets and Internet providers has also facilitated Russian intelligence penetration.

In its annual report for 2000, Czech counterintelligence asserted that Russian intelligence agencies were attempting to penetrate Czech ministries for the purpose of collecting classified information.[100] Official reports by BIS in 1996 and 1997 claimed: "The activities of these intelligence services are posing one of the most significant security risks to the Czech Republic." The number of agents was unusually high given the country's size; the Russian embassy staff in Prague was three times larger than in Warsaw. Russian networks constructed a web of lobbying agencies to try and "influence the decision making process in local governments, to disseminate misinformation, to undermine the country's credibility abroad, and to make the Czechs suspicious as regards the course of action taken by the authorities." The latter included casting doubts about the country's NATO's membership and the high cost of Czech involvement in foreign military missions, with corresponding cuts in public welfare benefits.

According to BIS reports, there was a link between the increased activity of Russia's secret services and Putin's appointment. One half of the Russian diplomats in Prague are believe to be spies out of a total embassy staff of about 400. Russian intelligence services have displayed an increased interest in nuclear, chemical, and biological warfare following the beginning of testing operations at the Temelín nuclear power plant. The BIS also claims that Russia was building "a system of pressure agencies" to influence decisionmaking at the local administrative level, as well as spreading false information aimed at discrediting the Czech Republic abroad. These efforts were intended to raise questions about Czech participation in NATO peacekeeping operations and the purchase of new fighters for the Czech air force. In February 2000, the BIS uncovered a spy among diplomats at the Russian embassy and the suspect was expelled.[101] Russia immediately retaliated by expelling an officer in the military section of the Czech embassy in Moscow. This case was the first of its kind in the Czech Republic on the public record. The agent was an assistant of the military attaché who was collecting information on NATO equipment. In October 1999, press reports in

Britain alleged that Russia was constructing a large spy network in the Czech Republic directed against NATO.[102]

Czech secret services note an increased interest of Russian intelligence, especially the GRU, in information concerning modern military equipment, which NATO was reportedly moving to the Czech Republic. This included information from the Aero Vodochody aircraft maker, in which a majority stake was held by America's Boeing company, whose fighters represented a significant part of the NATO air force. Czech military secret services placed several officers into companies in which data from NATO was used and the expelled Russian diplomat contacted one of the Aero employees who turned out to be a counterintelligence agent. The Russian wanted the employee to provide him with "technical documents" that could be used in modernizing Russia's armed forces and offered a high sum for the information. Western intelligence agencies also reported a high volume of secret communications between the GRU's Prague Field Office and its stations in Germany and Austria, indicating a regionwide coordination of military espionage.

Russian agents have constructed an espionage network focusing on high-priority groups, including leftists, ambitious young politicians, trade unionists, businessmen with Russian connections, and students. Policemen and army officers have also been approached. Former Communist secret police agents in senior business or government positions are primary security risks because they are potentially open to extortion. Vulnerable themselves, these people usually also possess information that can be used for blackmailing others.[103] Fears surfaced in Prague that some personnel in the state apparatus and the intelligence services were unreliable in sharing classified information with NATO because of their ties with Russian secret services.[104] In January 2002, Czech services blocked investigation of a former Communist-era intelligence officer with close links to Moscow, raising concerns whether they were trustworthy partners for Western intelligence.[105] The individual in question met regularly with members of Russia's SVR, including the chargé d'affaires of the Russian consulate in Brno.

Czech analysts have complained about the unwillingness of successive governments to reform the country's four intelligence services (two civilian and two military), indicating that some senior officials continue to cooperate with Moscow. In 2000, Interior Minister Václav Grulich resigned, exasperated with efforts to derail his investigations into organized crime: "no objective police investigator or intelligence officer will investigate Russian espionage or organized crime activities in the Czech Republic for fear of losing his or her position, or worse."[106] Success in combating organized crime is not a guarantee for promotion in the Czech police service. Several police officials who oversaw the arrest of Russian and Ukrainian mobsters at Prague's U Holubů restaurant in April 1995 were later dismissed. The U Holubů incident was one of the largest roundups of Russian and Ukrainian gangster bosses that revealed a wealth of information on the criminal underworld. However, the attention drawn by the raid to the activities of the Russian mafia was unwelcome to some officials with purported ties to Moscow.

In February 2002, the Czech media reported that American officials were pondering whether to provide Prague with access to top-secret information on its nuclear weapons. Premier Miloš Zeman's close adviser Miroslav Slouf, who had a Communist past, together with several other individuals close to the Prime Minister, allegedly jeopardized the credibility of the Czech Republic among NATO allies. In August 2003, the Czech media reported that military intelligence (VZS) continued to employ people who served the Communist regime. The VZS's most important department, intelligence operations, was headed by Jan Kocourek, who was dismissed as military attaché at the Czech embassy in Bonn in 1994 because of his past links with the Communist government.[107] Paradoxically, allegations about links with the Soviet past served Moscow's interests as it sowed distrust within the expanding Alliance.

SLOVAKIA

Moscow viewed Slovakia as the "weak link" in Central Europe and together with Serbia the country was described as a "bulwark" of Russian policy in the region. This was a direct consequence of Bratislava's foreign policy approach during most of the 1990s under the Vladimír Mečiar regime. The governing elite considered relations with Russia as a strategic alternative to NATO and European integration. This was largely a product of self-serving economic calculations by the ruling party.[108] Some Slovak leaders viewed the country as a bridge between Russia and the West, thus justifying close relations with Moscow. They calculated on acquiring significant economic benefits from such an arrangement while preventing a potential loss of power that would have resulted from opening the country to stronger Western influences. Slovak "exceptionalism" was also based on historic grounds where fear and resentment of Russia were muted.

Slovakia under Mečiar became the only Central European state that accepted the "Kvitsinsky Doctrine" and signed a basic treaty with Russia. The doctrine was named after the Soviet deputy foreign minister Yuliy Kvitsinsky who led negotiations in 1991 to forge bilateral treaties with all former Warsaw Pact members incorporating a security clause denying their right to enter into "hostile alliances." Slovakia's exclusion from the first round of NATO enlargement was considered a diplomatic success in Moscow. In the aftermath of Alliance expansion, Moscow warned about the creation of any multistate alliances in the region that would exclude Russia from one of its traditional "spheres of influence."[109] With the election of a democratic government in Bratislava in September 1998 Moscow's influences came under greater scrutiny. The Putin administration also had to accept Slovakia's NATO invitation at the November 2002 Prague summit.

Moscow had little need for propaganda attacks and disinformation campaigns against the Mečiar regime, which was perceived as a valuable outpost of Russian interests in the heart of the Western-oriented region. Criticisms of the democratic coalition government elected in September 1998 became more commonplace and Russian services bribed or blackmailed editors and journalists to transmit material that would benefit Moscow. There were suspicions in Bratislava that some of the negative reports about government security agencies were manufactured or disseminated by Russian intelligence services. These included claims about the unreliability of Slovak security services and the illicit sale of weapons to internationally sanctioned regimes.[110]

Moscow offered security guarantees for Slovakia's neutrality in an effort to keep the country outside NATO. The Mečiar government welcomed such assurances and was the only Central European administration that stressed Russian objections to NATO enlargement while distancing itself from the Alliance. Tensions with the West over the regime's authoritarian policies pushed Bratislava closer to Russia. The failed May 1997 referendum on NATO membership was well received in Moscow, which had signed several agreements with Bratislava on military cooperation weeks before the ballot.[111] Tensions were raised between the two capitals following the decision of the Mikuláš Dzurinda government in March 1999 to cancel the planned purchase of Russian antimissile systems. Russian officials also objected to Slovakia's NATO bid but did not issue specific threats. During a visit to Bratislava in January 2001, Foreign Minister Ivanov reiterated Moscow's negative stance on NATO enlargement, but did not specify Russia's reaction to the alleged "threat to its national security."[112]

Approximately 98 percent of Slovakia's oil supplies and over 80 percent of gas supplies are imported from Russia. In 1993 Slovakia joined the Surgut Agreement, a CIS-based energy council intended to develop Russian energy exports on a multinational basis. Slovakia became the first country outside the former Soviet Union that joined a CIS body. The Surgut arrangement proved a failure and ceased to exist by the close of 1994. Nevertheless, Russia and Slovakia maintained their "strategic energy cooperation" throughout the Mečiar era. The agreements signed in April 1997 involved increases in the transit of Russian gas through Slovak territory, thus deepening dependence on Russian energy without significantly expanding Slovak trade and exports to Russia. If realized, plans to construct a pipeline system through Belarus and Poland to the West could lessen Slovakia's importance as a transit country while upholding its position as an energy dependent state.

The Mečiar government did not attempt to curtail Slovakia's dependence on Russian energy, which by the mid-1990s exceeded the level before the collapse of Communism. Under both the Mečiar and Dzurinda

administrations, Bratislava signed long-term contracts for increased oil supplies and allowed for major Russian purchases of energy facilities. In January
2002, Yukos acquired 49 percent of Transpetrol, Slovakia's state-owned monopoly pipeline operator. It gained significant managerial powers and greater
control of an important transit route through Europe.[113] The Transpetrol system runs through Slovakia from Ukraine to the Czech Republic and a southern branch connects with the Adria system to Croatia's coast. In January 2002,
Yukos purchased a substantial share in a Slovak pipeline and planned to buy
several Slovak refineries.

In purely economic terms, Russia was less interested in a free trade zone
with the small Slovak market and more focused on buying key strategic sectors and energy transit facilities. During premier Chernomyrdin's visit to
Bratislava in April 1997, eight new Slovak-Russian agreements were signed,
including the establishment of a joint Slovak-Russian company, Slovrusgas,
that was to become the owner of gas transit pipelines over Slovak territory.
In March 2002, Gazprom, in tandem with several West European companies, bought a 49 percent share in Slovakia's gas pipelines.[114] Because
Slovakia's gas pipeline network remains essential for Russian exports to Western Europe, Moscow aspires to fully control the system. Russia is also focused on Slovakia's nuclear capacity and supplies nuclear fuel for two nuclear
power plants, Mochovce and Bohunice, constructed with Russian assistance.
Muscovite companies are hoping to take part in the decommissioning of two
units of the Bohunice plant and the modernization of two other units. They
also plan to participate in the rebuilding of the Mochovce plant.[115] Russia's
RAO UES is interested in purchasing the state-held share in Slovakia's electricity producer Slovenské Elektrárne.

Mečiar established close economic ties with Moscow in order to revive
strategic industrial sectors beneficial to the government and geared to trade
with Russia and the CIS.[116] This helped to ensure the maintenance of large
state-run enterprises, such as the Slovak machine building and arms industries, which were an important component of the ruling Movement for a
Democratic Slovakia (MDS) support base. These heavy industries were
threatened by streamlining or closure in the event of economic reform and
Slovakia's Western integration.[117] By supporting their maintenance, Mečiar
assured himself of a significant voting bloc. He could also distance himself
from Western criticism and receive Moscow's acquiescence for his authoritarian rule, styled as the "Slovak way of transition." Mečiar's Slovakia was
the only Central European state that signed a free trade agreement with
Moscow, received a major Russian loan, and expanded its military dependence on Moscow by acquiring Russian military hardware. Moscow steadily
paid off its $1.3 billion Soviet-era debt to Bratislava: the total debt dropped
to under $100 million by 2003.[118] Bratislava planned to recoup some of
Russia's debt through contracts with Russian companies in high technology
manufactures.[119]

Russian capital has been especially active in banking, energy, and transportation. With the planned privatization of several major strategic industries in 2004, Russian corporations positioned themselves to benefit from the deals. Slovak economists warned that the government needed to be careful about selling remaining shares in the energy sector because it risked endangering the country's independence.[120] The EU and Prague also expressed their disagreement with the proposed free trade zone between Slovakia and Russia. Although Bratislava hesitated in forging such an agreement, pressures from Moscow continued.

During the Mečiar era, the Russian authorities remained largely silent on any conflictive ethnic questions in Slovakia, as Bratislava was a promising ally in the region. Although the Slovak administration was criticized by Western countries and by international organizations for its discriminatory policies toward the large Hungarian and Roma minorities, this had little echo in official Moscow.

The Mečiar regime provided a valuable opportunity for Moscow to influence Slovak foreign policy and to maintain some leverage in Central Europe. The Mečiar regime itself deliberately cultivated its connections with Russia as a form of balance against Western pressures and to delay political and economic reforms. Officials and businessmen within the ruling MDS upheld close links with their Russian counterparts, while President Yeltsin publicly affirmed Kremlin support for Mečiar's reelection in September 1998.

Mečiar's MDS was closely allied with extremist groupings that supported Slovakia's isolation from the West and closer relations with Russia. He was dependent on the Slovak National Party (SNP) and the Association of Slovak Workers (ASW) to ensure a parliamentary majority throughout much of the 1990s. The leader of the ASW, Ján L'á L'upták, declared on a visit to Moscow in May 1996 that Slovakia should remain a neutral country and avoid NATO membership.[121] Connections were also reported between the ultranationalist and anti-NATO Slovak National Party and Russian interest groups. After the victory of democratic forces in September 1998, the MDS went into opposition and maintained its ties with Russian compatriots, the ASW disappeared from the political scene, and the SNP split into two competing factions.

With the election of a pro-Western coalition government in September 1998, Russia lost a reliable partner in Bratislava. Rumors immediately began to circulate that some of the coalition partners were unreliable, corrupt, and tainted with a Communist past. One such persistent allegation in the Slovak and Czech press concerned Pavol Rusko, the leader of the New Citizen Alliance (ANO).[122] Rusko allegedly had ties to Mečiar without whose support he would not have obtained a license in 1996 to establish the Markýza television station. There were also implications that Rusko had ties with Russian secret services and business networks. Scandals surrounding the Slovak intelligence services during 2003 led to suppositions that this was orchestrated by outside powers that sought to discredit Bratislava as a NATO member.

During the Mečiar period, pro-Russian officials and businessmen accumulated sizable assets from dubious privatization schemes in banking, energy, steel, and telecommunications. Some of these arrangements involved illicit practices, including price manipulation, insider information, extortion, and connections with Russian criminal networks.[123] The MDS establishment included some of Slovakia's wealthiest individuals based on the Russian oligarchic model as well as former police chiefs with criminal connections who were dismissed by the government of premier Dzurinda. The most notorious case concerned Ivan Lexa, the head of Slovak counterintelligence under Mečiar. Lexa fled Slovakia after the September 1998 elections charged with overseeing in 1995 the kidnapping of the son of President Michal Kováč, Mečiar's chief political opponent. Lexa was also accused of conspiracy to sabotage the entry of Slovakia and its neighbors into NATO and the EU by manufacturing political scandals.[124] He received assistance from the Russian mafia and was linked with the criminal underworld and Russian intelligence services before his capture in July 2002. According to the Slovak Intelligence Service (Slovenská Informačná Služba, SIS) annual report in 2001, organized crime is controlled by powerful international mafia groups, especially from Russia, Albania, and Italy.[125] Criminal groups focus on drug trafficking and procurement of privatization tenders. Slovakia is also a transport corridor for weapons smuggling, whereby Russian and Ukrainian mafias use their links to the Slovak underworld to smuggle small arms to third countries.

In January 2003, allegations were made by the British defense journal *Jane's Intelligence* that the SIS was involved in arms trafficking, collaborated with Russian intelligence, conducted illegal phone tapping against critical journalists, and engaged in smear campaigns against politicians.[126] Instead of recruiting younger and well-educated pro-Western individuals into the service, the SIS opted for older people previously employed by the former Czechoslovak Communist regime's state security apparatus, which was closely linked with Moscow. Some also served as senior SIS and police officials under the Mečiar regime and were believed to have active ties with the Russian SVR, including SIS director Vladimír Mitro.[127]

NATO leaders expressed concern that the penetration of Slovak intelligence services could compromise its national security and the Alliance as a whole. NATO secretary-general Lord Robertson asserted that Bratislava must persuade the Alliance that its security bodies can be entrusted with classified information and that it has a reliable and independent system of security screening. The Slovak authorities strongly criticized reports that the condition of the SIS was raising serious doubts about the country's eligibility for NATO and EU membership.[128] There were suspicions that the reports were grossly exaggerated and doctored by activists associated with

Mečiar, who maintained active connections with Russian intelligence, in a deliberate antigovernment smear campaign.

A report delivered to parliament in June 2003 by Ladislav Pittner, the director of the SIS, claimed that Russian secret services have stepped up their activities in Slovakia.[129] That same month, a Russian diplomat was expelled from the country on suspicion that he tried to obtain secret information from several Slovak ministries, including Defense. Slovak interior ministry investigators uncovered evidence that intelligence originating within SIS was sold secretly to individuals known to have connections with Russian and Ukrainian intelligence services, as well as with organized crime groups.[130] Speculations grew that Russian services were benefiting from the disarray in the SIS to gather compromising material on pro-Western political figures that could be used to garner political influence in Bratislava.

7

Exploiting Crises: Adriatic Balkans

NO PAIN, NO GAIN: RUSSIA'S BALKAN AMBITIONS

Russia harbors a long-term ambition for a permanent presence in the Balkans. Throughout the post–World War II period, the Soviet Union was determined to retain control in the eastern part of the region while seeking to reestablish its influence in Yugoslavia and Albania. Since the end of the Cold War, Moscow's Balkan policy has been two-tracked: to limit U.S. and NATO influence and to upgrade Russia's presence. Even when its influence was limited, Moscow endeavored to uphold the appearance of great power status. According to one Russian commentator, Kremlin leaders were "preoccupied with inventing national interests for Russia," so they could then publicly defend them. Moscow's Balkan policy was one such invention.[1] Although in a clearly inferior military position to that of the United States and NATO, Russia viewed the Balkans as an opportunity to gain leverage through crisis and to create a counterbalance to growing American influence. Furthermore, the emerging Caspian–Black Sea energy network invigorated Russian concerns that it not be excluded from a major transit region: "Russia more often than not displays a self-serving attitude in its apparent pursuit of milieu goals. Russian partisanship in the wars in ex-Yugoslavia, allegedly in order to help their Serbian brethren, has above all been instrumental for propelling Russia into a position of influence."[2]

During the 1990s, the Kremlin obstructed an effective Western policy toward former Yugoslavia in order to enhance its prestige and to weaken the credibility of NATO's projected new missions in Europe's troublespots. Prime Minister Primakov favored a strategy that focused on states and regions where the West was facing problems such as the Balkans. Moscow adopted a pro-Serbian stance during the wars in Croatia, Bosnia-Herzegovina, and Kosovo, undermined international efforts to apply effective pressure on Belgrade, and sought to prevent NATO deployments in the former Yugoslavia. Despite its concentration on the region, Moscow suffered various setbacks. The restoration of the Serbian-occupied territories to Croatian control after 1995 was perceived as a serious defeat for Moscow's Yugoslav project. Even more troublesome, NATO's relative success in Bosnia-Herzegovina from the summer of 1995 onward was viewed negatively by Russian policymakers as it enhanced the credibility of the Alliance as the key institution of collective security in Europe.

Russia's military leadership desired some degree of confrontation with the West in order to increase military spending and undermine liberal influence in the political establishment. The Yugoslav wars presented opportunities for disputes with NATO, while for the Foreign Ministry any divisions between Europe and the United States over fundamental policy interests benefited Russia's long-range strategy.[3] NATO's military operation against Serbia in the spring of 1999 was condemned as an aggressive war against a "brother Slavic" nation. Milošević's attempted expulsion of Albanian residents from Kosovo was either ignored, downplayed, or depicted as a justifiable policy directed against "Albanian terrorists." With the NATO victory and the emplacement of Alliance troops in Kosovo, Moscow participated in the peace deployment in order to maintain its foothold and prestige in Yugoslavia.

After 1998, Moscow lost a traditional ally in the Balkans when the new democratic government in Bulgaria declared its intention to join NATO and curtail political and economic dependence on Russia. Moscow employed a legion of measures, including diplomatic threats and energy blackmail, to coerce Sofia back into line but its efforts backfired. The Kremlin's heavy handed approach merely stiffened Bulgarian resolve. Russian leaders expressed concern that NATO would assume a prominent role throughout the Balkans and permanently exclude Moscow as a serious regional player. With Bulgaria and Romania poised for NATO membership, with NATO in control in Bosnia and Kosovo, and with strong American influence in Albania, Croatia, and Macedonia, Russia possessed few strong cards at its disposal. Officials charged that Washington deliberately undermined the authority of the UN. During the bombing of Yugoslavia in the spring of 1999, the UN was bypassed while the "system of international relations was destabilized."[4] Russia wanted a strong UN that would promote Russian interests and to which NATO would be subservient. According to commentators, Washington raised NATO to a status whereby it could use force regardless of the decision of the UN Security Council. NATO's New

Strategic Concept, adopted at the height of the Kosovo war in April 1999, was purportedly designed to weaken the decisionmaking role of the Security Council.

In Moscow's view, during the 1990s NATO was transformed into a tool of exclusively American global interests and each instance of military force was depicted as a blow "objectively" aimed at Russia's security. NATO action disrupted the "geopolitical balance" and called into question state sovereignty and "the entire international legal order."[5] In Moscow's estimations, the White House was determined to preserve American dominance and to sabotage the creation of a European defense organization. Officials warned about the "Yugoslav variant" in NATO policy, whereby an aggressive military posture could be applied to other crisis spots including the former USSR.[6] Some Russian military figures and parliamentarians suggested that Yugoslavia was being used aa rehearsal for an invasion of Russia.[7] The Kosovo war demonstrated that under the cover of peacemaking, the United States was intent on deploying its growing military power to "shape its new global policy" regardless of the interests of other states.[8] Because Washington could interfere with impunity in the internal affairs of all post-Soviet republics, Moscow had to respond with a tough counter strategy.

NATO's New Strategic Concept was described as an instrument for intervention around the globe. Moscow warned that if Russia dismantled its intercontinental missiles, it would become an ideal target for the United States to carve up the country. Officials were especially fearful over a Chechen debacle, which could provide an opportunity for future NATO engagement according to the principles of "humanitarian intervention" and support for separatist movements.[9] Moscow condemned NATO air strikes against Belgrade as illegal, canceled military cooperation with the Alliance, recalled Russia's military representative from NATO headquarters, expelled Alliance representatives from Russia, and terminated the Partnership for Peace (PfP) agreement. However, Moscow was powerless to influence Allied decisionmaking although its condemnations of NATO may have stiffened Belgrade's resistance against meeting the conditions for ending the bombing campaign.

In the aftermath of the NATO operation, pro-Western states in the Balkans expressed concern over a rapid U.S. departure. They pushed for NATO and EU integration to ensure their security. Meanwhile, Russia could not afford to keep thousands of peacekeepers in the Balkans and its troops vacated Bosnia and Kosovo during 2003.[10] Officials stressed that their military contingent had no further security tasks to perform, while NATO officials declared that the security situation would not be affected by the withdrawal. In a gesture of justification for the evacuation, Andrey Nikolaev, head of the Duma Defense Committee, claimed that Russia intended to increase its influence in the region through "military-technical cooperation," presumably referring to arms sales.[11] Russia will "build up its presence in the region to meet current tasks and interests, including joint efforts in developing defense institutions in Serbia and Montenegro and involvement in improving the defenses of Greece and Bulgaria." Nikolaev called these countries the "strongholds of Russia's policy in the Balkans."[12] Russia may acquire fresh opportunities as the EU assumes greater military responsibility in the region and will exploit differences between the European powers.

> The withdrawal of our military contingents from Kosova and Bosnia should not be interpreted as total withdrawal of Russia from the Balkans. Regarding the Balkans, the Russian Federation will remain active in the UN Security Council as well as the Contact Group. When it comes to economic aspects, I believe that Russia will keep coming back more and more, at the same time enlarging its political influence in the region. Just as it came back to Romania (which has more than 200 business arrangements with small Russian firms), Bulgaria (economic exchange between two countries has almost reached $1.3 billion), and even Slovenia and Croatia (economic exchange around $1 billion). Russia's intention is not to commit itself to any kind of military or ideological role in the Balkans. Our goal is to put emphasis on economic relations which we see as fundamental in our new presence and influence in the region.[13]

According to Russia's ambassador to Serbia and Montenegro, Vladimir Ivanovski, Russia has significant economic interest in the Balkans, especially in the context of EU enlargement.[14] The transit of Russian pipelines to the EU attracts Russian energy companies, which are gaining strength in the region. Moscow intends to develop "economic cooperation" with all Balkan states by "participating in the privatization of companies and by investing in industry and agriculture." Russia claims to be switching its focus and the form of its presence in a region that "still plays a very important role in establishing European security" and a "Russian sector of interest." Putin's first trip to the Balkans in June 2001 was designed to send three messages. First, Russia wanted to assert itself as a significant decisionmaker despite its economic weakness. Second, the Kremlin sought to demonstrate that although Central Europe had largely slipped from its grasp and the Baltics were heading toward NATO membership, the Balkans remained contested territory. And third, Putin's visit to Belgrade was intended to cement the alliance against threats to Yugoslavia's survival.

Russia's failure to regain significant influence in Bulgaria and its slender role in Romania and Albania made Serbia even more imperative for Moscow as a bridgehead in the region. It was also intent on pulling Macedonia into an "Orthodox bloc" and exploited the Albanian insurgency as an opportunity to offer assistance and protection to Skopje. Moscow was also determined to preserve the remnants of Yugoslavia and Putin proposed holding an international conference where "territorial integrity and the inviolability of borders" would be guaranteed. Economic instruments, especially in the energy sector, are a pivotal element in the reassertion of Russian influence. Indeed, the authorities consider both Bulgaria and Romania as central for increasing the amount of fossil fuels pumped into Europe and bypassing the Bosphorus straits.

SLOVENIA AND CROATIA

With the eruption of the Yugoslav wars in the summer of 1991, Russian policy wavered between support for the integrity of Yugoslavia and its cool relationship with Milošević, who had backed the coup attempt in Moscow in August 1991. A central aim of Russian diplomacy was to preserve Yugoslavia and to maintain Serbia's dominance. According to the Soviet Foreign Ministry before the breakup of the USSR, a position inherited by its Russian successor, a single independent Yugoslavia was "an important element of stability in the Balkans and in Europe as a whole."[15] Belgrade in turn viewed Russia as a useful ally because of Moscow's veto powers in the UN Security Council during Belgrade's endeavors to carve out a Greater Serbia. Yeltsin eventually recognized the independence of Slovenia and Croatia in February 1992, after it became clear that Socialist Yugoslavia was defunct. However, during the early stages of the Bosnian war in 1992 Russian policy became fervently pro-Serbian and coincided with the emergence of a more assertive foreign policy.[16]

According to Russian analysts, the United States was intent on acquiring new protectorates in the Balkans, whereby Croatia, Bosnia-Herzegovina, and Kosovo provided valuable inroads into the region.[17] Moscow claimed that the White House sought to expand its influence through military occupations cloaked as peacekeeping deployments. The Kremlin consistently opposed NATO and American involvement in the former Yugoslavia. Russian contingents participated in the UN deployments in Eastern Slavonia, a territory occupied by Serbian paramilitary forces in Croatia during the war for independence. Russian "blue helmets" in Croatia established close ties with local Serbian forces and earned a reputation for their involvement in black marketeering. The Croatian military offensive in the summer of 1995 to recapture lost territories was described in Moscow as an American deployment of proxy forces to defeat the Serbian cause and as evidence of escalating U.S. interference in the Balkans.

After Croatia declared its independence in June 1991, it came under regular attacks in the Moscow press. There were three main elements of this assault: Croatia was allegedly the most vociferous enemy of Yugoslavia and Serbia; the government was clamoring for NATO military involvement in the Balkans; and Croatia was seeking Alliance membership.[18] All three policies, shared by Slovenia, "objectively" diminished Russia's position in the region.

Russia became a member of the Contact Group for the former Yugoslavia in April 1994, alongside five major Western powers. This increased Moscow's stature as a regional player, especially because of its ties to Belgrade. Moscow's inclusion in the group prevented NATO from acting without Russian consent. Croatia's military victory in the Serb-occupied areas of Krajina in August 1995, together with successful Bosniak offensives in western Bosnia, diminished Moscow's role as a key factor that could influence Serb leaders in both countries. The Kremlin protested Zagreb's offensive but lost the Krajina Serbs as a bargaining chip in Balkan politics. Russia's weakness was underscored in the rejection by Croatian president Franjo Tudjman of Yeltsin's invitation to attend a conference in Moscow in August 1995. A subsequent Russian attempt to hold a trilateral meeting with Tudjman, Milošević, and Bosniak Muslim leader Alija Izetbegović was also unsuccessful and Western powers were blamed by Moscow for undermining the initiative.

For the first time in its history, Russia accepted the role of a peacekeeper under a UN mandate in the Serb-occupied areas of Croatia and subsequently in the Implementation Force (IFOR) and Stabilization Force (SFOR) missions in Bosnia. The Russian component in Croatia in June 1992 within the UN Protection Force (UNPROFOR) included some 1,000 soldiers out of a total 14,000 deployed. This enabled the Kremlin to claim that it was taking a responsible and positive role in Balkan security. The increasing activism of NATO in peacekeeping operations was perceived negatively in Moscow. NATO's New Strategic Concept was viewed as a recipe for institutional expansion and military action. The projection of the Alliance as the main force for conflict resolution in the Balkans was condemned as a means for marginalizing Russian influence.

Russian companies established working relationships with the Croatian oil pipeline enterprise that carried oil from the Adriatic to Central Europe. They are seeking to reverse the flow and transmit Russian oil to the Mediterranean.[19] Yukos won a contract with Zagreb to reconstruct the Adria pipeline and connect it with the Druzhba pipeline system in Central Europe. This would enable Russian oil to be transported directly to the Adriatic coast at a substantial saving in costs, bypassing the Bosphorus straits.[20] In December 2002, several states including Croatia signed an agreement to integrate and expand the capacity of the Druzhba and Adria pipeline systems to facilitate the pumping of Russian oil to Croatia's deepwater port of Omisalj. Slovenia also announced that it was considering Russia's proposal for the expansion of a gas pipeline through its territory. In addition to oil supplies and pipeline opportunities, Yukos sought shares in oil refining companies in Croatia. Russian oil giants remained in the race for the privatization of INA, Croatia's state owned oil company.[21] Besides TNK (a major Russian oil company) and Lukoil, which already possesses storage facilities in Croatia, Yukos is the main candidate for the takeover of INA. Yukos named Lord David Owen, former peace negotiator for the Balkans, as the front man for the project.

Since the breakup of Yugoslavia, Croatian-Russian economic relations have steadily developed, although the bulk of this trade has consisted of Russian exports. In 2002, Croatian exports to Russia reached $83 million, compared to $163 million in 1997 and 1998. Since then Zagreb has registered a negative trend.[22] Statistics show a different pattern in the opposite direction, as Russia exported $309 million of merchandise to Croatia during 1995 and $797 million by 2002. About 90 percent of the total were oil products. Russian businessmen also invested in Croatian real estate, especially along the Adriatic coast. Regarding Slovenia, during a trip by Foreign Minister Ivanov to Ljubljana, several agreements were finalized and it was noted that economic cooperation was steadily improving.[23] Slovenian businessmen stepped up their presence in Russia as the volume of investment increased. Slovenia and Russia are planning to expand trade from the current $600 million annually to at least $1 billion by 2006. Talks also focused on Russia's debt to the countries of post-Yugoslavia. Slovenia is entitled to $207 million of the total $1.29 billion that Russia owes to the Yugoslav successor states.

In Slovenia, Russia had little opportunity to exploit ethnic differences as the country is largely homogeneous and there are no territorial claims among its neighbors. In the case of Croatia, the demands of the large and radicalized Serbian minority provided ammunition for undermining the independent state during much of the 1990s and for defending Belgrade against Western pressure. During the Serbo-Croatian war in the early 1990s, Moscow imitated Belgrade in its condemnations of the Tudjman regime as a reincarnation of the World War II Ustaše fascists. Moscow had few opportunities to influence the political processes in either Slovenia or Croatia. There were limited personal or institutional links between the defunct Yugoslav and Soviet Communist systems. In addition, most of the parties that came to prominence in both states were anti-Yugoslav and proindependence—positions that were contrary to Kremlin policy. In both Zagreb and Ljubljana, Moscow was seen as siding decidedly with the Yugoslav and Serbian causes. Nevertheless, Moscow is counting on making longer-term political inroads in both Ljubljana and Zagreb through its economic penetration and business investments.

BOSNIA-HERZEGOVINA

In the early stages of the Bosnian war that erupted in April 1992, Moscow tacitly supported Western peace initiatives. This included the imposition of sanctions against Yugoslavia in May 1992 as punishment for openly backing the Bosnian Serb separatists. It also approved the dispatch of a UN mission to deliver humanitarian assistance to Bosnia and even backed the creation of a no-fly zone for all military aircraft over the country in October 1992. The Kremlin pressed for a "dual key" approach to military action, in which NATO air strikes had to be approved by the UN. This mechanism paralyzed decisionmaking and timely responses to Serb offensives. As the war progressed, Yeltsin came under mounting criticism at home for his alleged servility toward the West at the expense of Serbian and Yugoslav interests. Domestic pressures coupled with the inability of the Western countries to find an acceptable peace settlement encouraged Russia to adopt a more pro-Serbian stance just as the Western powers condemned Serb atrocities and threw more of their weight behind the Bosniak Muslims. Moscow and Washington began to diverge in their policy prescriptions to end the war.

Moscow lost significant influence during the Bosnian war after President Bill Clinton appointed Richard Holbrooke as a special envoy to forge a permanent peace settlement. This signaled more intensive U.S. involvement in terminating the war and demonstrated that the United States remained the most respected power. The Russian side was excluded from the Dayton peace process that culminated in the signing of the accords in November 1995. The Kremlin was not treated as an equal partner and its influence over Serbian politicians looked hollow. Russia appeared impotent in the face of American determination and its claim to great power status was dented.

By vocally and materially supporting Belgrade and the militant Serbian separatists in Croatia and Bosnia, Russia inadvertently encouraged the brutality on the battlefield by Serbian militias and the intransigence of the Bosnian Serb leadership during international negotiations. In public forums, Moscow claimed that no side should be favored on the battlefield, thus justifying the "ethnic cleansing" campaign committed predominantly by Serbian forces. Russian commentators also asserted that Serbs were threatened with genocide.[24] After the hostilities subsided, Moscow continued to support a policy of "equalization," in effect backing the efforts of the Serb Republic entity in blocking the central government in Sarajevo from functioning in a unified state.

The Yeltsin regime played on the notion of a deeply rooted Serbian-Russian friendship in order to discourage resolute Western action against the Bosnian Serb military. This alleged pan-Slavic solidarity (despite the fact that all other Yugoslav republics were Slavic) was useful for both foreign and domestic consumption.[25] Internationally, it helped to raise Russia's stature as a global power. Domestically, it undercut the position of ultranationalists and Communists who berated Yeltsin for his acquiescence to "NATO imperialism." Moscow portrayed itself as a serious political and military player and depicted the Bosnian war as being in its strategic area. In February 1994, Russia countered a NATO ultimatum to Serb forces to withdraw heavy weapons from around Sarajevo or face bombing. It issued a guarantee that Russian peacekeeping units would monitor the deployment of heavy artillery around the Bosnian capital. Russia's move prevented NATO military strikes and thrust Moscow forward as a major player in the conflict. Between 1992 and 1995, Moscow exploited divisions in Alliance responses to the Bosnian crisis. NATO military actions against Serbian forces, ranging from the interception of Serbian aircraft to the bombing of Bosnian Serb positions in the spring of 1994 and the summer and fall of 1995, were condemned. Yeltsin complained about the lack of consultation by NATO leaders when taking major decisions such as bombing Serbian forces in retaliation for the shelling of UN-designated "safe areas."

Russia repeatedly rejected military intervention, including air strikes against Serb targets and only grudgingly supported sanctions against Yugoslavia. Concerns over deteriorating relations with Moscow contributed to dissuading the Clinton administration from pursuing more forceful measures that it initially demanded.[26] The Kremlin supported the cantonization of Bosnia that would have consolidated substantial Serb territorial gains and it was subsequently omitted from the U.S.-sponsored rapprochement between Croatian and Bosniak leaders that resulted in the creation of the Bosnian Federation in March 1994. The Kremlin was also unable to control its nominal Bosnian Serb allies who were increasingly provoking NATO military strikes. NATO's military intervention signaled its first substantial offensive and a potential precedent for other conflict zones where Moscow believed it had security interests. NATO's nonconsultation with Moscow was interpreted as an act of betrayal and implicit aggression against Russia itself. NATO was denounced as an expansive organization that disregarded Russian interests.[27]

Moscow vehemently opposed military strikes against Serbian forces despite ongoing massacres of civilians, military attacks on UN "safe areas," and the capture of UN troops as hostages. It consolidated the Serbian position by concluding a military agreement with Belgrade in February 1995. Russian officials urged the strengthening of the UN deployment in Bosnia even though the mission had failed to protect vulnerable civilians from systematic military assaults. With more intensive U.S. engagement by the summer of 1995, the Russian reaction became less restraining for the Allies. In August and September 1995, NATO bombed Serb targets throughout Bosnia and intensified its pressures prior to the signing of the Dayton accords in November 1995. Kremlin protests were largely ignored by Alliance leaders and Moscow was excluded from the political process as its weight in the Bosnian conflict became more transparent than real. Russia was exposed as a minor player in a region where it claimed historical and strategic interests.[28]

Russia contributed troops to NATO's mission in order to maintain its stature among Bosnian Serbs. However, it was not permitted to acquire its own sector in the divided country. The Russian brigade was subordinated to an American general who was also the commander of IFOR. In effect, the Russian contingent remained under NATO control. Such an arrangement disabled Russia from playing a determining role in Bosnia's postwar evolution. Nevertheless, it accepted the two-entity status quo in which it pursued especially cordial relations with the political leadership in Bosnia's Serb Republic who opposed the consolidation of an authoritative central government in Sarajevo.

Moscow supported the various partition plans, including the Vance-Owen proposal in January 1993, which would have divided the country into ten ethnic cantons and given Serbs the lion's share of conquered territory. Washington urged a "lift and strike" strategy, by lifting the arms embargo on Sarajevo together with selective NATO air strikes against Serbian military targets to halt "ethnic cleansing." This strategy was strenuously opposed by the Kremlin. While the United States argued that the Muslims should be better armed to resist the Serbian onslaught, Moscow and several West European powers contended that the Muslims had already lost the war and hostilities should be swiftly terminated.

An initial Russian peacekeeping deployment took place in February 1994 after the Bosnian Serb military refused NATO demands to withdraw their heavy weapons from around Sarajevo. Russia's special envoy Vitaliy Churkin obtained a Serb agreement to NATO's conditions in return for the deployment of 400 Russian troops to prevent the Bosnian Muslims from taking over positions evacuated by Serbs. This arrangement was received domestically as a great success for Russian diplomacy.[29] In effect, the Russian side was providing protection for Serbian forces around the Bosnian capital while doing nothing to prevent further atrocities in other UN "safe areas." When it suited Serb leaders, they ignored Russian requests to curtail their offensive. The bombardment of Goražde and other "safe areas" continued regardless of Moscow's intervention. Such incidents weakened Kremlin argument that it had significant leverage over the Serbian side.

Although it was excluded from the final peace process, Moscow was eager to become involved in its implementation. Difficulties were encountered in reaching an agreement on the Russian troop presence, as Moscow did not want its forces placed formally under NATO command. The Russian contingent was put under the command of a Russian officer while tactically it was under the control of a U.S.-led multinational division. This move outraged some military commanders who complained that Russia had submerged its distinct identity by placing its soldiers at the disposal of U.S. officers.[30]

Russian energy and business interests have made most noticeable inroads in the Serbian entity. According to sources in the government of Bosnia's Srpska Republic, the oil refinery in the town of Brod on the Sava River would most likely be privatized by Russian companies.[31] Under Putin, Moscow also became involved in the Bosnian Federation in seeking out lucrative energy supply contracts and business acquisitions.

Bosnia's economic relations with Russia were insignificant when compared to the prewar period. During 2000, economic exchanges with Russia only amounted to 1 percent of Bosnia's total economic interaction with all other countries. The figures reached 1.6 percent in 2002. This trade was largely based on the import of Russian gas, although there were attempts by Russian companies to return to the Bosnian market.[32] During a visit to Sarajevo in September 2003, Foreign Minister Ivanov declared that Moscow would expand its economic influence.[33] Russia's debt to the country was settled and Bosnian officials expressed interest in attracting Russian companies to participate in the privatization process. Moscow firms were especially interested in acquiring or modernizing companies that were built with Soviet technical assistance before the collapse of Yugoslavia.

In mirroring Belgrade's perspective, the anti–civil war in Bosnia was portrayed by Russian authorities as an interethnic struggle in which the Serbs were defending their interests and preventing annihilation or expulsion by Bosniak Muslims and Catholic Croats. Moscow grudgingly accepted the Dayton accords and voiced displeasure at being omitted from the process. Subsequently, it politically defended the Serbian entity and opposed any revision of Dayton that would have weakened this statelet.[34] The Russian media continued to portray Bosnia's Muslim leaders as Islamic fundamentalists with an anti-Serb agenda.

Russia's overriding motive in Bosnia is to strengthen the Serbian position in relations with Sarajevo and international actors. Officials have tried to discredit the policies of the central government, the UN High Representative, and NATO as discriminatory against Serbs. They protested against the seizure of Bosnian Serb television and radio stations in 1997, despite the fact that these outlets were broadcasting inflammatory material to undermine the Dayton agreements. NATO's capture of war criminals was depicted as a cavalier policy that disregarded Russian opinion and was slanted against Serbs.[35]

During the 1990s, Moscow exerted greater political influence over the Bosnian Serb side than any of the Western powers and was able to arrange various concessions. Nonetheless, Pale (the Bosnian Serb capital) was not always cooperative and when the Vance-Owen Peace Plan was rejected by the Bosnian Serb assembly in August 1994 and Milošević severed Yugoslavia's economic ties with Pale, Moscow sided with Belgrade and froze relations with Bosnia's Serb leadership. The Kremlin intensified its relations with Milošević, seeing Belgrade as a more reliable and strategically important partner. It pressed for the lifting of economic sanctions against the Federal Republic of Yugoslavia.[36] Because of its restricted influence in Pale, Moscow was more accommodating toward the Dayton accords and the subsequent NATO mission, seeing the peace agreement as ultimately beneficial for Belgrade.

After the signing of the Dayton accords, officials in Moscow continued to give tacit support to former Bosnian Serb leaders, many of whom had been indicted by the Hague Tribunal as war criminals. A range of political groups, government officials, and parliamentarians in Russia condemned NATO actions in capturing Serbian commanders and politicians.[37] In effect, they encouraged Radovan Karadžić, Ratko Mladić, and other indicted mass murderers to believe that they had some international legitimacy and protection from Moscow.

Close ties developed during the Bosnian war between Serbian and Russian criminal gangs, militia groups, Russian volunteers, and intelligence agencies. These relations were maintained during the ensuing peace as Bosnia proved a lucrative fulcrum of the illicit international trade in weapons, people, drugs, and goods. Russia remained part of the international group monitoring developments in Bosnia, alongside the United States and the EU, and this provided opportunities for penetrating Bosnia's intelligence networks and gaining information on NATO operations. In November 2003, Western acquiescence to Russian intelligence involvement in Bosnia was evident when Paddy Ashdown, chief international representative in the country, visited Moscow for talks with Foreign Minister Ivanov.[38] Their discussions focused on reforms in Bosnia's defense and intelligence structures.

ALBANIA AND KOSOVO

Diplomatic relations between Albania and the Soviet Union were restored in July 1990, almost thirty years after they were severed by the Enver Hoxha regime in Tirana. As a result of the Albanian-Soviet split, Moscow lost its largest naval base in the Mediterranean, at Pashaliman in southern Albania. The first official visit to Moscow by a post-Communist Albanian head of government, Prime Minister Alexander Meksi, took place in April 1995 when a number of political and economic agreements were signed. However, ties remained frosty throughout much of the 1990s, primarily because of differing approaches to the Balkan crises. Russian authorities were unwilling to sacrifice their good relations with Belgrade to improve ties with Tirana.[39] During a trip to Moscow in June 2000, Foreign Minister Paskal Milo was attacked in the Russian press and by Duma deputies in commentaries interpreted by Tirana as "open threats" to Albanian interests. The escalating conflict over Kosovo worsened relations following a letter from Foreign Minister Primakov to the Albanian premier, in which he charged Tirana with exacerbating the crisis and pressed the government to eliminate "Albanian terrorism" in Kosovo. Albanian authorities dispatched a strong-worded response to Kremlin accusations.[40]

According to Albanian analysts, Russia was desperate to gain legitimacy and a voice in regional politics.[41] Russian officials claimed that NATO was tacitly supporting Albanian "ethnoterrorists" in Kosovo in its war against Belgrade because their goals coincided.[42] The NATO intervention was perceived as a method for restricting Russian influence by sideling the UN Security Council. Belgrade's resistance to NATO and U.S. pressure was interpreted as a defense of Russian global interests.[43] The Kremlin felt vindicated in criticizing NATO enlargement, which coincided with offensive Alliance missions that could set a precedent for operations near Russia's borders.[44] The director of Moscow's European Security Institute claimed that NATO's action in Serbia in 1999 would not only provoke a new Cold War but possibly a third world war.[45] The Defense Ministry argued that NATO's war with Yugoslavia marked a new era in international relations characterized by the escalating danger of U.S. military aggression against Russia.[46]

Despite its criticism of U.S. unilateralism, Moscow was first to dispatch troops to Kosovo without prior UN approval in a move designed to preempt NATO. Russian authorities also petitioned Tirana to accept a Russian military presence in Kosovo. This was the main purpose of Foreign Minister Ivanov's visit in June 1999. The Kremlin's belligerent stance throughout the NATO campaign was intended to gain a better postwar bargaining position.[47] It calculated that the West would offer Russia valuable incentives to avoid a permanent West-East rupture. The authorities acted in a hostile manner to gain advantages but restarted cooperation at a calculated moment so as not to be left out of decisionmaking. Despite the concerted diplomatic campaign to obtain advantages from the Kosovo conflict:

> Russia's Balkan diplomacy has failed to accomplish any of its proclaimed or hidden goals. Moscow managed neither to become a genuine partner to the West, nor to create an effective anti-Western outpost in Yugoslavia. It did not do what it could do to prevent the conflict in Kosovo. Russia remained indifferent to the sufferings of Kosovo Albanians and has failed to protect the Kosovo Serbs. Even on its own (misguided) terms, Moscow's worst-case scenario has come true: NATO troops are now in Yugoslavia.[48]

Moscow's postconflict proposals for the creation of a new Balkan "collective security system" were lambasted in Tirana as a renewed attempt to regain regional influence and to weaken the American position. Albanian officials pointed out that the security system proposed by the Kremlin was designed to bypass NATO and to include states such as Serbia, which were not even participants in NATO's PfP program. The proposal was intended to consolidate existing state borders and forestall Kosovo's and Montenegro's independence. During a visit to Prishtina in June 2001, Putin tabled the idea of recognizing the territorial integrity of all Balkan countries, claiming that any change of borders was "extremely dangerous and destructive."[49] In September 2001, Defense Minister Igor Sergeyev confirmed that Russia supported the concept of Kosovo remaining an "integral part of Yugoslavia."[50] Foreign Minister Ivanov revived the idea of an international conference in September 2003 during his trip to the Balkans.[51]

Russia persistently employs the anti-Albanian card to serve its strategic interests. Since NATO's intervention in Kosovo, Russian officials have depicted the Albanian nation as the chief danger to stability in the Balkans. They accuse the Alliance of having trained and deployed Kosovo Liberation Army (KLA) "terrorists" and "criminal drug runners" and charge Tirana with encouraging instability by calling for NATO's deployment in Kosovo. Russian commentators refuse to acknowledge that NATO took action over Kosovo in response to potential genocide. Officials assert that NATO engagement was a pretext to further fracture Yugoslavia—the only Balkan country not aspiring to join the Alliance—and to increase its military presence in the region.[52] Russian state propaganda claimed that conflicts in Southeast Europe were deliberately provoked to justify NATO expansion and its "out of area" missions, thus failing to acknowledge the ethnic cleansing of Kosovo's Albanians by Serbian security forces. Instead, the mass flight of hundreds of thousands of residents was depicted as a consequence rather than a cause of the NATO campaign. In July 1999, Foreign Minister Ivanov also asserted that "ethnic cleansing" was fabricated by the Western media in the service of NATO.

Support for "Albanian separatists" in Kosovo was viewed as encouraging secessionist forces in Russia, particularly among Muslims in the north Caucasus, as well as in other CIS states. Russian authorities blamed NATO after its takeover in Kosovo for failing to disarm the KLA, for allowing atrocities against the Serbian minority, and for attacks on Russian peacekeepers.[53] NATO stood accused of maintaining the KLA through the creation of the Kosovo Protection Corps (KPC), as the basis of a new Kosovo security structure. This would result in the permanent exclusion of the Serbian military and contribute to Yugoslavia's disintegration.[54] Moscow did not want NATO to set a precedent whereby military intervention enabled a region to secede from a recognized state.

Russian politicians warned that Albanians were incapable of democratic government but were inherently violent. As proof, they pointed to unstable developments in Albania and the emergence of the KLA with its supposed criminal empire. It alleged that any Albanian state generated regional instability, undermined the process of European expansion, acted as a conduit of illicit materials, and provided a gateway for fundamentalist Islamic forces.[55] Albania was denounced as a training base and transit point for terrorists. Tirana responded by expressing regret that the Kremlin had failed to condemn Serbian terrorism in Kosovo and the slaughter of innocent civilians.[56] Moscow's support for Belgrade created a highly negative image among Albanian and Kosovar politicians and citizens. Russia is viewed as the major supporter of the Greater Serbia project. Statements by Putin during a trip to Belgrade in June 2001, claiming that the main source of "national and religious intolerance and extremism" was in Kosovo, did not endear him to Albanians.[57] Russian criticism of the UN framework for self-rule in Kosovo, because it evidently surrendered too much to radicals, was resented in Prishtina and viewed as a method for returning the territory to Serbian jurisdiction. Frequent Russian assertions that a major plot existed to create a Greater Albania contributed to stoking tensions between Moscow and Tirana.[58]

Russian officials assign collective blame on Albanians for much of the organized crime in the Balkans. In March 2001, two days before an official visit to Tirana, Foreign Minister Ivanov declared that wherever there was an Albanian majority, crime and human trafficking were rampant.[59] Russian policy toward Kosovo and Macedonia was described in Tirana as a concerted effort to create a Slavic-Orthodox axis. During his meeting with Albanian officials, Ivanov complained that the international Islamic terrorist network began in Afghanistan, operated through Chechnya, and ended with Albanians in Kosovo and Macedonia. This stretch of territory was described as the "arc of instability." Such comments underscored how Moscow sought to link liberation struggles in both Yugoslavia and Russia with a vast terrorist conspiracy. The Russian press reported that Chechen fighters were being recruited by Albanian separatists in Kosovo and that Washington had a hidden agenda to dominate the region.[60] This justified reports that Russia's Defense Ministry was supplying Belgrade with intelligence on KLA and NATO operations in the Balkans.

Officials in Moscow aim to undermine Western support for the Kosovars and to present the KLA as an anti-Western, anti-Yugoslav, and anti-Russian grouping. The Russian public has been fed on a steady diet of Albanian ethnic cleansing against Serbian allies. Demands for Kosovo's independence allegedly provided a springboard for pan-Albanian nationalism and posed a risk of "Balkanization" for the entire Euro-Atlantic region. Analysts also claimed that only radicals supported Kosovo independence, thus misrepresenting the views of the overwhelming majority of Albanian residents.[61]

Moscow attacked Tirana for its position on Kosovo in an effort to disinform world opinion and to pressurize Albania to desist from pursuing close ties with Prishtina. In September 2000, the Foreign Ministry claimed that Albania had violated the UN Security Council resolution concerning the sovereignty and territorial integrity of the FRY.[62] Tirana had assigned an official representative to Prishtina following the opening of a "contact mission" with the consent of Bernard Kouchner, special representative of the UN Secretary-General. Moscow charged that any state representatives to Kosovo first needed to gain Belgrade's consent despite the fact that Serbia no longer controlled the territory.

Notwithstanding Russian charges, Tirana is cautious in its approach toward Kosovo, balancing the aspirations of the Kosovars for independence and its own dependence on the international community.[63] Indeed, Tirana has been criticized by Prishtina for not being more outspoken on the final status question. The Albanian government is also a staunch supporter of the territorial integrity of Macedonia and condemns the actions of militant Albanians. While Moscow accuses Albania of negative interference in Serbia's and Macedonia's internal affairs, Tirana remains suspicious of Russia's active support for Belgrade's positions.

The Kremlin consistently opposed NATO operations in Southeast Europe and distrusts the evolution of relations between the Alliance and individual Balkan states. In July 1998, Moscow complained about NATO air maneuvers in Albania and Macedonia that were intended to threaten Belgrade.[64] Throughout the NATO bombing campaign over Kosovo, Russian leaders threatened a military response, which did not materialize. According to Sergey Karaganov, head of a policy institute close to Prime Minister Primakov, NATO needed to suffer a political defeat in Serbia to undercut its ambitions to become "the world's policeman."[65] Despite hawkish statements by some military and political leaders, more realistic views predominated, as Moscow was cognizant of the self-defeating nature of confrontation with NATO. Some jet fighters were dispatched to Serbia but were intercepted and impounded in Azerbaijan. Military leaders announced an intention to send an expeditionary fleet to the Adriatic. Ultimately, only one Russian intelligence-gathering vessel reached Montenegrin waters in mid-April 1999 in a largely symbolic gesture. The Yeltsin administration made it clear that it would not be drawn into the NATO-Serbian war regardless of its political sympathies.

Moscow supplied the Yugoslav military with intelligence information during the war and the NATO assault was closely monitored by Russian radar and space-based observation systems. Military leaders claimed that their data avoided more substantial human losses in Serbia. Reports also surfaced in 1999 that Russian mercenaries including officers assisted Serbia's military during the Kosovo war.[66] A number of Russians were killed in combat, although it was unclear whether they were volunteers or on official training duties. The Kremlin's ultimate helplessness over Kosovo was criticized by Communists and nationalists as an indication of weakness, diplomatic failure, and foreign policy bankruptcy. This provided political fuel for the emergence of a stronger leadership under Putin.

As NATO prepared to deploy its ground troops in Kosovo, the Russian authorities dispatched a contingent of 200 soldiers from their location in Bosnia to Prishtina airport to create a fait accompli of a separate Russian sector. Both Prishtina and Tirana were highly suspicious of any Russian role in Kosovo as this would dissuade the return of Albanian refugees and promote partition.[67] Indeed, condemnation of the Russian intervention in Kosovo proved to be one of the few issues that united both government and opposition in Albania.

Russia's intrusion provided a temporary illusion of military success, which quickly dissipated. Russian sources claim the deployment was part of a more elaborate plan by Yeltsin to establish a major presence in the territory.[68] Moscow intended to transfer another 4,000 troops into Kosovo through Prishtina airport to gain control of a broad area next to the Serbian border and claim it as a Russian sector in advance of NATO deployments. The Foreign Ministry was not apprized of a plan approved directly by Yeltsin on the advice of Chief of the General Staff Anatoly Kvashnin and Defense Minister

Sergeyev.[69] The entire military operation was to be coordinated with Belgrade, but was unsuccessful because Hungary, Romania, and Bulgaria refused to provide overflight rights to Russian forces. Governments in all three states consulted with Washington and denied such rights until an accord was reached between Russia and NATO on a unified peacekeeping command.[70]

Kremlin attempts to carve out a Russian zone of control in Kosovo proved unsuccessful as NATO leaders feared partition and renewed Albanian-Serbian conflicts.[71] Kosovars vehemently opposed the creation of a Russian sector, as this would have given Moscow a voice in the final status of the province.[72] Hashim Thaci, the KLA commander and head of Kosovo's provisional government, declared that Russian troops had entered the territory in contravention of NATO commands and would be considered as soldiers of an occupying power.[73] Albania's prime minister stated that any separate Russian command in Kosovo would constitute a factor of regional instability and warned that Russian forces could face a situation similar to that of Afghanistan under the Soviet occupation.[74]

During the Russian deployment, protests were staged by Albanian residents and several soldiers were wounded in attacks on checkpoints.[75] Albanian analysts were concerned that Russian soldiers could intimidate returning Kosovars, tolerate Serbian violence, and bypass NATO command structures. They pointed to a Russian disregard of the chain of command in Bosnia when they rushed their contingent to Prishtina without announcing their departure. Moscow possessed few diplomatic or military levers to press its case for a distinct role in Kosovo and had to be satisfied with a small force under overall NATO command. Moscow also lacked modern peacekeeping units while being unable to bear the financial costs of a substantial deployment. Russian peacekeepers were dispersed among NATO's "occupation zones" and were not in a position to take control in the most densely populated Serbian areas despite claims that they were protecting minority Serbs against Albanian violence:

> Once again in Kosovo, the Russians have taken a strong public line that they cannot back up. If the seizure of the airport had been followed by its use to airlift in thousands of troops who could have then moved into the northwest of Kosovo, they might have left NATO with no choice but to accept a *de facto* partition. But a military short of funds, fuel, serviceable transport aircraft and disciplined, well-equipped units, with minimal international support, was in no position to build on its tactical success. The result is to illustrate their weakness rather than their strength.[76]

For Moscow, the postintervention instability in Kosovo proved that NATO's concept of "humanitarian intervention" did not contribute to a stable European security architecture. During the war, influential Russian commentators even applauded the conflict as it could initiate the "collapse of the U.S. global empire."[77] Strategists argued that a U.S. quagmire in Yugoslavia would ultimately serve Russian interests in the Balkans. If the NATO missions in Bosnia and Kosovo were to face serious challenges, Russian policymakers could claim that NATO's Strategic Concept was a failure. Such a scenario could undermine support for further rounds of Alliance enlargement and any subsequent NATO missions.

Moscow periodically threatened to withdraw its contingent from Kosovo, allegedly in protest against NATO backing for an independent state. In reality, the authorities faced financial pressures to evacuate. In January 2003, Russian commanders issued a directive to their peacekeeping contingents in Bosnia and Kosovo in preparation for withdrawal.[78] The Kremlin concluded that existing deployments were no longer bringing any political advantage and did not justify the annual expenditures. In sum, Russia failed to gain any political leverage with NATO through its deployments. An additional reason for the troop departure was low morale and the involvement of officers in criminal activities that undermined Kremlin contentions that it was still a reputable military power.

Albania has avoided dependency on Russian energy, trade, and markets. However, Russia intends to include the country in its growing energy grid in Europe. In June 2000, both governments announced that they planned to restart negotiations to stretch a gas and oil pipeline to Albania and to increase the volume of trade and investment. Moscow also expressed a strong interest in supplying electricity to Albania through Russia's Unified Energy System. During the visit of Albanian Foreign Minister Ilir Meta to Moscow in December 2002, the two countries agreed to establish joint economic committees and to sign bilateral agreements in agriculture and crime fighting.[79] A cooperation agreement between the two chambers of commerce was also initialed.

Moscow regularly deployed the ethnic card in its criticisms of U.S. and NATO policy toward Kosovo. It accused Albanians of expelling and murdering Serb residents after the NATO liberation in June 1999. The mass exodus of Serbs, the majority fleeing the NATO advance and fearful of returning Albanian residents who were expelled from their homes by Belgrade, was presented as a form of systematic ethnic cleansing.[80] The Alliance allegedly conspired in this process as Russian officials trumpeted charges of Albanian genocide against Kosovar Serbs to discredit the NATO mission. In November 2001, Russia's ambassador to the UN, Sergey Lavrov, declared that in Kosovo "ethnic discrimination continues, international terrorism is spreading to other places, while criminal activity is increasing."[81] Albanian officials viewed Lavrov as Belgrade's chief advocate at the UN. Officials in Moscow also discussed the partition of Kosovo as a variant of reincorporation in Serbia, thereby echoing the position of some Serbian spokesmen. The premise was that peace would remain elusive without ethnic partition in which Belgrade is entitled to the northern portion of Kosovo adjacent to Serbia. Albanians strongly oppose such plans, as they would remove the most industrialized part of the territory from where Albanians were expelled by Serbian security forces.

Moscow had little opportunity to engage in social manipulation in Albania or Kosovo among a largely Albanian population where Russia exerts little respect or influence. Nonetheless, Albanian analysts believed that Serbian intelligence forces with Russia's involvement are active in both states to generate social tensions and instability. Because Moscow does not possess close ties or have influence with any major political forces in Tirana or Prishtina, it has been unable to promote extremist political formations that could challenge the popularity of the consistently pro-Western governments.

Russian authorities campaign to discredit the legitimacy of the elected Kosovo government in order to undermine the drive for statehood. Most party leaders and government officials have been described as extremists. Following the first general elections, Ambassador Lavrov claimed that an "institutional vacuum" existed in the territory, evidently proving that the November 2001 elections were premature.[82] Lavrov also claimed that election results did not consolidate the position of "moderate Kosovo leaders" who were being "ruthlessly persecuted by former leaders of the KLA." Putin reaffirmed Moscow's negative attitude to the creation of a constitutional framework for Kosovo, claiming that this made too many concessions to Albanian radicals by creating the positions of president and government chairman.[83] Putin asserted that such an arrangement violated UN Security Council Resolution 1244 regarding Kosovo's status as an integral part of Yugoslavia. According to the Foreign Ministry, Russia opposes any discussion over final status for the territory.[84]

The pervasive presence of organized crime and official corruption in the Balkans has given Moscow fertile ground for drumming home its anti-Albanian and anti-Kosovar message. Albania is regularly depicted as the center of regional crime and this has led to some diplomatic incidents. In April 2002, the Albanian Foreign Ministry strongly protested statements by a group of foreign monitors styling itself as the "Friends of Albania," which had criticized Tirana for its shortcomings in the fight against crime and corruption. The "Friends" consisted of several OSCE states, including Russia, Ukraine, and Macedonia.[85]

After the ouster of Milošević and with an internationally relegitimized Serbia, Russia tried to assure itself of a major ally from where it could project its influence. Under Putin, the Kremlin supported the Vojislav Koštunica administration in its attempt to restore Belgrade's authority over Kosovo and charged KFOR with failing in its mission. According to Putin, during his trip to Belgrade in June 2001, the Balkans were seriously threatened by "religious intolerance and extremism, which have their main sources in Kosovo."[86] Foreign Minister Ivanov claimed that NATO's "passive reaction" to the spread of the Kosovo conflict into Macedonia threatened peace in the entire region. During Putin's visit to Kosovo in June 2001, he stressed Russia's regional interests and expressed support for Belgrade.[87] Putin also lashed out at the November 2001 elections and asserted that Kosovo's Serbs should boycott the ballot and not participate in setting up joint democratic institutions. Both Putin and Koštunica proposed a regional conference to chart the future of the Balkans. Implicit in this suggestion was the maintenance of current borders and the preservation of Yugoslavia.[88]

Although organized crime is a multiethnic international enterprise, direct Russian penetration in Albanian-majority areas of the Balkans is limited. Russian gangs are primarily suppliers of human cargo and various illicit materials into the region. During the 1990s, the size of the Russian embassy in Tirana has grown threefold in its staffing. This indicates a substantial increase in the number of intelligence operatives in the country. Albania's close relationship with NATO and the United States has provided additional reasons for espionage among Russian agencies based in Tirana. Similarly, Kosovo with its large NATO and U.S. presence has become an information-gathering bonanza for Russian civilian and military intelligence units.

SERBIA

In March 1998, Soviet leader Mikhail Gorbachev visited Belgrade and expressed support for Yugoslavia's independence and voiced sympathy for Serbian leader Milošević. Although Yeltsin was not enamored of Milošević, Belgrade remained Moscow's major Balkan partner by default throughout the 1990s. The Milošević regime gave substantial opportunities for Russia to create wedges between the United States and its European allies, weakening the case for NATO enlargement and mission expansion, and raising Russia's prestige throughout the region. Moscow's support for Serbia and the preservation of the federal structure had little to do with pan-Slavic "Orthodox solidarity" and more with the desire to promote Russian state interests: "it was not ethnic nationalism but rather state nationalism that prompted Russia to take side with the Serbs."[89] The Yugoslav crisis helped Russia to restore a position in Southeast Europe. The international sanctions imposed on Belgrade for fomenting war isolated the country from the West and stimulated pro-Russian sentiments. While Moscow publicly opposed the sanctions regime, it also benefited politically from their imposition as it could depict itself as the sole friend of Belgrade.

The Kremlin favored continuing crisis in the Balkans to divert Western attention from its own policies inside the CIS. The turmoil complicated transatlantic relations and prevented the progress of Balkan states toward NATO membership. Conflict provided the Kremlin with renewed leverage through involvement in the six-nation "contact group" designed to resolve the Yugoslav crises. Yeltsin also assumed hard and soft diplomatic approaches, veering between the tougher position of Foreign Minister Primakov and the more accommodating approach of former Prime Minister Chernomyrdin who was appointed special envoy to the Balkans. When it became clear that Yugoslav disintegration could not be averted, Moscow supported the Greater Serbia project as this could fortify its regional leverage. Political forces in Moscow with the blessing of the Kremlin assisted militant ethnonationalist groups in Serbia. Throughout the sanctions regime, Moscow acted as an economic lifeline for Belgrade especially through its energy supplies. In sum, the pro-Belgrade position contributed to prolonging the Yugoslav wars and gave succor to Milošević.[90]

The Milošević regime exploited Russian opposition to Yugoslavia's disintegration and NATO involvement.[91] They manipulated the image of a strong Russia to convince the public that Moscow was Serbia's protector and would intervene in the event of a showdown with NATO. Notions that Yugoslavia would join the Russia-Belarus Union were propaganda ploys employed by the embattled Serbian leadership. Moscow capitalized on these statements, as during a visit to the region by Russian Defense Council secretary Yuriy Baturin in October 1996. He suggested that Russia was interested in establishing a military base on the Montenegrin coast to counter the growing NATO presence in Croatia and Bosnia. During the NATO war over Kosovo, Russia's Duma adopted a resolution to invite the FRY to join the Russia-Belarus Union. Yeltsin also floated the idea of Serbia joining the "fraternal pan-Slavic Union." Such statements were subsequently downplayed, as Moscow was not prepared to defend Belgrade against NATO or assume any onerous new economic obligations.

The Yugoslav wars provided opportunities for Russian politicians and media to lambast the West. The disintegration of Yugoslavia was presented as a Western plot to diminish the role of Serbia, which remained Russia's most dependable ally in the region.[92] NATO involvement was depicted as a hegemonic design to dominate Europe and to rein in any powers that opposed Alliance enlargement.[93] For Russian nationalists, Serbia was viewed as the key western pillar of "Eurasia." Yeltsin played the pro-Serb and anti-Albanian card to pacify the Russian parliament and avoid impeachment charges. In May 1999, he warned that Moscow might withdraw from the Kosovo peace process if NATO persisted in ignoring Russian proposals for a settlement.[94] But despite such bravado, Moscow accommodated the NATO plan that amounted to Belgrade's surrender. Yeltsin again came under criticism from the Duma, this time for acquiescing to Milošević's capitulation.

During NATO's war against Serbia, the Russian media engaged in a ferocious campaign depicting the Alliance as an aggressive organization whose intervention led to a "massive loss of human life and considerable material destruction."[95] They distorted NATO's motives, exaggerated the number of casualties among Serbs, repeated Belgrade's propaganda claims that dozens of NATO planes had been shot down, and underreported the victimization of the Kosovo Albanian population. According to Russian conspiracy theories, NATO's military operation was primarily directed against Russia in order to remove its influence from the Balkans and terminate its balancing act in the Yugoslav conflicts.[96] The Kosovo war provided a valuable opportunity to openly vent frustration with Russia's greatly diminished role in the post–Cold War world. The Russian Orthodox Church also participated in disinformation campaigns about the allegedly victimized Serbs. During the Milošević years, the Moscow patriarchate supported its Serbian counterpart by repeatedly claiming that Serbs were victims of Western military action and of prevalent anti-Serbian sentiments.[97] Its religious intolerance also buttressed antiminority and antiforeigner sentiments among some sectors of Serbian society. The head of Russia's Orthodox Church, Patriarch Aleksey II, stirred up the conflict by visiting Belgrade in April 1999 and proclaiming Kosovo a Serbian and Orthodox Christian holy ground.

Shortly before the collapse of the USSR, Moscow was intimately involved in the arms trade with Communist Yugoslavia. In August 1991, Soviet defense minister Dmitriy Yazov negotiated a secret $2 billion arms deal with Belgrade. It failed to be enacted because of the hard-line coup attempt in Moscow later that month. As a result of Yeltsin's victory, Milošević temporarily lost a reliable ally in Moscow, especially as he had backed Yeltsin's opponents during the revolt. This alliance was restored once Russian foreign policy became geared toward preserving Yugoslavia. Serbia's opposition to NATO intervention in Bosnia (1995) and Kosovo (1999) was applauded across Russia's political spectrum as it provided opportunities to open an anti-NATO "front" in the Balkans.

Moscow provided weapons systems to Belgrade during the 1990s. The Yugoslav air force was supplied with long-range surface-to-air missiles and the Yugoslav army with various rocket systems. In addition to sending spare parts for existing weaponry, Russia provided assistance in training Serbia's special forces. Russia's antiterrorist group Alfa helped train the particularly vicious Special Operations Unit of Serbia's State Security Service.[98] Belgrade imported military equipment through a multitude of illicit channels that implicated Russian officials. One connection led to the Swiss-based bank Compagnie Bancaire Genève, whose client was the Russian Valery Tcherny, known by Interpol under the name of Victor Vasillevich Dudenkov.[99] His company Aviatrend was part of the financial network used by Milošević to make transfers of more than a billion dollars to purchase weapons. Milošević possessed a secret import network and to conceal the source, cash was deposited in the accounts of eight fictional companies registered in Cyprus. Borka Vučić, former director of the Yugoslav Belgrade Bank in Nicosia, Cyprus, "organized money transfers to persons that supplied (Yugoslav) armed forces and battle units of the (Serbian) Ministry of Internal Affairs with weapons and equipment." Financial documents, delivered in August 2001 to the Hague Tribunal by the Swiss Ministry of Justice, showed that these companies transferred money to Switzerland and to Aviatrend accounts and the transactions were related to arms shipments.

The Duma and the Defense Ministry declared that NATO military action would trigger a new Cold War and scuttle the 1997 Founding Act between Russia and the Alliance. Military planners warned that the NATO assault would encourage Moscow to include contingencies for deploying tactical nuclear weapons in conventional threat scenarios.[100] According to the commander of Russia's strategic missiles forces, General Vladimir Jakovlev, strategic ballistic units equipped with modern launchers and missiles were placed in a "state of highest alert."[101] Moscow opposed NATO's military action to demonstrate its prowess and pro-Serb credentials but avoided a major rupture with the West. The outcome was a combination of hot rhetoric and cool action and an eventual restoration of relations. Instead of direct military assistance, Russia provided Serbia mostly with intelligence data during the Alliance intervention.[102] Calls by Russian parliamentarians to supply Milošević with "antimissile complexes" were not heeded by the Kremlin for fear of provoking a serious conflict with the United States.[103]

Russian leaders condoned the recruitment of Russian "volunteers" to participate in the Yugoslav wars.[104] Russian mercenaries, or *kontraktniki* (contract soldiers), consisted of former servicemen lured by money and booty and active-duty Russian military dispatched by the Defense Ministry. At the beginning of the conflict in Bosnia, Serb forces did not have enough pilots and hired Russians to fill the gap.[105] In Croatia, in April 1995, the commander of the UNPROFOR Sector East, Russian general Aleksander Pereljakin, who had been replaced for dereliction of duty, was appointed as an adviser to the commander of the Baranja division of the Army of Serbian Krajina. According to Bosnian sources, Russian volunteers fought in units of between ten and twenty-five soldiers, organized on a national basis. One of the first squadrons, consisting of Russian volunteers named the Tsar's Wolves, appeared in Bosnia-Herzegovina in late 1992. Russians collaborated with the Serb mobster Arkan's Serb Volunteer Guard and with Vojislav Šešelj's White Eagles. They also escorted fuel delivery convoys and participated in smuggling operation.

The number of Russian volunteers fighting for local Serbs in Croatia and Bosnia was estimated at somewhere between 2,000 and 3,000. Serbia's Interior Ministry recruited *kontraktniki* through construction and international trade companies, such as Yugoimport, working on restoration projects in Russia. Milošević's brother Borislav, in his capacity as Serbian ambassador in Moscow, acted as the coordinator for Russian mercenary recruitment, as well as for smuggling war materiel to Serbia. Russian reservists and military retirees also participated in the fighting in Kosovo. Russian *kontraktniki* included servicemen, members of elite paramilitary police units, military intelligence (GRU) commando brigades, and Spetsnaz (special forces) who committed atrocities against Albanian civilians in Kosovo. Several militant parties in Russia were also active in enlisting volunteers, including the Liberal Democrats.[106]

Moscow's hard-line stance against NATO gave a false signal to Belgrade that the bombing would be avoided or short-lived. This may have prolonged the NATO campaign between March and June 1999 by stiffening Milošević's resistance. When it became clear that NATO would not back down, Russian authorities assumed the role of mediators under the leadership of special envoy Chernomyrdin. Russian analysts subsequently complained that Chernomyrdin simply imposed NATO's *diktat* on Belgrade while posing as an independent peacemaker to salvage some semblance of Russian prestige.[107]

Serbia has been greatly dependent on Russian gas supplies even before the break-up of Yugoslavia. During the Milošević era, 94 percent of total imports from Russia consisted of oil and gas shipments.[108] Throughout the sanctions regime, Moscow sought to have the blockade officially lifted so it could export energy to Belgrade. Russia's UN representatives threatened to unilaterally withdraw from the sanctions committee if it did not reconsider its embargo on gas deliveries. However, the Kremlin was playing a double game: demonstrating solidarity with the Serbs while not openly defying the international community and the major Western powers. Energy flows continued and Serbia incurred a large debt to Russia, estimated at over $270 million by 1998, for natural gas deliveries. Because Russia needs Belgrade as a dependable ally in the region, energy exports have been maintained despite nonpayments after the lifting of international sanctions. In a visit to Belgrade in June 2001, Putin promised Koštunica that Russia would not cut its supplies of natural gas despite the country's fiscal problems. Such statements underscore that energy is a political issue rather than simply a business proposition. In April 2003, Russia's Finance Ministry announced that Moscow was looking at the possibility of building a nuclear power plant in Serbia to pay off the remaining Soviet debt to Yugoslavia.[109]

Serbia figures centrally in Russia's plans to expand energy supplies and industries in the Balkans. Lukoil has explored the purchase of Serbian refineries including ones damaged by NATO bombing, such as the facility in Novi Sad, Vojvodina.[110] In September 2003, Lukoil signed a deal with Belgrade to purchase a 79.5 percent stake in its second largest fuel chain, Beopetrol, for approximately $134 million.[111] Beopetrol operates almost 200 filling stations, covering roughly 20 percent of Serbia's retail fuel market. Russia's oil lobby believed that Milošević could secure Russian business interests in the Balkans. Economic tools were therefore used to reinforce the Milošević government and to gain long-term control over strategic sectors. The Progresgas company was registered as a private concern after being formed in 1992 as a mixed Russian-Yugoslav project by Progres Belgrade and Gazprom.[112] Mirko Marjanović, prime minister under Milošević, was the owner of Progres. Progresgas took the gas import business away from Energogas Belgrade and NAP Novi Sad, both large, state-owned companies. Marjanović established the gas import monopoly after Moscow insisted on having a major private energy company under its control. Russia's energy monopolization has continued after Milošević.

Trade networks between Serbia and Russia deepened throughout the Milošević years. Serbian companies closely linked with officials in Belgrade developed a lucrative business in oil and grain.[113] Similar deals were made in the telecommunications and banking sectors. Members of Milošević's administration benefited financially through many of these joint ventures, which helped to prop up the internationally sanctioned regime. The Koštunica government discovered that gas deliveries to Yugoslavia had been monopolized by Progresgas and the company was identified as forming the financial base of Milošević's regime. Progres chairman Marjanović was an old acquaintance of Gazprom's former chairman and former Russian premier Chernomyrdin.[114] Progres specialized in barter arrangements with Gazprom. It paid for gas supplies by selling grain from Serbia's strategic reserves, resulting in a crisis in the agricultural sector in 1997. All details on these deals were kept in a separate computer that disappeared from the company's headquarters after Milošević fell from power.

In addition to sanctions busting during the UN embargo, Moscow provided the country with credits, as during the visit of Belgrade's foreign minister to Moscow in May 2000 when he was promised a $102 million loan. Russia consistently campaigned on Serbia's behalf for the lifting of economic sanctions despite the opposition of major Western powers. And on the eve of Milošević's ouster in July 2000, Moscow signed a free trade agreement with the FRY to assist the faltering dictator. In September 2003, Russia finally settled the repayment of its $1.29 billion debt to all former Yugoslav republics. Moscow planned bilateral agreements with the five successor states on repayment schedules.[115] In addition to Russian debts to Belgrade, Serbia owed Gazprom about $246 million.

During the Milošević era, Russian state propaganda mirrored official Belgrade in denouncing an assortment of domestic and external conspiracies directed against Yugoslavia. Some of Serbia's largest minorities, including Albanians, Hungarians, Muslims, and Croatians, figured in this media barrage as real or potential fifth columnists whose ambitions needed to be curtailed. This helped to justify Belgrade's discriminatory policies.

Moscow's consistent support for Milošević indicated its preference for isolationist leaders who obstructed NATO expansion and kept the United States at a distance. It suited both Milošević and Yeltsin to claim that Russian-Serbian relations were fully harmonious. However, it is debatable how much political influence Moscow actually exerted over Belgrade, despite the fact that it convinced Western leaders that its word was heeded. There were several occasions when mediators came away empty-handed in discussions with Milošević who played the Russian card to deter more intensive Western pressures. Close contacts were maintained between the two militaries and

Orthodox churches as well as between parliamentary and executive bodies. Following NATO's 1999 campaign, Moscow conferred awards on several Yugoslav military leaders including the army chief of staff and future defense minister General Dragoljub Ojdanić for their "heroic defense of the country." Ojdanić, one of several Serbian leaders indicted for war crimes by the Hague Tribunal, paid a clandestine visit to Moscow in May 2000. Despite protests by Western leaders, he met with top Russian military and defense officials.[116]

Serbia's regime promoted the notion that Russia was fully supportive of Milošević's policies and would defend the country against Western intervention. Moscow consistently displayed Serbia as the victim of Western aggression and disregarded the culpability of Belgrade for provoking and fuelling the Yugoslav wars. It described these conflicts as either internal power struggles or Western conspiracies to carve up Yugoslavia. In official Russian estimations, U.S. policy toward Serbia was designed to suppress Serbian national interests and to establish a puppet regime. Belgrade's "independent stance" allegedly thwarted NATO's plans for regional domination and set an example for other East European states to exert their sovereignty.

Although the Yeltsin government sought to prevent NATO intervention in both Kosovo and Bosnia, it was ultimately powerless to intercede. Once Western leaders realized that Moscow's influence in Belgrade was limited they ignored Russian protests. The Kremlin convinced itself that the West would not venture a clash with Russia over former Yugoslavia. Hence, NATO's military action came as a shock to Yeltsin.[117] Nevertheless, the crisis in former Yugoslavia provided Moscow with an avenue for reinvolvement. Moscow's role in the Contact Group gave Belgrade some diplomatic leverage vis-à-vis the international community. Belgrade insisted on Moscow's engagement in all aspects of the "peace process" and thereby helped to raise Russia's prestige as a regional player.

As the Milošević regime disintegrated during the fall of 2000, it became clear that Washington and Moscow had fundamentally different objectives. While the United States wanted Serbia to emerge as an anchor of regional stability with a pro-Western administration, Russia preferred to maintain the country as a source of regional uncertainty that undermined the process of NATO's institutional and operational expansion. Putin and the Duma expressed fears that Serbia could swing in a pro-Western direction after Milošević's ouster. The Serbian leader had been a useful partner and Moscow displayed a lukewarm reaction to the election victory of Koštunica in October 2000. Kremlin support for Milošević was evident in its acceptance of fraudulent election results despite international condemnation and mass protests by Serbian citizens. Moscow calculated that Milošević would ride out the storm and recover his position as he had in the past. As a result, Russian credibility was eroded even in Serbia.[118]

Russian authorities only recognized Koštunica's electoral triumph once the public revolt unnerved Milošević's supporters and Serbian security forces took the side of the opposition. Moscow then attempted to pose as a power broker in order to regain its influence. It had to rapidly adapt to new political realities as the supporter of Serbian democrats. Despite some pungent anti-U.S. statements by Koštunica during the election campaign, Putin remained uncertain about his policies once he was in power. There were fears that a post-Milošević Serbia, similarly to its neighbors, would petition for NATO membership and strengthen its ties with the American military. Nevertheless, once Moscow realized that the Milošević era was over it courted the new Yugoslav leadership and even claimed that Foreign Minister Ivanov was instrumental in ensuring a smooth transition of power between Milošević and Koštunica.[119] The Kremlin threw its weight behind the new Serbian president and sought to ingratiate itself with Belgrade by claiming that the West needed to atone for its 1999 bombing by bearing the costs of Serbia's reconstruction.[120]

Yugoslavia's new president displayed a cool approach toward the United States and paid his first foreign visit to Moscow in October 2000. During a subsequent visit to Moscow in October 2001, Koštunica issued a joint statement with Putin declaring a "strategic commitment" between the two states in several spheres, including political, economic, and scientific relations.[121] Koštunica wanted to use Serbia's ties with Russia as a lever against Western influences. He calculated that Moscow's political support would be substantial as Russia remained concerned about its diminishing influence in the Balkans. However, Russia had only limited economic potential other than energy that it could offer Belgrade in comparison with Western powers.

Russia was one of the few countries where Milošević's extradition to The Hague was greeted with widespread outrage. Duma deputies expressed their willingness to mount a large-scale public relations campaign in defense of the Yugoslav former dictator and some accused the Serbian authorities of treason for extraditing Milošević.[122] Even Foreign Minister Ivanov, who maintained that the extradition was Yugoslavia's internal affair, stated that it "does not contribute to stability in Yugoslavia" and "plays into the hands of the separatists in Kosovo and Montenegro who are advocating withdrawal from the federation."

Close ties developed between the Russian and Serbian mafias during the UN sanctions regime and involved a variety of illicit endeavors. Russian criminal organizations were active in Serbia as their operations were facilitated by close connections between state officials, international smugglers, security services, and intelligence networks.

Under the Milošević regime, Serbia and Russia established close security and intelligence ties as a form of mutual self-defense against Western penetration. After the demise of Yugoslavia and Koštunica's loss of office in

2003, the government in Belgrade pursued a more Western-oriented policy. It focused on reforms in the security system in order to enable the country to qualify for NATO membership. This included a purge of pro-Milošević military officers. Russian intelligence either became more active or the new government was more determined to reveal instances of espionage. In September 2003, the Serbia-Montenegrin Defense Ministry confirmed the arrest of three senior army officers on suspicion of gathering secret military information for a "large eastern country."[123] Two army colonels and a lieutenant colonel were arrested after they were paid for revealing secrets to an intermediary working for Russia's secret service. The Montenegrin daily, *Vijesti*, claimed that an espionage ring was uncovered at the heart of the military leadership. The detention of Russian agents was linked to the dismissal of the head of Serbia-Montenegro's Intelligence Service in the Military General Staff (Obavestajna Uprava Generalstaba), Radoslav Skorić, in August 2003 for suspected links to Russian intelligence.[124]

MONTENEGRO

During and after the Milošević era, the Russian authorities remained adamant about the necessity of preserving Yugoslavia, even if it only consisted of two units, Serbia and Montenegro. For the Kremlin, the existence of Yugoslavia was important as it maintained a sizable ally in the Balkans. The Montenegrin government was encouraged by Moscow to remain in a federal structure and moves toward independence were described as nefarious Western attempts to dismember the country. After the ouster of Milošević in October 2000, Western powers sought to discourage the Montenegrin administration from pressing forward with a referendum on regaining independence. Because this goal coincided with its own, Moscow took a backseat in the dispute between Belgrade and Podgorica. In essence, EU pressures against Montenegrin statehood were supported by Moscow and served Russian interests. The state agreement between Serbia and Montenegro forged by EU security high representative Xavier Solana in March 2002 was welcomed as a mechanism for keeping the federation or "union" together. The Kremlin claimed that Serbia and Montenegro constituted "one of its priority partners in the Balkans." According to the Russian Foreign Ministry, the "successful accomplishment of Serbia and Montenegro's formation as a state would respond to the interests of enhancing Balkan stability."[125]

Moscow has not applied substantial pressure on Montenegro to remain in one state with Serbia, but Russian sources regularly criticized the West for seeking to break up Yugoslavia. Officials also implied that Albanian radicals were keen to profit from the potential crumbling of the FRY and from the campaign for Montenegrin independence in their drive for a Greater Albania.[126]

Montenegro remains highly dependent on Russian energy supplies and Russian companies have sought to penetrate the Montenegrin economy. For example, Lukoil maneuvered itself into a position to be the main candidate to gain control over Montenegro's oil company Jugopetrol-Kotor.[127]

Russian officials took the side of pro-Yugoslav formations while highlighting the divisions in Montenegrin society between pro- and anti-independence groups. Rather than exploiting ethnic, historical, and identity divisions between Montenegrins and Serbs, Russian officials claim the existence of a single ethnos (much as they do in the case of Russians, Ukrainians, and Belarusians) while pinpointing the Albanian minority as the chief source and beneficiary of conflicts in the republic. Russian Orthodox Church leaders have also attacked the proindependence Montenegrin authorities. In January 2002, Russian Patriarch Alexey II and Serbian Patriarch Pavle, who was visiting Russia, announced that the two Churches would concentrate their efforts to overcome schisms in Montenegro, Macedonia, and Ukraine. They claimed that "Montenegrin renegades" who reestablished the Montenegrin Orthodox Church during the breakup of Yugoslavia were supported by the government in Podgorica.[128]

Russian officials have allowed themselves to be used by Montenegrin supporters of a joint Yugoslav state in various public campaigns. The pro-Yugoslav federal prime minister (from Montenegro), Zoran Žižić, was photographed in the 2001 election campaign with the Russian ambassador Valeriy Jegoskin. At an election rally of the Together for Yugoslavia Coalition, the Russian ambassador claimed that "it is in the interest of Montenegro, Serbia, and Russia to preserve the Federal Republic of Yugoslavia."[129] Russian Patriarch Alexey II also attempted to exert influence on the Montenegrin electorate in favor of a Yugoslav state. Before Montenegro's April 2001 parliamentary ballot, he subscribed to an appeal issued by the Serbian Orthodox Church in a special message to the Together for Yugoslavia Coalition. According to Alexey, "I am backing efforts geared toward the revival of spirituality and the cultural, economic, social, and political unity of the brotherly peoples of Montenegro and Serbia united in a common Yugoslav state." Russian Church commentators have parroted the contentions of Serbian bishops that the Montenegrin nation is a "Communist invention."

MACEDONIA

In 1992, President Yeltsin recognized Macedonian independence. It was a difficult decision as he risked alienating the nationalist-Orthodox bloc who opposed the disintegration of Yugoslavia and favored Serbia in all regional conflicts. Moscow's calculation was to build on a future alliance with Macedonia and to draw the country closer to a pro-Russian Serbia. Several incidents, including the Albanian insurgency in 2001 and Western pressures on Skopje to reach an agreement with Albanian minority leaders, provided a valuable entry point for Russian diplomacy. Moscow posed as a champion of the Macedonian state, claiming that Albanians were intent on dismembering the country. In October 2003, Macedonian Prime Minister Branko Crvenkovski visited Russia in a gesture intended to strengthen relations between the two countries.

Russian authorities have depicted ethnic tensions in Macedonia as a consequence of "Albanian terrorism" and expansionism stemming from Kosovo. Officials warned that just as Kosovo could be torn away from Serbia, similarly parts of Macedonia could also be severed. In this manner, they ingratiated themselves with the government in Skopje. During Putin's visit to Serbia in June 2001, he warned that Macedonia could become a repeat of Kosovo if Western pressures forced Skopje to negotiate with Albanian rebels.[130] He suggested that Macedonia's borders be tightly sealed to prevent the movement of guerrillas and weapons, thus implying that the rebellion in Macedonia was a purely external imposition. Comparisons were regularly made between Albanian militants in Macedonia and armed Chechen groups that attacked neighboring republics in the Russian Federation. Both Albanian and Chechen guerrillas were labeled as Islamic fundamentalists and drug traffickers with alleged ties to Al-Qaeda. All Albanian political and guerrilla leaders, who are vehemently pro-American, have vigorously denied such connections.[131]

Echoing some of the propaganda emanating from Belgrade, the Russian media claimed that "Albanian terrorists" from Kosovo were also operating throughout western Macedonia and northern Greece. The aim was twofold: to demonstrate Russia's political support for the Macedonian government and to discredit any moves toward Kosovo's statehood as destabilizing for the wider region.[132] At the EU summit in Stockholm in March 2003, Putin complained that nothing had been done to disarm "Albanian extremists" and that the situation in Macedonia reminded him of the conflict in Chechnya where terrorists took advantage of the existing vacuum.[133] He blamed NATO for the constant threat of violence because it had not disarmed Albanian rebels in Kosovo. Putin claimed that the source of conflict in Macedonia was NATO's support for Albanian separatism.[134] Pro-Russian Macedonian politicians mimicked Moscow's disinformation campaign. Macedonian National Assembly speaker Stojan Andov claimed that the hidden agenda of Western countries was Russia's withdrawal from the region through the manipulation of the Albanian rebellion.[135]

As NATO involvement in Macedonia grew in the 1990s, Russia stepped up its pressures on Skopje to buy Russian arms and arbitrarily set a date for an agreement on military cooperation.[136] It strongly opposed the replacement of the UN military mission in Macedonia with a NATO force and vehemently supported the more militant elements in the Macedonian government during the armed conflict in the summer of 2001 with ethnic

Albanian rebels of the National Liberation Army (UCK). Moscow complained that it was not consulted in NATO's efforts to head off civil war in the country. Despite opposition from the White House, the Macedonian authorities obtained substantial stocks of military equipment from Ukraine, which had become a close partner for Russia under Putin. This included T-72 tanks, MI-24 helicopters, and Sukhoi-25 aircraft.[137] Macedonian military personnel were also sent to Ukrainian training centers and there were persistent reports of clandestine weapons supplies from Russia during and after the Albanian rebellion.[138] Western powers were concerned that the weaponry was being earmarked for Interior Ministry forces and were especially wary as Minister Ljupćo Boškovski advocated a hard line against the Albanian minority.

During Macedonian president Boris Trajkovski's visit to Moscow in October 2001, the Kremlin declared that Albanian gunmen in northern Macedonia were terrorists and compared the situation with Chechnya.[139] Trajkovski fell in line with Kremlin assertions that Russia was a great friend in the battle against international terrorism.[140] However, although a protocol on military cooperation was signed, the Russians were reportedly hesitant in providing specialized military equipment to the Macedonians so as not to antagonize the EU and the United States.

Russia has not been involved in peacekeeping deployments in Macedonia either in the UN Preventive Deployment (UNPREDEP) mission in the 1990s or in the postconflict NATO-led mission in 2001–2002. Both of these deployments were small-scale and focused on patrolling Macedonia's northern borders with no active rules of engagement. Moscow portrayed the Alliance deployment as a failure and a means for expanding NATO influence in the Balkans. Russian sources claimed that Skopje was disenchanted with Western peacekeeping efforts and appealed to Moscow for assistance based on "Russian counter-terrorist experience in Chechnya."[141]

Putin became personally involved in pushing for an agreement for the participation of Lukoil and Yukos in the privatization of the Greek Hellenic Petroleum company, which was due to build an oil pipeline from Thessaloniki in Greece to Skopje, with an extension to Nis in southern Serbia and to Kosovo.[142] Plans were drafted to extend the gas pipeline to other nearby countries. Moscow also set its sights on participating in road infrastructure projects cutting across Macedonian territory.[143] It is looking toward greater involvement in the power sector, especially in facilities constructed with Russia's technical assistance, and studying possible participation in the modernization of existing hydro and steam power plants as well as in building new electric power plants. In order to balance bilateral trade and increase the volume of exports to Russia, Macedonia was granted a preferential regime, which reduces customs tariffs by 25 percent. A free trade agreement between Russia and Macedonia has also been pursued.[144]

Russia has endeavored to develop economic relations with all former Yugoslav republics and comes fifth in the total volume of Macedonia's foreign trade and third in Macedonia's imports. During a meeting in Moscow in January 2003 between Foreign Ministers Ivanov and Ilinka Mitreva, talks focused on economic cooperation. Ivanov proposed that Macedonian construction companies participate in tenders for housing projects in Russia and expressed interest in the development of gas and oil pipelines and the modernization of Macedonian power plants.[145] The ministers signed a consular agreement easing the bilateral visa regime and declared the imminent signing of a free trade agreement. In December 2002, Skopje and Moscow local governments signed a cooperation program for the 2003–2006 period in a number of areas, including city and economic governance, architecture and construction, tourism, sports, health care, and local self-government.[146]

During the spring of 2001, Albanian insurgents in Macedonia played into the hands of the anti-Albanian lobby in Belgrade and Moscow. Kremlin intentions were to transform the perceptions of Albanians from that of victims of ethnic war into terrorists determined to destabilize the region. This propaganda strategy strengthened its case for preserving Yugoslavia and increased Russian influence. According to proponents of the Belgrade-Moscow axis, Albanian political leaders in each state were secretly plotting for a Greater Albania. Consistent condemnations of guerrilla attacks in Macedonia by Albanian politicians and their recognition of Macedonia's borders were dismissed as duplicitous. Serbian and Russian propaganda was determined to retool public perceptions of Albanians in the West as the equivalent of Afghanistan's Taliban menace. Either NATO was being duped into supporting their cause or the United States was deliberately creating a "stronghold of crime and terrorism" in the Balkans.

Armed conflict between Albanian guerrillas and Macedonian security forces assisted Moscow's position. It undercut calls for Kosovar statehood, because this was depicted as promoting militancy and regional instability. It reinforced arguments that Albanians were ill-suited for self-government and needed to remain under international wardship and eventual Serbian control. And it reinforced calls in Moscow for the preservation of the Yugoslav state as an important counterweight to the specter of "Albanian expansionism." Both Belgrade and Moscow pursued closer political and military links with Skopje in evident "Slavic solidarity" against rising pan-Albanianism. The Ohrid agreement arranged by the EU and United States in the summer of 2001 to integrate the Albanian minority more fully into state institutions was perceived in Moscow as giving too many concessions to Albanian nationalists. Russian officials felt vindicated in highlighting the operations of a small guerrilla group, the Albanian National Army (ANA), in Macedonia in the summer of 2003, which claimed to be fighting for a Greater Albania.[147] They asserted that the new rebellion proved the fragility of the Ohrid agreement and that the goal of all Albanian activists was to split the country. The accords were purportedly only a tactical maneuver allowing them to regroup for the continuing struggle.

While it has not launched campaigns to discredit the Macedonian authorities, Moscow has warned Skopje against joining NATO, claiming that this would clash with Russian interests.[148] Skopje has been criticized for failing to realize that NATO itself presented a danger to Macedonia's territorial integrity because of its alleged support for "Albanian extremism" and its objective of turning Macedonia into a U.S. protectorate.[149] In order to increase its profile in Macedonia, Russian officials appealed to Slavic brotherhood, Orthodox solidarity, and other standard clichés. This was the case during the visit to Moscow of Macedonia's Foreign Minister Mitreva in January 2003.[150] Mitreva spoke at the Duma where she asserted that the struggle against terrorism and to survive under "postimperialist conditions" were the principal priorities of both Skopje and Moscow and that Macedonia desired the restoration of a close friendship with Moscow. Foreign Minister Ivanov claimed that Russia was prepared to support Macedonian government efforts to "protect the country's sovereignty and integrity." In appealing to nationalist sentiments, Russia's ambassador to Macedonia, Agaron Asatur, distanced himself from the Ohrid agreement, emphasizing that "Russia is not one of the countries that prepared or signed that document."[151] In sum, Russia posed as the defender of Macedonian statehood and territorial integrity while depicting the NATO powers as untrustworthy and primarily concerned with Albanian interests.

8

Exporting Influence: Black Sea Balkans

BULGARIA

The Black Sea states of Bulgaria and Romania are considered strategically significant by Moscow for several reasons. First, their control can help project Russian influence throughout Southeast Europe, while the Black Sea itself is considered a zone of Russian dominance. Second, they form an infrastructural and energy linkage between Europe and the Caucasus-Caspian regions. And third, Bulgaria is viewed as an historic ally that can help restore Russia's outreach. Traditionally, Russia sought to keep open the Bosphorus straits between the Black Sea and the Mediterranean for its navy and raw materials. This was accomplished in the late nineteenth century at the expense of all states in the region, including Bulgaria and Serbia, which became Russian quasi-protectorates. Currently, Russian strategic ambitions primarily focus on the unhindered flow of Russia's energy supplies westward but not necessarily through the Bosphorus. Moscow intends to secure alternative routes through the Balkans as a shield against potential blockages in Turkey.

In the early 1990s, politicians in Moscow believed that they could draw Bulgaria into a closer political orbit, through membership in the CIS or in an alliance with the pro-Russian quadrilateral inner core of the Commonwealth (Russia, Belarus, Kazakhstan, Kyrgyzstan). Such proposals, declared by Yeltsin, were viewed with dismay in Sofia, leading President Zhelyiu Zhelev to declare them an "insult to Bulgarian sovereignty and national dignity."[1] Moscow concluded a bilateral treaty with Bulgaria during Yeltsin's visit to Sofia in August 1992. Nevertheless, relations did not develop smoothly and there was no agreement on the repayment of Russia's debt to Bulgaria. The issue was not resolved until May 1995 and trade between the two countries plummeted, largely as a result of disputes over gas prices.

Russia was intent on using Bulgaria as an outpost for its strategic penetration in the region, relying on the country's cultural and historical links with Russia and its valuable location. The disintegration of the Soviet bloc raised the question of how Sofia could protect its independence and promote economic development while maintaining balanced relations with Moscow.[2] Russia continued to display a superiority complex toward the smaller Slavic state and expected Bulgaria to remain part of the post-Soviet political, economic, and security space. Such expectations were disappointed when Bulgaria elected a pro-NATO reformist government in April 1997 and its progress toward NATO entry generated tensions with Moscow.

Putin's policy has proved more focused and politically active than Yeltsin's. In addition, Russian businesses have sponsored public relations campaigns aimed at redirecting Bulgaria's national strategy toward Moscow. However, Russian leaders were perturbed once again in "losing" Bulgaria after the parliamentary election victory of the King Simeon movement in June 2001. This prevented the Bulgarian Socialists from regaining power and potentially redirecting the country toward Moscow as they did in the mid-1990s. The Socialists finished a distant third in the ballot. The new Bulgarian authorities made it clear that they would seek NATO membership even after Socialist Georgi Parvanov was elected president in November 2001. Putin sought to revive the Russian-Bulgarian relationship, which had floundered during the administration of the Union of Democratic Forces (UDF). During a visit to Bulgaria in March 2003 to mark Bulgaria's liberation from the Ottoman Empire and the 125th anniversary of the Russo-Turkish war, Putin stressed that Russo-Bulgarian collaboration "will significantly contribute to the development of a prosperous and self-determining Europe."[3]

During the 1990s, much of the old Communist propaganda networks were active in Bulgaria in new disguises, whether as Socialists, agrarians, or nationalists. An essential component of their message was the benevolence of Russia, a sentiment still shared by substantial numbers of Bulgarian citizens. Pro-Russian propaganda in Sofia and Moscow played on historic themes of "Slavic solidarity" and Russian sacrifices on behalf of Bulgarian independence.[4] When Moscow realized that the cause was lost for Bulgaria's omission from NATO, a new twist on the "Slavic Orthodox" concoction emerged with some Russian commentators claiming that the Bulgarians were not fully Slavic.[5] The intent was to maintain the propaganda illusion that NATO was essentially a Catholic-Protestant organization aimed against the Eastern Slavic world.

Moscow was consistently opposed to Bulgaria's NATO membership but failed to dissuade Sofia from canvassing for entry.[6] Instead, Russia's intelligence services engaged in a campaign to discredit the Bulgarian government by planting rumors that circulated widely in Bulgaria that the new Prime Minister, Simeon Saxcobourgotski, was a marionette in the hands of the Russian mafia. Moscow also claimed that the United States was forcing Bulgaria into NATO and pressing on Sofia to downgrade its relations with Russia.[7] A Russian connection was also suspected by Bulgarian commentators over press reports that surfaced in March 2002 claiming that a secret meeting of Al-Qaeda took place in Sofia to identify U.S. and European embassy targets in Sarajevo. Bulgarian authorities strenuously denied the reports and launched a full investigation into its source.[8] According to a prominent Bulgarian journalist:

> It does not take much of an effort to recognize the familiar tactics of Moscow. Moscow understood that it cannot stop NATO's enlargement, neither can it distract Bulgarian institutions from achieving their goal to receive an invitation to NATO in November in Prague. This is why during the last two months, Russia adopted a new strategy—it does everything possible to discredit Bulgaria before its NATO allies. During their visits to Sofia recently, the *Duma*'s president Genadiy Seleznyov and other Russian parliamentarians suddenly started saying that relations between the two countries have never been more promising.[9]

There were no direct Russian military threats against Bulgaria but Moscow periodically voiced displeasure with Sofia's closer moves toward NATO and Washington. In the early 1990s, the Kremlin decided to pay off its outstanding debt to Sofia through the supply of military hardware and fuel. However, by early 2003, much of this debt had still not been returned and stood at some $50 million.

Moscow was angered by its exclusion from plans for a regional peacekeeping initiative in which the United States was involved. All the south Balkan countries, including Greece and Turkey, agreed during 1998 to establish the Multinational Peace Forces South East Europe (MPFSEE) to be trained and deployed in future crisis points. The brigade headquarters were located in the Bulgarian city of Plovdiv. The Foreign Ministry strongly criticized Russia's omission from the decisionmaking process as an attempt to push the country out of the Balkans.[10] It also complained that the peacekeeping force would be "fully bonded" to certain "nonregional organizations and countries." It viewed the new arrangement as an attempt by Washington through its Balkan allies to gain preponderance in the region and eliminate Russian influence.

Moscow complained when it was not invited to participate in a NATO defense ministers meeting with PfP representatives from Southeast Europe held in Sofia in October 1997. Russia's exclusion so angered officials that they publicly questioned Bulgaria's desire to develop good relations with Moscow and asserted that the entire Balkan area was a sphere of "vital interest" for the Kremlin.[11] At the close of NATO's war over Kosovo, Bulgaria refused to grant Russia overflight rights to position its troops in the province until an agreement was concluded between NATO and Russia on a unified command for the peacekeeping force. Yeltsin's aide, Andranik Migranian, described this as a hostile act by Sofia that would "intensify anti-Bulgarian feelings in Russia and risked influencing economic relations."[12] Sofia's opposition was denounced as an impudent and unfriendly act that would be long remembered by Moscow. Russian authorities were more angered by Bulgaria's action than that of Hungary and Romania, which also refused overflight rights:

> First, the Sofia bureaucracy did indeed drive the Russians completely up the wall. Diplomats familiar with the basic nature of the problem conceded that when it came to "uncooperative actions," the Bulgarians far surpassed both the Hungarians and the Romanians. At times their treatment of Russian officials bordered on outright scorn. The second reason is historical. Russia's history of relations with Hungary and Romania is too complex and controversial for us to be able to demand support from those countries at a critical time. Bulgaria is a different story. Moscow had the right to expect greater sympathy and more tact from a country that owes Russia its independence, and from a people who so love to swear "eternal love" for their "dear Russian brothers," whether it's appropriate to do so or not. But Sofia has new friends these days.[13]

Bulgaria's determination to join NATO sparked official protests in Moscow. In August 2000, the Foreign Ministry accused Bulgaria of forging excessively close relations with NATO, warning that this damaged the country's traditional ties with Russia. Bulgaria's Foreign Ministry responded with a sharp rebuke: "The discussion of national security issues is the sovereign right of the Bulgarian state. Any pronouncements or interpretations on this subject by any other country are unacceptable."[14] A simmering conflict between Moscow and Sofia concerns the planned opening of U.S. bases or military staging points in Bulgaria. Rebasing has been welcomed by the Bulgarian authorities as a means for reinforcing ties with Washington and bringing economic benefits to the country. The Kremlin signaled to Sofia that it strongly opposes this initiative and demands participation in negotiations over the proposed bases.[15]

Bulgaria remains overwhelmingly dependent on Russian gas supplies, while Russia views the country as an important energy hub for Southeast Europe and a major transit point for increasing supplies into Europe.[16] Of the $200 million Russian FDI in Bulgaria, by far the largest share was in the gas and oil industry. Russia seeks a monopolistic position over energy transit and consumption and is determined to prevent alternative sources and routes from the Caspian that bypass Russian territory. Proposals for such alternatives have included the southern gas pipeline, which is planned to connect energy supplies from Turkmenistan to Europe through Turkey and the Balkans.

About 80 percent of primary consumption in Bulgaria is based on imported energy resources.[17] Plans have also been drawn up to route two oil pipelines from the Caspian to Western Europe across Bulgarian territory: the Burgas-Alexandroupolis and the Albania-Macedonia-Bulgaria pipelines. While Russia seeks to gain control over this system to ensure regional energy dominance, Bulgaria wants to diversify its sources in order to buttress its independence. During the last decade, Russia increased its export of crude oil to Bulgaria: between 1992 and 1995 the import of oil grew from 30 percent to over 73 percent. According to Bulgarian analysts, "this enormous increase, especially in 1993–1994, is probably geopolitically directed to tie Bulgaria to Russia."[18]

Gazprom has taken an active part in Russian diplomacy and its directors have accompanied the Russian president and prime minister abroad. "Gas diplomacy" has been one of the most important elements of Russian policy toward Bulgaria.[19] Gazprom has systematically attempted to monopolize the state-owned Bulgarian gas transmission network and dominate supplies throughout the region. Pressures exerted on Bulgaria, including threats to reduce energy supplies when Sofia's foreign policies were not in tandem with Moscow's, provoked charges that Gazprom was a tool of Russian imperialism. This was highlighted when the company demanded that Bulgaria pay for its gas supplies in convertible currency. Throughout the 1990s, Bulgaria experienced various forms of energy blackmail implemented largely by Gazprom. When the Bulgarian government declined to sell its gas transmission system to Gazprom in the mid-1990s, Russian business exerted enormous political pressure for the privatization of pipelines through the Russian-linked Multigroup Corporation—a semilegal cartel with high-level political and security service connections.

The joint Bulgarian-Russian venture Topenergy also served as a conduit for Russian pressure and was established with the consent of Socialist prime minister Andrey Lukanov in the early 1990s. Although the treaty between the two countries required that they acquire equal shares in the venture to be held by state-owned enterprises, by 1997 Gazprom possessed over 54 percent (a blocking quota) in Topenergy. In the summer of 1997, 17 percent of Topenergy shares were held by private Bulgarian companies, such as Overgas, also connected to Gazprom and Multigroup. Bulgaria's portion, owned by several state enterprises, amounted to a mere 28.3 percent.[20]

Bulgaria was left dependent on Russia's gas supplies and could not impact on business decisions by the energy monopoly. Through the penetration of Gazprom and Topenergy, Russia was selling gas to Bulgaria for a price higher by one third than that offered to Germany. After a pro-Western government took power in Sofia in 1997, this arrangement was revoked, although Gazprom continued to control Topenergy. Simultaneously, the state-owned Bulgarian gas company Bulgargas, the sole supplier to Bulgarian consumers, signed a contract with Turkmenistan to diversify supplies. However, Russia continued to pressure Bulgaria to buy significant quantities through Gazprom as a condition for obtaining a lower price. Moscow clearly preferred to have a Socialist administration in place in Sofia, as it was more accommodating to Russian interests.

In February 2003, Gazprom expressed a strong interest in purchasing the state-owned gas company Bulgargas, which was due to be privatized in 2004.[21] Gazprom CEO Aleksey Miller also held consultations with President Parvanov and Prime Minister Simeon Saxecoburggotski to increase gas supplies to Bulgaria as well as to Greece, Macedonia, Serbia, and Turkey. Gazprom was keenly interested in gaining control over gas transit, distribution, storage, and import.[22] Bulgaria is in the process of liberalizing its gas market in line with EU directives, allowing large volume gas consumers to negotiate rates directly with importers and gas distribution companies. Gazprom is currently Bulgaria's main gas supplier and Bulgargaz purchases gas from Overgas, in which Gazprom holds 50 percent shares. Gazprom has been keen to eliminate intermediaries and sell gas directly to Bulgarian consumers; it has also offered closer cooperation with the Bulgarian chemical industry.

At a news conference with President Parvanov in March 2003, Putin claimed that Russian investment in Bulgaria's energy sector is of key interest to the Russian economy.[23] The transit of Russian gas via Bulgaria was to be increased by one-third. Moscow also wanted to participate in the proposed modernization of the Kozloduy nuclear power plant and the construction of a second nuclear power station near Belene. The Kostov government, before it lost elections in 2001, promised the EU that it would close Kozloduy's first and second power-generating units by 2003, and the third and fourth units by 2006. In return, the EU offered financial assistance. Two reactors were shut down, but this decreased the capacity to meet Bulgaria's electricity needs. As a result, the government rescinded the decision to deactivate two further reactors.[24]

Kozloduy produces above 40 percent of the country's electricity but is reliant on nuclear fuel imported from Russia. This gives Moscow a decisive role in the country's electricity sector. Bulgaria hopes to solve its energy problem by modernizing the Kozloduy plant, a task that Russian specialists have promised to undertake. According to a plan proposed by Moscow for paying off its Soviet-era debt, Russia would supply fuel for the nuclear power plant and spare parts for Russian military hardware still used in Bulgaria, including MiG fighter jets. The Russian company RSK "MiG" also established a joint venture with Bulgaria's Defense Ministry to repair MiG jets and service the Balkan region, thus pushing out a European consortium EADS that had bid for the project.[25]

In the oil sector, Lukoil owns several refineries and purchased 58 percent of Bulgaria's Neftochim refinery, one of the largest in the Balkans, in October 1999 and planned to expand its operations in other energy enterprises. Two Russian companies, Naftex and Lukoil, through their Bulgarian subsidiaries, dominate Bulgaria's oil market and endeavored to purchase other strategic economic sectors, including oil refineries.[26] Construction of the Bourgas-Alexandroupolis oil pipeline was scheduled to begin by the end of 2003. Talks were ongoing with Russia's energy ministry and with officials from Kazakhstan, which can provide huge quantities of oil from western Siberia through Russia's Novorosiisk to Burgas on Bulgaria's Black Sea coast, and from there to Alexandroupolis in Greece on the Aegean.[27] This project will provide an alternative to the Bosphorus route. While Russia would prefer to sell its own oil through the system, Sofia and Athens have tried to synchronize their actions and attract Moscow to sign the tripartite memorandum on the project.

Lukoil became the leading contender to privatize the Greek oil corporation Hellenic Petroleum, which is the largest oil company in the Balkans.[28] It was prepared to pay $454 million for a 23 percent stake in the company. The Greek government referred to Lukoil as "the exclusive contender" for the stake. Even after the sale, Athens will retain over 58 percent of the company and control its management. However, the minority stake would give Lukoil access to Hellenic Petroleum's infrastructure of more than 1,500 retail gasoline outlets throughout the Balkans and open up new opportunities for expansion. The Greek government was warned by a consortium of foreign investors against allowing sale of Hellenic Petroleum to Lukoil, as this would adversely affect profitability and investment. Lukoil faced charges that it had used its control over the Nefotochim Burgas refinery in Bulgaria to overcharge for crude oil supplies and underpay for processing at the refinery. The evident purpose was to "strip value from the Bulgarian company and its plant" and increase Sofia's vulnerability to Russian energy interests.[29]

During Putin's visit to Bulgaria in March 2003, ten bilateral documents were signed.[30] Moscow declared its intention to increase the quantity of gas transited through Bulgaria from 12 billion cubic meters to 18 billion. Putin expressed readiness to take part in the development of the gas-transportation network and the gasification of the entire country. If Gazprom was willing to give $50 million for the development of this network, the Russian government would grant a credit of $150 million. Putin also announced that Russia and Bulgaria would work together to increase sales of electricity in the region through the creation of a joint venture for electricity exports with Bulgaria's National Electric Company (NEK).[31] Russia's United Electric Systems (UES), run by former deputy prime minister Anatoliy Chubais, planned to expand overseas and considered the privatization of Bulgaria's electric distribution system to be strategically important.[32] The Bulgarian government, hoping to avoid the scandals associated with previous privatization deals, stated that eligible companies should have experience in a liberalized energy market and refused to accept offshore bids or consortiums formed specifically for the tender. The purpose was to achieve more transparency in privatization. UES did not meet these criteria and company leaders aggressively negotiated with Sofia to change them. UES decided to participate in the privatization through its subsidiary Nordik OU, an offshore venture.

Sofia's chief economic interest in Russia has been to restore Bulgarian exports on the Russian market after a precipitous decline following the collapse of the CMEA. But its success has been limited. Moscow discriminated against Bulgarian industries, denying them special status for lower import duty rates that it accorded to several other former satellites.[33] High customs duties coupled with the lack of an adequate banking system and Russia's inability to pay for imports curtailed Bulgarian businesses from operating on the Russian market. To exert political leverage on Sofia, Moscow imposed high customs duties, perpetuated a negative trade balance, and maintained Bulgarian dependence on Russian energy. This policy backfired, as Sofia turned increasingly westward in its political orientation and protested against comments by Yeltsin in early 1996 that Bulgaria may seek to join the economic union between Russia, Belarus, Kazakhstan, and Kyrgyzstan.[34]

The UN economic embargo on Serbia throughout the 1990s isolated Bulgaria from EU markets and provided opportunities for corruption and criminal groups to flourish. Moscow was intent on making the region more profitable for its own oligarchic lobbies and criminal cartels linked with the reenergized FSB structure. Bulgaria and the nearby region provided a potential bonanza for quasi-legal Russian businesses. Their expansion faced little competition from the West and Bulgaria had little choice but to accept Russian investments. In addition, during the UN embargo against Serbia, Moscow tried to persuade Bulgaria to open a "humanitarian corridor" to Belgrade, in violation of international sanctions. Sofia refused to be drawn into machinations designed to pull the country more closely into Russia's ambit.

In early 2001, a project for setting up an "economic growth council" provoked controversies when it transpired that this could greatly increase Russian influence over the country's economy.[35] The new body was intended to be a permanent consultative organ with the government on issues of economic policy, including investment priorities, utilization of EU and World Bank funds, and promotion of private business. Four of the nine members of the council were representatives of the Vazrazhdane Business Club, thus ensuring the dominance of an organization with close ties to Russian business interests. The initiative was postponed after an outcry by Bulgarian officials, economists, and business groups who charged that the council would create a monopoly for an organization that was involved in large-scale corruption.

Russian investments in Bulgaria amounted to $500 million by 2003, with Lukoil accounting for $340 million. Bulgaria's Economy Minister Nikolai Vassiliev claimed in January 2002 that his country hoped to attract $1 billion in Russian investments over the next few years.[36] Sofia viewed Russia as "an immense market and a considerable source of investment whose potential has not yet been fully captured."

Russia employed suspect tactics to gain possession over valuable Bulgarian companies. In the most glaring example, in July 2002 the Russian authorities claimed substantial shares in the largest state enterprise, Bulgartabak, on the grounds that under a post–World War II agreement the Soviet Union gained control over a substantial portion of Bulgartabak as part of Bulgaria's postwar "reparations" to the USSR.[37] Moscow subsequently granted Bulgartabak estate on indefinite lease to Bulgaria, with the option of a one-month notice of unilateral abrogation.[38] Putin's representative announced that Russia would open procedures for repossessing its property. Bulgarian officials responded that Russia's claim lacked any legal grounds. During the 1950s, Bulgaria acquired from the USSR domestic assets seized by the invading Red Army at the close of World War II. It gained ownership unconditionally on the basis of valid international agreements. According to Vassilev, "Russia has no reason to claim property and link that issue with the privatization of Bulgartabak." The enterprise was slated for a major privatization deal with a Western company when Russian authorities sabotaged the deal to eliminate business competition by claiming 21 percent of Bulgartabak's assets, or twelve of the twenty-two factories owned by the complex. As a result of this maneuver, several Western tobacco companies withdrew their offers for the company.[39] Grandtabak (the Russian Association of Distributors of Tobacco Products) announced that if its interests were ignored Bulgarian tobacco products would be barred from the Russian market. In December 2003, parliament approved a new strategy in which Bulgartabak would be carved up prior to its sale. The move was welcomed by Western tobacco giants.

During a visit to Moscow by Bulgarian Prime Minister Saxecoburggotski in June 2002, several agreements were signed, including the reduction of Russia's debt to Bulgaria in return for Sofia acceding to have its MiG-29 jet fighters serviced in Russian factories.[40] One controversial aspect of the visit was a link between the debt settlement and the registration of former Soviet property in Bulgaria as Russian-owned. In addition to opening up claims to Bulgarian business, this stipulation risked a dispute between Bulgaria and Ukraine, which also claimed some of the assets. In addition, Moscow offered to pay off some of its debts to Sofia by investing in Bulgaria.

Another controversy centered around Moscow's failure to deliver on its contracts. In July 2003, Minister of Defense Nikolay Svinarov announced that he would seek a compensation of $500,000 from Russia for breaking its contract for the repair of MiG-29s.[41] There were numerous postponements by

Moscow and parts for only three planes were delivered although six jets were
to be refurbished by April 2003. Due to delays, a joint venture between RSK
"MiG" and the Bulgarian company Terem had to be created, but these negotiations also came to a deadlock. Russia scorned legal commitments,
sought close involvement in modernizing Bulgaria's military to NATO standards; and promoted a joint venture through which it could gain control
over Terem. In such conditions, Bulgaria endeavored to increase Western
investment and technological modernization, while counterbalancing Russian
economic involvement.

The ethnic question has barely figured in Russia's policy toward Bulgaria.
It would be a difficult contortion according to "Slavic solidarity" for Moscow to foment conflict or to accuse Sofia of discrimination against its Muslim
populations (Turkish, Roma, Pomak), which form the country's largest minorities. Nonetheless, the Turkish minority has figured in Kremlin calculations because its main party, the Movement for Rights and Freedoms
(MRF) often finds itself as "king-maker" given the split between Socialists
and center-rightists in parliament. Russia's claims to Bulgartabak assets had
broader political implications. In addition to being a profitable industry,
tobacco production has also been a source of populist politics. A significant
percentage of the Turkish minority is employed by Bulgartabak. The MRF
has lobbied for the interests of its supporters and proved influential during
the privatization process. As a political formation with a steady electorate,
it is known to be a vote-swinging party and all other parties aim at building
a coalition with it. In this respect, whoever controls the tobacco industry
controls the income of a sector of the population that can promote political
change in their favor.

When the center-right government declined to sell the state-owned gas
transmission network, Russia's corporate lobby exerted enormous political
pressure against Sofia. Shortly before the parliamentary elections in June
2001, Russian secret services were involved in a calumny against the Union
of Democratic Forces (UDF) government.[42] Evidence emerged of Russian
involvement in an anti-UDF campaign financed by Michael Chorny, a notorious Russian businessman operating in Bulgaria. Documents were circulated to the mass media charging that Jordan Sokolov, chairman of the
National Assembly under the Ivan Kostov government, volunteered to cooperate with Russia's secret services. Another package of documents accused
Anelia Atanassova, wife of the director of the National Security Agency, and
Elena Kostova, wife of premier Kostov, of receiving astronomical sums of
money from Deutsche Bank. Such smear campaigns were also Moscow's
response to the expulsion of several criminally connected Russian businessmen from Bulgaria.

Some Bulgarian enterprises have been implicated in arms exports scandals to rogue regimes, including potential dual-use equipment to Middle
Eastern governments. Although the government has attempted to crack

down on such unauthorized sales and tighten controls over the arms trade, the disclosures have occurred at critical political junctures and dented Sofia's international reputation. One such scandal involving spare parts for armored personnel carriers destined for Syria was reported in the press on the eve of NATO's Prague summit in November 2002.[43] Suspicions were raised that the timing of the story was intended to throw into question Bulgaria's NATO invitation. According to Bulgarian security analysts, the entire episode was provoked and manipulated by anti-NATO groups including former members of the security forces with close ties to Kremlin intelligence services and the Russian mafia.

For much of the 1990s, Bulgaria's Socialists remained closely tied with Russia. When they returned to power in December 1994, Moscow's influence increased and it viewed Sofia as an opponent of NATO enlargement. During a visit to Sofia in March 1996, Yeltsin mentioned Bulgaria as the only East European country that could become a member of the Russian Commonwealth.[44] In March 1996, Duma chairman Genadiy Seleznev claimed that Russia and Bulgaria shared a common strategic aim and supported Bulgarian neutrality. By contrast, the oppositionist UDF was perceived as a dangerous element that would move the country closer to NATO. The UDF's election victory in April 1997 was seen as a major setback by the Kremlin, as the new Bulgarian administration embraced the prospect of NATO entry. Moscow endeavored to divide the Union by seeking to corrupt officials and parliamentarians with lucrative business propositions. It invested large amounts of money to undermine the government between 1997 and 2001. Resources were earmarked for the mass media and several political parties to discredit the UDF and to promote the more trusted Socialists. Pro-Russian lobbying groups in the BSP canvassed on behalf of Moscow's economic interests and against Bulgaria's NATO membership.

Bulgaria's center-right forces did not oppose good relations with Russia but expressed anxiety that Moscow was intent on influencing Bulgarian foreign policy to the detriment of relations with the United States. During Putin's visit to Bulgaria in March 2003, UDF supporters claimed that he attempted to influence Sofia's position on Iraq and worsened relations with Washington.[45] To counterbalance the center-right government, Putin cultivated ties with Socialist President Parvanov. Moscow's ITAR-TASS news agency claimed in September 2002 that Putin meets with Parvanov more often than with any other leader from the former Soviet bloc.[46] By September 2003, they had met five times during the course of one year and Parvanov was expected in Moscow again at the beginning of 2004.

The Kozloduy issue also became a source of political struggle. Sofia made a commitment to the EU that two of Kozloduy's reactors were to be shut down by 2006. However, it also conducted major repair work, claimed that the reactors were safe, and requested the EU to conduct a new inspection and change the closing date. Putin subsequently intervened by offering to repair the two reactors, thus undermining Bulgaria's competence and credibility.[47] EU experts had suggested that wholly new facilities be built in Kozloduy to replace the Russian-built plant. Putin retorted that Bulgaria should not spend an estimated $2 billion but instead pay Russia $300 million for repairs. The entire episode could bring the Kremlin several dividends: profits from Kozloduy repairs, greater political influence among the Socialist opposition that resists Kozloduy's closure, public criticism of the pro-Western government, and conflicts between Sofia and the EU that could complicate Bulgaria's accession.

Russian criminal groups have financed espionage operations in Bulgaria that "create purposeful feelings of insecurity and inspire civil discontent."[48] Bulgarian analysts contend that criminal attacks are not simply turf battles or score settling between rival groups, but a deliberate method for making the public feel insecure in order to raise popular opposition to pro-Western governments and to influence election results.

The layered connections between former Communist officials, intelligence services, and criminal networks linking Bulgaria and Russia were most evident in the operations of the financial organization, Multigroup. It was extremely active throughout the 1990s and maintained close ties with Russian criminal networks.[49] Multigroup was originally formed by high Bulgarian officials at the end of the 1980s with the assistance of the intelligence services. Seeing the writing on the wall for Communism, the organization was established to help transform the political monopoly of the Communist Party into economic strength, which could later be translated into a political comeback under different ideological labels. Multigroup maintained contacts with the post-KGB and criminal groups sponsored by Russia's intelligence services and was closely linked with the Russian-Bulgarian company Topenergy. One of the major figures in Multigroup, Iliya Pavlov, was closely tied to former prime minister and Gazprom head Chernomyrdin.

Several illicit deals were uncovered by Bulgarian intelligence services on the part of Russian companies, including money-laundering schemes. Five Russian businessmen were expelled from Bulgaria during 2000; the most notorious were Michael Chorny and Deniz Ershov. Chorny was involved in purchasing several Bulgarian banks, media outlets, telecommunications companies, and a football team, Levski FC.[50] He was known as a kingpin in Russia's Solntsevskaya crime syndicate and for having intimate relations with Russian oligarchs and officials. He also possessed a substantial stake in Metatabak, one of the bidders for Bulgartabak, and was involved in Tobacco Holding, another company that entered the final bidding for Bulgartabak.

Bulgaria prevented Chorny and other Russian crime figures from re-entering the country. In June 2003, Interior Minister Georgi Petkanov announced that his ministry would challenge a decision by the Sofia city court to lift a government order issued in 2000 that bars Chorny because of his connections to organized crime.[51] There were speculations that Sofia's improved relations with Moscow were opening the floodgates to a variety of Russian business interests. However, in October 2003 National Security Service head General Ivan Chobanov issued a new order barring Chorny from Bulgaria on the grounds that he posed a threat to national security.[52]

Several incidents demonstrated the intersection between crime, corruption, political influence, and Russian state and business interests. Iliya Pavlov, Bulgaria's wealthiest and most powerful businessman, was shot dead in Sofia in March 2003 after testifying in a trial of the October 1996 killing of former prime minister Andrey Lukanov.[53] Investigators concluded that Pavlov's killing was linked to business interests as he was a key figure in the Bulgarian-Russian energy trade and headed the MG Corporation (formerly Multigoup), which held stakes in tourism, banking, food production, and energy sectors. In 1996, Pavlov became the director of the joint Russian-Bulgarian company Topenergy, which coordinated the gas and oil trade and which later became a subsidiary of Gazprom.

Russia's intelligence services remained particularly active in Bulgaria and in March 2000 a major spying scandal erupted when Bulgaria's Foreign Ministry gave Moscow one week to withdraw three high-ranking diplomats from Sofia.[54] One of the diplomats was the military attaché who had been recalled from Poland in 1993 over a similar espionage scandal. The three suspects were implicated in the arrest of a retired senior Bulgarian military intelligence officer, Colonel Yani Yanev, and the chief of a Defense Ministry archive. They were accused of delivering military secrets and other classified intelligence material to Russian diplomats in Sofia. The expulsions were an unprecedented event in the history of Bulgarian-Russian relations and indicated the seriousness of the charges. On a visit to Sofia in March 2001, FBI director Louis Freeh praised Bulgaria for expelling the three diplomats and for fighting Russian crime groups. Freeh stated that it was important to "identify and prevent agents of other countries from conducting intelligence operations in our democracies."[55] He also announced plans to build a permanent FBI office in Sofia.

Bulgaria's Foreign Minister Nadezhda Mihailova asserted that the Interior Ministry possessed evidence that officials at the Russian embassy systematically committed actions that "threatened Bulgaria's national interests and security as well as being a direct intrusion into its domestic affairs."[56] Moscow reacted angrily to the incident and reciprocated by expelling three Bulgarian diplomats. The Kremlin also issued a standard accusation to deflect attention from its espionage activities by claiming the Bulgarian government was conducting an "anti-Russian campaign" and pandering to U.S. interests. Deputy Foreign Minister Aleksander Avdeev warned that Sofia's determination to draw closer to NATO would undermine its friendly relations with Russia.[57] In a patronizing "big brother" posture, Russian authorities claimed that Bulgaria's national interests did not correspond to the government's policies.

The Bulgarian government was rocked by a scandal in September 2003 over the planned appointment of Brigo Asparuhov, a former Communist intelligence operative, to act as special adviser to the prime minister on security issues and coordinator of the special services of the Bulgarian defense and interior ministries. Following strong NATO and U.S. pressure and heated domestic controversy, the Soviet-trained general reluctantly turned down the nomination in October 2003. Some observers voiced suspicions that Russian services had a hand in the planned appointment and influenced the premier to nominate him.[58]

ROMANIA

Relations between Romania and Russia were distant under the Nicolae Ceauşescu regime and barely improved after the fall of the dictator. Only in September 1993 did Romanian leaders travel to Moscow to sign agreements on restoring economic ties. Romania became the only country in the region with which Russia failed to sign a bilateral political treaty throughout the 1990s. Bucharest insisted that any treaty include a joint condemnation of the 1939 Nazi-Soviet Pact under whose terms Romania lost its Moldovan province. Moscow feared that this would legitimize moves toward a Romanian-Moldovan union. The Treaty on Friendly Relations and Cooperation was finally signed in July 2003, during a visit by President Ion Iliescu to Moscow.[59] The Duma ratified the treaty in the fall of 2003. The accord was preceded by the signing of a bilateral declaration that dealt with outstanding issues, such as the repatriation to Romania of gold and cultural items kept by the Soviet Union after World War I. The two parties agreed to set up a joint commission of experts to resolve the issue. The declaration condemned the 1939 Ribbentrop-Molotov Pact as well as Romania's participation in World War II on the side of Nazi Germany. Defense Minister Ivanov promised to support Romania's candidacy for a nonpermanent seat on the UN Security Council. A Romanian Consulate was opened in St. Petersburg, with a diplomatic and an economic role. Nonetheless, relations between the two countries remained fraught with mutual suspicion, especially as Bucharest was concerned about Moscow's policies toward the wider region, especially Moldova.

During the 1990s, Russian state propaganda depicted Romania as a regional expansionist power with ambitions toward Moldova and parts of Ukraine that it lost to the USSR after World War II. Moscow fostered animosities among Bucharest and Chisinau and Kyiv in order to appear as the defender of the territorial integrity of Romania's northern neighbors.

Bucharest initially accepted the "Kvitsinsky Doctrine" propounded by Moscow on the eve of the Soviet collapse. In negotiations over a bilateral treaty, a clause was inserted whereby both parties were prohibited from joining any military alliance that was perceived by either side to be hostile. Following the disintegration of the USSR, the treaty remained unratified by Bucharest and Romania began to adopt a more openly pro-NATO position to the chagrin of the Kremlin. Although no direct military threats were made against the country, it was understood that Russia strongly opposed Bucharest's foreign and security policies.

Romania remains dependent on Russian oil and gas, which constituted some 90 percent of Romanian imports, and Russian companies sought to purchase refineries, pipelines, and other energy infrastructure. In December 1999, Lukoil acquired a controlling stake in the Petrotel refinery, one of the largest consortiums in the country. In August 2003, Romania opened the bidding for control of its national oil company SNP Petrom.[60] The sale of a controlling stake in Petrom was expected to be worth up to $1 billion and was a key element of the country's accords with international lenders. Analysts believed that three companies that have been most active in the region, Lukoil, Hungary's MOL, and Austria's OMV, would form a consortium to purchase controlling shares. In July 2003, during a visit to Moscow to sign a bilateral treaty, President Iliescu met with representatives of Gazprom and other gas companies regarding the possibility of establishing a joint consortium to transport gas from Russia to Romania. They also discussed the possibility of building a pipeline from Russia to the Romanian port of Constanța. Russian companies were also planning to purchase major stakes in Romania's petrochemical industry.

During the 1990s, more than 200 Russian companies became involved in the Romanian economy, with investments reaching more than $400 million.[61] A steel complex, based in the town of Targoviste, was purchased in August of 2002 by the Conares Trading company, controlled by Russian business. This complex is now called "little Russia." Russia's prime minister stated in Bucharest that "the Russian government will continue to support our companies in the process of privatization in Romania." They were expected to participate in the privatization of several large enterprises, including Distrigaz, Carom, and Petrotub. Romanian officials believe that "big Russian investment incursions" were intended to strengthen their position in preparation for Romania's EU entry, expected around 2007. Russian companies would then have an opportunity to act more freely on the European market.

In his 1999–2000 and 2001 reports to parliament, the director of Romanian Security Intelligence (RSI), Alexandru-Radu Timofte, claimed that "foreign interest groups" posed a danger to the country's economy, including threats "under the guise of strategic investments."[62] These groups "have thrown great sums of money into the ring" and individuals who acted on their behalf received warnings from the judicial system and left the country before being detained. Timofte mentioned the collapsed National Investment Fund, which was manipulated from abroad; there was little doubt that he was referring to Russian business groups. He also warned that corruption posed "a direct threat aimed at constitutional democracy" and endangered national security. He implied that foreign agents could also be involved in the process to gain favors from government officials.

The persistent political crisis in neighboring Moldova has been manipulated by Moscow to cast Romanian foreign policy in a negative light. This was evident as the conflict heated up in Chisinau between the government and protestors in February 2002. There were demonstrations by the opposition movement against the enforced introduction of Russian as a state language by Moldova's Communist administration. However, Russian officials presented the demonstrations as a Romanian provocation aimed at annexing Moldova. Romanian authorities charged Moscow with fueling a crisis in the torn state in order to break the pro-Romanian block, to more fully subordinate Moldova, and to discredit the government in Bucharest. Russian officials thereby cast aspersions on Romanian foreign policy and questioned Bucharest's reliability as a potential NATO ally. Communist authorities in Moldova, with close ties to Moscow also fueled speculations that Bucharest would promote "revanchism" toward Moldova if it were admitted into NATO.[63]

Since the reelection victory of President Iliescu in November 2000, Moscow has made various overtures toward Bucharest. In particular, the Russians were eager to develop closer economic ties in the energy and transport sectors. Some analysts speculated that Iliescu maintained secret ties with the Russian political establishment and there were rumors of the supposed existence of a telephone hotline to the Russian president, which Iliescu strenuously denied.[64] The Kremlin believed that a social democratic president and government in Bucharest would be more accommodating than a center-right administration on the Moldovan question and this would play to Moscow's advantage.

With Romania poised for NATO accession, conflicts erupted in September 2003 concerning parliamentary oversight over the country's secret services. Western agencies applied pressure on Romanian deputies to clean up the intelligence network by purging former members of the Securitate (Ceauşescu's secret police). The process was opposed by secret service chiefs who resisted greater civilian control over their operations. Following the dismissal of Vasile Iancu, Romania's deputy head of intelligence, parliament demanded an explanation from the director of the service, as the removal of deputy spy chiefs had to be decided by the Supreme Defense Council. Western intelligence services remain concerned about possible connections between former Communist intelligence officers and Russian services. Washington demands greater civilian control over the intelligence services of all NATO invitees together with transparency in their budgets.

9

Conclusions: Looking Ahead

OBSESSIVE-COMPULSIVE: RUSSIA AND EAST EUROPE

If the Russian Federation was a mirror image or an understudy of the United States or other Western powers, the expansion of Moscow's political and economic influence in Eastern Europe could be considered benign. If Russia had a thriving liberal democracy, a vibrant civil society, an effective multi-ethnic system, a productive capitalist economy, and a genuine peace policy in Chechnya, then its influences may have even been welcomed in Eastern Europe, regardless of historical experiences with Russian imperialism. Unfortunately, this is not the case and current Russian influences are largely negative and underpinned by the strategic goal of long-term dominance. For an expansive country with great power aspirations, foreign policy becomes an instrument of domestic policy while domestic policy is exported abroad. In this context, characterizing President Putin as a "pragmatist" does not address the question of Russia's objectives, but simply describes the means employed to achieve six strategic goals in and through Eastern Europe.

1. *Expanding foreign policy influences.* Capturing and exerting predominant if not exclusive influence over the foreign policy orientations and security postures of nearby states formerly in the Soviet zone of influence. This goal is depicted as a means for stemming and reversing Moscow's decline as a major international player. It is primarily intended to restore Russia's

regional status and hegemony. Some states are more vulnerable to Kremlin pressures, especially Russia's CIS neighbors, but none is fully immune from attempted domination.

2. *Promoting economic monopolization.* Obtaining economic benefits and monopolistic positions through targeted foreign investments and strategic infrastructure buyouts. This strategy can also gain Moscow substantial influence over a country's economic, financial, trade, and investment policies as neighboring capitals became increasingly dependent on Moscow for their economic functioning. This approach revolves around a calculation that Russia can regain its position as a continental and global power on the basis of a strong and expansive economy.

3. *Consolidating political dependence.* Increasing East European dependence on Russian energy supplies and capital investments. This dependence can then be steadily converted into long-term and predictable intergovernmental political influence. Close connections between the Kremlin and large Russian companies, whether through executive appointments, the promotion of overseas operations, or financial, legal, and police instruments, demonstrates that foreign and economic policy are closely interwoven and coordinated. Revenues from energy sales and foreign investments will enable Russia's economic recrudescence to be transformed into predominant political influence.

4. *Limiting Western enlargement.* Limiting the pace and scope of Western penetration in Russia and its "zone of interest" and constricting Western enlargement, especially with regard to the security arena in the CIS states. NATO control in the Balkans and Central Europe and increasing U.S. involvement in Central Asia and the Caucasus are viewed as springboards for American domination in "Eurasia" that would place Russia at a geopolitical and economic disadvantage. Obstructing Alliance enlargement and operations is viewed as a means for restricting American "hegemony" and strengthening Russian security. This would also enable Moscow to prevent or limit neighboring governments from participating in U.S.-led political or military coalitions opposed by the Kremlin.

5. *Rebuilding global influence.* Using the broader East European region as a springboard for rebuilding a larger sphere of predominant influence and great power status. The region could thereby become a gateway to Moscow's political influence throughout the continent rather than a barrier against it. Russia is seeking a hierarchical system of international relations in which security agreements between the major powers take precedence over and determine the position of medium and small states. Such a strategy would also counteract any obstructions to expanding Russian influence around its borders from the Baltic Sea to Central Asia.[1]

6. *Eliminating U.S. unipolarity.* Gradually but systematically undercutting and restricting the transatlantic or Europe–United States relationship as well as Eastern Europe's direct ties to Washington. By steadily expand-

ing political influence in targeted countries, Russian agencies aim to prevent closer regional cooperation with the United States. The ultimate purpose is to reinforce the European-Russian or "Eurasian" strategic "poles" to counterbalance the global predominance of the United States. Transatlantic disputes also provide fertile terrain for Moscow to augment conflicts and maneuver itself into a stronger position to determine European security.

The struggle over Eastern Europe revolves around two opposing strategic concepts—"Eurasian" and "Euramerican." The "Euramerica" option envisages the close engagement of the United States in European security, whether through NATO or in various bilateral and subregional arrangements. In marked contrast, the "Eurasian" variant would consist of a Brussels-Moscow axis in which the EU achieves a greater security role in close collaboration with Russia. The Kremlin could thereby exercise veto powers over major European decisions in foreign and security policy. While most of the new democracies support the "Euramerica" structure, competition with the "Eurasian" alternative is most pronounced in Belarus, Ukraine, and Moldova. All three countries are now defined as "strategic partners" by Moscow, which calculates that their close integration with Russia can counter the process of NATO enlargement and limit American involvement in Eastern Europe.

East Europeans harbor mixed feelings about a potentially stronger and more prosperous Russia. If indeed Russia were to stage sustained economic modernization accompanied by the consolidation of a strong state, its pressures throughout the region will increase. While an unstable and economically backward Russia could become a source of regional insecurity, the most palatable solution would be a politically stable but relatively weak Russia with growing links to the West but with restricted foreign policy capabilities. A prosperous Russia does not signify a more cooperative government. If Russia rapidly bolsters its economy without undergoing profound democratization, it could become more aggressive and expansive. It may be preferable to have an economically weak or domestically entangled Russia as long as this does not precipitate violent disintegration or the destabilization of neighboring countries. Although Russia's actions remain restricted by its capabilities, Moscow will seek to expand its maneuverability, especially in the former Communist sphere. Western moves to integrate the CIS states or to construct energy lines that bypass Russia will continue to be seen as directly threatening Russian security interests.

For Eastern Europe, EU and NATO membership are viewed as overarching goals. Some capitals also seek a coordinated strategy toward Russia and a common energy policy. As several states moved closer to the EU, they have proposed an "Eastern dimension" toward Russia and the CIS although they possess limited tools in influencing Moscow's foreign policy. However, political leaders in Russia do not treat their former proxies as equal partners. Instead, they endeavor to reach accords with power centers in Washington and Brussels over the heads of former satellites, whose security concerns they disregard.[2] Relations between East European states and Moscow will impact on a range of issues, from economic and energy policy to security postures and military capabilities. Potential vulnerability to Russian pressures may complicate their Western integration and their relations with Washington. The EU may prefer that Ukraine, Belarus, Moldova, and other former Soviet republics reintegrate with Russia as this would supposedly ensure greater political and economic coherence and guarantee vital energy supplies to Western Europe. At present, Moscow supplies over 15 percent of fuel provisions in the EU and this dependence is likely to accelerate in the coming years. Russia is keenly interested in increasing supplies and fostering European dependence. This would be one important foundation of Putin's characterization of the EU as a "strategic partner."

Russia's eagerness to establish closer ties with Western powers following 11 September 2001 was a strategic calculation to gain political and economic benefits.[3] For Putin, modernization of the economy is a high priority and he needs Western cooperation to reestablish Russian power. East Europeans remain suspicious about Moscow's strategic intentions and the NATO-Russia Council is criticized because it "brought Russia into our house again; through the back door."[4] The U.S.-Russian relationship is viewed as one based on size and strength and not on adherence to "shared values" such as democracy and human rights. However, size and strength will not be enough to sustain the relationship:

> It seems that politicians from the Czech Republic, Hungary, and Poland are somewhat less enthusiastic about integrating Russia more fully into Transatlantic structures, such as NATO, than, for example, the United States and some other countries, because they are not entirely convinced that Russia has really become a full-fledged democratic country that can be entirely trusted.[5]

Russian officials have not opposed East European entry into the EU, with seven states gaining membership in May 2004. Paradoxically, EU enlargement may be more unpredictable for Russian interests than NATO expansion.[6] The economic gap between Europe and Russia could accelerate and undermine Moscow's ambitions as an equal player. An expanding EU will affect border controls and visa requirements under the restrictive Schengen requirements to the detriment of excluded countries.[7] The introduction of economic and trade legislation and ecological and accounting standards according to EU requirements could mean new hurdles for CIS producers and exporters. EU regulations also require greater transparency in financial transactions and this could discourage Russian companies from operating in the region.[8] EU-standard import duties will be levied on Russian goods and new restrictions will be introduced on the transit of Russian cargo. East Europeans fear that a strict application of Schengen will negatively affect their relations with eastern neighbors who will be excluded from the EU for the foreseeable future.[9]

Moscow has sought closer links with the EU, initially through the Partnership and Cooperation Agreement (PCA), formalized in June 1994 in the economic and trade arenas. Putin has pushed the notion of a "Unified Space" (*Odinnoye Prostranstvo*) when negotiating postenlargement issues such as visas, travel, and commerce. But this also assumes cooperation in other domains, including political and security issues. However, Russian authorities have made it clear that they are not seeking EU membership or even associate status, as they are unwilling to submit to any supranational authority. They see the country as a regional power in its own right and not as a subordinated state. Full assimilation would mean becoming a nonimperial middle-level power on a relatively meager economic level with restricted global capabilities.

Moscow seeks a "strategic partnership" with the EU that could remove NATO's rationale, marginalize the smaller East European states, and limit U.S. influences.[10] The Kremlin favors the development of a European security pillar with a close relationship with Russia and a scaled-back U.S. role. It has supported a permanent EU-Russia Council and regular EU-Russia summits that can implement joint decisions in the security arena. This would contribute to giving Moscow a more prominent official role in Eastern Europe. In May 2003, Putin reiterated that "[i]f Europe wants to be independent and a full-fledged global power center, the shortest route to this goal is good relations with Russia."[11] Moscow is also pushing for more substantial influence over states excluded from the EU and NATO and aims to neutralize the maneuverability of Central Europeans, even though they are already NATO members:

> The diminution of Central Europe to a group of client states was quasi-institutionalized when European Commission president Romano Prodi signed a protocol with Putin establishing monthly meetings between Russia's defense establishment and the EU's Political and Security Committee. This EU move to establish a permanent security mechanism with Russia was a humiliation for Poland, the Czech Republic, and Hungary, which, although NATO members, were not afforded a similar consultative mechanism.[12]

The Kremlin requires West European and U.S. acquiescence or neutrality in reconstructing much of the post-Soviet zone under its political and security umbrella. Russia has promoted itself as a regional stabilizer, on guard against the threats of weak states, authoritarian governments, Islamic fundamentalists, and terrorist networks. It has suited Moscow to have internally unstable or authoritarian regimes on its doorstep that not only cast Russia in a positive light, but also reinforce its contention that Russian influences can benefit the region: "Focusing exclusively on Russia's real or politically manipulated sensibilities is inappropriate for a variety of reasons. While the West should not provoke Russia's nationalist passions, it should neither be a hostage to often politically manipulated hypersensitivity nor encourage it."[13]

Moscow has viewed the EU's Common Foreign and Security Policy (CFSP) as a potential counterbalance to "NATO-centrism" in Europe.[14] In seeking to restrict U.S. influence, Moscow has traditionally sought an independent European bloc. Such hopes have yet to be realized as the EU has evolved into a vehicle for economic and institutional integration devoid of a coherent security and foreign policy. Most East European capitals express concern that the emerging European Security and Defense Policy (ESDP) could push the United States out of Europe while lacking any military credibility. Hence, there is hesitation in supporting the ESDP among staunchly Atlanticist governments who fear that Europe cannot stand up to Moscow's pressures on its own. Anxieties are expressed about a Kremlin "divide and rule" strategy that could decouple the Alliance and leave the East Europeans stranded.

In order to tie the EU closer to Russia and to exert more effective influence over its economic, foreign, and security policies, Moscow will push for increased Union dependence on Russian energy supplies.[15] As dependence increases, Russia can maneuver itself into an indispensable position in decisions pertaining to Euro-Atlantic security and use energy as a source of pressure and blackmail as it has among former satellites. Russia's neighbors also express fears about the authoritarian drift of Russian politics and the negative impact this could have in the region. Putin's assertiveness at home is likely to be matched by increasing aggressiveness abroad, thus posing greater threats to the new European democracies.

BIPOLAR DISORDER: RUSSIA AND
THE UNITED STATES

Russian elites have exploited the "conflict potential" of relations with the United States as a means for fostering national unity and constructing a state identity.[16] Under Yeltsin and Putin, the anti-U.S. card was occasionally played to mobilize public opinion. Moscow was aggrieved that the bipolar world order had been transformed into a unipolar one and Russia was no longer in a pole position. The international "equilibrium" had been disturbed and needed to be restored; otherwise, Russia would sink under the overwhelming weight of U.S.-led globalization. Furthermore, U.S. unilateralism under the George W. Bush administration accentuated Moscow's fears that it would be ignored by Washington in any major international crisis. The undermining of the authority of the UN Security Council during the Iraqi war in 2003 was seen as vetoing the Russian veto and diminishing Moscow's prestige and power on the international arena.

Putin's foreign policy concept published in July 2000 described the necessity of combating the dangerous trend of U.S. "unipolarity." One purported means for achieving U.S. dominance was the pursuit of globalization through economic and political control.[17] The "global correlation of forces" was "visibly imbalanced," hence a new international security configuration had to be created: "We cannot overlook the increasing aggressiveness of very influential forces in some countries of the world and the diminishing effectiveness of international security and conflict-resolution institutions."[18] According to Foreign Minister Ivanov, it was important for Russia to work with various power centers, including the EU as "the largest integration association in the world and a major pole of an emerging world multipolar system."[19]

In the post–11 September environment, Moscow has become more cooperative with the United States and less verbally vehement against NATO enlargement. Russian leaders initially believed that Washington would legitimize Russia as the "regional superpower" and peacekeeper in Central Asia, the Caucasus, and elsewhere.[20] Instead, the United States decided on direct military involvement. Putin calculated that this could also benefit Russia if the U.S. presence was short-termed, helped to provide economic assistance to unstable regions, and spared Moscow any substantial costs. Meanwhile, Russia would maintain its military presence and its political influence while acting as a U.S. partner. This was a form of "bandwagoning" in which Russia would opportunistically benefit from U.S. strength by gaining concessions in other arenas. Such a policy could be abandoned if the Kremlin envisaged greater advantages from noncooperation with Washington.

One intriguing question is whether the Kremlin prefers a weak and ineffective NATO, in which the United States acts unilaterally, or a more capable NATO that can influence and modify U.S. policy. Any substantial role by Russia in NATO's decisionmaking structures through the NATO-Russia Council will serve to weaken the Alliance, especially if the United States is convinced that most EU countries are unreliable and have limited military capabilities. Moscow's involvement in any phase of NATO policymaking is of grave concern to East Europeans who fear that NATO could become ineffective and bereft of American leadership.

Since 11 September, Moscow has argued that NATO is in crisis and enlargement will further weaken the organization. It posits that NATO will wane as a security structure as Washington will not engage the organization for major combat operations.[21] The competition between U.S. and Allied chains of command plus the difficulty of running a war in a committee of nineteen-plus members could make NATO increasingly redundant. Any transformation from a defense organization into a political association with a supplementary military role will make it more palatable to Moscow despite NATO's enlargement eastward. Russian involvement through the Russia–

North Atlantic Council (R-NAC) could increase its leverage in Alliance planning. The new organism, formally inaugurated at a Russia-NATO summit meeting in Rome in May 2002, started with a limited agenda focusing on such issues as terrorism, arms proliferation, and peacekeeping. However, the East Europeans were concerned that its mandate could expand as the Council gave Moscow a voice in Alliance deliberations.

Some analysts argued that Putin rejected the doctrine of "multipolarity" in his dealings with Washington.[22] Such premature hopes were dented when Moscow sided with France and Germany during the Iraq crisis in early 2003. Putin once again publicly elevated "multipolarity" as a strategic objective, meaning the pursuit of multiple power centers in order to diminish U.S. dominance.[23] In May 2003, Foreign Minister Ivanov claimed that a new system of international relations should be based on the principles of "multipolarity" and "multilateral global cooperation."[24] Moscow seeks the creation of multiple power centers to diminish U.S. power. "Multilateral cooperation" is viewed as a pyramid with the UN Security Council at the apex of a structure supported by various regional organizations and bilateral ties. Before he was elected president, Putin chaired the meeting of the Russian Security Council, which revised the country's national security concept and its military doctrine to include "unipolarity" as a threat to Russian security.[25] To be accepted as a major "pole," Moscow believes that it has a strategic imperative to integrate the CIS and project its influence: "Retired General Makhmut Garayev's perspective, widely shared across the entire Russian military-political elite, also logically entails the precept, enshrined in official policy documents, that Russia must expand territorially and politically as a central pole of the multipolar world if it is to survive at home."[26]

Putin hailed the joint statement on Iraq, issued on 13 February 2003 by Russia, France, and Germany, as "the first brick in the construction of a multi-polar world."[27] Apparently, Russia, France, and Germany were determined to work together toward that alternative, thus enabling Moscow to extend its influences in European affairs. Putin claimed the joint statement was adopted spontaneously on the initiative of French President Jacques Chirac. "Paris is the best place for it. If it had been done in Russia, everybody would be saying that we are trying to split Europe and the United States." In sum, Putin restated his pre–11 September position by calling for international containment of the U.S. superpower so that he could strengthen Russia's global status.[28]

U.S. policymakers should soberly reflect on the premature conclusion that Putin's Russia has been transformed into a reliable ally and a trusted partner. Russian-U.S. divergencies in basic objectives are too often presented as mere tactical differences.[29] There is a naive and simplistic supposition that the United States and Russia share a common enemy of "international terrorism" and that Moscow has substantial experience in combating "Islamic extremism." Shared enemies do not necessarily ensure enduring friendship, especially if they are exploited to one side's advantage. The Kremlin will offer cooperation in combating common threats, but in return will expect economic benefits, enhanced status, and a freer hand to deal with domestic opposition, separatist movements, and awkward neighbors. Putin's approach can be described as either pragmatism or opportunism calculated to restore Russia's "balance" with the United States.[30] Domestic critics of Putin's policy believe that Russia has already given too much away to the United States:

> The West is expanding to Central Asian republics. NATO's troops play the master in Kazakhstan, Kyrgyzstan, Uzbekistan and Tajikistan. US intelligence planes, including the AWACS, fly near the Russian border under the pretext of combating *Al Qaeda*. Everyone promised that the flights would stop after the end of the operation in Afghanistan. The operation has not ended yet—it will never end, why should the West withdraw troops from a potentially rich region? It is natural that it's an expensive task for Russia to stop NATO's expansion. But it shouldn't be forgotten that many Russians live in these republics. Russia must take care of these people by exerting influence on local politics and politicians. However, Russia has not done anything in this direction.[31]

Washington's new doctrine of preemptive strikes against terrorist networks and "rogue regimes" encourages Russia to employ a similar doctrine in its self-declared "spheres of security." Moscow will insist on substantial prerogatives toward neighboring countries seen as threatening to Russian interests.[32] In October 2003, Defense Minister Ivanov declared that Russia reserved the right to intervene militarily in the CIS in order to settle disputes that cannot be solved through negotiation. Putin added that the pipelines carrying oil and gas to the West were built by the Soviet Union and it was Russia's right to protect "even those parts of the system that are beyond Russia's borders."[33] Ivanov additionally claimed that the use of nuclear weapons remains a key tenet in Russia's defense strategy, and that Moscow does not exclude the possibility of preemptive strikes to defend Russia's interests or those of its allies.

POSTTRAUMATIC STRESS: RUSSIAN FUTURES

Instead of idealistic pronouncements about a new dawn of West-East partnership, analysts need to determine who was likely to benefit most from the new rapprochement. Unable to prevent NATO expansion, Moscow seeks to influence the Alliance through closer political collaboration. East European capitals carefully monitor NATO's relations with Moscow as this has a direct bearing on their security. The three Central European countries (Poland, Hungary, and the Czech Republic) that were already NATO members

228   COLD PEACE

opposed giving Russia a voice in decisionmaking. Although they recognized that Putin had become more cooperative and that it was preferable to have a stable NATO-Russia relationship, they remain concerned that Moscow could block NATO initiatives. Czech president Vaclav Havel has been the most outspoken over the new rapprochement between Moscow and Brussels. According to him, any attempt to integrate Russia into NATO would hurt the identity of the Alliance and turn it into another "talking shop." NATO aspirants are perturbed that Russia's involvement in the Alliance will jeopardize its effectiveness as a union for mutual defense, bolster Moscow's assertiveness vis-à-vis former satellites, and undermine the stringent criteria for NATO membership that they labored so hard to meet. If a quasi-authoritarian Russia can delay, dilute, or determine NATO policy, then this could fundamentally damage the Alliance.

The R-NAC ran the risk of undermining cohesion in NATO decisionmaking. All decisions within NATO were consensual while membership was derived from a common commitment to shared national security interests. The R-NAC envisaged a structure in which Russia and the current nineteen NATO members would deliberate on joint security actions. Such an organism would parallel the North Atlantic Council (NAC) and unlike the previous consultative council (in which NATO and Russia met as one-on-one), the new organism could provide Moscow with equal footing among the twenty states. This was a potential recipe for obstruction and paralysis. If the R-NAC evolves in this direction, Moscow would become a de facto participant in NATO's decisions on critical security issues. Such an arrangement could either turn NATO into a replica of the OSCE or rupture the Alliance into competing blocs.

During a visit to Brussels in October 2001, Putin stressed his yearnings for NATO to become a "political organization" and not a security alliance.[34] The notion of Russian membership became primarily a means for undercutting NATO's rationale as an effective military structure that could operate outside the zone of member states. It was also an attempt to weaken the U.S.-European security relationship and to expose the former Soviet satellite states to renewed Russian influence. In December 2002, shortly after NATO's Prague summit, presidential aide Sergey Yastrzhembskiy emphasized that Russia "calmly disapproved" of NATO's decision to invite seven new countries, including the three Baltic states, to join the alliance.[35] Yastrzhembskiy claimed that NATO was a Cold War relic that has "revealed its inability to respond to new challenges" and that the Central Europeans wanted to join "mostly because of their historical complexes." Putin understood that Russia was too weak to prevent further NATO enlargement and that failed opposition would hurt him domestically and internationally. Putin also realized that NATO itself was weakening as a coherent institution as Washington was increasingly acting with "willing coalitions" during international crises.

The Putin presidency concluded that a European security structure remained in its infancy and a "multipolar world" would take several years to develop. As a result, Russia wanted to be a "security partner" for the United States on a global scale. Simultaneously, it endeavored to exploit the "European card" to undercut U.S. influence and raise Moscow's status without provoking retaliation from Washington. Russia's informal "axis" with France and Germany over the Iraqi crisis was an instructive example as it provided Moscow with an opportunity to restate its "multipolar" doctrine. During visits to Germany and France in February 2003, Putin publicly reanimated Primakov's concept for reshaping the international system with the creation of regional counterbalances to the United States.[36] Such statements were usually reserved for domestic audiences, but the new consensus with Paris and Berlin evidently emboldened the Kremlin.

Following 11 September, the Kremlin calculated that the global position of the United States would be enhanced. It responded quickly in support of Washington and exploited the international antiterrorism campaign by manipulating Western fears of global terrorism to consolidate its dominance in the CIS. The Kremlin desired U.S. "recognition of Russian vital security interests across the entire post-Soviet space, including the three Baltic republics."[37] The cooperative Kremlin set its sights on gaining strategic advantages from the eagerness of the United States to forge a global coalition against terrorism. In October 2002, Putin ordered a revision of the country's national security doctrine in the wake of the hostage crisis in Moscow.[38] Defense Minister Ivanov stressed the increased role of the army in the international aspects of combating terrorism, claiming that threats to national security, including those from abroad, were growing. Russia was prepared to use military force against terrorists and those who sponsored them. Since unilateralism and preemptive strikes were practiced by the United States, Russia also upheld its right to protect and project its "national interests."

The Kremlin canvassed for an international seal of approval as the primary "peacekeeper" or "conflict manager" in Central Asia, the Caucasus, and other former Soviet territories. This would entail a free hand in dealing with domestic separatist movements and conducting military operations in neighboring states regardless of the opposition of indigenous governments. Throughout the 1990s, Moscow expanded its peacekeeping operations in the former Soviet space with little regard for a UN mandate.[39] It claimed that Muslim radicalism constituted a threat to Russia and its neighbors and camouflaged attempts to extend its influence as a struggle against fundamentalism and terrorism. Moscow calculated that Washington would accede to Russia's increasing influences in the "near abroad" while it was preoccupied on other fronts.

"International terrorism" has provided an excellent aide for Russian purposes. The inherent vagueness of the concept has provided Russia (and other states)

with room to instrumentalize the "war" for more narrow state interests.
. . . While Putin has rejected George W. Bush's notion of an "axis of evil," he
accepted the broad point that "from the Balkans to the Philippines a certain
arc of instability has emerged."[40]

Moscow seeks to exploit this arc of instability to its strategic advantage.
In contrast to that of Russia, it is clearly in the "national interest" of the
United States to have secure and democratic countries throughout the eastern half of Europe and among all former Soviet republics that will assume
membership in international and Atlanticist institutions. Washington also has
several dependable allies in Eastern Europe that can assist it in its wider security missions through diplomatic, political, and even specialized military
support. But to guarantee such a scenario, the United States will need to
remain closely engaged throughout the region and not abandon its long-
term interests to Russian ambitions or West European weaknesses. The
fundamental competition between the United States and Russia has not
evaporated in the wake of 11 September, but has simply assumed novel forms.
Putin's policy is focused on maintaining stable relations with the major military and economic powers and working from within existing transnational
organizations, such as the EU and NATO, or influencing them as a buffer
against U.S. hegemony. Putin is playing the role of a "European integrationist" in his relations with EU officials.[41] In the short term, this can be viewed
as pragmatism, or a rational calculation focused on economic and political
advantages. In a longer-term perspective, pragmatism becomes strategic
opportunism in pursuit of Russia's great power status. One cannot assume
that Putin's conversion to "Westernism" can be taken at face value or that
it is durable.

There is visible distrust among Russia's military and security circles over
Putin's turnaround in relations with the West. But this resistance is neither
open nor organized.[42] The Kremlin takes all important cadre decisions and
forestalls the emergence of any significant political opposition. A number of
powerful Russian interest groups would prefer to maintain open confrontation with the West, including the security establishment and the military-
industrial complex.[43] Some differences between Putin and the Russian
military and security services have been evident, despite the fact that these
are his traditional bases of support.[44] Military and security service officials
have expressed their displeasure with Putin's policies and his disregard of the
opinions of security chiefs in designing foreign and security policy. While they
have not threatened Putin's position, they "have been openly unhappy with
what they see as a series of concessions to the West, and to Washington in
particular."[45] If Putin's foreign policy strategy does not bring Russia concrete gains then the security establishment may increasingly question his
approach.

CONTAINMENT AND PREEMPTION

The strategic issues examined in this book have far-reaching policy implications for the United States and its European allies. They raise questions about the international politics of "postreform Russia." Three points need to be underscored. First, Russia maintains a long-term foreign policy objective to recapture and expand its great power status. Such a focus was dissipated during the Yeltsin years, but has been sharpened under the Putin regime. Second, Moscow has sought to combine its limited current capabilities with emerging opportunities while not forsaking its long-term aspirations. Hence, cooperation with the Western powers (mirroring the policy of "peaceful coexistence" during the Cold War) does not contradict its long-range goals, but may be essential during times of relative weakness. And third, while under Yeltsin governmental and corporate foreign policies sometimes diverged, under Putin private business concerns have increasingly been mobilized to serve specific state interests.

Long-range Russian policy cannot be understood in response to a particular event (such as 11 September) or a particular campaign (such as the global antiterrorism struggle). Urgently needed is a comprehensive assessment of Moscow's strategic objectives in various regions of the globe. In this context, Russian policy toward Eastern Europe is a valuable test case of Russia's commitment to forging cooperative bilateral and regional relations and its alleged discarding of any imperial impulses. The United States possesses only limited influence over developments inside Russia. However, major international players can impact on Russian foreign policy, whether by discouraging unwelcome expansionist moves, providing political, economic, and military support to East European, Caucasian, and Central Asian governments, or integrating these states in the major international institutions. A series of steps could be undertaken not only to strengthen the new democracies but also to help ensure their commitment to the transatlantic relationship and to the U.S. alliance. This would help undercut Russia's expansionist maneuvers that rebound negatively throughout the region. Ultimately, each of these steps would be beneficial for Russia itself, as they would restrain moves that will prevent the country from becoming either a functioning democracy or a genuine security partner for its neighbors or for the United States.

1. *Security commitment.* Reaffirming the enduring commitment of the United States to European security. U.S. engagement cannot be seen as a passing phase, as this would not only encourage radicals, populists, and nationalists in various countries but could also embolden Russia to become more assertive toward its East European neighbors. Washington must consistently demonstrate that the security of any part of Europe will not be sacrificed to Russia's expansive "national interests." In this context, the opening

of U.S. bases in any East European state must be a bilateral decision in which Moscow exercises no influence as U.S. troops pose no threat to Russia's security.

2. *Partnership and alliance.* Ensuring that the East European democracies are internationally elevated as full partners and that any decisions pertaining to their security and regional relations cannot be influenced, pressured, or vetoed by Moscow. In this context, NATO membership for the remaining Balkan states, including Croatia, Albania, Macedonia, Serbia, Montenegro, Bosnia-Herzegovina, and Kosovo, can prevent their exploitation by outside actors as unstable "gray zones." Likewise, the pursuit of Alliance accession for Belarus, Ukraine, Moldova, and other Black Sea states must become a priority for Brussels in the coming years and a timetable of criteria needs to be determined as was the case with the first two rounds of NATO expansion.

3. *Energy focus.* Minimizing Russia's long-term political influences through its control over energy supply and distribution networks, by encouraging diversity in gas and oil supplies, developing domestic energy sources, and encouraging alternative infrastructural investments in the East European region. A long-term strategy needs to be developed to ensure that Caspian Sea oil and gas flow to the West through pipelines that bypass Russia and thereby lessen the chances for economic disruption or political blackmail. East European states are strategically positioned to benefit from the expansion of supplies from the Caspian to the EU both as consumers and transit routes, thus ensuring greater stability than Russia can provide. Washington should not yield to Moscow's demands for fixing prices on world oil market and reject a Russian quasi-monopoly on the transit of Caspian oil and gas.

4. *Curtailing dominance.* Restricting Russia's attempts to strengthen its regional power at the expense of its East European neighbors and not accede to Kremlin moves to bring Belarus, Ukraine, and Moldova under its direct control. In this context, federalization plans for Moldova, if approved by Washington, in which Moscow gains enduring influence over Chisinau will set a dangerous precedent for other potentially unstable states such as Ukraine. Simultaneously, support for human rights, democratization, the rule of law, and open societies must be redoubled, and the struggle against official corruption, organized crime, and authoritarianism intensified.

5. *Intelligence work.* Supporting and enhancing counterintelligence capabilities in the East European states in order to counter Russia's subterfuge, hostile espionage activities, including penetration of security and intelligence forces, and destabilizing "active measures." Links between Russian government, business, and criminal organizations must be of special concern to Washington as Eastern Europe is a major international hub for Russia's criminal "Atlanticism."

6. *Promoting Atlanticism.* Underscoring the yawning gap between "Atlanticist" and "Eurasian" values in order to embrace all European countries in an expanding Atlantic international structure and preventing any new West-East divisions in Europe. The most effective way to convince Russia not to pursue "zero-sum games" in its western neighborhood is to promote Atlanticist positions among all East European states. Above all, Russia respects clarity, strength, and determination. Weakness and indecision will make future decisions that much more difficult and conflictive, for the United States and for its new European allies.

Notes

CHAPTER 1

1. The term "Eastern Europe" or "Europe East" is used to describe that part of the continent (minus Russia, which defines itself as "Eurasian") that was forced to live under Soviet-imposed Communism. The book examines four subregions of this broad area: Central Europe, the Baltic states, the Balkans or Southeast Europe, and the European Commonwealth of Independent States (CIS), but not including the Caucasus.

2. Some Western policy analysts prefer to focus on "Russian interests" in Eastern Europe while ignoring East European security interests in protecting themselves from unwelcome Russian interference. See Owen Harries, "The Collapse of 'The West,'" *Foreign Affairs* 72, no. 4 (September–October 1993): 42–43. Russia's "national interests" actually conflict with American interests where they dismiss the aspirations of America's closest allies in Eastern Europe.

3. Vladimir Socor, "Perspectives from the 'Near Abroad' on Relations with Russia," *Policy Briefings* no. 9 (Washington, D.C.: Institute for Advanced Strategic and Political Studies, 9 December 2002).

4. Agnieszka Kowalczewska, "Wschód Zachodzi," *Polityka Online* (Warsaw) no. 1 (2001): 2279, polityka.onet.pl.

5. Marek Ostrowski, "Patrzyć Putinowi W Oczy," *Polityka Online* (Warsaw) no. 4 (2002): 2334, polityka.onet.pl.

6. Especially disconcerting in the region is the view among some U.S. analysts that Russia was entitled to a "sphere of influence" in Eastern Europe. In effect, this entails political dominance and the determination of each country's security and

foreign policy. For one such perspective, see Ted Galen Carpenter, "Casting NATO Line Perilously Far to East," *Washington Times*, 2 December 2002.

7. Ilya Prizel, "Putin's Russia, the Berlin Republic, and East Central Europe: A New Symbiosis?" *Orbis* 46, no. 4 (Fall 2002): 679–693.

8. Christian Haerpfer, Cezary Miłosiński, and Claire Wallace, "Old and New Security Issues in Post-Communist Eastern Europe: Results of an 11 Nation Study," *Europe-Asia Studies* 51, no. 6 (1999): 989–1011.

9. Michael Radu, "Why Eastern and Central Europe Looks West," *Orbis* 41, no. 1 (Winter 1997): 40.

10. Gregory O. Hall, "NATO and Russia, Russians and NATO: A Turning Point in Post–Cold War East-West Relations?" *World Affairs* 162, no. 11 (Summer 1999): 22–28.

11. Ian Bremmer, "Russia's Total Security," *World Policy Journal* 16, no. 2 (Summer 1999): 31–41.

12. Astrid S. Tuminez, "Russian Nationalism and the National Interest in Russian Foreign Policy," in Celeste A. Wallander, ed., *The Sources of Russian Foreign Policy After the Cold War* (Boulder, Colo.: Westview, 1996), 41–68.

13. Vladimir Shlapentokh, "Is the 'Greatness Syndrome' Eroding?" *Washington Quarterly* 25, no. 1 (Winter 2002): 132.

14. Andrey P. Tsygankov, "The Final Triumph of the Pax Americana? Western Intervention in Yugoslavia and Russia's Debate on the Post–Cold War Order," *Communist and Post-Communist Studies* no. 34 (2001): 133–156.

15. Mette Skak, *From Empire to Anarchy: Postcommunist Foreign Policy and International Relations* (New York: St. Martin's Press, 1996), 140.

16. Vera Tolz, *Russia: Inventing the Nation* (London: Arnold, 2001), 12, 15. Tolz believes that the phrase "Russian nationalism" is a misnomer as the phenomenon is better depicted as Russian imperialist ideology based on the expansive state rather than the expansive nation. Nevertheless, Russian prejudice pertaining to an alleged cultural superiority over neighboring Slavic and non-Slavic populations is a form of expansive nationalism manifested in assimilation and Russification. Rupnik adds: "But what is Russia without its empire? No one has yet provided an answer to the question, which touches the very heart of Russian identity but also the contours of Russia's borders." See Jacques Rupnik, "Europe's New Frontiers: Remapping Europe, Political Aftermath of the End of the Cold War; After Communism, What?" *Daedalus* 123, no. 3 (22 June 1994): 91–106.

17. William Zimmerman, *The Russian People and Foreign Policy: Russian Elite and Mass Perspectives, 1993–2000* (Princeton: Princetin University Press, 2002), 91–92. The biggest security threats to Russia in the perceptions of the public were the "growth of U.S. power" and the "spread of NATO in Eastern Europe" (p. 92).

18. Frank Umbach, "Russia as a 'Virtual Great Power': Implications for Its Declining Role in European and Eurasian Security," *European Security* 9, no. 3 (Autumn 2000): 106.

19. Karen Dawisha and Bruce Parrott, *Russia and the New States of Eurasia: The Politics of Upheaval* (Cambridge: Cambridge University Press, 1994).

20. Peter Truscott, *Russia First: Breaking with the West* (London: I. B. Tauris, 1997).

21. From personal conversation with officials and analysts in Lithuania.

22. Jeff Chinn and Robert Kaiser, *Russians as the New Minority: Ethnicity and Nationalismin the Soviet Successor States* (Boulder, Colo.: Westview, 1996), 75.

23. Celeste Wallander, "Lost and Found: Gorbachev's 'New Thinking,'" *The Washington Quarterly* 25, no. 1 (Winter 2002): 117–129. A useful synopsis of the collapse of the Soviet bloc can be found in Ronald D. Asmus, J. F. Brown, and Keith Crane, *Soviet Foreign Policy and the Revolutions of 1989 in Eastern Europe* (Santa Monica: Rand, National Defense Research Institute, 1991). The "Brezhnev Doctrine" of limited sovereignty in the "socialist camp" was merely a continuation of the Lenin and Stalin "Doctrines."

24. Gorbachev first expounded freedom of choice for the East Europeans in a speech at the UN General Assembly on 7 December 1988. The term "Sinatra Doctrine" was initially used by Genadiy Gerasimov, head of the Information Department of the USSR's Foreign Affairs Ministry, based on the song "I Did It My Way." See Gerhard Mangott, "Russian Policies on Central and Eastern Europe: An Overview," *European Security* 8, no. 3 (Autumn 1999): 77, n. 2.

25. The dates of full Soviet military withdrawal from Central Europe and the Baltic states were as follows: Hungary, June 1991; Czechoslovakia, June 1992; Poland, October 1992; Lithuania, August 1993; Estonia, August 1994; and Latvia, August 1994.

26. Aleksei Pushkov, "Russia's Foreign Policy," *Nezavisimaya Gazeta* (Moscow), 16 November 1995.

27. Mangott, "Russian Policies," 46.

28. Paul Marantz, "Russian Foreign Policy During Yeltsin's Second Term," *Communist and Post-Communist Studies* 30, no. 4 (1997): 345–351. During 1991–1993, Yeltsin was struggling to consolidate his rule, to establish Russian independence, and to prevent a social explosion as a result of wrenching market reforms.

29. Suzanne Crow, "Why Has Russian Foreign Policy Changed?" Radio Free Europe/Radio Liberty (RFE/RL), *Research Report* 3, no. 18 (6 May 1994): 1–6. Also see Neil Malcolm et al., *Internal Factors in Russian Foreign Policy* (New York: Oxford University Press, 1996), 21–25. For a helpful volume on how Russian foreign policy was transformed from an "internationalist" to a "national patriotic" position in the early 1990s, see Leon Aron and Kenneth M. Jensen, eds., *The Emergence of Russian Foreign Policy* (Washington, D.C.: U.S. Institute of Peace, 1994).

30. James H. Brusstar, "Russian Vital Interests and Western Security," *Orbis* 38, no. 4 (Fall 1994): 607. Brusstar uncritically accepts certain Muscovite premises and recommends, "The West should concede that Russia has a vital interest in Central Europe being neutral and excluded from any alliance that is hostile to Russia" (p. 617).

31. Roger E. Kanet and Susanne M. Birgerson, "The Domestic-Foreign Policy Linkage in Russian Politics: Nationalist Influences on Russian Foreign Policy," *Communist and Post-Communist Studies* 30, no. 4 (1997): 335–344.

32. Kozyrev's statement on 14 February 1994, quoted by *Interfaks*, 14 February 1994.

33. Kozyrev's address to the Federation Council on 6 July 1995, in *Segodnya* (Moscow), 7 July 1995. Even Russian liberals assumed that all CIS states wished to remain in a democratic federal structure that would succeed the USSR. Nationalists were more determined to restore a new transcontinental state structure led by Russia

and shielded from corrupting Western influences. For Communists, the "Russian idea" of a restored superstate was simply a continuation of the Communist idea. The nationalist and Communist concepts were supported by the Russian Orthodox Church, which feared the penetration of alien religions if Russia integrated with the West.

34. Vera Tolz, "Conflicting 'Homelands Myths' and Nation-State Building in Postcommunist Russia," *Slavic Review* 57, no. 2 (Summer 1998): 267–294.

35. Aleksander Iudin, "Apologia Natsionalizma," *Den* (Moscow) no. 38 (September 1993): 24–30.

36. *Nezavisimaya Gazeta* (Moscow), 22 September 1993.

37. Primakov's positions can be found in *Gody v Bol'shay Politike* (Moscow: Sovershenno Sekretno, 2000).

38. For an exposition of "national patriotism," see Sergey Kortunov, "National Supertask: An Essay in Russian Ideology," *Nezavisimaya Gazeta* (Moscow), 7 October 1995. For an analysis of this new Russian ideology justifying a strong state and great power ambitions, see Henrikki Heikka, "Beyond Neorealism and Constructivism: Desire, Identity, and Russian Foreign Policy," in Ted Hopf, ed., *Understandings of Russian Foreign Policy* (University Park: Pennsylvania State University Press, 1999), 93–104.

39. Konstantin Eggert, "A Great Power Foreign Policy Is Too Expensive," *Izvestia* (Moscow), 16 December 1995.

40. Andrzej Czarnocki, "Russia and East-Central Europe," in Andrzej Dumała and Ziemowit Jacek Pietras, eds., *The Future of East-Central Europe* (Lublin: Maria Curie-Skłodowska University Press, 1996), 208–218.

41. Ilya Prizel, *National Identity and Foreign Policy: Nationalism and Leadership in Poland, Russia, and Ukraine* (Cambridge: Cambridge University Press, 1998), 267.

42. Statement by Foreign Minister Primakov at a press conference on 12 January 1996, published in *Moskovskiye Novosti* (Moscow), 14–21 January 1996.

43. A helpful Russian analysis of "Eurasianism" can be found in V. L. Tsymbursky, "Geopolitika kak Mirovidenie i Rod Zaanyati," *Polis* (Moscow) no. 4 (1999): 7–28.

44. For a discussion of Primakov's "multipolarity," consult Eitvydas Bajarunas, *Putin's Russia: Whither Multi-Polarity?* (London: Conflict Studies Research Centre, UK Ministry of Defence, March 2002).

45. Witold Rodkiewicz, "Rosja i jej Sąsiedzi : Postimperialny Syndrom," in *Russia and Its Neighbors* (Kraków, Poland: Meritum, 2000), 11–21.

46. For an example of Russian defensiveness, see Alexey Arbatov, "A Moscow Perspective," in Christopher Lord, ed., *Central Europe: Core or Periphery?* (Handelshojskolens Forlag: Copenhagen Business School Press, 2000), 181–192.

47. The "moderate" Kozyrev once remarked that all Moscow had lost in Eastern Europe were "false allies that we never trusted anyway." See Mikhail Tretiakov, "How Do We Answer Warsaw's Trybuna?" *Pravda* (Moscow), 23 June 1993.

48. Jane Perlez, "In Bulgaria, Russia Eyes a Renewal of Old Ties," *New York Times,* 21 May 1995.

49. Brusstar, "Russian Vital Interests," 609–610.

50. Leon Aron, "The Foreign Policy Doctrine of Postcommunist Russia and Its Domestic Context," in Michael Mandelbaum, ed., *The New Russian Foreign Policy* (New York: Council on Foreign Relations, 1998), 27.

51. N. Narochnitskaia, "Russia and the 'Eastern Issue,'" *International Affairs* (Moscow) 45, no. 3 (1999): 25.

52. Stephen Blank, "Russia, NATO Enlargement, and the Baltic States," *World Affairs* 160, no. 3 (Winter 1998): 115–125.

53. "Can Russia Ever Be Secured?" *The Economist,* 7 December 1996.

54. Bruce D. Porter, "Russia and Europe After the Cold War: The Interaction of Domestic and Foreign Policies," in Celeste A. Wallander, ed., *Sources of Russian Foreign Policy* (Boulder, Colo.: Westview, 1996), 136.

55. For a Western rendition of Russian fears of NATO enlargement, see Roland Dannreuther, "Escaping the Enlargement Trap in NATO-Russian Relations," *Survival* 41, no. 4 (Winter 1999–2000): 145–164. Russian blackmail and threat in response to NATO enlargement was repeated by some Washington-based institutions, including the Cato Institute and the Carnegie Endowment for International Peace. For some savory quotes naively repeating Moscow's "Armaggedon scenario" of nuclear annihilation, see Ronald J. Laurenzo, "NATO Expansion Could Make Russia Go Nuclear," *Washington Times,* 22 March 1998.

56. Adrian Karatnycky, "Don't Believe the New Red Scare," *Washington Times,* 24 March 1997. According to Karatnycky, "The scare-mongering and brinkmanship is reminiscent of Soviet-era diplomacy" (p. 15).

57. Alvin Z. Rubinstein, "A U.S. Policy for Russia," Foreign Policy Research Institute, 25 April 2001, *E-Notes.*

58. For a valuable exposition of Russian self-perceptions in the Putin era by a leading professor at Moscow State University, see A. S. Panarim, "Położenie Geopolityczne Rosji: Alternatywne Scenariusze U Progu XXI Wieku," in *Political Science Studies,* vol. 4, *History and Geopolitics: Russia on the Threshold of the Twenty-First Century* (Warsaw: Institute of Political Sciences, University of Warsaw, 2000), 38–78.

59. M. Ponomarev, "V Vashingtone Reshili Otkrit Karti?" *Krasnaya Zvezda* (Moscow), 10 August 1993.

60. *Ob Osnovnyye Polozheniya Voyennoy Doktriny Rossiyskoy Federatsiyi* (Moscow, Sobranie Aktov Presidenta i Pravitelstva Rossijskoy Federatsii, no. 45, 2 November 1993).

61. Alla Kassianova, "Russia: Still Open to the West? Evolution of the State Identity in the Foreign Policy and Security Discourse," *Europe-Asia Studies* 53, no. 6 (2001): 821–839. After the 1999 Kosovo war, the military leadership underscored its determination to employ nuclear weapons if it could not conduct an adequate conventional response to military aggression.

62. A. Gousher, "External Challenges to Russia's National Interests," *International Affairs* (Moscow) 45, no. 2 (1999): 162–167.

63. Peter Rodman, "Russia: The Challenge of a Failing Power," in Robert Kagan and William Kristol, eds., *Present Dangers* (San Francisco: Encounter Books, 2000), 84.

64. Based partly on the author's participation with General Anatolii Kvashnin at a conference at the Russian Foreign Service Academy in Moscow in November 1999.

65. Richard F. Staar, "Moscow's Plans to Restore its Power," *Orbis* 40, no. 3 (Summer 1996): 375.

66. Jan S. Adams, "Russia's Gas Diplomacy," *Problems of Post-Communism* 49, no. 3 (May–June 2002): 14–22. Adams also describes the operations of the Gazprom-linked Itera gas corporation, which became the world's second largest gas company. As a private company, Itera is not restricted by government regulations that mandate Gazprom's less profitable domestic sales. The company was a means for gas magnates and their political connections to gain handsome profits without state monitoring.

67. Leonid Gankin, "As Russia Is Sidelined," *Kommersant* (Moscow), 18 November 1997.

68. David E. Hoffman, *The Oligarchs: Wealth and Power in the New Russia* (New York: PublicAffairs, 2002), 2. According to Hoffman, the oligarchs "bought up the Russian mass media, especially television, and they seized not only factories but also the assets of the state itself, including the budget, the law enforcement system, and the Kremlin leadership" (p. 3).

69. CSIS Task Force Report, *Russian Organized Crime and Corruption: Putin's Challenge* (Wahsington, D.C.: Global Organized Crime Project, Center for Strategic and International Studies, 2000).

70. Martin McCauley, *Bandits, Gangsters, and the Mafia: Russia, the Baltic States, and the CIS* (Harlow, England: Longman, 2001), 8.

71. Sergey Medvedev, "Power, Space, and Russian Foreign Policy," in Ted Hopf, ed., *Understandings of Russian Foreign Policy* (University Park: Pennsylvania State University Press, 1999), 42.

72. V. Shlapentokh, "Putin's First Year in Office: The New Regime's Uniqueness in Russian History," *Communist and Post-Communist Studies* no. 34 (2001): 371–399. For an optimistic analysis of Putin's democratic credentials, see Thomas E. Remington, "Russia and the 'Strong State' Ideal," *East European Constitutional Review* 8, nos. 1–2 (Winter 1999–Spring 2000): 65–69.

73. For a Russian perspective on Putin's foreign policy decisionmaking, see V. Kremeniuk, "The Ideological Legacy in Russia's Foreign Policy," *International Affairs* (Moscow) 47, no. 3 (2001): 18–26.

74. Stuart D. Goldman, "Russia," Congessional Research Service, *Issue Brief for Congress,* 22 June 2001, Washington D.C.

75. Timothy J. Colton and Michael McFaul, "Russian Democracy Under Putin," *Problems of Post-Communism* 50, no. 4 (July–August 2003): 13. According to the authors, Putin has preserved formal democratic practices and simultaneously weakened "the actual democratic content of these political rules and norms."

76. Anatolii Kostiukov, "Kumir Nashemu Domu," *Sovetskaya Rossiya* (Moscow), 15 May 2001.

77. Some American academics have accepted such a "neutral" or positive view of Putin, as evident in Angela Stent and Lilia Shevtsova, "America, Russia, and Europe: A Realignment?" *Survival* 44, no. 4 (Winter 2002–2003): 121–134.

78. Peter Rutland, "Putin and the Oligarchs," in Dale R. Herspring, ed., *Putin's Russia: Past Imperfect, Future Uncertain* (Lanham, Md.: Rowman & Littlefield, 2003), 134–136. The oligarchs consisted of two broad groups: former members of the Soviet nomenklatura who retained control of state enterprises that were privatized (such as Gazprom), and young businessmen who had grown immensely wealthy during the process of market reform. Some of the latter came from the criminal

underground. These groups made a deal with Yeltsin: gaining economic and financial privileges from the state in return for helping his reelection in 1996. They were able to offer the president leadership, money, organizational skills, media access, and Western contacts.

79. In support of Putin's policies, in June 2001 the first conference of Russian, Belarusian, and Ukrainian nations was held in Moscow. The leader of the Russian delegation was the chairman of parliament, Genadiy Seleznyov, who claimed the conference was a platform for the extensive unification of the three nations and an enticement to other states to voluntarily join the emerging union.

80. According to Françoise Thom, in an essay titled "Putin's Russia," delivered at a conference organized by the Prague Institute for National Security on 26 April 2002: "In the West, the party that wins an election forms the government. But in Russia the victorious administration forms its own party."

81. According to Reporters Without Borders, in its 2003 edition on worldwide freedom of the press, Russia ranked 148 out of 166 countries investigated. See Reporters Without Borders, "Second World Press Freedom Ranking," 23 October 2003, www.rsf.org.

82. In October 2003, police arrested Yukos CEO Mikhail Khodorkovsky and froze the government portion of Yukos shares. Putin's circle objected that Khodorkovsky intended to use his considerable economic resources for political purposes. Khodorkovsky had gained increasing international stature, providing him with a more solid base for political activity than former oligarchs Boris Berezovsky and Vladimir Gusinsky, both of whom fled Russia under intense pressure from the Kremlin. The Interior Ministry and the FSB assembled a number of cases against big business that can be activated whenever the Kremlin issues the directive. Yukos became one of the world's biggest oil companies in 2003 when it merged with Sibnef. Its offer to sell a controlling stake to the U.S. company Exxon-Mobil alarmed the Kremlin. Yukos has also led a trend in Russian business toward increased openness and transparency: "This too is not in the interests of Kremlin officials, who have more influence when the game is played under the old Russian system, with its traditions of secrecy and backroom deals." See Stephen Mulvey, "Analysis: The Yukos Puzzle," *BBC Online,* 27 October 2003, bbc.co.uk.

83. Charles Grant, "Russia's Future in Balance: Putin Versus Khodorkovsky?" *Russia Weekly,* 7 August 2003. Grant suggests one of two scenarios given the actions against Russia's oligarchs: either Putin believes he can strengthen Russia without adopting liberalism and civic democracy, or the security establishment is in control and believes that Putin has moved too far toward the West and is trying to steer the country toward protectionist authoritarianism. Such forces believe that private capital with Western ties in Russia's key industries constitutes a direct threat to national security.

84. Comments by the president of the Institute of Strategic Forecasting, Aleksandr Konovalov, reported in RFE/RL, *Newsline* 7, no. 141, pt. 1 (28 July 2003).

85. In its Global Survey of Media Independence for 2003, the Washington-based Freedom House listed Russia as "not free" for the first time since the disintegration of the Soviet Union. See the chapter on Russia in *Freedom in the World, 2003: The Annual Survey of Political Rights and Civil Liberties* (New York: Freedom House,

2003), 458–465. Russian analysts believe that Putin supports the interests and methods of the *siloviki*—all security agencies that supported the application of force.

86. For full texts of the two documents, see *Nezavisimoye Voennoe Obozrenie (Independent Military Review)* (Moscow) no. 1 (14–20 January 2000) (for the National Security Concept), and *Nezavisimaya Gazeta* (Moscow), 22 April 2000 (for the Military Doctrine).

87. For useful analyses of the 2000 National Security Concept, see Nikolai Sokov, "Russia's New Concept of National Security," *East European Constitutional Review* 9, nos. 1–2 (Winter 1999–Spring 2000): 83–87; and Jakub M. Godzimirski, "Russian National Security Concepts 1997 and 2000: A Comparative Analysis," *European Security* 9, no. 4 (Winter 2000): 73–91.

88. RFE/RL, *Newsline* 7, no. 129, pt. 1 (10 July 2003).

89. See Putin's speech in *Nezavisimaia Gazeta: Stsenarii* (Moscow), April 2001.

90. Vladimir Putin, "Prezidentskoe Poslanie Federalnomu Sobraniu," *Rossiiskaia Gazeta* (Moscow), 11 July 2000.

91. In June 2000, Putin approved the National Security Information Doctrine, which focused on the need to broaden governmental control over the flow of information. For some facts on the doctrine, see Oleg Odnokolenko, "Everyone Is Free: Security Council Introduces Concept of 'Abuse of Media Freedom,'" *Segodnia* (Moscow), 24 June 2000.

92. Robert H. Donaldson and Joseph L. Nogee, *The Foreign Policy of Russia: Changing Systems, Enduring Interests* (Armonk, N.Y.: M. E. Sharpe, 2002), 146.

93. Irina Kobrinskaya, "'Parallels' and 'Verticals' of Putin's Foreign Policy," PONARS Policy Memo no. 263, PONARS (Program on New Approaches to Russian Security) Policy Conference, Center for Strategic and International Studies, Washington, D.C., 6 December 2002, 91. Putin also benefited from the foreign policy advice of trusted "hard-liners" such as Primakov.

94. Jim Nichol, "Russian President Putin's Prospective Policies: Issues and Implications," Congressional Research Service, *Report for Congress*, 17 April 2000, Washington, D.C.

95. Kobrinskaya, "'Parallels' and 'Verticals,'" 96.

96. See comments by Aleksander Dugin, one of the leading exponents of Eurasianism, in *Financial Times* (London), 2–3 December 2000.

97. Dale R. Herspring and Peter Rutalnd, "Putin and Russian Foreign Policy," in Herspring, *Putin's Russia*, 250.

98. According to Donaldson and Nogee, in an attempt to stymie the emerging foreign relations of Russia's regions and the two major cities of Moscow and St. Petersburg, "The January 1999 Law on Coordination of the Foreign Relations and International Trade of the Subjects of the Russian Federation required that they submit drafts of proposed international agreements to the foreign ministry for approval. The law also required advance notice when negotiations were to be conducted with foreign entities, as well as approval for opening offices abroad." See Donaldson and Nogee, *Foreign Policy of Russia*, 171–172.

99. RFE/RL, *Newsline* 7, no. 13, pt. 1 (22 January 2003).

100. William D. Jackson, "Encircled Again: Russia's Military Assesses Threats in a Post-Soviet World," *Political Science Quarterly* 117, no. 3 (2002): 395–396.

101. Based on conversations in Moscow in September 2003.

102. Flemming Splidsboel-Hansen, "Past and Future Meet: Aleksandr Gorchakov and Russian Foreign Policy," *Europe-Asia Studies* 54, no. 3 (May 2002): 1–21.

103. Vladimir Putin, "Russia at the Turn of the Millennium," 31 December 1999, found at the Russian government Web site, www.government.ru. In an indication of how economic relations became a tool of foreign policy, the "multipolar" former premier Primakov was elevated president of the Russian Chamber of Commerce.

104. Splidsboel-Hansen, "Past and Future Meet," 10.

105. Thomas E. Graham, "Russia's Foreign Policy," paper delivered at a symposium at the Royal Defense College, Evere, Belgium, 1 March 2000, and located at the Web site of the Carnegie Endowment for International Peace, ceip.org.

106. F. Stephen Larrabee and Theodore W. Karasik, *Foreign and Security Policy Decisionmaking Under Yeltsin* (Santa Monica, Calif.: RAND, 1997).

107. Jerrold L. Schecter, *Russian Negotiating Behavior: Continuity and Transition* (Washington, D.C.: U.S. Institute of Peace, 1998), 41. Schecter provides a useful assessment of Russian negotiating techniques and strategies. He concludes that the old Soviet style (or Bolshevik Code) still persists among current Russian diplomats. It consists of marked suspicion of the outside world, zero-sum calculations in negotiations, and an intent to trick or cajole the opponent.

108. Allen C. Lynch, "The Realism of Russia's Foreign Policy," *Europe-Asia Studies* 53, no. 1 (January 2001): 7–31.

109. Neil Malcolm and Alex Pravda, "Democratization and Russian Foreign Policy," *International Affairs* 72, no. 3 (July 1996): 537–552.

110. Ibid, 547.

111. Stephen J. Blank, *Threats to Russian Security: The View from Moscow* (Carlisle, Pennsylvania: Strategic Studies Institute, U.S. Army War College, July 2000).

112. Consult *Nezavisimoye Voyennoye Obozreniye* (Moscow) no. 42 (6–12 November 1998).

113. In November 2003, the Foreign Ministry and the Russian Union of Oil and Gas Producers signed an agreement on cooperation to "regulate mutual information feeding in order to help each other to achieve our common goal, to realize Russia's national interest." The agreement "realizes the two parties' desire to increase the efficiency of energy diplomacy, which is acquiring an ever more important role in international relations and in bilateral cooperation between states." According to the Foreign Ministry, "virtually no large project related to investment of Russian fuel and energy companies can be carried out without active assistance on the part of the state." See *RIA Novosti* (Moscow), 5 November 2003.

114. RFE/RL, *Newsline* 7, no. 8, pt. 1 (14 January 2003).

115. In February 2003, Valeriy Golubev assumed a leadership position with a Gazprom subsidiary. Golubev is a former KGB officer and, like Putin, worked in the administration of former St. Petersburg mayor Anatoliy Sobchak. Another former intelligence officer from St. Petersburg, Sergey Ushakov, was appointed Gazprom's deputy chairman for administration. See RFE/RL, *Newsline* 7, no. 34, pt. 1 (21 February 2003). Aleksandr Bespalov, chairman of the pro-Kremlin Unified Russia's General Council and its Central Executive Committee, was named head of Gazprom's information-policy department. Bespalov was one of Putin's colleagues at the St. Petersburg regional office of the KGB. See RFE/RL, *Newsline* 7, no. 39, pt. 1 (28 February 2003).

116. Sergey Karaganov, quoted in Dov Lynch, *Russia Faces Europe,* European Union, Chaillot Paper no. 60 (Paris: Institute for Security Studies, May 2003), 23.

CHAPTER 2

1. Bulgarian political analyst Ognyan Minchev, from Sofia's Institute for Regional and International Studies, stated in personal conversations in April 2002: "A derisive type of skepticism has become common among a number of western observers, who mocked Russia's postimperial helplessness to uphold its position as a first-rate world power. However, even if Russia is not in a position to decisively influence the key power factors of international life, this does not mean that Moscow is helpless to exert pressure on smaller and weaker partners in the international community."

2. Among the U.S. commentators regularly and favorably quoted on NATO enlargement by the Russian press were George Kennan; Susan Eisenhower, who formed an organization against NATO enlargement; Ted Carpenter of the Cato Institute; former ambassadors Jack Matlock and Richard T. Davies; former secretary of defense Robert McNamara; and professors Richard Pipes and Marshall Shulman.

3. William D. Jackson, "Imperial Temptations: Ethnics Abroad," *Orbis* 38, no. 1 (Winter 1994): 16.

4. RFE/RL, *Newsline* 7, no. 134, pt. 1 (17 July 2003).

5. RFE/RL, *Newsline* 7, no. 190, pt. 1 (6 October 2003); and Denis Trifonov, "'Ivanov Doctrine' Reflects Moscow's Growing Confidence in the CIS and Beyond," *Central Asia-Caucasus Institute Analyst* (Washington, D.C.: Johns Hopkins, 19 November 2003).

6. Paul Kubicek, "End of the Line for the Commonwealth of Independent States," *Problems of Post-Communism* 46, no. 2 (March–April 1999): 19.

7. Bobo Lo, *Vladimir Putin and the Evolution of Russian Foreign Policy,* Royal Institute of International Affairs, Chatham House Papers (London: Blackwell, 2003), 92. According to the author, the real importance of conflict resolution for Moscow is "not intrinsic but instrumental."

8. Amy Myers Jaffe and Robert A. Manning, "Russia, Energy, and the West," *Survival* 43, no. 2 (Summer 2001): 133–152. During the Gorbachev years, Moscow's decision to end subsidized energy exports to Eastern Europe helped to push the region toward the West.

9. Mark A. Smith, *Russian Business and Foreign Policy,* F82 (London: Conflict Studies Research Centre, UK Defence Academy, May 2003). According to Vagit Alekperov, the president of Lukoil, in a statement to an international oil forum in November 2001, the company considers itself a "national Russian company, and we do not accept the ideology of the division into state, private, and other companies." See www.lukoil.ru/presscenter/artic.htm?artid=286.

10. Sabrina Tavernise and Peter S. Green, "Oil Concerns in Russia Branch Out," *New York Times,* 2 April 2002. According to the authors, Russia's oil companies are "moving to secure market outlets and captive customers for their crude," section W, p. 1.

11. "Comrade Capitalist," *The Economist* (London), 15 February 2001.

12. Gazprom's dissident board member, Boris Fyodorov, the former Russian finance minister, alleges that "$2 billion to $3 billion disappears from Gazprom each

year through corruption, nepotism, and simple theft." See Maria Antonenko and Kevin Krogmann, "License to Steal?" *Transitions Online,* 23 May 2001, tol.cz.; and Michael Lelyveld, "Russia: New Suspicions Emerge Over Gazprom Dealings," www.rferl.org/nca/features/2001/05/24052001111543.asp.

13. FE/RL, *Newsline* 7, no. 31, pt. 1 (18 February 2003).

14. Lukoil owns refineries in Russia, Ukraine, Romania, and Bulgaria, and has acquired 3,590 gas stations, including about 900 in Eastern Europe and the former Soviet Union. See "Lukoil Eyes Foothold in the Balkans," *Moscow Times,* 11 August 2003.

15. The International Relations Department at Moscow State University is now training specialists in "energy diplomacy."

16. Andrzej Krzysztof Wróblewski, "Broń Gazowa," *Polityka Online* (Warsaw) no. 4 (2001): 2282, polityka.onet.pl.

17. Kari Liuhto and Jari Jumpponen, "The Internationalisation Boom of Russian Corporations," *Research Report* no. 135 (Lappeenranta: University of Technology, Department of Industrial Engineering and Management, 2002).

18. Jeff Chinn and Robert Kaiser, *Russians as the New Minority: Ethnicity and Nationalism in the Soviet Successor States* (Boulder, Colo.: Westview, 1996), 279.

19. Elizabeth Teague, "Russians Outside Russia and Russian Security Policy," in Leon Aron and Kenneth M. Jensen, eds., *The Emergence of Russian Foreign Policy* (Washington, D.C.: U.S. Institute of Peace, 1994), 81–105.

20. According to Donaldson and Nogee, "Yeltsin's government was under considerable domestic pressure to act on behalf of the 25.2 million Russians in the 'near abroad.' Russian refugees from the Baltics were among the organizers of the Congress of Russian Communities . . . which demanded the 'protection of the interests of Russian citizens regardless of their place of residence.' The Congress of Russian Communities, with General Aleksandr Lebed among its leaders, became a potent force in Russian politics." See Robert H. Donaldson and Joseph L. Nogee, *The Foreign Policy of Russia: Changing Systems, Enduring Interests* (Armonk, N.Y.: M. E. Sharpe, 2002), 212.

21. Russian voting behavior in the Baltics and Ukraine weakens claims by Russian liberals who argue that Communism was not a Russian phenomenon because Russians were also its victims. The Russian diaspora votes overwhelmingly for Communist or Soviet restorationist parties. See Michael Radu, "Why Eastern and Central Europe Looks West," *Orbis* 41, no. 1 (Winter 1997): 43.

22. Jackson, "Imperial Temptations," 1. Jackson believes that the large Russian populations concentrated in regions such as Crimea (Ukraine) and Narva (Estonia) present challenges to territorial integrity.

23. Michael Radu, "The Burden of Eastern Orthodoxy," *Orbis* 42, no. 2 (Spring 1998): 297.

24. Moscow could also stage assassinations or coup attempts in a targeted country that was moving permanently out of Russia's orbit, but has thus far avoided such scenarios. Nikolas Gvosdev, "Moscow Nights, Eurasian Dreams," *National Interest* (Summer 2002): 157.

25. Dmitriy Gornostaev, "Trebovaniia k Kandidatam NATO," *Nezavisimaia Gazeta* (Moscow), 5 July 1996.

26. Nikolas K. Gvosdev, "The New Party Card? Orthodoxy and the Search for

Post-Soviet Russian Identity," *Problems of Post-Communism* 47, no. 6 (November–December 2000): 29–38. Russian Orthodox leaders continue to seek the resurrection of the "Holy Rus," which signifies a common pan-Slavic national community of Russia, Ukraine, and Belarus.

27. Yuriy Mamleiev, "Russia Between Eternity and Love," *Literaturnaia Gazeta* (Moscow), 28 January 1998.

28. Louise Shelley, "Transnational Crime: The Case of Russian Organized Crime and the Role of International Cooperation in Law Enforcement," *Demokratizatsiiya: The Journal of Post-Soviet Democratization* 10, no. 1 (Winter 2002): 51.

29. Daniel R. Kempton with Richard M. Levine, "Soviet and Russian Relations with Foreign Corporations: The Case of Gold and Diamonds," *Slavic Review* 54, no. 1 (Spring 1995): 104–105. The Yeltsin government subsequently sought to trace an estimated $14 billion in hard currency and goods.

30. CSIS Task Force Report, *Russian Organized Crime and Corruption: Putin's Challnge* (Washington, D.C.: Global Organized Crime Project, Center for Strategic and International Studies, 2000), 16.

31. Prague Institute for National Security, *National Security Newsletter* no. EN-01/03-00 (March 2000), www.pins.cz/main-en.htm.

32. Martin McCauley, *Bandits, Gangsters, and the Mafia: Russia, the Baltic States, and the CIS* (Harlow, England: Longman, 2001), 75. According to McCauley, nine major mafia organizations emerged controlling approximately half of the Russian economy.

33. Yuriy A. Voronin, "The Emerging Criminal State: Economic and Political Aspects of Organized Crime in Russia," *Transnational Organized Crime* 6, no. 2 (Summer–Autumn 1996): 54.

34. RFE/RL, *Newsline* 7, no. 153, pt. 1 (13 August 2003).

35. Donaldson and Nogee, *Foreign Policy of Russia,* 164. According to the authors, Yeltsin "did not truly curb the powers of these agencies, but rather chose to coopt their support, not only to perform foreign intelligence functions, but also to assist him in his struggle against his political opponents" (p. 165).

36. Mark Kramer, "Oversight of Russia's Intelligence and Security Agencies: The Need for and Prospects of Democratic Control," PONARS Policy Memo no. 281, PONARS (Program on New Approaches to Russian Security) Policy Conference, Center for Strategic and International Studies, Washington, D.C., 6 December 2002, 200. Kramer asserts that the existence of this repressive structure is a major hindrance to democratic oversight of the intelligence and security forces.

37. "The Russian Offensive (2)," *Jane's Intelligence Digest,* 16 April 2001.

38. "Slovak Intelligence Looks to the Past," *Jane's Intelligence Digest,* Briefings, 1 August 2003. Russian intelligence services received a direct order from Putin to "radically increase foreign intelligence gathering activities." See "Russia Steps Up Espionage," *Jane's Intelligence Digest,* Briefings, 29 November 2002. In particular, Moscow has increased its efforts to recruit Russian emigres as informers and agents.

39. "NATO's Intelligence Concerns," *Jane's Intelligence Digest,* 5 September 2003.

40. Stephen J. Blank, "Putin's Twelve-Step Program," *Washington Quarterly* 25, no. 1 (Winter 2002): 147–160.

41. An example of this was the confirmed bugging of the Moscow offices of the independent Czech daily *Lidove Noviny* in March 2000. See Petra Prochazkova,

"Russian Intelligence Is Bugging Journalists," *Lidove Noviny* (Prague), 7 March 2000.

42. McCauley, *Bandits, Gangsters, and the Mafia,* 231.

43. Links between terrorist cells and Russian security agencies in Chechnya could be replicated in parts of Eastern Europe. For growing evidence on links between some Chechen terrorist groups and Russian security agencies, see regular reports in *Chechnya Weekly,* Jamestown Foundation, Washington, D.C.

CHAPTER 3

1. Russian policymakers view the post-Soviet states as unviable. See Igor Kliamkin, "Russian Statehood, the CIS, and the Problem of Security," in Leon Aron and Kenneth M. Jensen, eds., *The Emergence of Russian Foreign Policy* (Washington, D.C.: U.S. Institute of Peace, 1994), 107–118.

2. Robert H. Donaldson and Joseph L. Nogee, *The Foreign Policy of Russia: Changing Systems, Enduring Interests* (Armonk, N.Y.: M. E. Sharpe, 2002), 178. According to the authors, "the failure of the CIS to integrate economically or militarily did not prevent Russia from using the organization to establish its dominance over the former Soviet territorial space" (pp. 189–190). Moscow's strategy was also intended to forestall any separatist waves within the Russian Federation.

3. Richard Pipes, "Is Russia Still an Enemy?" *Foreign Affairs* no. 76 (September–October 1997): 72–73.

4. Donaldson and Nogee, *Foreign Policy of Russia,* 157.

5. The term "near abroad" was reportedly first coined by Russian foreign minister Andrey Kozyrev in an interview with *Izvestia* (Moscow) on 2 January 1992.

6. Paul Kubicek, "End of the Line for the Commonwealth of Independent States," *Problems of Post-Communism* 46, no. 2 (March–April 1999): 15–24.

7. Henry E. Hale, "The Rise of Russian Anti-Imperialism," *Orbis* 43, no. 1 (Winter 1999): 111–125. In the early 1990s, Moscow pressed ahead with radical domestic economic reforms without consulting with its allies and thus undermined the premise of CIS coordination in economic policy. This contributed to accelerating the breakdown of economic ties between former Soviet republics.

8. "Russia's Old Imperial Map Is Still Shrivelling," *The Economist* (London), 22 May 1997.

9. Vera Tolz, *Russia: Inventing the Nation* (London: Arnold, 2001), 271.

10. For analysis of the uses of national identity in the post-Soviet states, see Taras Kuzio, "History, Memory, and Nation-Building in the Post-Soviet Colonial Space," *Nationalities Papers* 30, no. 2 (2002): 241–264.

11. *Nezavisimaia Gazeta* (Moscow), 14 January 2000.

12. Allen C. Lynch, "The Realism of Russia's Foreign Policy," *Europe-Asia Studies* 53, no. 1 (January 2001): 11.

13. John Lough, "The Place of the 'Near Abroad' in Russian Foreign Policy," RFE/RL *Research Report* 2, no. 11 (12 March 1993): 21–29.

14. *Izvestia* (Moscow), 7 August 1992.

15. See the Russian Foreign Intelligence Service report titled *Rossiia-SNG, Nuzhdaetsia li v Korrektirovke Pozitsiya Zapada?* (Moscow, 1994).

16. *Vozroditsia li Soyuz? Budushtshee Postsovetskovo Prostranstva: Tezisy po*

Vneshnei i Oboronnoi Politike (Moscow, 1996). Excerpts from the Council report can also be found in *Nezavisimaya Gazeta* (Moscow), 23 May 1996.

17. See the collection of writings by advisers to Russia's major intelligence agencies in *Belaia Kniga Rossiiskikh Spetssluzhb* (Moscow: Obozrevatel, 1995).

18. William D. Jackson, "Encircled Again: Russia's Military Assesses Threats in a Post-Soviet World," *Political Science Quarterly* 117, no. 3 (2002): 373–400.

19. Paul A. Goble, "Russia as a Eurasian Power: Moscow and the Post-Soviet Successor States," in Stephen Sestanovich, ed., *Rethinking Russia's National Interests*, Significant Issues Series 16, no. 1 (Washington, D.C.: Center for Strategic and International Studies, 1994), 42–51.

20. Stanislaw Bieleñ, "Geopolityczne Uwarunkowanie Nowej Tożsamości Rosji," in Stanisław Bieleñ and Witold Góralski, ed., *Nowa Tożsamośc Niemiec i Rosji w Stosunkach Międzynarodowych* (Warsaw: Foundation of International Studies, 1999), 73–117.

21. Some Russian analysts viewed the EEC as an alternative to U.S.-dominated "globalization." See Sergey Baburin, "Eurasian Economic Community as a Form of Russian Reintegration and Alternative to Globalization," *Russia and Central Europe in the New Geopolitical Realities,* Russian Academy of Sciences, Fourth International Scientific Conference, Moscow, 14–16 June 2001, 33–46.

22. Liz Fuller, "Back to the USSR?" RRFE/RL, *Newsline* 5, no. 147, pt. 1 (6 August 2001), 11–13.

23. "Putin Plans 'Russian EU,'" *Jane's Intelligence Digest,* Briefings, 16 May 2003.

24. Comments by Evgeniy Primakov, then director of the Russia's Foreign Intelligence Service, "Russia and the CIS: Does the West's Position Need Adjustment?" *Rossiiskaya Gazeta* (Moscow), 22 September 1994.

25. Oksana Antonenko, "Russia, NATO, and European Security after Kosovo," *Survival* 41, no. 4 (Winter 1999–2000): 133.

26. Martha Brill Olcott, "Sovereignty and the 'Near Abroad,'" *Orbis* 39, no. 3 (Summer 1995): 353–367.

27. See the commentary by Konstantin Zatulin and Andranik Migranyan in the monthly supplement to *Nezavisimaya Gazeta* (Moscow) no. 1 (December 1997). The translation is contained in "Russian Foreign Policy, 1994–1998: Charting an Independent Course," in Gordon Livermore, ed., *Current Digest of the Post-Soviet Press,* 6th ed. (Columbus, Ohio: American Association for the Advancement of Slavic Studies 1999), 97–100.

28. Richard Sakwa and Mark Webber, "The Commonwealth of Independent States, 1991–1998: Stagnation and Survival," *Europe-Asia Studies* 51, no. 3 (1999): 379–415. For an assessment that takes Kremlin policy at face value, see Mikhail A. Alexseev, "The Challenge of Relations with Former Republics," in Stephen K. Wegren, ed., *Russia's Policy Challenges: Security, Stabiluty, and Development* (Armonk, N.Y.: M. E. Sharpe, 2003), 38–57.

29. V. Zemskii, "Collective Security in the CIS," *International Affairs* (Moscow) 45, no. 1 (1999): 97–104.

30. Roland Dannreuther, "Escaping the Enlargement Trap in NATO-Russian Relations," *Survival* 41, no. 4 (Winter 1999–2000): 148.

31. From an interview with Andranik Migranyan, director of the CIS Center of the Russian Academy of Sciences Institute of International Economic and Political

Research, in *Rossiiskaya Gazeta* (Moscow), 4 August 1992. Migranyan encouraged the government to recognize the independence of several national autonomous regions, such as Transnistria in Moldova, pending their possible inclusion in the Russian Federation, as well as the separatist Serbian territories in Croatia and Bosnia-Herzegovina.

32. Liz Fuller, "Introducing the 'Other' Guam," RFE/RL, *Newsline* 1, no. 169 (1 December 1997), rferl.org/newsline/1997/12/011297.asp.

33. Martin McCauley, *Bandits, Gangsters, and the Mafia: Russia, the Baltic States, and the CIS* (Harlow, England: Longman, 2001), 354.

34. Roman Solchanyk, *Ukraine and Russia: The Post-Soviet Transition* (Lanham, Md.: Rowman & Littlefield, 2001), 107.

35. Antonenko, "Russia, NATO, and European Security,"128.

36. Lena Jonson, "Russia, NATO, and the Handling of Conflicts at Russia's Southern Periphery: At a Crossroads?" *European Security* 9, no. 4 (Winter 2000): 45–72.

37. RFE/RL, *Newsline* 7, no. 175, pt. 1 (15 September 2003).

38. The CIS Counter-Terrorism Center, established in June 2000, was headed by General Boris Mylnikov, who served in the KGB from 1975 to 1991 and was first deputy head of the FSB department responsible for the "protection of constitutional order and the struggle against terrorism."

39. For some examples on how particular economic benefits dispensed by Moscow were linked to specific political and foreign policy decisions by a targeted country, see Yuliya Mostovaya, "Politicheskii Rezus-Konflikt," *Zerkalo Nedeli*, 19 August–1 September 2000.

40. Useful details can be found in "Will the Union Be Reborn?" which analyses a document produced by Moscow's Council on Foreign and Defense Policy, in *Transition* 2, no. 15 (26 July 1996): 32–35, 62.

41. *Finansovaya Rossiya* (Moscow), 31 January 2002.

42. V. Kremeniuk, "The Ideological Legacy in Russia's Foreign Policy," *International Affairs* (Moscow) 47, no. 3 (2001): 18–26. According to the author, "Russia is still measuring its might and the might of others by the number of missiles and warheads rather than by the level of living and the amount of capital free for investments. It seems that the minds of Russian politicians are still clogged with vague ideological patterns and the division of the world into 'us' and 'them'" (p. 26).

43. RFE/RL, *Newsline* 7, no. 74, pt. 1 (17 April 2003). In February 2003, the four countries reached agreement on the creation of a "joint economic space." The four states agreed to create a supranational commission on trade and tariffs that will be based in Kyiv and initially headed by a representative of Kazakhstan. This commission would not be subordinate to the governments of the four countries. The ultimate goal of the economic alliance is the creation of a "regional-integration organization" that will be open to other countries but will not replace the CIS. The planned zone will require uniform customs, currency, and budgetary policies.

44. *Komsomolskaya Pravda* (Moscow), 27 August 2002, quoted in RFE/RL, *Newsline* 6, no. 162, pt. 1 (28 August 2002).

45. RFE/RL, *Newsline* 7, no. 194, pt. 1 (10 October 2003).

46. Herman Pirchner Jr. and Ilan Berman, "Reviving Greater Russia," *Washington Times*, 24 October 2002; and Ilan Berman, "Putin's Problem," *National Review Online*, 8 January 2002, www.nationalreview.com.

47. "Russia's New 'Warsaw Pact,'" *Jane's Intelligence Digest,* Briefings, 9 May 2003. In the aftermath of the ousting of Saddam Hussein's regime in Iraq, many authoritarian leaders in the CIS felt threatened by U.S. "unilateralism" and could turn to Russia in search of security guarantees.

48. Vladimir Socor, "Eurasian Military-Political Bloc Mooted at CSIS Summit," Institute for Advanced Strategic and Political Studies, Washington, D.C., *Policy Briefing* no. 1 (23 October 2002).

49. RFE/RL, *Newsline* 7, no. 76, pt. 1 (22 April 2003). According to Moscow's *Nezavisimaya Gazeta* on 21 April 2003, the new treaty formalizes a split in the CIS between countries oriented toward Moscow and those openly following U.S. interests.

50. Vladimir Mikhailov, Russia's air force commander in chief, headed the CIS air defense coordination committee.

51. Diana Bazyliak, "Young People Evade the Draft, While Russia Competes for Conscripts," *The Day* (digest of Ukrainian daily newspaper online), 15 April 2003, day.kiev.ua.

52. "Putin's CIS Strategy," *Jane's Intelligence Digest,* Briefing, 7 March 2003.

53. Marko Mihkelson, "Russia's Policy Toward Belarus, Moldova, and the Baltic States," in Janusz Bugajski, ed., *Understanding Russia: New European Perspectives* (New York: Council on Foreign Relations, 2002), 97–115.

54. Lena Jonson and Clive Archer, "Russia and Peacekeeping in Eurasia," Lena Jonson and Clive Archer, eds., *Peacekeeping and the Role of Russia in Eurasia* (Boulder, Colo.: Westview, 1996), 3–28.

55. Roy Allison, "The Military Background and Context to Russian Peacekeeping," in Jonson and Archer, *Peacekeeping,* 35.

56. Anatoly Rozanov, "Belarus: Foreign Policy Priorities," in Sherman W. Garnett and Robert Legvold, eds., *Belarus at the Crossroads* (Washington, D.C.: Carnegie Endowment for International Peace, 1999), 19–36.

57. Margarita M. Balmaceda, "Myth and Reality in the Belarusian-Russian Relationship: What the West Must Know," *Problems of Post-Communism* 46, no. 3 (May–June 1999): 3–14.

58. Adrian Karatnycky, "Does Russia Want Another Empire?" *Washington Times,* 27 May 1997. Primakov called for a union with Belarus "at any cost" as a response to NATO enlargement. According to Balmaceda, "In many ways, Lukashenka has become a mouthpiece for some highly odious views, beliefs the Russian leadership cannot voice openly without endangering their tenuous, but polite, relations with the West." Balmaceda, "Myth and Reality," 7.

59. Siargej Ausiannik, "Zagadnienie Równoprawności w Stosunkach Między Białorusi a Rosji," in *Russia and Its Neighbors* (Kraków: Meritum, 2000), 31–41.

60. Heinz Timmermann, "Putin: Harder Method Toward Minsk: The Relationship Between Russia and Belarus with Regard to the Union Treaty" (Köln: Bundesinstitut für Östwissenschaftliche und Internationale Studien, June 2000).

61. RFE/RL, *Newsline* 6, no. 153, pt. 1 (15 August 2002).

62. Taras Kuzio, "Will Lukashenka Survive as Putin Loses Interest in Union with Belarus?" RFE/RL, *Newsline* 6, no. 131, pt. 1 (16 July 2002).

63. RFE/RL, *Newsline* 7, no. 47, pt. 2 (12 March 2003); and RFE/RL, *Newsline* 7, no. 62, pt. 2 (1 April 2003).

64. Hrihoriy Perepelitsa, "Belarusian-Russian Integration and its Impact on the Security of Ukraine," in Garnett and Levgold, *Belarus at the Crossroads*, 81–103.

65. A typical speech by Lukashenka stressing the global significance of the Russia-Belarus Union can be found in "A New Stage in Uniting the Fraternal Belarusian and Russian Peoples Has Begun," *Narodnaya Hazeta* (Minsk), 22 January 1999.

66. For an analysis of Russian influence in Belarus, see Marcin A. Piotrowski, "Security Above All," *Rocznik Strategiczny 2000/01* (Warsaw: Foundation of International Relations, 2001), 220–239.

67. RFE/RL, *Newsline* 7, no. 20, pt. 2 (31 January 2003).

68. Jeff Chinn and Robert Kaiser, *Russians as the New Minority: Ethnicity and Nationalism in the Soviet Successor States* (Boulder, Colo.: Westview, 1996), 142.

69. S. J. Main, *Belarus-Russian Military Relations (1991–1998)* (London: Conflict Studies Research Center, 1998).

70. RFE/RL, *Newsline* 6, no. 209, pt. 2 (5 November 2002); and RFE/RL, *Newsline* 6, no. 208, pt. 2 (4 November 2002).

71. RFE/RL, *Newsline* 6, no. 211, pt. 2 (11 November 2002).

72. Vladimir Socor, "Putin and Gazprom in Belarus: One Hand Giveth, One Hand Taketh Away," Institute for Advanced Strategic and Political Studies, *Policy Briefings* no. 7, Washington D.C., 19 November 2002. In addition to fossil fuels, Russia committed itself to loaning $20 million to Belarus and $20 million to Ukraine for the completion of the Rivne and Khmelnitsky nuclear power plants. See the *Interfax News Agency* (Moscow), 2 July 2003.

73. RFE/RL, *Newsline* 7, no. 119, pt. 2 (25 June 2003). In July 2003, the Belarusian Energy Ministry stated that the privatization of Beltranshaz on Russia's terms would be pointless: "If we sold control of *Beltranshaz*, we would sell control of the country." See RFE/RL, *Newsline* 7, no. 144, pt. 2 (31 July 2003). Minsk wanted to sell a minority stake in the company, while Gazprom maintained that the price was inflated and sought a controlling interest.

74. "Belarus, Gazprom Unable to Agree on a Price for Beltransgaz," *Interfax News Agency, Petroleum Report*, 2 July 2003. Gazprom prepared to raise the price of gas to Belarus from a fixed wholesale price reserved for Russian consumers to a level charged to independent consumers. Gazprom's proposal was agreed upon by the Kremlin as evidence of a "hardening of Russia's foreign-policy course in relation to Belarus." See RFE/RL, *Newsline* 7, no. 172, pt. 1 (10 September 2003). Prime Minister Kasyanov announced that subsidized prices for natural gas would terminate as of January 2004. See RFE/RL, *Newsline* 7, no. 175, pt. 1 (15 September 2003).

75. Vital Silitski, "The Devil Is in the Details: Stalemate in Economic Integration with Russia," RFE/RL, *Poland, Belarus, and Ukraine Report* 5, no. 10 (18 March 2003).

76. *The Belarus Issue*, Working Paper no. 1 (Vilnius: Institute of International Relations and Political Science, Vilnius University, 2002).

77. Elena Daneiko, "The Economic and Monetary Relationship Between Belarus and Russia" (Köln: Bundesinstitut für Östwissenschaftliche und Internationale Studien, May 2000).

78. Martin Sieff, "Treaty of Union with Belarus Could Divide Russia," *Washington Times*, 6 April 1997.

79. RFE/RL, *Newsline* 6, no. 232, pt. 1 (12 December 2002).

80. Russian companies feared Lukashenka's popularity inside Russia and the dangers he would pose to private business if he were elected president of the Russia-Belarus Union. See Vladimir Dorokhov, "Starii-Novyi Kandidat," *Belruskaia Delovaia Gazeta* (Minsk), 5 February 1998.

81. RFE/RL, *Newsline* 7, no. 12, pt. 2 (21 January 2003).

82. RFE/RL, *Newsline* 7, no. 111, pt. 2 (13 June 2003). According to the draft agreement, both the Belarusian National Bank and the Russian Central Bank would retain their status, but the National Bank would have "limited control" over the printing of money as well as over exchange-rate and monetary policies. The Russian Central Bank would supply Belarus with ruble notes after 1 January 2005. The two banks would coordinate monetary policy but the Russian side's decisions would prevail in issues directly affecting the stability of the ruble.

83. "Belarus to Transit to Russian *Ruble*," *Vedomosti* (Moscow), 9 June 2003. During the summer of 2003, there was growing speculation that the currency union would be scuttled because it would require Lukashenka to relinquish some of his powers. The key issue for Lukashenka was Russia's agreement to his third presidential term; the currency union was a bargaining chip. Failure of the currency union could appear as a failure in Putin's attempts at CIS integration. See Igor Semenenko, "Setbacks to Ruble Union May Signal Its Demise," *Moscow Times*, 4 July 2003.

84. RFE/RL, *Newsline* 7, no. 115, pt. 2 (19 June 2003); and Vital Silitski, "Minsk Postpones Introduction of Russian Ruble in Noncash Transactions," RFE/RL, *Newsline* 7, no. 138, pt. 2 (23 July 2003). According to Silitski: "The Belarusian government's action only confirms the suggestion of some of its opponents who maintain that no progress in integration is possible before the economic systems and policies of the two countries converge. But Lukashenka himself denies the possibility of such convergence" (pp. 11–12).

85. RFE/RL, *Newsline* 7, no. 11, pt. 2 (17 January 2003).

86. Vital Silitski, "The Pitfalls of Belarus's Economic Integration with Russia," RFE/RL, *Newsline* 7, no. 56, pt. 2 (24 March 2003).

87. Rafał Sadowski, *Belarus-Russia: Whither Integration?* (Warsaw: Centre for Eastern Studies, May 2003).

88. RFE/RL, *Newsline* 7, no. 123, pt. 2 (1 July 2003).

89. From papers presented by Rafał Sadowski and Jan Maksymiuk at a conference on Belarus organized by the American Enterprise Institute (AEI) in Washington, D.C., on 14 November 2002. Also see A. Wierzbowska-Miazga and Rafał Sadowski, *Belarus in the World Arms Market* (Warsaw: Center for Eastern Studies, 2001).

90. RFE/RL, *Newsline* 7, no. 162, pt. 2 (26 August 2003).

91. *Interfax News Agency* (Moscow), 8 July 2003.

92. RFE/RL, *Newsline* 7, no. 60, pt. 2 (28 March 2003).

93. Vladimir Socor, "The OSCE in Belarus: On Lukashenka's and Putin's Sufferance?" Institute for Advanced Strategic and Political Studies, Washington, D.C., IASPS *Policy Briefings: Geostrategic Perspectives on Eurasia* no. 13 (27 January 2003).

94. Jan Maksymiuk, RFE/RL, *Newsline* 6, no. 235, pt. 2 (17 December 2002). According to the author, "[H]e might succeed in making this option a reality, since Moscow appears to be more interested in making Lukashenka more 'docile' in issues

of interest for Russian businesses than in expanding democracy in Belarus"
(pp. 11–12).

95. *Interfax News Agency* (Moscow), 3 February 1995.

96. Phil Williams, "Drug Trafficking and Organized Crime in Belarus: Threat and
Response," www.google.com/search?q=cache:WCm45SpYksAJ:www.rol.home.by pub-
lications drtraf.html+%22drug+trafficking+and+organized+crime+in+Belarus%22&hl
=en&ie=UTF-8

97. "Slavic Disunion?" *The Economist* (London), 22 July 1999.

98. Valentin Romanov, "Kaliningrad as an Integral Part of Russia," *International
Affairs* (Moscow) no. 6 (1995): 42–49; and Vladimir Shumeiko, "Kaliningrad Region: A Russian Outpost," *International Affairs* (Moscow) no. 6 (1995): 1–7.

99. Katarzyna Pełczyńska-Nałęcz, Alexander Duleba, László Póti, and Vladimir
Votapek, *Eastern Policy of the EU: The Visegrad Countries' Perspective* (Warsaw: Centre for Eastern Studies, 2003), 43.

100. Graeme Herd, "Competing for Kaliningrad," *World Today* (London) 55,
no. 12 (December 1999), 7–8. The commonly held view is that Moscow is living
at the expense of the regions and that Moscow keeps getting richer while the regions become poorer.

101. RFE/RL, *Newsline* 7, no. 141, pt. 1 (28 July 2003).

102. Brian Vitunic, "Enclave to Exclave: Kaliningrad Between Russia and
the European Union," *Intermarium On-Line Journal*, Vol. 6, no. 1 (2003),
www.columbia.edu/cu/sipa/REGIONAL/ECE/vol6no1/enclave.pdf.

103. See the comments by Admiral Feliks Gromov, the commander in chief of
the Russian navy, in "Znachenie Kaliningradskogo Osobogo Raiona dlia Oborono-
sposobnosti Rossiiskoi Federatsii," *Voennaya Mysl* no. 5 (September–October 1995):
13.

104. David R. Sands, "Baltics' Bid to Join NATO Gets Touchy," *Washington
Times*, 17 January 2001. Some analysts believed that U.S. intelligence reports on
the incident were delibertely supressed for political reasons as Washington sought
cooperative relations with Moscow. See Bill Gertz, "U.S. Yet to Query Moscow on
Nukes," *Washington Times*, 4 January 2001.

105. Michael Mrozinski, "Poland Fears It May Be on a Nuclear Front Line,"
Agence France Presse, 5 January 2001.

106. "Conflict over Economic Zone Looming?" *RFE/RL Russian Federation
Report* 3, no. 27 (3 October 2000).

107. Alexander Bubenets, "Eskadrennyi Subiekt Kaliningrad," *Nezavisimaia
Gazeta* (Moscow), 24 February 2001.

108. Keith C. Smith, "Baltic-Russian Cooperation: Opportunities Resulting from
Baltic EU and NATO Membership," Europe Program Working Paper (Washington,
D.C.: Center for Strategic and International Studies, March 2003), 28.

109. For an analysis of how western regions of Russia bordering actual and potential NATO member states are more pro-Western than the central government in
Moscow, see Jakob Hedenskog and Ingmar Oldberg, "Russia's Western Border
Regions: Gateway to Europe?" Slavic Research Center, Hokkaido University, Japan,
5 March 2002.

110. Katarzyna Pełczyńska-Nałęcz, *Seven Myths About Kaliningrad*, Policy Briefs
(Warsaw: Centre for Eastern Studies, July 2002), 17.

254   Notes

111. Vygaudas Usackas, Lithuania's deputy foreign minister, in an article titled "Linking Russia with New Europe: Kaliningrad Could Become Gate of Opportunity," *Washington Times*, 12 January 2000.

112. "Central European Risk Pointers: Kaliningrad Oblast," *Janes Online*, 18 February 2002, www.janes.com.

113. *NTV* (Moscow), 20 February 2000.

CHAPTER 4

1. Vera Tolz, *Russia: Inventing the Nation* (London: Arnold, 2001), 209–232. Russian nationalists believe that the Kyivan Rus state in the ninth century was the ethnic, religious, and cultural predecessor of the Russian state. Ukrainian historians point out that the Kyivan heritage was neither Russian nor Muscovite and that the true successor to Kyivan Rus was the subsequent Galicia-Volhynia state, which was predominantly Ukrainian.

2. Nico Lange, "Ukraine: Eleven Years after the Change: Decisions Between East and West?" *Eurasisches Magazine* (Germany), November 2002.

3. Taras Kuzio, "Is Ukraine a Member of the CIS?" RFE/RL, *Newsline 7*, no. 11, pt. 2 (17 January 2003).

4. Tor Bukkvoll, "Off the Cuff Politics: Explaining Russia's Lack of a Ukraine Strategy," *Europe-Asia Studies* 53, no. 8 (December 2001), 1141–1157.

5. Margarita M. Balmaceda, "Ukraine, Central Europe, and Russia in a New International Environment," in Margarita M. Balmaceda, ed., *On the Edge: Ukrainian-Central European-Russian Security Triangle* (Budapest: Central European University Press, 2000), 1–34. Also see Jeremy Lester, "Russian Attitudes to Ukrainian Independence," *Journal of Communist Studies and Transition Politics* 10, no. 2 (June 1994): 193–233.

6. L. Gankin, "Brat'ya Stali Partnerami," *Moskovskie Novosti* (Moscow), June 1997: 1–8.

7. Among other threatening statements, Foreign Minister Andrey Kozyrev called for the defense of Russian minorities and St. Petersburg mayor Anatolii Sobchak warned of "forced Ukrainianization" of the Russian minority and a potential territorial conflict.

8. Ilya Prizel, *National Identity and Foreign Policy: Nationalism and Leadership in Poland, Russia, and Ukraine* (Cambridge: Cambridge University Press, 1998), 377. According to Prizel, "Initially, this Western focus of Kravchuk's foreign policy did not inspire the same level of support in Russian-speaking eastern and southern Ukraine as it did among nationalist intellectuals." Nevertheless, Kravchuk's "Western paradigm" gained general support in the early 1990s.

9. Taras Kuzio, "Public Opinion, Unions, and Nationalism in the Three Eastern Slavic States," RFE/RL, *Newsline 6*, no. 172, pt. 1 (12 September 2002).

10. "Fleet Accord Paves Way to Russia-Ukraine Treaty," *Rossiiskie Vesti* (Moscow), 30 May 1997.

11. *Financial Times* (London), 12 July 2001. As a former prime minister and head of Gazprom, Chernomyrdin was involved in corrupt business practices and maintained close ties with several oligarchs.

12. "Ukraine Strives for Membership of the European Union as One 'Strategic Goal,'" *Blickpunkt Bundestag* (Germany), January 2001.

13. In Prizel's words: "Polish analysts initially envisioned that their country would serve as a 'bridge' between Ukraine and Europe, but many Ukrainian nationalists saw Poland as an escape hatch from Russian domination." See Prizel, *National Identity and Foreign Policy*, 139.

14. RFE/RL, *Newsline* 7, no. 195, pt. 2 (14 October 2003); and RFE/RL, *Newsline* 7, no. 196, pt. 2 (15 October 2003). See also "Ukraine Ready to Defend Itself from Russia," *Pravda* (Moscow), 21 October 2003.

15. According to Russian deputy foreign minister Valery Loshchinin, "unilateral attempts" by Ukraine to demarcate the border in the Azov-Kerch water area "run counter to international law envisaging that a border can only be demarcated by mutual consent." Moscow wanted the region to be registered as an economic complex in common use for shipping, extracting natural resources, and fishing. It did not recognize any state border between Crimea and the Krasnodar region in Russia. See *RIA Novosti* (Moscow), 5 November 2003.

16. According to Dmitry Rogozin, chairman of the Russian Duma's International Affairs Committee and a close Putin ally, Ukraine unlawfully seized Tuzla when it gained independence. In reality, the Tuzla islet and the deep navigation channel in the Kerch Strait formed an administrative part of the Kerch municipality in Crimea, and therefore a part of Soviet Ukraine. The Russian-Ukrainian "friendship treaty" enshrined existing borders between the two countries. See Vladimir Socor, "A Naval Dustup over a Mad Too Far," *Wall Street Journal*, 24 October 2003.

17. *Rossiiskiye Vesti* (Moscow), 25 September 1997.

18. Konstantin Zatulin and Andranik Migranyan in the monthly supplement to *Nezavisimaya Gazeta* (Moscow) no. 1 (December 1997). The translation is contained in "Russian Foreign Policy, 1994–1998: Charting an Independent Course," in Gordon Livermore, ed., *Current Digest of the Post-Soviet Press*, 6th ed. (Columbus, Ohio: American Association for the Advancement of Slavic Studies, 1999), 97–100. For periodic Ukrainian government support for NATO enlargement during the first Kuchma administration, see Roman Woronowycz, "Lisbon Summit of OSCE Discusses Future Course for European Security," *Ukrainian Weekly* no. 49 (8 December 1996).

19. "Sour Slavs in the Slow Lane," *The Economist* (London), 30 May 2002.

20. "A New Misery Curtain," *The Economist* (London), 31 May 2002.

21. RFE/RL, *Newsline* 7, no. 136, pt. 2 (21 July 2003).

22. Charles Clover, "Kiev-Moscow Pact Could Threaten NATO Links," *Financial Times* (London), 22 January 2001.

23. Olexiy Haran, "Ukraine at the Crossroads: Velvet Revolution or Belarusification," PONARS Policy Memo no. 261, PONARS (Program on New Approaches to Russian Security) Policy Conference, Center for Strategic and International Studies, Washington, D.C., 6 December 2002, 81.

24. RFE/RL, *Newsline* 7, no. 135, pt. 1 (18 July 2003).

25. Marcin A. Piotrowski, "Ukraine in Search for Lost Time," *Rocznik Strategiczny 2000/01* (Warsaw: Foundation of International Relations, 2001): 208–220.

26. Paul J. D'Anieri, *Economic Interdependence in Ukrainian-Russian Relations* (Albany: State University of New York Press, 1999). President Kravchuk's opposition to a single economic space with Russia paradoxically increased Ukraine's economic

dependence because Moscow imposed a higher price for energy imports and vastly increased Kyiv's debt.

27. Oles M. Smolansky, "Ukraine's Quest for Independence: The Fuel Factor," *Europe-Asia Studies* 47, no. 1 (1995): 67–90.

28. Margarita Mercedes Balmaceda, "Gas, Oil, and the Linkages Between Domestic and Foreign Policies: The Case of Ukraine," *Europe-Asia Studies* 50, no. 2 (1998): 257–286.

29. Ilya Prizel, "Putin's Russia, the Berlin Republic, and East Central Europe: A New Symbiosis?" *Orbis* 46, no. 4 (Fall 2002): 685.

30. Jan S. Adams, "Russia's Gas Diplomacy," *Problems of Post-Communism* 49, no. 3 (May–June 2002): 14–22. Many Ukrainian leaders viewed Gazprom's proposals as a threat to the country's independence. Ukrainian activists also charged that Russia had cheated Ukraine in the division of assets following the Soviet breakup in 1991.

31. U.S. ambassador Carlos Pascual in a speech titled "Ukraine: The Road to Energy Security," delivered to the sixth annual conference "Energy Security of Europe in the XXI Century," Kyiv, Ukraine, 28 May 2003.

32. Taras Kuzio, "Moscow's Energy Strategy," *Jane's Intelligence Digest*, 20 December 2002; and Vladimir Socor, "Putin, Gazprom Seek Control of Ukraine's Gas Pipelines to Europe," Institute for Advanced Strategic and Political Studies, Washington, D.C., *Policy Briefing* no. 3, 27 October 2002.

33. F. Stephen Larrabee, "Ukraine's Balancing Act," *Survival* (London) 38, no. 2 (Summer 1996): 143–165.

34. Moscow tried to shield itself from potential Ukrainian instability by decreasing its dependence on Ukraine as a major transit country for energy supplies to Western Europe. See Arkady Moshes, "Russian Policy Towards Ukraine, Belarus, and the Baltic States in the Putin Era," PONARS Policy Memo no. 123, Institute of Europe. Gazprom became active in planning alternative routes for Russian exports, with pipelines projected through Belarus, Poland, and Slovakia to bypass Ukraine.

35. *Current Digest of the Post-Soviet Press* 54, no. 24 (10 July 2002). Source: Viktor Matveyev, Svetlana Stepanenko, and Fyodor Lukyanov, "Natural Gas Entente," *Vremya Novostei* (Moscow), 11 June 2002: 1–2.

36. *ITAR-TASS* (Moscow), 20 August 2001.

37. Ariel Cohen, "The New Tools of Russian Power: Oil and Gas Pipelines," *Johnson's Russia List* no. 5003 (2 January 2001).

38. RFE/RL, *Newsline* 7, no. 134, pt. 2 (17 July 2003).

39. Oles M. Smolansky, "Fuel, Credit, and Trade: Ukraine's Economic Dependence on Russia," *Problems of Post-Communism* 46, no. 2 (March–April 1999): 49–58.

40. RFE/RL, *Newsline* 5, no. 241, pt. 1 (21 December 2001); and *Komsomolskaya Pravda* (Moscow), 20 December 2001.

41. Elizabeth Piper, "Russia, Ukraine Vow to Create Economic Power," *Moscow Times*, 19 March 2002.

42. RFE/RL, *Newsline* 7, no. 39, pt. 2 (28 February 2003).

43. RFE/RL, *Newsline* 6, no. 235, pt. 2 (17 December 2002); and RFE/RL, *Newsline* 7, no. 19, pt. 2 (30 January 2003).

44. RFE/RL, *Newsline* 6, no. 230, pt. 1 (10 December 2002).

45. *Political Commentary* no. 3 (September 2003). A European Commission spokesman stated that Kyiv's plan to sign the SES cast doubts on its sincerity for

257

EU integration. See RFE/RL, *Newsline* 7, no. 158, pt. 2 (20 August 2003). It also indicated a success for Moscow in keeping Ukraine distant from Europe's integration process lest it lose influence over the country. Moscow was seeking a coordinated approach with Kyiv in their international integration. To reassert some measure of independence, in August 2003 Ukrainian foreign minister Anatoliy Zlenko stated that Ukraine would not coordinate its entry into the WTO with Russia. See RFE/RL *Newsline* 7, no. 163, pt. 2 (27 August 2003).

46. Paul A. Goble, "Russia and Its Neighbors," *Foreign Policy* no. 90 (Spring 1993). 79–88.

47. Serge Schmemann, "Russia Votes to Void Cession of Crimea to Ukraine," *New York Times,* 22 May 1992.

48. Dzintra Bungs, "Russian Vice President on Crimea," RFE/RL, *Research Report,* 17 April 1992, 61.

49. V. Skachko, "Gde Naiti Mekhanizmy, ili kto Okonchatel'no Reshit Krymskii Vopros," *Zerkalo Nedeli,* 25 March 1995.

50. Nikolas K. Gvosdev, "The New Party Card? Orthodoxy and the Search for Post-Soviet Russian Identity," *Problems of Post-Communism* 47, no. 6 (November–December 2000): 35.

51. Reported in *1999 Country Reports on Human Rights Practice: Ukraine* (Washington, D.C.: U.S. Department of State, Bureau of Democracy, Human Rights, and Labor, 25 February 2000).

52. Reported in *2002 Country Reports on Human Rights Practice: Ukraine* (Washington, D.C.: U.S. Department of State, Bureau of Democracy, Human Rights, and Labor, 31 March 2003).

53. Adrian Karatnycky, "Meltdown in Ukraine," *Foreign Affairs* 80, no. 3 (May–June 2001): 73–86.

54. A. Kasaev and V. Timoshenko, "Leonid Kuchma Makhnul na Rossiyu Rukoi," *Nezavisimaya Gazeta* (Moscow), 12 October 1999.

55. For Putin's statements in Kyiv, see *Ukrainska Pravda* (Kyiv), 2 October 2000, www.pravda.com.ua.

56. Taras Kuzio, "Russian President Gives Ukrainian Counterpart a Helping Hand Against the Opposition," RFE/RL, *Newsline* 6, no. 153, pt. 1 (15 August 2002). With Russian assistance, criminal cases were also launched against business supporters of the opposition Our Ukraine bloc.

57. Taras Kuzio, "Russia Gives Ukraine a Helping Hand in Elections," RFE/RL, *Newsline* 6, no. 13, pt. 1 (22 January 2002).

58. RRFE/RL, *Newsline* 6, no. 53, pt. 2 (20 March 2002).

59. Vladimir Socor, "Perspectives from the 'Near Abroad' on Relations with Russia," Institute for Advanced Strategic and Political Studies, Washington, D.C., *Policy Briefing* no. 9 (9 December 2002).

60. "Putin Plans 'Russian EU,'" *Jane's Intelligence Digest,* Briefings, 16 May 2003.

61. Paweł Wołowski, *Ukraine: Another View* (Warsaw, Centre for Eastern Studies, 2003), 15.

62. Louise I. Shelley, "Organized Crime and Corruption in Ukraine: Impediments to the Development of a Free Market Economy," *Demokratizatsija: The Journal of Post-Soviet Democratization* 6, no. 4 (Fall 1998): 648–663.

63. "NATO's Intelligence Concerns," *Jane's Intelligence Digest,* 5 September 2003.

64. "If Russia loses control over Moldova, this will be the beginning of its complete and final loss of control in the entire Black Sea region. We should not forget that Euroatlantic forces are relentlessly moving into Central Asia. In this way, Europe is subtly and inconspicuously strengthening its position within the area of the former USSR. Furthermore, it should be clear that when we say 'Europe' in the military sense, we actually mean NATO, or at least its 'European wing.'" From Mikhail Lavrov, "Europe Is Sending Troops into the Trans-Dniester Region and Russia Can Sit and Watch," *Press Center Russia, Information Agency*, 18 July, 2003, www.presscenter.ru.

65. Jeff Chinn, "The Case of Transdniestr (Moldova)," in Lena Jonson and Clive Archer, eds., *Peacekeeping and the Role of Russia in Eurasia* (Boulder, Colo.: Westview, 1996), 103–119.

66. Sherman W. Garnett and Rachel Lebenson, "Ukraine Joins the Fray: Will Peace Come to Trans-Dniestria?" *Problems of Post-Communism* 45, no. 6 (November–December 1998): 22–32.

67. For an interview with Voronin in which he criticizes the lack of a sufficient Russian presence in Moldova and the threat of a Romanian takeover, see "Moldova: Years of Missed Opportunities," *International Affairs*, Moscow 47, no. 2 (2001): 146–152.

68. Eugen Tomiuc, "Moldova and Russia Initial Bilateral Agreement," RFE/RL, *Newsline* 5, no. 212, pt. 2 (7 November 2001).

69. *RIA Novosti* (Moscow), 16 July 2001.

70. Vladimir Socor, "Will This OSCE Guard Dog Ever Bark?" *Wall Street Journal Europe*, 16 November 2002.

71. In August 2003, fifteen Moldovan NGOs criticized the of Moldova's federalization plan. In an official communique, the organizations state that Transnistrian separatism serves Russia's geopolitical agenda. In May 1997, Moscow "imposed the existing 'pentagonal' negotiating format, in which the secessionists enjoy an equal footing with the Moldovan state, alongside the 'trilateral' Russia-Ukraine-OSCE 'mediating' and 'guaranteeing' formats, both dominated by Russia." According to the NGOs, the Transnistrian authorities "and Moscow behind them" are "using the 'federalization' project for turning Moldova into a Russian protectorate." Reported in RFE/RL, *Newsline* 7, no. 155, pt. 2 (15 August 2003).

72. Claus Neukirch, "Russia and the OSCE: The Influence of Interested Third and Disinterested Fourth Parties on the Conflicts in Estonia and Moldova," in Pal Kolsto, ed., *National Integration and Violent Conflict in Post-Soviet Societies: The Case of Estonia and Moldova* (Oxford: Rowman & Littlefield, 2002), 235.

73. According to Neukrich, "The official declarations by Foreign Minister Andrey Kozyrev and President Yeltsin in 1992 notwithstanding, the overall influence of Russian actors on the Moldovan conflict played a major role in its escalation." See Neukrich, "Russia and the OSCE," 236.

74. According to ststements by the Russian Foreign Ministry in *RIA Novosti* (Moscow), 4 November 2003.

75. Kate Litvak, "The Role of Political Competition and Bargaining in Russian Foreign Policy: The Case of Russian Policy Toward Moldova," *Communist and Post-Communist Studies* 29, no. 2 (1996): 213–229.

76. "The Black Sea Region: New Economic Cooperation and Old Geopolitics," 22 May 2003, www.gazetasng.ru.

77. "Russia Seeks Ways to Keep Its Troops in Moldova," *Monitor* 5, no. 164 (8 September 1999). Russia's Defense Ministry and its General Staff in particular have pushed to keep Russian troops in Transnistria regardless of any political settlement.

78. Suzanne Crow, "Russia's Peacekeeping: Defense, Diplomacy, or Imperialism?" RFE/RL, *Research Report* 1, no. 37 (18 September 1992).

79. Andrea M. Lopez, "Russia and the Democratic Peace: The Decision to Use Military Force in Ethnic Disputes," in Ted Hopf, ed., *Understandings of Russian Foreign Policy* (University Park: Pennsylvania State University Press, 1999), 203.

80. Allen C. Lynch, "The Realism of Russia's Foreign Policy," *Europe-Asia Studies* 53, no. 1 (January 2001), 7–32.

81. RFE/RL, *Newsline* 6, no. 200, pt. 2 (23 October 2002).

82. "Moldova: Years of Missed Opportunities," *International Affairs* (Moscow) 47, no. 2 (2001): 139–152.

83. Vladimir Socor, "Moscow Pushes for Basing Rights in Moldova," *Prism* 1, no. 9 (30 June 1995).

84. Vladimir Socor, "The OSCE and 'Federalization' Failing in Moldova," Institute for Advanced Strategic and Political Studies, Washington, D.C., *Policy Briefing* no. 13 (27 January 2003).

85. RFE/RL, *Newsline* 6, no. 229, pt. 2 (9 December 2002).

86. RFE/RL, *Newsline* 7, no. 7, pt. 2 (13 January 2003); and RFE/RL, *Newsline* 7, no. 12, pt. 2 (21 January 2003).

87. Stephen J. Blank, "Putin's Twelve-Step Program," *Washington Quarterly* 25, no. 1 (Winter 2000): 155. The article presents a level-headed assessment of Putin's domestic and foreign policy ambitions.

88. Fiona Hill and P. Jewett, *Back in the USSR: Russian Intervention in the Internal Affairs of the Former Soviet Republics and the Implications for United States Policy Toward Russia* (Cambridge: JFK School of Government, January 1994), 61.

89. RFE/RL, *Newsline* 7, no. 183, pt. 2 (25 September 2003).

90. Consult the article by Jon Preasa in *Tara* (Chisinau), 26 September 2002.

91. Igor Munteanu, "Social Multipolarity and Political Violence," in Kolsto, *National Integration*, 200. Munteanu maintains that most of the support for the anti-Moldovan separatists was found among "retired military staff, pensioners, and employees of the party bureaucracy and security forces in the region" (p. 215).

92. For a pro-Russian perspective on Transnistrian radicalization in the early 1990s, consult Alla Skvortsova, "The Cultural and Social Makeup of Moldova: A Bipolar or Dispersed Society?" in Kolsto, *National Integration*, 159–196.

93. "Dniester Leader's Revelation on Russian Support," RFE/RL, *Research Report*, 9 October 1992.

94. RFE/RL, *Newsline* 7, no. 27, pt. 2 (11 February 2003).

95. *Jane's Intelligence Digest*, Briefings, 15 February 2002.

96. Vladimir Socor, "How to Discredit Democracy and Federalism," *Wall Street Journal Europe*, 6–8 June 2003. According to the author, "Trans-Dniester is the sole case of minority rule in contemporary Europe. Russians are the third-largest population group there, behind Moldovans and Ukrainians. Yet the authorities are mainly Russian; and the top leaders, mostly Russians from Russia (as distinct from local Russians). Moldovans and local Ukrainians are disenfranchised peasants, still toiling in *kolkhozes* (collective farms). They are unrepresented politically, and an object of

Soviet-style linguistic russification by the authorities. The Russian population is concentrated in the city of Tiraspol, while all of the five rural districts have overwhelming Moldovan and/or Ukrainian majorities. Yet, OSCE and other Western officials in practice treat Trans-Dniester as a 'Russian' area, and its self-imposed leadership as though it were legitimate. . . . The advocates of Moldova's 'federalization' would hand legal power precisely to the police regime in Transnistria. In sum, 'federalization' in this case is a democratic-looking label that covers something entirely different: a shabby deal with Moscow's proxies in this country."

97. Based on conversations with officials and experts in Chisinau, Moldova, in February 2003. See also Eugen Tomiuc, "In Moldova-Trannsdniester Dispute, Many Plans But Few Solutions," RFE/RL, *Newsline* 7, no. 162, pt. 2 (26 August 2003).

98. Irina Sandul, "Moldova Seeks Help from Moscow; Communists Seen as Saviors," *Washington Times*, 1 April 2001.

99. RFE/RL, *Newsline* 6, no. 196, pt. 2 (17 October 2002).

100. RFE/RL, *Newsline* 7, no. 19, pt. 2 (30 January 2003).

101. Vladimir Socor, "Federalization Experiment in Moldova," *Russia and Eurasia Review* 1, no. 4 (16 July 2002); and Bruno Coppieters and Michael Emerson, "Conflict Resolution for Moldova and Transnistria Through Federalization?" (Brussels: Center for European Policy Studies, 2002). Also see RFE/RL, *Newsline* 7, no. 28, pt. 2 (12 February 2003).

102. Moldova's chief negotiator with Transnistria, Vasile Sturdza, was especially critical of the Ukrainian position and speculated that Kyiv had turned into a "lobbyist for the interests of the separatist regime." RFE/RL, *Newsline* 6, no. 238, pt. 2 (20 December 2002); and RFE/RL, *Newsline* 7, no. 29, pt. 2 (13 February 2003).

103. Michael Shafir, "Russia's Self-Serving Plan for Moldova's Federalization," RFE/RL, *Newsline* 7, no. 221, pt. 2 (24 November 2003).

104. RFE/RL, *Newsline* 7, no. 74, pt. 2 (17 April 2003).

105. RFE/RL, *Newsline* 7, no. 106, pt. 2 (6 June 2003).

106. "Russia's Interest in Moldova," *Jane's Intelligence Digest*, Briefings, 4 July 2003; and Jacek Wrobel, "Transnistria," *Armed Conflicts in the Post-Soviet Region: Present Situation, Prospects for Settlement, Consequences* (Warsaw: Center for Eastern Studies, 2003), 53.

107. "Moscow's Energy Strategy," *Jane's Intelligence Digest*, 20 December 2002.

108. Viktor Alksnis, a former member of the Russian State Duma committee on Transnistria, calculated that the enclave runs a $3–4 billion business, supplying weapons to rogue states and terrorist groups. The enclave is heavily subsidized by Moscow to which it owes $800 million for energy supplies. See "Putin's CIS Strategy," *Jane's Intelligence Digest*, Briefings, 7 March 2003.

109. Taras Kuzio, "Moscow's Energy Strategy," *Jane's Intelligence Digest*, 20 December 2002.

110. "Moldova: No Quick Fix," International Crisis Group Europe (Chisinaa/Brussels), *Report* no. 147 (12 August 2003): 6. The report offers a thorough critique of the OSCE-sponsored federalization plan.

111. *Jane's Intelligence Digest*, Briefings, 4 July 2003.

112. *Flux* (Chisinau), 8 August 2002; *ITAR-TASS News Agency* (World Service) (Moscow), 25 November 1995; and *ITAR-TASS News Agency* (World Service) (Moscow), 6 November 1997.

113. According to Christian Democratic general secretary Ion Neagu in October 2003, as reported by RFE/RL, *Newsline* 7, no. 203, pt. 2 (24 October 2003).

CHAPTER 5

1. Soviet troops in the Baltic states were placed under Russian jurisdiction in January 1992, although the armed forces of the Russian Federation were only formally established in May 1992. Russian troops were withdrawn from Lithuania by August 1993 and the last soldiers left Estonia and Latvia one year later.

2. In March 1993, Russia's Defense Ministry declared that scheduled troop withdrawals would be delayed because of a lack of progress in the status of Russians in the Baltic states. The Kremlin wanted to use the issue in order to obtain greater Western aid in constructing housing for returning military personnel. See "Moskva Priostanavlivaet Vyvod Voisk iz Baltii," *Nezavisimyia Gazeta* (Moscow), 31 March 1995.

3. Seth Faison, "Three Baltic Nations Ask UN to Help Get Troops Out," *New York Times,* 4 October 1992; and Serge Schmemann, "Yeltsin Suspends Baltic Troop Pullout," *New York Times,* 30 October 1992.

4. Sven Gunnar Simonsen, "Compatriot Games: Explaining the 'Diaspora Linkage' in Russia's Military Withdrawal from the Baltic States," *Europe-Asia Studies* 53, no. 5 (July 2001), 771–791. Moscow refused to consider any compensation payments for damages caused by fifty years of Soviet occupation. A Lithuanian task force estimated that damages to the country reached $20 billion, and the three Baltic republics planned to bring a joint action in the sum of $60 billion against Russia. In response, Moscow issued documents charging that the Balts owed Russia vast amounts of money for the infrastructure built during Soviet times.

5. *Izvestiya* (Moscow), 6 July 1996; and *Novoe Vremya* (Moscow), 20 April 1997. One persistent argument against Baltic accession was that they had failed to sign the Conventional Forces in Europe treaty. In reality, all three states were prepared to sign the document.

6. Atis Lejins and Zaneta Ozolina, *Small States in a Turbulent Environment: The Baltic Perspective* (Riga: Latvian Institute for International Affairs, 1997); and Sergey Medvedev, "Geopolitics and Beyond: The New Russian Policy Toward the Baltic States," in Mathias Jopp and Sven Arnswald, eds., *The European Union and the Baltic States* (Helsinki: Finnish Institute of International Affairs, 1998). Only in September 1997 did Russian premier Chernomyrdin announce that Moscow would sign border agreements with the three Baltic states.

7. Peter Truscott, *Russia First: Breaking with the West* (London: I. B. Tauris, 1997), 68–69. Russian hypocrisy is striking given Moscow's systematically brutal policies toward the Chechens.

8. "Putin Stirring Trouble in the Baltic States," *Monitor* 8, no. 2 (3 January 2002).

9. Sherman W. Garnett, "Europe's Crossroads: Russia and the West in the New Borderlands," in Michael Mandelbaum, ed., *The New Russian Foreign Policy* (New York: Council on Foreign Relations, 1998), 65.

10. Stephen Blank, "Russian Policy on NATO Expansion in the Baltics," *Meet-*

ing Report no. 151 (Washington, D.C.: East European Studies, Woodrow Wilson Center, 27 January 1998).

11. Graeme P. Herd, *Russia-Baltic Relations, 1991–1999: Charactersistics and Evolution*, F66 (London: Conflict Studies Research Centre, August 1999), 4.

12. RFE/RL, *Newsline* 6, no. 228, pt. 1 (6 December 2002).

13. "Is Moscow Renouncing Differentiation Tactics?" *Monitor* 6, no. 125 (27 June 2000)

14. Keith C. Smith, "Baltic-Russian Cooperation: Opportunities Resulting from Baltic EU and NATO Membership" Europe Program Working Paper (Washington, D.C.: Center for Strategic and International Studies, March 2003), 13. According to Smith, Moscow was more likely to accept the EU as a forum for regional cooperation than any U.S.-sponsored programs for North West Russia arranged in tandem with the Baltic states.

15. RFE/RL, *Newsline* 6, no. 211, pt. 2 (11 November 2002).

16. RFE/RL, *Newsline* 6, no. 32, pt. 2 (19 February 2002).

17. See the report by Mart Helme, Estonia's former ambassador to Russia in *BNS* (Tallinn), 2 August 2001.

18. Keith C. Smith, *Baltic-Russian Relations: Implications for European Security* (Washington, D.C.: Center for Strategic and International Studies, Europe Program, 2002), 15. Estonia's Foreign Minister Toomas Hendrik Ilves urged that Russian propaganda attacks should be left without response in order to lessen their impact. See *BNS* (Tallinn), 27 March 2000.

19. Andrea M. Lopez, "Russia and the Democratic Peace: The Decision to Use Military Force in Ethnic Disputes," in Ted Hopf, ed., *Understandings of Russian Foreign Policy* (University Park: Pennsylvania State University Press, 1999), 197–198.

20. Reported in *Hommikuleht* (Tallinn), 10 December 1993, 3.

21. Toivo U. Raun, "Estonia: Independence Redefined," in Ian Bremmer and Ray Taras, eds., *New States, New Politics: Building the Post-Soviet Nations* (Cambridge: Cambridge University Press, 1997), 404–433. Among issues raised by the Kremlin were the rights of retired Soviet servicemen, changes to the Estonian citizenship policies, and compensation for Soviet property in Estonia.

22. "CIS and Baltic Countries Are Focus of Russia's Immediate Vital Interests," *Krasnaya Zvezda* (Moscow), 19 January 1994.

23. Simonsen, "Compatriot Games."

24. "Good Fences," *The Economist* (London), 17 December 1998.

25. Andrus Park, "Russia and Estonian Security Dilemmas," *Europe-Asia Studies* 47, no. 1 (1995): 27–45.

26. *BNS* (Tallinn), 21 July 2000. Such a scenario was outlined by Estonia's former chief of staff, Major-General Ants Laaneots, head of the Baltic Defense Studies Center.

27. RFE/RL, *Newsline* 7, no. 103, pt. 1 (3 June 2003).

28. "Comrade Capitalist," *The Economist* (London), 15 February 2001.

29. V. Elagin, "A Difficult Road from Tallinn to Moscow," *International Affairs* (Moscow) 47, no. 3 (2001): 152–160.

30. Francis Fukuyama, "The Ambiguity of 'National Interests,'" in Stephen Sestanovich, ed., *Rethinking Russia's National Interests,* Significant Issues Series 16, no. 1 (Washington, D.C.: Center for Strategic and International Studies, 1994), 10–23.

31. Aleksei Semjonov, "Estonia: Nation-Building and Integration—Political and Legal Aspects," in Pal Kolsto, ed., *National Integration and Violent Conflict in Post-Soviet Societies: The Case of Estonia and Moldova* (Oxford: Rowman & Littlefield, 2002), 109–110. Semjonov claims that Intermovement, the United Council of Labor Collectives, and the pro-Moscow wing of the Communist Party did not represent the "silent majority" of Russian speakers in Estonia.

32. *BNS* (Tallinn), 20 November 2000.

33. "Statement of the Delegation of the Russian Federation," cited in Dov Lynch, *Russia Faces Europe,* Chaillot Paper no. 60 (European Union, Paris: Institute for Security Studies, 2003), 41.

34. Paul Goble, "Russian Presence in Former Republics Declines," RFE/RL, *Newsline* 5, no. 149, pt. 2 (8 August 2001).

35. *BNS* (Tallinn), 18 November 1999.

36. *BNS* (Tallinn), 17 March 1999. The leader of the Russian Party in Estonia, Nikolay Maspanov, confirmed the accusations during Estonia's election campaign and claimed that the penetration of Russian business in politics has been evident since the 1995 general elections.

37. *Molodezh Estonii* (Tallinn), 3 March 1993, 1.

38. Stephen Blank, "Russia, NATO Enlargement, and the Baltic States," *World Affairs* 160, no. 3 (Winter 1998): 115–125. According to Winner, "The combination of ethnic Russians, trade and investment linkages left over from the Soviet era, and relatively young governing institutions cause some worry that Moscow will use these gangs to undermine the sovereignty of the three small states." See Andrew C. Winner, "The Baltic States: Heading West," *Washington Quarterly* 25, no. 1 (Winter 2002): 213.

39. Paddy Rawlinson, *Russian Organised Crime and the Baltic States: Assessing the Threat,* Working Paper no. 38/01 (Wales: Center for Comparative Criminology and Criminal Justice, University of Wales, 2001).

40. *ETA News Agency* (Tallinn), 23 November 2000.

41. *BNS* (Tallinn), 31 August 2000. The economic counselor of the Russian embassy, Sergey Andreyev, was also expelled from Estonia in 1996 "for activity incompatible with diplomatic status."

42. *Interfax* (Moscow), 3 February 2000.

43. "Russian Spies Seek to Manipulate Estonian Diplomat," *Agence France Presse* (Tallinn), 18 September 2003.

44. Interview with Normans Penke, Latvia's Ambassador to Russia, in "Latvian Envoy Predicts No Early Breakthrough in Relations with Russia," *Lauku Avize* (Riga), 7 August 2003.

45. *Novosti* (Moscow), 6 September 2003. Moscow did not mention that the human rights records of many members of this and other UN committees leave a lot to be desired.

46. *ITAR-TASS* (Moscow), 3 May 2000.

47. "Latvian Foreign Ministry Rebuffs Russia's Criticism of War Veteran Trials," *BNS* (Riga), 14 January 2002.

48. *BNS* (Tallinn), 29 March 2000.

49. "Newspapers in Latvia Help Russian Politicians in Smear Campaign," *Lauku Avize* (Riga), 26 June 2003, in *BBC Monitoring International Reports,* 26 June 2003.

50. Mel Huang, "Latvia's Marching Season," *Central European Review* 0, no. 25 (26 March 1999).

51. Andrey Fedorov, member of the board of directors of the Moscow-based Council on Foreign and Defense Policy, in "Rossiia i Pribaltika: Chto v Perspektive?" *Rossiiskaya Gazeta* (Moscow), 15 July 1997.

52. *BNS* (Tallinn), 7 March 2002. The Macedonian authorities would not have been pleased with such disparaging comments from Moscow, which had so strongly signaled its support for Skopje in the struggle against "Albanian terrorism."

53. A similar violent confrontation was planned by the Kremlin in Tallinn but was abandoned after Soviet failures in both Latvia and Lithuania.

54. *Nezavisimaya Gazeta* (Moscow), 17 May 1995. In May 1992, the chief of Russia's Military Academy, General Igor Rodionov, declared that the Baltic states must remain neutral or face potential military force.

55. Vladimir Socor, "Have Oil, Won't Let It Travel Via Latvia," *Wall Street Journal Europe*, 31 January 2003.

56. RFE/RL, *Newsline* 7, no. 13, pt. 2 (22 January 2003); RFE/RL, *Newsline* 7, no. 25, pt. 1 (7 February 2003); RFE/RL, *Newsline* 7, no. 34, pt. 2 (21 February 2003); and RFE/RL, *Newsline* 7, no. 35, pt. 2 (24 February 2003).

57. Sabrina Tavernise, "Latvia's Oil Routes Dry Up as Russia Alters Flow," *New York Times*, 21 January 2003.

58. "Andris Berzins, a Hard-Pressed Latvian," *The Economist* (London), 22 June 2000.

59. Keith C. Smith, "Baltic-Russian Cooperation: Opportunities Resulting from Baltic EU and NATO Membership," Working Paper (Washington, D.C.: Center for Strategic and International Studies, Europe Program, 2003), 27–28.

60. RFE/RL, *Newsline* 6, no. 238, pt. 2 (20 December 2002).

61. M. Demurin, "The Prospects of Russian-Latvian Relations," *International Relations* (Moscow) 47, no. 1 (2001). See also Aleksandr Shinkin, "U Liuda 'Vtorogo Sorta' v Latvii Obshchii Priznak—Russkie," *Rossiiskaya Gazeta* (Moscow), 18 January 1998.

62. Paul Goble, "Exploiting Ethnic Issues as a Foreign Policy Strategy," RFE/RL, *Security Watch* 2, no. 3 (22 January 2001).

63. "Self-Strangulation," *The Economist*, 7 June 2003.

64. RFE/RL, *Newsline* 7, no. 136, pt. 2 (21 July 2003).

65. RFE/RL, *Newsline* 7, no. 128, pt. 2 (9 July 2003). Kobzon was also declared *persona non grata* in the United States, Canada, Israel, Australia, and a number of European countries, according to *Baltic News Service*, 5 July 2003. Extremist Russian groupings, including the National Bolsheviks, have also staged provocative actions, such as the occupation of a church in Riga. Several members were jailed in Latvia on terrorist charges. Although the Russian government was not implicated in these incidents, its constant media attacks against Latvia set the stage for Russian extremism.

66. RFE/RL, *Newsline* 7, no. 195, pt. 1 (14 October 2003).

67. J. L. Black, *Russia Faces NATO Expansion: Bearing Gifts or Bearing Arms?* (Lanham, Md.: Rowman & Littlefield, 2000), 215–216.

68. Yevgeny Vostrukhov, "Panic Mongers Have Nothing to Do with It: Sprats Will Bring Down the Cabinet," *Rossiiskaya Gazeta* (Moscow), 15 April 1998.

69. *BNS* (Tallinn), 23 November 2001.

70. Stephen J. Blank, "Russia and the Baltics in the Age of NATO Enlargement," *Paremasters* (U.S. Army War College Quarterly) (Autumn 1998): 50–68.

71. Yevgeniy Vostrukhov, "Slippery Slope: Why Am I Against an Economic Blockade of Latvia" *Rossiyskaya Gazeta* (Moscow), 7 April 2000.

72. Sergey B. Stankevich, "Toward a New 'National Idea,'" in Sestanovich, *Rethinking Russia's National Interests,* 24–32. In a warning to all former Soviet satellites, the author asserts that "citizens of the newly independent states must remember that it is only because democracy now prevails in Russia that they too are able to enjoy democracy" (p. 29). The logic of such assertions is that if Russia devolves into a more authoritarian system it will threaten democratic development among its neighbors.

73. RFE/RL, *Newsline* 7, no. 96, pt. 1 (22 May 2003).

74. "Knocking at the Clubhouse Door," *The Economist* (London), 30 August 2001.

75. Ceslovas Laurinavicius, Raimundas Lopata, and Vladas Sirutavicius, *Military Transit of the Russian Federation through the Territory of the Republic of Lithuania* (Vilinius: Institute of International Relations and Political Science, Vilnius University, 2002).

76. RFE/RL, *Newsline* 7, no. 20, pt. 1 (31 January 2003).

77. RFE/RL, *Newsline* 7, no. 78, pt. 1 (24 April 2003). Putin pushed for visa-free travel throughout Europe for all Russian citizens. This is unlikely to happen given the problems of organized crime and migration from and through the Russian Federation.

78. Vladimir Socor, "Russia's Energy Giants Muscling Their Way into the Baltics," Institute for Advanced Strategic and Political Studies," Washington, D.C., *Policy Briefing* no. 6 (17 November 2002). Moscow viewed the Lithuanian oil company as a valuable gateway into Western markets.

79. Lithuanian president Valdas Adamkus was persuaded by former British foreign secretary David Owen, chairman of Yukos's international division, who pledged that the company was a "transparent, profit-oriented, long-term investor." Owen agreed to serve on the supervisory board of the refinery. Yukos also planned to establish a Balticwide filling station network. See "A Slippery Patch for Russian Oil," *Business Week Online,* 13 January 2003. Vilinius was outraged that operational control of Mazeikiu was transferred from Williams to Yukos without the knowledge of the Lithuanian government.

80. Michael Wines, "Vilnius Journal: Is Big Brother Being Replaced by Big Oil Company?" *New York Times,* 19 September 2002. The opposition Conservatives warned that Russian capital could in the long-term challenge Lithuanian democracy and a Western model of development regardless of NATO and EU membership. See *BNS* (Vilnius), 30 August 2002.

81. RFE/RL, *Newsline* 7, no. 183, pt. 2 (25 September 2003). Conservative Party leader Andrius Kubilius urged the government to suspend the planned sale of Lietuvos Dujos shares to Gazprom until the economic and political situation in Russia became clearer following the crackdown on Yukos. He also warned that in the event of Yukos's collapse, Vilnius would have to buy out the Yukos stake in Mazeikiu or risk a threat to national security. Reported in RFE/RL, *Newsline* 7, no. 205, pt. 2 (29 October 2003).

82. RFE/RL, *Newsline* 7, no. 62, pt. 2 (1 April 2003).

83. "Lithuanian Nuclear Plant Closure Seen as Increasing Dependency on Russia," *BNS* (Tallinn), 13 April 2001. Moscow has also suggested assistance in keeping open the Ignalina plant, which is scheduled for a two-phased closure in 2005 and 2009.

84. According to remarks by Vladas Gaidys, director of the Vilmorus marketing and opinion research center in Vilnius. See Nicholas Kralev, "Tiny Baltic States Have Big Hopes for NATO Membership," *Washington Times*, 16 November 2002.

85. RFE/RL, *Newsline* 7, no. 203, pt. 2 (24 October 2003).

86. *BNS* (Tallinn), 2 October 2000.

87. "Lithuanian MP Claims Russian Money Being Used in Election Campaign," *BBC Monitoring International Reports*, 3 January 2003.

88. RFE/RL, *Newsline* 7, no. 209, pt. 2 (4 November 2003). Parliament formed a commission to investigate allegations that international criminal groups attempted to influence members of the presidential office. Publication of a classified State Security Department document prompted parliament to take action. Department Director General Mecys Laurinkus testified that there were clear efforts to influence the president's staff. The Lithuanian media also reported that Russia intended to destabilize Lithuania and ensure a victory for the Liberal Democratic Party in the 2004 parliamentary elections. The alleged plan called for discrediting the ruling Social Democrats by finding "documents" in Russia about how Yukos gained control of Mazeikiu by bribing the Social Democrats.

89. Rawlinson, *Russian Organised Crime*, 17–19.

90. RFE/RL, *Newsline* 7, no. 205, pt. 2 (29 October 2003).

91. RFE/RL, *Newsline* 7, no. 208, pt. 2 (3 November 2003).

92. Vladimir Socor, "Lithuanian President Impeached over Russian Penetration of His Office," Institute for Advanced Strategic and Political Studies, Washington, D.C., *Policy Briefing* no. 49 (16 January 2004).

93. "Lithuania: Baltics Seen as Target for Russian Intelligence Service," *Interfax* (Moscow), 7 August 1998.

94. *BNS* (Vilnius), 21 December 1999.

95. "Lithuania Will Not Play "Spy Games" with Russia—Security Chief," *BNS* (Tallinn), 4 July 2000.

96. "Russian Spies Seek to Manipulate Estonian Diplomat," *Agence France Presse* (Tallinn), 18 September 2003.

CHAPTER 6

1. Russian officials have tended to avoid the term "Central Europe," particularly as it has connotations of resistance to Moscow. The term itself was a banner of opposition to Soviet Communism throughout the latter part of the post–World War II period. Russian officials prefer to talk about a more vaporous "common European identity" that apparently includes Russia.

2. For the 2000 version of Russia's foreign policy concept and references to Central and Eastern Europe, see *Diplomaticheskiy Vestnik* (Moscow) no. 8 (2000).

3. Deputy Foreign Minister Kvitsinski was the head of the Soviet delegation negotiating new bilateral treaties with the East European states.

4. "Russia's Foreign Policy Concept," *International Affairs* (Moscow), January 1993: 14–16.

5. Gerhard Mangott, "Russian Policies on Central and Eastern Europe: An Overview," *European Security* 8, no. 3 (Autumn 1999): 44–81.

6. Scott Parrish, "Russia Contemplates the Risks of Expansion," *Transition* 1, no. 23 (15 December 1995): 11–14, 64.

7. Aleksander Dugin, *Osnovy Geopolitiki: Geopolititsheskaya Budushtsheye Rossii* (Moscow: Arktogeya, 1997).

8. Yuriy Monich, "The Role of East-Central Europe in Russian Foreign Policy and Trade in the 1990s," *Russian and East European Finance and Trade* 31, no. 5 (September–October 1995): 63–76.

9. Mangott, "Russian Policies," 48.

10. Leonid Gankin, "A Gift for Stubborness," *Moskovskiye Novosti* (Moscow) no. 50 (15–22 December 1996).

11. Vladimir Nadein, "Helsinki Defeat: American View of Results of Summit Meeting," *Izvestia* (Moscow), 28 March 1997. Nadein posits the question: "If Russia, currently weak, unstable, and dependent on Western generosity, is fighting tooth and nail for the right to decide the fate of the Hungarians and the Poles as it sees fit, how would it deal with them if it really were backed by forces having 'parity' with NATO?"

12. Marek Calka, "The Warsaw-Kyiv-Moscow Security Triangle," in Margarita Balmaceda, ed., *On the Edge: Ukrainian-Central European-Russian Security Triangle* (Budapest: Central European University Press, 2000), 35–67.

13. Margarita M. Balmaceda, "Economic Relations and the Ukrainian-Central European-Russian Triangle," in Margarita Balmaceda, ed., *On the Edge: Ukrainian-Central European-Russian Security Triangle* (Budapest: Central European University Press, 2000), 165–218.

14. Helena Khotkova, "Russia's Relations with Central-Eastern European Countries: Beginning of a New Stage?" *Slovak Foreign Policy Affairs* (Bratislava) 2, no. 1 (Spring 2001): 75–81.

15. A. S. Panarim, "Położenie-Geopolityczne Rosji: Alternatywne Scenariusze U Progu XXI Wieku," in *Political Science Studies,* vol. 4, *History and Geopolitics: Russia on the Threshold of the Twenty-First Century* (Warsaw: Institute of Political Sciences, University of Warsaw, 2000), 66–68.

16. "North Central Europe," Energy Information Administration, U.S. Department of Energy, May 2003, www.eia.doe.gov.

17. Sarah Meiklejohn Terry, "Poland's Foreign Policy since 1989: The Challenges of Independence," *Communist and Post-Communist Studies* no. 33 (2000): 20. According to Kozyrev, "The countries of this region have never fallen out of Russia's field of interest." Another Foreign Ministry official revived the German expansionist specter by asserting, "Whether they like it or not, the small nations of Eastern Europe will be forced with time to resign (their) separatism and conclude an alliance with Russia beceause otherwise they will be crushed politically and economically by Germany" (p. 24).

18. Ilya Prizel, *National Identity and Foreign Policy: Nationalism and Leadership in Poland, Russia, and Ukraine* (Cambridge: Cambridge University Press, 1998), 128.

19. Ilya Prizel, "Warsaw's Ostpolitik: A New Encounter with Positivism," in Ilya Prizel and Andrew A. Michta, eds., *Polish Foreign Policy Reconsidered* (New York: St. Martin's Press, 1995), 95–128.

20. Witold Żygulski, "An Exchange of Blows," *Warsaw Voice*, 5 March 2000, 593. The Duma passed a resolution condeming the "Poznań provocation" and demanding an investigation into the passivity of the Polish police. The Russian police did not intervene during much more vicious attacks against Polish diplomatic missions in Moscow and St. Petersburg, as a result of which the Polish Ministry of Foreign Affairs issued a protest and demanded protection for its diplomatic corps in Russia.

21. Zdzisław Raczyñski, "Zimny Pokój Na Bugu," *Polityka Online* (Warsaw) no. 38 (1999): 2211, polityka.onet.pl.

22. Margarita Balmaceda, "Ukraine, Russia, and European Security: Thinking Beyond NATO Expansion," *Problems of Post-Communism* 45, no. 1 (January–February 1998).

23. After a long dispute between Warsaw and Moscow, it was agreed in July 2003 that residents of Kaliningrad could travel to Poland on free visas after Poland introduced a visa regime for Russian citizens in October 2003. The agreement provided for a simplified procedure for issuing visas to Russian citizens who permanently live in Kaliningrad. See RFE/RL, *Newsline* 7, no. 138, pt. 2 (23 July 2003).

24. "Eastern Policy of the EU: The Visegrad Countries' Perspective. Thinking about an Eastern Dimension: Policy Recommendations," in Katarzyna Pełczyńska-Nałęcz, Alexander Duleba, László Póti, and Vladimir Votapek, eds., *Eastern Policy of the Enlarged European Union: A Visegrad Perspective* (Bratislava: Slovak Foreign Policy Association, 2003), 251–263.

25. Nikolay Bucharin, "Prognosis of Russian-Polish Relations in the First Decade of the Twenty-First Century," *International Dialogue* (Moscow: Russian Academy of Sciences), 2000/2: 160–170.

26. "Patriarch Alexy: A Powerful Russian," *The Economist* (London), 25 April 2002.

27. Nikolas K. Gvosdev, "The New Party Card? Orthodoxy and the Search for Post-Soviet Russian Identity," *Problems of Post-Communism* 47, no. 6 (November–December 2000): 29–38.

28. Kai-Olaf Lang, "Poland's Relations with Russia: Between Suspicion and Cooperation," *Bericht des BIOst* (Germany: Bundeninstitut für Östwissenschaftliche und Internationale Studien) no. 31/2000 (13 November 2000).

29. "A Russian Base in the Baltics Is Reported to Have Nuclear Arms," *Associated Press*, 4 January 2001.

30. Anatolyy Skychko, "Just What We Need—Russian Nuclear Warheads," *Vseukrainskiye Vedomosti* (Kyiv), 26 March 1998.

31. Michael Radu, "Why Eastern and Central Europe Looks West," *Orbis* 41, no. 1 (Winter 1997): 51.

32. Anatolii Shapolev, "Pospeshish—Kogo Nasmeshish," *Rossiiskaya Gazeta* (Moscow), 26 February 1998.

33. RFE/RL, *Newsline* 7, no. 105, pt. 2 (5 June 2003).

34. Russian commentators complain that radar stations are mushrooming on Russia's borders to monitor developments inside the country, and contrary to provisions of the NATO-Russia Founding Act, the United States is creating military bases in Poland and moving 42,000 troops to Russia's borders. See *RIA Novosti*, 5 November 2003.

35. Based on conversations at the Russian Academy of Sciences in September

2003. Evidently, U.S. military bases in states that are "Russophobic" will create new conflicts, especially as the notion of containment remains a guiding principle in both Russian and American foreign policy. Any increase in the capabilities of the opponent will be viewed as a hostile act. Instead, Moscow is proposing a multinational force with Russian participation in the Central-East European states, an idea that is rejected throughout Central Europe.

36. Aleksander Chuikov, "NATO Asks Russia to Go Away," *Rossia* (Moscow), 31 July 2003.

37. Terry, "Poland's Foreign Policy since 1989," 22.

38. Karel Hirman, "Visegrad Country in Energy Relations Between Russia and the EU," *Slovak Foreign Policy Affairs* 2, no. 1 (Spring 2001): 82–96.

39. Adam Grzeszak, "Rosyjska Ruletka," *Polityka Online* (Warsaw) no. 32 (2002): 2362. polityka.onet.pl.

40. Andrzej Krzysztof Wróblewski, "Gaz Bez Granic," *Polityka Online* (Warsaw) no. 10 (2001): 2288, polityka.onet.pl. According to Wróblewski, "Gas from Russia is relatively cheap, but places us in a position of excessive dependence on a monopolist. Gas from Norway is certain but expensive."

41. An agreement on gas supplies and pipeline construction was finally reached in January 2003 during Deputy Prime Minister Marek Pol's visit to Moscow. See *Gazeta Wyborcza* (Warsaw), 24 January 2003.

42. Jan Maksymiuk, "Opposition Wants to Sue Deputy Premier for Gas Deal with Russia," RFE/RL, *Poland, Belarus, and Ukraine Report* 5, no. 10 (18 March 2003). Wieslaw Walendziak, the chairman of the parliamentary Treasury Committee, claimed that the new contract makes Russia a monopolist gas supplier to Poland for prices higher than in the open market. He also predicted that Poland's chemical industry would collapse as a consequence of the gas deal.

43. Adam Grzeszak, "Orlen Dziobie Pierwszy," *Polityka Online* (Warsaw) no. 38 (2002): 2368, polityka.onet.pl.

44. *RIA-Novost* (Moscow), 10 June 2003.

45. Balmaceda, "Economic Relations," 192. See also Phil Williams, ed., *Russian Organized Crime: The New Threat* (London: Frank Cass, 1997).

46. "Comrade Capitalist," *The Economist* (London), 15 February 2001.

47. Marek Menkiszak, "Polish Policy Towards Russia, the Ukraine, and Belarus, 1991–2002," in Pełczyñska-Nałęcz et al., *Eastern Policy*, 130–135.

48. Andrzej Krzysztof Wróblewski, "Wokulskiemu Szło Lepiej," *Polityka Online* (Warsaw) no. 24 (2001): 2302; and Paweł Tarnowski, "Kółka Róblowa," *Polityka Online* (Warsaw) no. 40 (1998): 2161.

49. Vladimir Lapsky, "V NATO Probalsia 'Agent 8,'" *Rossiiskaya Gazeta* (Moscow), 14 April 1998.

50. Leonid Kornilov, "People Who Understand Russia Are Back in Power," *Izvestia* (Moscow), 14 December 1995.

51. Steven Erlanger, "Russia and Poland Seek to Heal Rift," *New York Times,* 21 May 2000.

52. See the interview with Poland's former minister of internal affairs Andrzej Milczanowski in *Sieć, Polska* (Washington, D.C.), 27 April 1997. According to Milczanowski, at one point Primakov assured Yeltsin that Russian intelligence services had the necessary means to influence Polish president Kwaśniewski to block Poland's entry into NATO.

53. Francis Harris and Krzysztof Leski, "NATO Fears Russian Spy Ring as Poles Are Held," *Sunday Telegraph* (London), 11 July 1999.

54. "Poland Expels Russian 'Spies,'" *BBC News Online Europe,* 20 January 2000, bbc.co.uk.

55. "The Russian Offensive (2)," *Jane's Intelligence Digest,* 16 April 2001.

56. Francis Harris, "Eastern Security Chaos Mars NATO's Enlargement Party," *Sunday Telegraph* (London), 7 March 1999.

57. "National Security Strategy of the Republic of Hungary, Budapest," Government Resolution no. 2144 (2002).

58. László Póti, "The Good, the Bad, and the Non-Existent: Hungarian Policy Towards Russia, the Ukraine, and Belarus: Lessons of the 1990s," in Pelczynska-Nalecz et al., 76.

59. "Moscow Goes Ballistic over Remarks by Hungarian Prime Minister," *Monitor* 5, no. 205 (4 November 1999). Orbán also spoke about "ominous political forces in Ukraine, Belarus, and Russia which would like to recreate a broad alliance which could pose a threat" to Hungary.

60. Vladimir Mukhin, "Russia's Weapons Makers Gunning for New Business," *Russia Journal,* 12 March 2003.

61. RFE/RL, *Newsline* 5, no. 172 (11 September 2001).

62. "Comrade Capitalist," *The Economist* (London), 15 February 2001.

63. A. Burzinkay, "The Borsodchem Affair and Political Dimensions," *Hospodarske Noviny,* 1 February 2001.

64. *Népszabadság* (Budapest), 3 February 1998.

65. "Russia and Hungary to Cooperate in IT Sector," *Moscow Times,* 9 September 2003.

66. "Russia and Hungary Settle Debt Problem," *Pravda* (Moscow), 20 January 2003.

67. "Russians Buy Ex-U.S. Ambassador's Bank," *Budapest Business Journal,* 3 June 1996.

68. RFE/RL, *Newsline* 6, no. 28, pt. 2 (12 February 2002).

69. László Póti, "The Hungarian-Ukrainian-Russian Triangle: Not Like Rubic's Cube," in Balmaceda, *On the Edge,* 127–163.

70. "The New Russian Offensive," *Jane's Intelligence Digest,* 23 February 2001. Information has also been planted in the Western mass media to discredit Budapest. A newspaper campaign in 2000 by the Dutch branch of Amnesty International led to the organization making an apology to the Hungarian police who had been accused of "knocking out the teeth" of Roma children. Hungary's deputy minister for the Secret Services, István Simicskó, charged that a professionally managed campaign was being orchestrated to besmirch the country's reputation. The former Socialist Party Secret Services minister, István Nikolits, confirmed that "externally coordinated propaganda operations" were uncovered during his time in office.

71. Peter Finn, "Gangs Find Budapest Appealing," *Washington Post,* 21 December 1998.

72. Raymond Bonner, "FBI Goes Global: New Hungary Office to Hunt for 'Russian Mafia,'" *Manchester Guardian,* 22 February 2000. U.S. officials reported that if the FBI office in Budapest succeeds, it could be a model in other countries struggling against Russian organized crime, including the Baltic states.

73. Robert H. Donaldson and Joseph L. Nogee, *The Foreign Policy of Russia: Changing Systems, Enduring Interests* (Armonk, N.Y.: M. E. Sharpe, 2002), 250–251.

74. *ČTK* (Prague), 2 February 2001. Relations had been damaged by a number of issues, including the abolition of visa-free travel by both sides in 2000.

75. *Česke Noviny* (Prague), 3 November 2003.

76. Peter S. Green, "New Arbitration Claim in Battle over Czech TV Station," *New York Times,* 9 August 2003. The legal fighting began in 1999, when Central European Media (CEM) accused Vladimír Železny, its partner in TV Nova, of skimming revenue. Ronald S. Lauder's company established TV Nova in 1995 and financed its early operations before the company was sold. CEM owns other television stations in Slovakia, Romania, Ukraine, and Slovenia. TV Nova has captured more than 70 percent of the Czech audience.

77. *ČTK* (Prague), 9 March 2000.

78. For a chronicle of bluff and bluster against NATO enlargement among Russian officials, see J. L. Black, *Russia Faces NATO Expansion: Bearing Gifts or Bearing Arms?* (Lanham, Md.: Rowman & Littlefield, 2000). The author points out: "Present day Russian politicians and journalists are almost all themselves products of the USSR. A mistrust of Western, and especially American, motivation was inculcated in them during their childhood school days and in their early professional careers" (p. 240).

79. *ČTK* (Prague), 1 March 2001.

80. *Agence France Presse* (Prague), 30 January 2001.

81. Christopher P. Winner, "Havel Warns Russians on NATO," *Prague Post Online,* 16 May 2001, www.praguepost.cz/news051601d.html. According to Havel, "I find it almost absurd that such a large and powerful country should be alarmed by the prospect of three small democratic republics at its borders joining a regional grouping which it does not control." Havel also dismissed the prospect of Russia becoming a NATO member, a position voiced by some Western politicians to assuage Putin.

82. *Jane's Intelligence Digest,* Briefings, 28 March 2003.

83. Vladimír Votápek, "Policy of the Czech Republic Towards Russia, the Ukraine, and Belarus," in Pelczynksa-Nalecz et al., 97.

84. "Moravian Oilers Reject British Accusations," *Pravo* (Prague), 4 August 2000.

85. *Jane's Intelligence Digest,* Briefings, 9 August 2002.

86. Tony Wesolowsky, "From Russia, with Love: Czech Republic," *Bulletin of the Atomic Scientists* 59, no. 1 (1 January 2003); and "The Two Headed Falcon—One Scenario," RFE/RL, *Crime, Corruption, and Terrorism Watch,* 11 February 2002. According to an interstate agreement in January 2001, the debt principal was to be paid over the course of twenty years beginning in 2002. Analysts point out that the Czech Republic must also prepare itself for the possibility that Russia will not pay. See *Pravo* (Prague), 12 January 2001.

87. *ČTK* (Prague), 17 February 2000.

88. Kate Connolly, "Jail Ends Saga of the Reporter, the Lemon and the Corrupt Official," *Sunday Telegraph* (London), 5 July 2003. According to Jiři Pehe, adviser to former president Havel, "The Srba case is just the tip of the iceberg."

Transparency International, a Berlin-based NGO that campaigns against corruption, notes that the Czech Republic has been steadily slipping in its corruption rankings from 37 in 1999 to 52 in 2002, out of 102 countries.

89. Francis Harris, "Russian Spies Trying to Sabotage NATO Expansion," *Daily Telegraph* (London), 18 February 1999.

90. *ČTK* (Prague), 22 August 2000; and *ČTK* (Prague), 4 August 2000.

91. *ČTK* (Prague), 25 April 2000.

92. "Russia Steps Up Espionage," *Jane's Intelligence Digest,* Briefings, 29 November 2002.

93. Walter Mayr, "Brothers, to the Sun, to Karlovy Vary," *Der Spiegel* (Hamburg), 24 April 2000. According to Mayr, "The fact that the Interior Ministry in Prague issues permanent residence permits primarily to those Russians who have 'expressly not been recommended' by the Czech Embassy in Moscow, suggests the unpleasant suspicion that not all channels between the former Communist fraternal states have been closed."

94. *ČTK* (Prague), 12 November 1999. According to Czech interior minister Vaclav Grulich, the promotion of "advantageous immigration" to the Czech Republic appears with increasing frequency in Russian newspapers, Web sites, and leaflets. Grulich believed it necessary to tighten the issuing of trade and work licenses. The introduction of visas for Russians will also improve the situation. Many Russians simply seek to legalize their incomes through residency in the Czech Republic. Unofficial numbers indicated that about 100,000 Russians were staying in the country by 1999.

95. *Jane's Intelligence Digest,* Briefings, 9 August 2002.

96. *ČTK* (Prague), 9 December 2000.

97. Prague Institute for National Security, *National Security Newsletter* (English), December 1999; see www.pins.cz/main-en.htm. Some of the bank's major losses were the result of financing barter trading with Russia and other CIS states.

98. *ČTK* (Prague), 25 November 1999.

99. Czech Security Information Service: Czech Republic, *Annual Report 2000,* www.bis.cz/eng/vz2000/vz2000_10.html; and *ČTK* (Prague), 17 February 2000.

100. *ČTK* (Prague), 24 October 2001.

101. Prague Institute for National Security, *National Security Newsletter* no. E-01/02-00 (February 2000); *Lidové Noviny* (Prague), 18 February 2000; and *ČTK* (Prague), 17 March 2000.

102. *Sunday Telegraph* (London, Internet version), 31 October 1999; *Daily Telegraph* (London), 31 October 1999; and *Interfax* (Moscow), 3 November 1999.

103. Prague Institute for National Security, *National Security Newsletter* no. E-01/01-00 (August 2000).

104. RFE/RL, *Newsline* 6, no. 35, pt. 2 (22 February 2002). Also see Francis Harris, "Prague's Secret Service Is at War with Itself," *Daily Telegraph* (London), 5 February 1999. Some former spies claim that Czech counterintelligence is riven by personal and political divisions: "One Western security source said it was split between younger officers in middle-to-senior ranks who were recruited after the 1989 revolution and older, lower-grade specialist staff who dated from Communist times. Western officers assumed information handed to the service was 'in Moscow within hours.'"

105. *Jane's Intelligence Digest,* Briefings, 22 January 2003. Allegedly, Czech services have conducted wiretaps and surveillance of journalists investigating intelligence

agencies who were ignoring the subversive activities of individuals with close links to Russian services. *Jane's* reported in September 2002 that some sections of the Czech intelligence and diplomatic community continue to have strong ties to Russian services. See *Jane's Intelligence Digest*, Briefings, 27 September 2002.

106. Observation by Petr Vančura, director of the Prague Institute for National Security, in *Jane's Intelligence Digest*, Briefings, 9 August 2002. According to Vancura, "The Russians today are behaving with incredible openness and confidence, indicating they have absolutely no intention of releasing the Czech Republic from their sphere of influence" (p. 3).

107. RFE/RL, *Newsline 7*, no. 160, pt. 2 (22 August 2003).

108. László Póti, "The Triangle with Five Sides: Patterns of Relations Between Poland, Slovakia, Hungary, Ukraine, and Russia," in Balmaceda, *On the Edge*, 220–230.

109. A Russian academic diatribe against Central Europeans is contained in Irina Aleksiejewna Wasilenko, "Rosja i Europa Srodkowa: Nowe Realia Geopolityczne," in *Political Science Studies*, vol. 4, *History and Geopolitics*, 79–84.

110. RFE/RL, *Newsline 7*, no. 204, pt. 2 (27 October 2003).

111. The chairman of the Democratic Party, Ján Langoš, asserted that Mečiar's policies supported Russia's interests: "The ties between Meciar and Russian premier Chernomyrdin are quite clear. Meciar has already pulled Slovakia into an unbelievable dependence on the Russian economy and has made Slovakia dependent on Russia militarily as well." See Jolyon Naegele, "Slovakia: Ties to Moscow Strengthen; Relations ith Brussels Strained," *RFE/RL Online*, Features, 22 May 1997, www. rferl.org.

112. *ČTK* (Prague), 31 January 2001.

113. "Marketing Activities," January 2002, www.yukos.com/rm/marketing.asp.

114. Sabrina Tavernise and Peter S. Green, "Oil Concerns in Russia Branch Out," *New York Times*, 2 April 2002.

115. "Russia Committed to Enlarged Europe Without Borders," *Interfax News Agency* (Bratislava), 1 July 2003.

116. Alexander Duleba, "Pursuing an Eastern Agenda," *Transition* 2, no. 19 (20 September 1996): 52–55.

117. Alexander Duleba, "The Slovak-Ukrainian-Russian Security Triangle," in Balmaceda, *On the Edge*, 69–125. Also see Alexander Duleba, *The Blind Pragmatism of Slovak Eastern Policy: The Actual Agenda of Slovak-Russian Relations*, Occasional Paper no. 1 (Bratislava: Slovak Foreign Policy Association, 1996).

118. A debt repayment scheme similar to that with the Czech Republic was arranged with Slovakia, amid suspicions that certain officials and business groups stood to benefit. See "The West Doubts That Russia Is Honest with Soviet Debt Settlement," *Pravda* (Moscow), 30 August 2002.

119. *Pravda Online* (Moscow), 4 July 2003, pravda.ru.

120. Juraj Porubský, "Slovak Government Wants to Sell Strategic Firms," *Bratislava Pravda* (Bratislava), 22 August 2003.

121. "Slovakia: Kovac Speaks Out Against Neutrality Option," *SME* (Bratislava), 28 May 1996: in *Foreign Broadcast Information Service (FBIS) East Europe*, 30 May 1996, 12.

122. "'Slovak Berlusconi' Rusko to Become Economy Minister," *ČTK National News Wire* (Prague), 3 September 2003.

123. "Power Struggles in Slovakia," *Jane's Intelligence Digest,* 14 February 2003.

124. For a summary of Lexa's activities before his arrest in South Africa in July 2002, see Buddy Naidu and Ronnie Govender, "Kidnapping Cop's Secret Life in SA," *Sunday Times* (South Africa), 21 July 2002.

125. *TASR* Web site (Bratislava), 29 May 2002, tasr.sk.

126. RFE/RL, *Newsline 7,* no. 10, pt. 2 (16 January 2003). For an updated report on Slovakia's intelligence services, see "Slovak Intelligence Looks to the Past," *Jane's Intelligence Digest,* Briefings, 1 August 2003; and "Slovakia: SIS Tapping Exposed," *Jane's Intelligence Digest,* Briefings, 25 July 2003. The scandal in the SIS culinated in the resignation of director Vladimí.

127. "NATO's Allies in Slovakia," *Jane's Intelligence Digest,* 20 December 2002.

128. RFE/RL, *Newsline 7,* no. 150, pt. 2 (8 August 2003).

129. *Sme* (Bratislava), 21 June 2003.

130. "Dzurinda under Pressure," *Jane's Intelligence Digest,* Briefings, 15 August 2003.

CHAPTER 7

1. Konstantin Eggert, "A Great Power Foreign Policy Is too Expensive," *Izvestia* (Moscow), 16 December 1995.

2. Mette Skak, "Back in the USSR? Russia as an Actor in World Politics," Working Paper no. 2000/7, Danish Institute of International Affairs, available at *Columbia International Affairs Online,* www.ciaonet.org.

3. "Transatlantic Relations in the Aftermath of Kosovo," *Special Report* (Washington, D.C.: U.S. Institute of Peace, 15 May 2000).

4. I. Klepatskii, "Russia's Foreign Policy Landmarks," *International Affairs* (Moscow) 45, no. 2 (1999): 18–28.

5. V. Kruzhkov, "NATO Action in Kosovo: Why Is Peace in Jeopardy?" *International Affairs* (Moscow) 45, no. 6 (1999): 85–95.

6. General Mikhail Kolesnikov, first deputy chief of the Russian General Staff, in *Nezavisimaya Gazeta* (Moscow), 1 August 1992.

7. *Interfax* (Moscow), 13 August 1992.

8. A. Fedorov, "New Pragmatism of Russia's Foreign Policy," *International Affairs* (Moscow) 45, no. 5 (1999): 46–52.

9. M. Deliagin, "America's Real Goals in Yugoslavia," *International Affairs* (Moscow) 45, no. 6 (1999): 75–84. Deliagin asserts that Europe had not developed reliable instruments to uphold its economic interests and remains subordinate to NATO's military goals.

10. RFE/RL, *Newsline 7,* no. 99, pt. 2 (28 May 2003).

11. RFE/RL, *Newsline 7,* no. 107, pt. 2 (9 June 2003).

12. "Russia Hoping to Be More Influential in the Balkans—Senior MP," *Interfax News Agency* (Moscow), 6 June 2003.

13. In the words of Vladimir Ivanovski, Russian ambassador to Serbia and Montenegro, in an interview in *Vecernje Novosti* (Belgrade), 25 April 2003.

14. Interview with Vladimir Ivanovski, titled "Russians Are Leaving the Balkans Forever, or Just to Be Back Again," *Weekly Telegraf* (Belgrade) no. 374 (25 June 2003).

15. *Pravda* (Moscow), 29 June 1991.

16. Mike Bowker, "The Wars in Yugoslavia: Russia and the International Community," *Europe-Asia Studies* 50, no. 7 (1998): 1245–1261. Bowker has a simplistic view of Russia's evident success in turning Milošević "from warmonger to peacemaker" priot to the signing of the Dayton accords.

17. A. Matvayev, "Washington's Claims to World Leadership," *International Affairs* (Moscow) 45, no. 5 (1999): 53–65.

18. "Croatia Seeks Membership in NATO," *Krasnaia Zvezda* (Moscow), 5 May 1997.

19. Sabrina Tavernise and Peter S. Green, "Oil Concerns in Russia Branch Out," *New York Times,* 2 April 2002.

20. "Adria Pipeline," www.yukos.com/rm/adria.asp.

21. "In the Arms of the Bear," *Ekonomist* (Belgrade) no. 18 (March 2002).

22. *Biznis.Infoforum.Hr (Infoforum News Service)* (Zagreb), 31 July 2003.

23. *Novosti* (Moscow), 8 September 2003.

24. An example of Russian hystrionics during NATO air raids on Serbia can be found in *Rossiiskaya Gazeta* (Moscow), 14 September 1995.

25. For an analysis of the mythical Russian-Serbian "historical friendship," see Slobodan Pavlovic, "Russia's Relations with Belgrade Are Far from Problem-Free," *Prism* 1, no. 13 (28 July 1995).

26. Hans-Joachim Hoppe, "Moscow and the Conflicts in Former Yugoslavia," *Aussenpolitik* no. 111 (1997).

27. According to one commentator, "The massive air attacks on the Bosnian Serbs from the summer of 1995 demonstrated that force, not patient negotiations, remained the principal instrument of diplomacy and that Moscow's position was only taken into account so long as it did not contradict the line taken by the United States. In the eyes of the majority of Russians the myth of the exclusively defensive nature of NATO was exploded." See *Nezavisimaia Gazeta* (Moscow), 14 March 1997.

28. Allen C. Lynch, "The Realism of Russia's Foreign Policy," *Europe-Asia Studies* 53, no. 1 (January 2001).

29. See the commentary in the army newspaper *Krasnaya Zvezda* (Moscow), 19 February 1994.

30. Stanislav Kondrashov, "Russia May Sell Too Cheap, in Bosnia and in General," *Izvestia* (Moscow), 21 November 1995.

31. "In the Arms of the Bear," *Ekonomist* (Belgrade) no. 18 (March 2002).

32. "Economic Capacity and Economy of the Russian Federation," *Chamber of Commerce Newsletter* no. 7 (February 2003), www.komorabih.com/servisi/glasnik/7sadrzaj.html.

33. "Russia Not to Leave Balkans," *Moscow Times,* 10 September 2003; and "Russia, Bosnia to Revive Contacts," *Pravda* (Moscow), 12 November 2001.

34. Josip Vricko, "The Russian Return to Bosnia-Hercegovina," *Vjesnik* (Zagreb), 30 August 1997.

35. For a press commentary attacking NATO policy in Bosnia, see Nikola Zhivkovich, "NATO i Bundeswehr Napialivaiut Ovechiu Shkuru: A General Nauman Blesnul Umom," *Sovetskaia Rossia* (Moscow), 18 October 1997.

36. *Izvestia* (Moscow), 3 August 1994.

37. Yevgeni Ivanov, "Nachalas Okhota Na Serbov," *Sovetskaia Rossiia* (Moscow), 12 July 1997.

38. *AFP* (Sarejevo), 14 November 2003.

39. A commentary on Albanian-Russian relations can be found in *AIM (Alternativna Informativna Mreza)* (Tirana), 20 June 2000.

40. "In Tirana: Diplomacy and Nationalism," *AIM* (Tirana), 10 March 1998.

41. Shaban Sinani, "Straight Northward! Straight Northward!" *Shekulli* (Tirana), 21 June 1999.

42. Aleksander Lukin, "NATO and Russia after the Kosovo Crisis," *Nezavisimaya Gazeta* (Moscow), 9 June 1999.

43. Pavel Kandel, "Eastern Europe after Kosovo: The Impact of the Crisis on Russian Politics," *East European Constitutional Review* 8, no. 3 (Summer 1999).

44. B. Kazantsev, "Serious Concern over New NATO Strategy," *International Affairs* (Moscow) 45, no. 2 (1999): 23–28.

45. Dimitri Danilov, "Implications of the NATO Attack Against Yugoslavia for European Security and Russian-Western Relations,"*Mediterranean Quarterly* 10, no. 3 (1999): 51–69.

46. I. D. Sergeev, "Osnovi Voenno-Tekhnicheskoi Politiki Rossuu v Nacale XXI Veka," *Krasnaya Zvezda* (Moscow), 9 December 1999.

47. Pavel K. Baev, "External Interventions in Secessionist Conflicts in Europe in the 1990s," *European Security* 8, no. 2 (Summer 1999): 42.

48. Oleg Levitin, "Inside Moscow's Kosovo Muddle," *Survival* 42, no. 1 (Spring 2000): 130.

49. *APS Diplomatic Recorder,* 23 June 2001; and Maura Reynolds, "Putin Pays a Call on Kosovo," *Los Angeles Times,* 18 June 2001. In an address to Russian troops in Kosovo, Putin claimed that "Russia has taken negatively the accelerated adoption of a constitutional framework for self-government in Kosovo," because "too many concessions have been made to radicals." Putin was the first Russian president to visit Serbia since the collapse of both Yugoslavia and the Soviet Union.

50. Sergeyev's comments in "Agreement for Cooperation of the Two Ministries," *Dnevne Vesti* (Podgorica, Montenegro), 2 September 2001.

51. *Novosti* (Moscow), 8 September 2003.

52. Oksana Antonenko, "Russia, NATO and European Security after Kosovo," *Survival* 41, no. 4 (Winter 1999–2000): 131.

53. Alexey G. Arbatov, "The Transformation of Russian Military Doctrine: Lessons Learned from Kosovo and Chechnya," *Marshall Center Papers* no. 2 (George C. Marshall European Center for Security Studies, Garmisch, Germany, 2000).

54. For Russian commentary on Kosovo's Protection Corps, see *Interfax News Agency* (Moscow), 23 December 1999.

55. Sergey Stefanov, "Serbs Will Never Resign Themselves with Kosovo's Separation," *Pravda* (Moscow), 22 March 2002.

56. *ATA* (Tirana), 9 March 1998. Yeltsin stated in the middle of the conflict that Milošević would never capitulate and Russia would not watch Kosovo turned into a NATO protectorate. Quoted in Celestine Bohlen, "Crisis in the Balkans: The Diplomacy; Russia Seeks to Mediate Kosovo Crisis," *New York Times,* 21 April 1999.

57. "Putin Urges Kosovo Crackdown," in *BBC News Online,* 18 June 2001, bbc.co.uk.

58. *ITAR-TASS News Agency* (Moscow), 23 September 1999.

59. *AIM* (Tirana), 24 March 2001. Ivanov previously served as Foreign Minister Primakov's deputy and was long involved in Russian diplomacy toward the Balkans.

60. Vladimir Kuznechevskii, "Chechnya v Tsentre Evropy?" *Rossiiskaya Gazeta* (Moscow), 19 June 1998.

61. Helena Khotkova, from the Russian Institute for Strategic Studies, in "The Russian View: Problems and Perspectives in the Balkans," *National Security and the Future* (Moscow) 3, nos. 1–2 (Spring–Summer 2002): 17–22.

62. *RosBusiness Consulting Database,* 27 September 2000. Disinformation originating from Belgrade is sometimes picked up by the Russian media, including "disclosures" that secret plans exist to create a Greater Albania with the involvement of Albanian emigres and even certain U.S. congressmen. See "Albanian-American Lobby Wants to Divide Macedonia by 2007," *Nedeljni Telegraf* (Belgrade), 21 June 2003.

63. Remzi Lani, "Albanian Foreign Policy: Closer to Geography Than to History," 2002, at the Albanian Ministry of Foreign Affairs Web site, www.mfa.gov.al/english/lajm.asp?id=205. Lani believes that "Albanian policy remains more a product of geography and pragmatism than of history and romanticism."

64. *Novye Izvestia* (Moscow), 8 August 1998.

65. "A Toothless Growl," *The Economist* (London), 29 April 1999. Karaganov argued that Russia should exploit any internal divisions in the Alliance, end all relations with NATO, pull out of or disrupt arms-control talks, modernize Russia's nuclear forces, and build counteralliances.

66. Anthony DePalma, "Kosovo Insurgents Report Killing Russian Officer in Battle with Serbs," *New York Times,* 22 May 1999. In addition to Russian casualties, the KLA reported intercepting radio communications in Russian and recovering military documents written in Russian.

67. Arben Kola, "Tirana: Wait, But Expect Nothing from Milošević," *AIM* (Tirana), 9 June 1999.

68. *Moskovsky Komsomolets* (Moscow), 2 July 1999.

69. Igor Korotchenko and Vladimir Mukhin in *Nezavisimaya Gazeta* (Moscow), 16 June 1999.

70. Eric Schmitt, "Crisis in the Balakns: The Military; NATO Bars Russia from Reinforcing Troops in Kosovo," *New York Times,* 3 July 1999.

71. "Russia's Military Role in Kosovo," *New York Times,* 19 June 1999.

72. "Straight Northward! Straight Northward!" *Shekulli* (Tirana) no. 21 (July 1999).

73. Quoted in *AIM* (Tirana), 23 June 1999.

74. Shaban Murati, "Cooling off with Albania and Russia's Role in the Balkans," *AIM* (Tirana), 23 June 1999.

75. Steven Erlanger, "Seven Checkpoints, Three of Them Russian, Are Attacked in Kosovo," *New York Times,* 7 August 1999.

76. Lawrence Freedman, "Russia Must Learn That It Is No Longer a Great Power," *The Independent* (London), 18 June 1999. The Kremlin preferred a UN force in Kosovo because a NATO deployment obliged each participating country to pay its share of the costs, which for Russia meant about $150 million a year. The Bosnian battalion alone consumed half of Moscow's annual budget for peacekeeping operations.

77. *Nezavisimaya Gazeta* (Moscow), 25 March 1999.

78. RFE/RL, *Newsline* 7, no. 15, pt. 1 (24 January 2003).

79. *Albanian TV* (Tirana), 13 December 2002.

80. Panayote Dimitras, "Kosovo Serb Refugees: Unimportant Detail or the Real Ethnic Cleansing?" *AIM* (Athens), 10 July 1999.

81. Kosovo home page of the Kosovo Information Center in a *QIK* news agency report from New York on 29 November 2001.

82. *ITAR-TASS News Agency* (New York), 26 February 2002.

83. *ITAR-TASS News Agency* (Prishtina), 17 June 2001.

84. *Novosti* (Moscow), 8 September 2003.

85. "Albania Rejects Criticism of International Monitors," *Makfax* (Tirana), 22 April 2002. Tirana threatened to suspend the OSCE mission in protest against what were perceived as unfair attacks that singled out Albania as the chief culprit in Southeast Europe.

86. *Tanjug* (Moscow), 17 June 2001.

87. Shkelzen Maliqi, "Putin Offers Kosovars Little: Backs Kostunica's Obstructionist Policy Towards Democratization of Kosova," *BCR* (Prishtina, Kosovo) no. 257 (20 June 2001).

88. See the interview with the chairman of the Albanian Assembly foreign affairs commission, Sabri Godo, in Tirana on 24 April 2001, in *FBIS-EEU-2001-0425*, 25 April 2001.

89. Pavel K. Baev, "The Influence of the Balkan Crisis on Russia's Peacekeeping in Its 'Near Abroad,'" in Lena Jonson and Clive Archer, eds., *Peacekeeping and the Role of Russia in Eurasia* (Boulder, Colo.: Westview Press, 1996), 69.

90. Scott Parrish, "Twisting in the Wind: Russia and the Yugoslav Conflict," in *Transition* 1, no. 20 (3 November 1995): 28–31, 70.

91. Stan Markotich, "Evolving Serbian Attitudes Toward 'Big Brother' Russia," *Transition* 2, no. 2 (13 December 1996): 54–56. An early discussion of Russia's Yugoslav policy can be found in Suzanne Crow, "Russia's Response to the Yugoslav Crisis," RFE/RL *Research Report* 1, no. 30 (24 July 1992).

92. Yelena Guskova, "NATO Starts War in Balkans," *Krasnaya Zvezda* (Moscow), 1 September 1995. Guskova was the director of the Center for the Study of the Present-Day Balkan Crisis with the Institute of Slavic and Balkan Studies at the Russian Acedemy of Sciences.

93. Andrey P. Tsygankov, "The Final Triumph of the Pax Americana? Western Intervention in Yugoslavia and Russia's Debate on the Post–Cold War Order," *Communist and Post-Communist Studies* no. 34 (2001): 133–156.

94. "Russia Warns the Alliance, While China Shows Restraint," *Nezavisimaya Gazeta* (Moscow), 13 May 1999.

95. V. Kozin, "Kremlin and NATO: Prospects for Interaction," *International Affairs: A Russian Journal* (Moscow) no. 3 (2000).

96. V. Baranovskii, "Kosovo: Russia's Interests Are Very Important," *International Affairs: A Russian Journal* (Moscow) no. 3 (1999).

97. Michael Radu, "The Burden of Eastern Orthodoxy," *Orbis* 42, no. 2 (Spring 1998): 299.

98. The former chief of state security in Belgrade, Goran Petrović, confirmed these reports. Referring to the reorganization of the Special Operations Unit, Petrović said that it could also be organized on the principles of the Russian group Alfa. See "Once There Were Red Berets," *Blitz News* (Belgrade), 18 July 2003. The chief of the General Staff of the Russian army, General Anatoliy Kvashnin, asserted that

Moscow could help Serbia by providing "personal, military equipment and military experts" See *Nin* (Belgrade), 8 April 1999.

99. "Even Americans Were Selling Weapons to Milošević," *Glas Javnosti* (Belgrade, Internet edition), 21 June 2002, glas-javnosti.co.yu.

100. Stephen J. Blank, *Threats to Russian Security: The View from Moscow* (Washington, D.C.: Strategic Studies Institute, U.S. Army War College, 2000), 10.

101. *Republika* (Belgrade) no. 211 (1999), www.yurope.com/zines/republika/arhiva/99/211/211_23.html; "Chronology of Attacks on the Federal Republic of Yugoslavia," *Nezavisna Svetlost* (Kragujevac, Serbia) no. 198, www.svetlost.co.yu/arhiva/99/195/hronologija-6.htm; and *Beta News Agency* (Belgrade), 26 March 1999.

102. In return for Russian assistance, parts of the U.S. stealth bomber F-117 that was gunned down in Serbia were transferred to Russia. See *Nin* (Belgrade) no. 2519 (8 April 1999); *Republika* (Belgrade) no. 211 (1999); and *Ilustrovana Politika,* www.politika.co.yu/ilustro/2099/drugi.htm.

103. In answer to charges by nationalists in both countries that Russia betrayed Serbia during the NATO war, former Russian premier Chernomyrdin's responded: "That is nonsense! Russia has supported Serbia even with weapons. That's not a secret. What else could we do? Start a third world war because of Kosovo?" See Chernomyrdin's interview in "We Haven't Betrayed Serbia," *Nin* (Belgrade), 14 October 1999. Russian parliamentarians were generally more verbally combative than state officials. Duma deputy Yuriy Kuznetsov claimed that the "Russian government will not try to stop volunteers . . . and if some NATO warship happens to sink in the Adriatic that won't be a coincidence." See Kuznetsov's statement in "Russian Volunteers Ready for NATO," *Glas Javnosti* (Belgrade), 20 February 1999, glas-javnosti.co.yu.

104. According to the Society of Serbian-Russian Friendship from Novi Sad and Moscow, released online, "Across Russia, thousands of volunteers are enlisted to defend Kosovo, Serbia and eventually Russia and the whole Slavic world," *Kosovo Archives Online* no. 4 (12 April 1999), www.yurope.com/kosovo/arhiva/kosovo-4/0058.html.

105. Ali M. Koknar, "The *Kontraktniki:* Russian Mercenaries at War in the Balkans," 3 August 2003, www.bosnia.org.uk.

106. Bosnian Islamic Youth newspaper *SAFF,* online edition, no. 75, www.saffbih.com/2002/broj 75/rusi.htm.

107. This hands-off military policy was maintained despite comments by Russian politicians and generals that they would defend Serbia. In March 2001, General Leonid Ivashchov claimed that Russia was willing to deploy its peacekeeping forces already in Kosovo to fight against Albanian rebels whom NATO was unable to disarm. See "Moscow Blames NATO," *Suddeutsche Zeitung* (Munich), 21 March 2001.

108. "Raw Deal," *Ekonomist* (Belgrade) no. 121 (16 September 2002).

109. The debt was estimated at some $1.2 billion. See "Russia Ready to Build a Nuclear Power Plant in Serbia to Pay Off Soviet Debt," 22 April 2003, www.mediapool.bg.

110. "Lukoil Eyes Serb Refinery at Novi Sad," *Reuters* (Sofia), 21 October 2000; and "In the Arms of the Bear," *Ekonomist* (Belgrade) no. 18 (2002).

111. "Serbia to Sell Beopetrol Fuel Chain to Lukoil," *Radio B-92 Online* (Belgrade), 25 August 2003, b92.net. In response to the impending sale, Croatia's

INA oil company charged that the Serbian decision was illegal because Beopetrol's assets belonged to INA and the company would take legal action to ensure the return of its property. See *Reuters* (Moscow), 29 September 2003.

112. "Three Roles of the Prime Minister," *Vreme* (News Digest Agency, Belgrade) no. 218 (3 December 1995). *Vreme* pointed out that during Yugoslavia's clash with the Russian-dominated Cominform, Stalin wanted to impose control over the Yugoslav economy through the creation of mixed companies.

113. "Serbia's Grain Trade: Milošević's Hidden Cash Crop," International Crisis Group Balkans Report no. 93, Washington/Brussels, 5 June 2000.

114. "Yugoslav Leaders Probe Milošević Gas Connections," *St. Petersburg Times*, 7 November 2000.

115. *Interfax News Agency* (Moscow), 17 September 2003.

116. *Monitor* 6, no. 98 (18 May 2000); and the editorial "Mr. Putin's Missteps," *New York Times*, 22 May 2000.

117. "Budapest Has Seen Brighter Days for Our Diplomacy," *Izvestia* (Moscow), 7 December 1994.

118. "Russia has played with only one card, this being Milošević, thus irritating everyone on the Balkans, including Serbs. At the beginning of the 1990s, Russia had an excellent starting position. It gained the trust of Serbs, but also of other nations. That trust was soon lost." The comment is by Andrey Piontkovski, director of the Moscow Center for Strategic Studies, reported in *Blitz News* (Belgrade), 17 June 2003. Milošević's wife, Mira Markovic, was given refuge in Russia to evade arrest and trial at The Hague.

119. A. Karasev, "Russia in Yugoslavia: Mission Accomplished," *International Affairs* (Moscow) 47, no. 1 (2001): 85–93.

120. *Monitor* 6, no. 199 (25 October 2000).

121. *Tanjug* (Moscow), 27 October 2001.

122. Boris Volkhonsky, "Slobodan Milošević Is Once Again of Great Value to His People: The West Has Appraised Him at $1.28 Billion," *Kommersant* (Moscow), 30 June 2001.

123. "Belgrade Confirms Army Officer Suspected of Spying," *B-92* Web site, b92.net; and *Associated Press* (Belgrade), 22 September 2003.

124. In June 2002, General Skoric, with the approval of Kostunica, became the director of the military secret service. After Skoric's dismissal, the Serbian media disclosed that many retired or dismissed high-ranking officers held "the Russian line" that made full cooperation with NATO impossible. See *Vijesti Online*, 23 September 2003, vijesti.cg.yu.

125. *Novosti* (Moscow), 8 September 2003.

126. Interview with Russia's first deputy foreign minister Aleksander Avdeyev in *Rossiyskaya Gazeta* (Moscow), 20 January 2001.

127. "In the Arms of the Bear," *Ekonomist* (Belgrade) no. 18 (March 2002).

128. *Tanjug* (Belgrade), 21 January 2002.

129. Helsinki Committee for Human Rights in Serbia, "Integration of the Region on New Foundations (Sustainability of the State Community of Serbia and Montenegro)," Belgrade, 10 January 2003, 8.

130. Carlotta Gall, "Putin Urges Global Pressure to Disarm Rebels in Kosovo," *New York Times*, 18 June 2001. In Putin's words, "Stability in the region is seri-

ously threatened, above all from national religious extremism and intolerance, the main source of which today is in Kosovo." Section A, p. 8.

131. *Agence France Presse* (Moscow), 23 November 2000. Macedonia's ambassador to Moscow, Dimitar Dimitrov, claimed in October 2001 that some 5,000 militants of Al-Qaeda and Islamic Jihad were participating in the Albanian National Liberation Army on Macedonian territory, with its headquarters in Kosovo or Albania. Reported in *ITAR-TASS* (Moscow), 17 October 2001.

132. "Putin Wants Definite Borders in the Balkans," *Suddeutsche Zeitung Online* (Munich), 17 June 2001, sueddeutsche.de.

133. "Russia's President Putin Attacked Massively the Western Countries' Actions in the Balkans," *Suddeutsche Zeitung* (Munich), 23 March 2003.

134. Chris Marsden, "Tensions Deepen as NATO Begins Macedonia Mission," 25 August 2001, World Socialist Web site, www.wsws.org/articles/2001/aug2001/mace-a25.shtml. During a visit to Skopje, Foreign Minister Igor Ivanov directly blamed the West for the spread of the Kosovo conflict into Albanian-populated areas of Macedonia.

135. A1 TV station in Macedonia, Web edition, 13 November 2001.

136. *MIC* (Skopje), 2 September 1996.

137. Reported on the Albanian-language Web site www.lajmet.com/arkivi/lajmet/2002/dhjetor, 8 December 2002; and by STB TV (Kyiv, Ukarine), 6 August 2001. Skopje has sold Ukraine some of its Russian debts to help pay for the armaments.

138. Justin Huggler, "Western Concern Over Arming Troops Puts Ukraine Under Pressure," *The Independent* (London), 6 August 2001.

139. "A Diplomatic Excursion to the East," *AIM* (Skopje), 30 October 2001.

140. Trajkovski's interview on *TV Moscow,* 29 October 2001.

141. Toby Westerman, "Russia's Influence in Balkans Growing: Macedonia Seeks Counter-Insurgency Techniques Uses in Chechnya," *WorldNetDaily*.com, 23 February 2002.

142. "In the Arms of the Bear," *Ekonomist* (Belgrade) no. 18 (March 2002).

143. "Macedonia Is Interested in Russia's Return to the Balkans," *Pravda* (Moscow), 22 November 2000.

144. Statement by Ambassador Vasiliy Likhachev, permanent representative of the Russian Federation to the European Union, to the Donors Meeting for the Former Yugoslav Republic of Macedonia, Brussels, 12 March 2002, www.seerecon.org/calendar/2002/Events/mdm/statements/russia.htm.

145. RFE/RL, *Newsline* 7, no. 9, pt. 2 (15 January 2003).

146. See www.lajmet.com/arkivi/lajmet/2002/dhjetor, 11 December 2002.

147. Valery Asriyan, in *Novosti* (Moscow), 10 September 2003.

148. *AIM* (Skopje), 30 October 2001.

149. Svetomir Shkarich, "NATO at Balkans and in Macedonia," *Russia and Central Europe in the New Geopolitical Realities,* Russian Academy of Sciences, Fourth International Scientific Conference, Moscow, 14–16 June 2001, 87–99.

150. Dmitry Babich "What Is Macedonia's Interest in Russia?" *Rosbalt News Agency* (St. Petersburg), 20 January 2003, www.rosbaltnews.com/2003/03/20/61068.html.

151. *MIA* (Skopje), 24 September 2001.

CHAPTER 8

1. President Zhelev in *BTA (Bulgarian Telegraph Agency)* (Sofia), 2 April 1996. Bulgaria's Foreign Ministry called Yeltsin's "invitation" to Bulgaria "a cause for concern." Leaders of the opposition UDF claimed that Russia's ultimate aim is the restoration of the Soviet Union in which Bulgaria would be a constituent element. In 1963, Bulgaria's Communist leader had offered to make Bulgaria the sixteenth republic of the USSR; the Kremlin seemed to believe that such offers were still valid. The incident mobilized the pro-NATO opposition against the Russian-oriented Socialist government led by Prime Minister Zhan Videnov and backfired against Moscow's policy.

2. Ognyan Minchev, "Bulgaria and Russia," in *Bulgaria for NATO* (Sofia: Institute for Regional and International Studies, 2002). Even though Bulgarian-Russian frienship has a long pedigree, relations have also been marked by conflicts as Russia's Tsars demanded that the newly liberated Bulgarian state in the late 19th century demonstrate "total economic and political dependence on Russia" (p. 120).

3. "Putin Expresses Aspirations for Russia and Bulgaria Together in a Self-Determining Europe," *Mediapool*.bg, 3 March 2003. Mediapool is an influential electronic news portal in Bulgaria.

4. Among the non-CIS states, Russia displays the most possessiveness toward Bulgaria. Russian elites believe that a bond exists between the two states, based on history, ethnicity, and religion, which commits Bulgaria to remain part of the post-Soviet space economically, politically, and militarily. In effect, this necessitates Sofia's subservience to Moscow.

5. Ira Straus, "Serbs' NATO Bid to Lead Way for Russia," *Russia Journal* (Moscow), 1 November 2002.

6. Comments by Russian Foreign Ministry representative A. V. Yakovenko on the eve of the visit of Bulgaria's prime minister to Moscow in June 2002, carried by the Information and Press Department of the ministry's *Information Bulletin,* 3 June 2002, www.mid.ru. According to Yakovenko, NATO's enlargement plans are a "mistake" and the "motivations for the expansion policy are groundless."

7. Rumen Angelov, "Who and How Tries to Force Bulgaria to Join NATO," *International Dialogue* (Russian Academy of Sciences, Moscow) no. 1 (2000): 61–79.

8. *Balkan Times Online,* 25 March 2002, balkantimes.ocm.

9. Kristina Georgieva, "Moscow Has an Interest in Mixing Sofia with Al-Qaeda," Bulgarian electronic paper *Mediapool*.bg, 25 March, 2002. During his visit to Sofia, Dmitriy Rogozin, the Duma's Foreign Relations Committee chairman, claimed that "Russia is not going to line up for NATO membership, we advise Bulgaria not to line up either." See *Dnevnik* (Sofia), 12 February 2002.

10. *Monitor* 4, no. 179 (30 September 1998).

11. Remarks by Russian deputy foreign minister Nikolai Afanasevskii, "Pro Rossiiu na Balkanakh Reshili Zabyt?" *Rossiiskaia Gazeta* (Moscow), 2 October 1997.

12. *Agence France Press* (Bucharest), 14 June 1999.

13. Maksim Yusin, "Russia Decides It Doesn't Want Bulgarian 'Air Corridor,'" *Izvestia* (Moscow), 21 July 1999.

14. Maksim Yusin, "Pointless Quarrel," *Izvestiya* (Moscow), 9 August 2000. According to Yusin, "Moscow was firmly put in its place and reminded of today's re-

alities. It was reminded that this isn't the 19th century, when "traditional ties" determined all policy in the Balkans and religious and ethnic kinship. We are living in an era of rationalism and pragmatism, when allies are chosen by very different criteria. The Russian Foreign Ministry appears to be alone in failing to recognize this. Today no country in Eastern Europe, however Slavic and Orthodox it may be, is going to sacrifice ties with the West for Russia's sake. The Bulgarians, the Romanians, the Slovaks and the Croats need loans, investments and state-of-the-art technology, and they dream of joining the European Union as soon as possible. They have no reason to want to join the CIS. After all, poverty-stricken Bulgaria can't ask Russia for loans. . . . The Foreign Ministry's position is perplexing, to put it mildly. Isn't it time to stop living in a world of illusions and historical myths? Why should our neighbors always be forced to make an artificial, contrived choice between Russia and the West? Especially when we already know the answer? But the Foreign Ministry just can't calm down. It follows debates in the Bulgarian parliament as closely as if they were taking place in a constituent republic of the Russian Federation, like Tataria or Kalmykia. It's as if Moscow has gone back to the Brezhnev era and is telling the Bulgarian authorities how to act in this or that situation."

15. Asked by journalists whether NATO or U.S. bases could pose a problem for Bulgaria's relations with Russia, Presidential Military Adviser Mikho Mikhov responded: "Of course there will be problems," but as a sovereign state, Bulgaria is obliged to make its own decisions regarding security. See RFE/RL, *Newsline 7*, no. 155, pt. 2 (15 August 2003).

16. Margarita Assenova, "Energy and the Transformation Process in Bulgaria and Romania," in *Energy and the Transformation Process in Southeast Europe* (Munich, Bertelsmann Foundation, 2000).

17. Georgi Ganev, "Bulgaria and Balkan Energy Flows: An Analysis of Strategies and Opportunities," paper delivered at a conference "Energy and the Transformation Process in Bulgaria and Romania," a Project of Partners in the Transatlantic Learning Community, 1998–2000, Bucharest, 16–17 January 1999.

18. Georgi Ganev, "Recent Past and Perspectives on Bulgarian-Russian Economic Relations," paper presented at a conference in Sofia, Bulgaria, entitled "Is There a Crisis of Bulgarian-Russian Relations?" organized by the Association Bulgaria and Russia and the Center for Liberal Strategies, November 1997.

19. Jakov Pappe, "Oil and Gas Diplomacy of Russia," *Business and Foreign Policy* no. 2 (1997).

20. *Capital Weekly* (Sofia) no. 30 (28 July–3 August 1997).

21. RFE/RL, *Newsline 7*, no. 24, pt. 2 (6 February 2003).

22. Andrew Neff, "State Gas Utility Looks to Exit Bulgarian Gas Distribution Market," *World Markets Analysis*, 11 July 2003.

23. RFE/RL, *Newsline 7*, no. 40, pt. 2 (3 March 2003).

24. Dmitry Babich, "Kozlodui Reborn," *Vremya MN* (Moscow), 31 January 2003.

25. Mira Yankova, "Russia Will Control Bulgaria's 'Benkovski' Military Plant," 24 March 2003, www.mediapool.

26. Galina Alexandrova, "Lukoil-Neftex Deal: Market Strategy or a Way to Survive," *Capital* (Sofia), 30 June 2001.

27. "Oil Sought from Kazakhstan for Bourgas-Alexandroupolis," *Financial Times Information*, Global News Wire, published by *Business Media Group*, 16 June 2003.

28. RFE/RL, *Newsline* 7, no. 5, pt. 1 (9 January 2003).

29. John Helmer, "Greeks Warned Against Lukoil Bid," *Russia Journal,* 1 March 2002. According to the investors, "*Lukoil's* transfer pricing, value destruction, and lack of fair and transparent practices with respect to minority shareholders set an extremely damaging precedent," russiajournal.com.

30. "Putin: The Credit for the New Impulse in Relations Should Be Given to President Parvanov," *Netinfo*.bg, 3 March 2003. Netinfo is an online news portal, known to be more informative than analytical.

31. Yassen Guev, "Russia Confirmed Its Interest in the Energy Sector and Bulgargaz," 2 March 2003, www.mediapool.bg.

32. Vladimir Karpov, "RAO UES Wants to Be on the Bulgarian Market," *Vedomosti*, 30 October 2003; and "The Government Cut the Russians off the Privatization of the Energy Distribution Systems," *Mediapool,* 24 October 2003.

33. *News From Bulgaria,* 20 September 1995, bulgaria@access1.digex.net. Bulgarian democrats argue that the emergence of any new "economic community" under Russia's aegis would reduce Sofia's chances for entry into the EU.

34. Robert H. Donaldson and Joseph L. Nogee, *The Foreign Policy of Russia: Changing Systems, Enduring Interests* (Armonk, N.Y.: M. E. Sharpe, 2002), 253.

35. Galina Alexandrova, "Bulgarian *Vazrazhdane* Business Club Attempt to Dominate Bulgarian Economy Fails for the Time Being," *Capital* (Sofia), 12 January 2001.

36. *ITAR-TASS* (Moscow), 21 January 2002.

37. Russia's spurious claims for post–World War II "reparations" are particularly galling to East Europeans for three reasons. First, World War II was made possible by the Nazi-Soviet alliance and the agreement between Berlin and Moscow to carve up Eastern Europe. Second, the USSR did not "liberate" the region at the close of World War II, but enslaved it under a Communist system for the next forty-five years. And third, Russia as the successor of the Soviet Union should pay reparations to its former satellites for the political repression, economic regression, and international isolation that each country experienced. In several states, former political prisoners and deportees have issued claims for material reparations from Moscow. This is an important symbolic gesture rather than a realistic expectation that Russia would actually deliver any financial payments to the victims of Sovietism.

38. "Russia and Bulgaria: Tobacco Fight," *Sofia Echo,* 15 July 2002. Russia's claims also included offices and real estate linked with the enterprise in several Bulgarian cities. In December 2002, the Russian authorities asserted that any property, which was originally transferred to the USSR after World War II as war reparations, was leased and not given to the Bulgarian state in the 1950s.

39. Delays in privatizing Bulgartabac harmed foreign investment prospects and led to criticisms from western capitals. Final bids for Bulgartabac were submitted by only four consortiums, three of which involved Russian capital. The winner in purchasing majority shares was Tobacco Capital Partners (TCP), a Dutch consortium backed by Deutsche Bank with no evident Russian connections. However, in October 2003, the government decided to break up the enterprise prior to its final privatization. See RFE/RL, *Newsline* 7, no. 189, pt. 2 (3 October 2003).

40. Ulrich Buechsenschuetz, "Are Bulgarian-Russian Relations Improving?" RFE/RL, *Newsline*, 18 June 2002. There were speculations in the Bulgarian press that the Bulgarian ambassador hesitated before signing the document because the

text had been changed at the last momemt by the Russian side to include passages not previously agreed.

41. Lyuba Budakova, "We Want a Compensation of Half a Million Dollars for the MIGs," *Mediapool*.bg, 31 July 2003. By the end of August 2003, there was no information on whether Russia was planning to pay the $500,000 compensation demanded by Sofia. The Terem deal was important to Bulgaria as the company was reliant on contracts to pay wages. As a result, Terem was forced to compromise, as it wanted to avoid strikes among its workforce. See "In September Terem-Plovdiv Will Pay Another Portion of Its Arrears to Its Employees," *Focus Information Agency*, 21 August, 2003, www.focus-news.net.

42. "Will the Tsar Keep Bulgaria in Russia's Orbit?" *Mediapool*.bg, 30 May 2001. The article summarizes a longer piece from *Moskovskie Novosti* from May 2001. The article was titled "The Tsar Returns" and was published before Bulgaria's parliamentary elections.

43. Plamen Petrov, "Bulgaria and NATO's Push East," *World Press Review* (Sofia), 2 December 2002.

44. "Bulgaria: Bulgarian Socialist Party to Issue Statement on Yeltsin," *Duma* (Sofia), 2 April 1996, in *Foreign Broadcast Information Service (FBIS), East Europe*, 2 April 1996. Yeltsin's remarks caused a furor in Sofia and the opposition attacked the Socialist government for failing to reject his proposals. Bulgaria was the last democratic country under former Communist rule to apply for NATO membership—in February 1997 under a UDF government.

45. Roumiana Buchvarova, "The Philes and Phobes Today," *Capital* (Sofia) no. 8 (March 2003), www.capital.bg. For a highly critical perspective on Bulgarian-Russian relations, see Peter Stoyanovich, "For Whom the Shipka Bell Tolls?" *Vseki Den* (Sofia), 5 March 2003, www.vsekiden.com. *Vseki Den* is an electronic portal comparable to *Mediapool*.

46. "Putin Will Ask Parvanov about the *Bulgargaz* Privatization," *Mediapool*, 5 September 2003, mediapool.bg/site/bulgaria/2003/09/05/18_050903bg.shtml.

47. www.evropa.bg, the Web site of the Delegation of the European Commission in Bulgaria; www.mediapool.bg/site/europa/bulg_ec/index.shtml, a site that follows Bulgaria's negotiations for EU membership; and the Kozloduy annual report at www.kznpp.org/eng/main.php?cont=4.

48. Ognyan Minchev, the director of the Institute for Regional and Internationak Studies in Sofia, in Matilda Nahabedian, "Looking to the Future: Bulgaria on Its Own," *Central Europe Review* 3, no. 12 (26 March 2001).

49. "Bulgarian International Octopus," *Nova Makedonija* (Skopje), 2 November 1995. Multigroup was also implicated in the failed assassination attempt on Macedonian president Kiro Gligorov in October 1995 because the Macedonian authorities were undermining its illicit operations.

50. For information on Russian business scandals in Bulgaria, see the following articles in the weekly *Capital* (Sofia): "Gazprom Interested in Acquiring Shares in Roseximbank," 26 August 2000; Yovo Nikolov, "Michael Chorny in UDF Land," 31 March 2001; and Velislava Popova, "Chorny Officially Named Standard Chief," 28 April 2001.

51. RFE/RL, *Newsline* 7, no. 108, pt. 2 (10 June 2003).

52. RFE/RL, *Newsline* 7, no. 196, pt. 2 (15 October 2003).

53. RFE/RL, *Newsline* 7, no. 45, pt. 2 (10 March 2003).

54. *Monitor* 7, no. 64 (2 April 2001).
55. Nahabedian, "Looking to the Future."
56. Ibid. Mihailova added that "the greatest gesture of goodwill towards our Russian partners is that we did not make public the facts about the illegal activity of diplomats from the Russian embassy."
57. *Nezavisimaya Gazeta* (Moscow), 22 March 2001.
58. Kalin Todorov, "Spy vs. Spy," *168 Tchasa* (Sofia), 3–9 October 2003. The episode cast a shadow over Bulgaria's credibility as a NATO invitee; this was also a Russian objective.
59. RFE/RL, *Newsline* 7, no. 126, pt. 2 (7 July 2003). According to Foreign Minister Ivanov, the document marks a new phase in bilateral relations, while Romanian Foreign Minister Mircea Geoana asserted that bilateral relations can "return to normalcy" after a "complicated decade."
60. "Lukoil Eyes Romania," *Moscow Times,* 28 August 2003.
61. "Russian Managers Appreciated," *Politika* (Belgrade), 12 April 2003.
62. RFE/RL, *Newsline* 7, no. 44, pt. 2 (7 March 2003).
63. RFE/RL, *Newsline* 6, no. 9, pt. 2 (28 March 2002).
64. "Will Romania Look East?" *Jane's Intelligence Digest,* Briefings, 10 November 2000.

CHAPTER 9

1. According to some analysts, Russia is using the ideological rationale of a new "liberal empire" to expand its controlling interests among neighbors, especially in regions prone to instability and authoritarianism. See Igor Torbakov, "Russian Policy Makers Air Notion of 'Liberal Empire' in Caucasus, Central Asia," *Eurasia Insight,* 27 October 2003, at EurasiaNet.org; and Roman Melnikov, "Can Russia Be a Liberal Empire?" *Pravda Online* (Moscow), 14 October 2003, english.pravda.ru. It is debatable to what degree Putin's model of empire is actually "liberal" and whether he would use purely "liberal" means to maintain its cohesion.
2. According to Prizel, "The Eastern Europeans, and Poles in particular, although welcoming the resumption of trade links with Russia, see any resumption of Russia's role as a great power allied with other great powers as a *prima facie* assault on their sovereignty." Ilya Prizel, *National Identity and Foreign Policy: Nationalism and Leadership in Poland, Russia, and Ukraine* (Cambridge: Cambridge University Press, 1998), 278.
3. "Russia and NATO: The Beginning of a New Relationship?" RFE/RL, *Russian Political Weekly* 2, no. 3 (21 January 2002).
4. A sentiment shared in conversations with analysts and officials in Prague in June 2003.
5. Jiri Pehe, "Attitudes of NATO's New Central European Members Toward Russia's Role in the Euro-Atlantic Structures," paper delivered at the conference "Euro-Atlantic Integration and Russia after September 11, 2001," Moscow, 29–31 May 2002.
6. Some Russian analysts claim that the inclusion of Central European and Baltic states could delay if not derail Russia's admission. See B. Pichugin, "Russia and the European Union's Eastward Expansion," *International Affairs* (Moscow) 42, no. 1 (January–February 1996): 90–96.

7. The Schengen agreement establishes conditions for the free movement of people in thirteen of the European Union's fifteen current member states. The EU expanded to include ten new countries in May 2004. Schengen also imposes tighter restrictions on the EU's "outer border" with nonmember states.

8. Todd Prince, "A Wary Eye Is Cast over EU's Influence on Trade," *Moscow Times,* 18 April 2002. East European entry into the EU could increase their exports to Russia as they will be looking for new markets, but much depends on the extent of Russian protectionism.

9. Joanna Apap, Jakub Boratynski, Michael Emerson, Grzegorz Gromadzki, Marius Vahl, and Nicholas Whyte, *Friendly Schengen Borderland Policy on the New Borders of an Emlarged EU and Its Neighbours,* Collective CEPS-Batory Foundation Paper, CEPS, Brussels, 6–7 July 2001. The authors claim that "the strict application of the Schengen border regime in general, and visa policy in particular, will directly affect and reinforce the growing socio-economic and psychological gap between the two parts of Europe" (p. 3).

10. Michael Emerson, *The Elephant and the Bear: The European Union, Russia, and Their Near Abroads* (Brussels: Center for European Policy Studies, 2001).

11. RFE/RL, *Newsline 7,* no. 99, pt. 1 (28 May 2003).

12. Ilya Prizel, "Putin's Russia, the Berlin Republic, and East Central Europe: A New Symbiosis?" *Orbis* 46, no. 4 (Fall 2002): 690.

13. Margarita M. Balmaceda, "Ukraine, Russia, and European Security: Thinking Beyond NATO Expansion," *Problems of Post-Communism* 45, no. 1 (January–February 1998): 21. East European governments believe that some EU states may be willing to sacrifice their interests in pursuit of closer relations with Moscow. The initial willingness of Brussels to forge a deal with Russia over transit rights to Kaliningrad without the input of the two directly effected states, Poland and Lithuania, provoked consternation.

14. See the commentary on the ESDP in *Krasnaya Zvezda* (Moscow), 14 October 1997.

15. Timofel Bordachev, "Russia and the 'Expanded Europe': New Risks and New Opportunities," Carnegie Moscow Center, *Briefing Papers* 2, no. 12 (December 2000). The EU currently depends on Russia for about 30 percent of its gas supplies.

16. Alla Kassianova, "Russia: Still Open to the West? Evolution of the State Identity in the Foreign and Security Discourse," *Europe-Asia Studies* 53, no. 6 (September 2001).

17. Alexander Zinovjev, "Globalization as a War of a New Type," *Russia and Central Europe in the New Geopolitical Realities,* Russian Academy of Sciences, Fourth International Scientific Conference, Moscow, 14–16 June 2001, 112–123.

18. RFE/RL, *Newsline 7,* no. 35, pt. 1 (24 February 2003). For a discussion of Russian foreign policy in the wake of 11 September, see the seven-part series "Poland and Russia after 11th September: Fragments of a Discussion," *Gazeta Wyborcza Online* (Warsaw), published between 17 May 2002 and 7–8 June 2002, wyborcza.pl.

19. Igor Ivanov, "Russia and the EU: Prospects for Strategic Partnership," *Europe Magazine* no. 5 (May 2001). Throughout the 1990s, Moscow endeavored to raise the prestige of the OSCE as a replacement for NATO. With Russia holding veto power, the OSCE was perceived as a useful tool in projecting Moscow's objectives and limiting NATO's impact.

20. Nikolas Gvosdev, "Moscow Nights, Eurasian Dreams," *National Interest* (Summer 2002): 157.

21. Such views are expressed by a range of Russian analysts—based on discussions in Moscow in September 2003.

22. Dmitri Trenin, *The End of Eurasia: Russia on the Border Between Geopolitics and Globalization* (Washington, D.C.: Carnegie Endowment for International Peace, 2002).

23. For Russian positions on multipolarity, see Thomas Ambrosio, "Russia's Quest for Multipolarity: A Response to U.S. Foreign Policy in the Post–Cold War Era," *European Security* 10, no. 1 (Spring 2001): 45–67. The author believes that Kremlin quests for a multipolar system are aimed at "creating conditions in which Russia can effectively resist American military, geopolitical, and economic encroachment." Such "encroachment" is implied to be negative and Russia's stance as purely defensive. The author also reveals his historical myopia when claiming that the strategic importance of Central Europe to Russia cannot be underestimated since it was the invasion route for Napoleon and Hitler. He fails to point out that it was also Russia's traditional invasion route westward.

24. RFE/RL, *Newsline* 7, no. 89, pt. 1 (13 May 2003).

25. Konstantin Zhukovsky, "Russian Security Council Updates Security Concept," *TASS* (Moscow), 5 October 1999.

26. Stephen J. Blank, *Threats to Russian Security: The View from Moscow* (Washington, D.C.: Strategic Studies Institute, U.S. Army War College, 2000), 35.

27. RFE/RL, *Newsline* 7, no. 28, pt. 1 (12 February 2003).

28. Vladimir Socor, "Geostrategic Perspectives on Eurasia," Institute for Advanced Strategic and Political Studies, Washington, D.C., *Policy Briefing* no. 15, 2 March 2003.

29. *The Twain Shall Meet: The Prospects for Russia-West Relations*, report of a joint working group of the Atlantic Council of the United States, the Centre for European Reform, and the Institute for U.S. and Canadian Studies at the Russian Acedamy of Sciences, policy paper, September 2002. The report contains a series of platitudes, including bland recommendations that "Russia should not use anti-terrorism as a foundation for establishing an exclusive Russian influence in neighboring states" or "greater western involvement in the former Soviet republics should not lead to a resumption of a traditional zero-sum game between Russia and the United States" (p. 18).

30. According to Lo, "It is not so much that Putin and members of his administration believe that the principle of the balance of power has become anachronistic, but that balance in practice is more likely to be achieved through collective efforts than by a severely weakened Russia on its own." See Bobo Lo, *Vladimir Putin and the Evolution of Russian Foreign Policy,* Royal Institute of International Affairs, Chatham House Papers (London: Blackwell, 2003), 80. Moreover, "In Russia, military power, territorial issues, threat perceptions, and notions of strategic balance have assumed a prominence unmatched anywhere else on the planet. In fact, so entrenched is the geopolitical mentality that the end of the Cold War, in most of the developed world a watershed in the transition to a new global politics, has had little positive impact on the Russian elite" (p. 72).

31. Aleksandr Chuikov, "NATO Asks Russia to Go Away," *Rossiya* (Moscow), 31 July 2003.

32. Nikolai Sokov, "*Quod Licet Iovi:* Preemptive Use of Military Force in Russian Foreign Policy," PONARS Policy Memo no. 254, PONARS (Program on New Approaches to Russian Security) Policy Conference, Center for Strategic and International Studies, Washington, D.C., 6 December 2002, 35.

33. Roman Kupchinsky, "The Putin Doctrine, RFE/RL, *Newsline* 7, no. 204, pt. 1 (27 October 2003).

34. Breffini O'Rourke, "Russia: Putin's Brussels Visit Underscores EU Ties," RFE/RL, 1 October 2001, www.rfer.org/nca/features; and "Speech by Russian President Vladimir Putin," *NATO Online Library,* 3 October 2001, www.nato.int/docu/speech.

35. RFE/RL, *Newsline* 6, no. 228, pt. 1 (6 December 2002).

36. Vladimir Socor, "The Grinding of a New Axis?" *Wall Street Journal Europe,* 21–23 February 2003.

37. Dmitri Trenin, "Less Is More," *Washington Quarterly* 24, no. 3 (Summer 2001): 141.

38. RFE/RL, *Newsline* 6, no. 205, pt. 1 (30 October 2002).

39. Pavel K. Baev, "External Interventions in Secessionist Conflicts in Europe in the 1990s," *European Security* 8, no. 2 (Summer 1999): 33.

40. Dov Lynch, *Russia Faces Europe,* Chaillot Paper no. 60 (European Union, Paris: Institute for Security Studies, 2003), 15.

41. Dimitri Trenin, "Vladimir Putin's Autumn Marathon: Toward the Birth of a Russian Foreign Policy Strategy," Carnegie Moscow Center, *Briefing Papers* 3, no. 11 (November 2001). The author marvels that Russia took its place alongside the EU after the attack on the United States. But there was little practical alternative for Moscow wihout discrediting itself in Washington. The Kremlin viewed the U.S. campaign as an opportunity to gain strategic benefits from a tactical move that bore few costs to Russia and could justify its own "antiterrorist" operations.

42. Marek Menkiszak, *The Pro-Western Turn in Russia's Foreign Policy: Causes, Consequences, and Prospects,* Policy Briefs (Warsaw: Center for Eastern Studies, Warsaw, 2002), 24–25.

43. Vitaliy Tsygichko, "S Amerikoy—Vmeste Ili Porozn," *Nezavisimaya Gazeta* (Moscow), 9 June 2001.

44. Ian Bremmer and Alexander Zaslavsky, "Bush and Putin's Tentative Embrace," *World Policy Journal* (New York) 18, no. 4 (Winter 2001–2002): 15.

45. David R. Sands, "Russians Criticize Putin on Treaty; Seen as Ceding too Much to U.S.," *Washington Times,* 15 May 2002. Russia's military leaders remain concerned over U.S. troop deployments to regions long viewed as part of Moscow's "natural sphere of influence" in Central Asia and the Caucasus.

Index

Moldova (*continued*)
in, 101–2; ethnicity in, 95–96; federalization of, 106, 259n96; Gagauz minority in, 103; intelligence in, 107–8; military and, 98–99, 101, 107; politics in, 105–6; Romania and, 95–96, 98, 103, 104, 216, 218; significance of, 29, 61–62; Transnistrian separatism, 95–101, 103, 104–6, 259n96; and treaty with Russia, 96–97
Montenegrin Orthodox Church, 197
Montenegro, 196–97. *See also* Balkan region
Moroz, Oleksandr, 93
Moskovskie Novosti, 21
Multigroup Corporation, 207, 214, 215
Multinational Peace Forces South East Europe (MPFSEE), 205

Naftex, 209
Naftogaz, 86–87
NAP Novi Sad, 192
National Electric Company (NEK), 209
Nationalism: ethnicity and, 40–41; Putin and, 18; rise of Russian, 3–4, 7–9, 18, 236n16
National Security Concept (2000), 21, 22
National Security Council, 22
NATO. *See* North Atlantic Treaty Organization
NATO-Russia Council, 137, 138, 222, 225–26
NATO-Russia Founding Act (1997), 14, 138, 191
Nazi-Soviet Pact (1939), 216
"Near abroad," 52, 54, 96
Nikolaev, Andrey, 171–72
Nordik OU, 209
North Atlantic Council (NAC), 228
North Atlantic Treaty Organization (NATO): Balkans and, 30, 34, 58, 169–70; Baltic states and, 109–14, 117, 154–55; Belarus and, 66; Bosnia and, 176–80; Bulgaria and,

170, 204–6, 213, 215, 285n44; Central Europe and, 3, 8–9, 13, 15–16, 136–38; CIS integration and, 56; continued expansion of, 232; Czech Republic and, 154–55, 157, 227; Eastern Europe and, 3, 8–9, 13, 15–16, 221; eligibility of Russia's neighbors for, 42, 111, 113, 121, 128, 205; Hungary and, 149–50, 227; intelligence links between Russia and new members of, 48; Kaliningrad and, 74; Kosovo and, 26, 34, 171, 181–88; Latvia and, 122–23; Lithuania and, 133; Macedonia and, 199; military and, 137; NATO-Russia Council, 137, 138, 222, 225–26; NATO-Russia Founding Act, 14, 138, 191; New Strategic Concept (1999), 26, 171, 174, 186; Poland and, 140–41, 143, 227; Romania and, 218; Russian opposition to, 2, 9, 12–15, 21, 25–26, 31, 33–35, 138, 150, 154, 170–71, 180–81, 220; Russian role in, 225–28 (*see also* NATO-Russia Council); Serbia and, 189–96; Slovakia and, 162–63, 165–66; Yugoslavia and, 169–70
Norway, 145, 155
Nuclear power, 131, 164, 192, 208, 213–14
Nuclear weapons, 34–35, 52, 74, 117, 137, 143, 150, 162, 227

Ohrid agreement (2001), 200, 201
Ojdanić, Dragoljub, 194
Oleksy, Józef, 148
Oligarchs, 16–17, 240n78
Olszewski, Jan, 149
Omelchenko, Oleksandr, 93
OMON. *See* Soviet Ministry of Interior troops (OMON)
OMV, 217
Orbán, Viktor, 150, 152
Organization for Security and Cooperation in Europe (OSCE), 13, 100, 104, 112, 119, 187, 228

About the Author

JANUSZ BUGAJSKI is Director of the East European Project at the Center for Strategic and International Studies in Washington, D.C. He has served as a consultant for both government and private organizations and has lectured at numerous American and European universities. He chairs the South-Central Europe area studies program at the Foreign Service Institute, U.S. Department of State, and is the author or editor of several books on the region.